W9-CAT-561

Marketing Classics

A Selection of Influential Articles

BEN M. ENIS
and
KEITH K. COX
University of Houston

Allyn and Bacon, Inc. Boston

Library of Congress Catalog Card Number: 70–75911

Printed in the United States of America

Fifth printing . . . February, 1972

CONTRIBUTORS

Wroe Alderson
Leo V. Aspinwall
Raymond A. Bauer
James A. Bayton
Theodore N. Beckman
Neil H. Bordon
Louis P. Bucklin
Robert D. Buzzell
Reavis Cox
Joel Dean
Peter F. Drucker
Leon Festinger
Jay W. Forrester
Foundation for Research on Human Behavior
Paul E. Green
Mason Haire
Stanley C. Hollander
Elihu Katz
George Katona
Robert J. Keith
Alfred A. Kuehn
Robert F. Lanzillotti
Robert J. Lavidge
Theodore Levitt
J. B. McKitterick
Phillip McVey
John F. Magee
Pierre Martineau
Alfred R. Oxenfeldt
Edgar A. Pessemier
Harry V. Roberts
Charles C. Slater
Wendell R. Smith
Gary A. Steiner
P. J. Verdoorn

PREFACE

Marketing is that phase of human activity that produces economic want-satisfaction by matching consumers' needs and the resources of business firms. From the firm's point of view, consumer-satisfaction is the result of its marketing strategy. Strategy is based on marketing philosophy and is derived from the analysis of consumers and their functional interrelationships with such market forces as economic conditions, competitors' actions, institutional change, and other environmental factors. This volume is a compilation of articles that provide broad insight into the field of marketing.

The authors consider these works to be among the classics of marketing literature. These articles are generally recognized by marketing scholars as being of enduring significance to marketing thought. They are widely quoted, have led to new directions in marketing research, and reflect the views of influential scholars. Consequently, these are works with which serious marketing students should be familiar, and to which they should have ready access. We believe the book will be a useful supplement to advanced undergraduate courses in marketing management and marketing strategy and to graduate courses in marketing fundamentals and marketing theory. The practitioner might also enjoy having these familiar works in his library.

The articles in this volume were chosen on the basis of extensive research in marketing literature, and the authors were fortunate to obtain the suggestions of a number of colleagues. Nevertheless, it would be presumptuous to imply that we have compiled *the* classic works of marketing. Marketing is too rich, too complex, too diverse a discipline to be subsumed in one volume. Our selections reflect our own perceptions of and biases about marketing; we assume full responsibility for errors of omission and commission in compiling this volume. We feel that the articles it contains are representative of the best work in the field of marketing.

B.M.E.
K.K.C.

CONTENTS

I

Marketing Philosophy 1

II

Consumer Analysis 90

I

Marketing Philosophy

Any discipline or area of human inquiry is based upon a philosophy, a set of underlying principles that provide the rationale for the existence of the discipline. The articles in this section present a cross-section of the philosophy of marketing. Wroe Alderson's paper provides, in his trenchant style, an overview of the nature of the marketing discipline: based on the economics of imperfect competition, composed of the problem-solving activities of consumers and firms, and illuminated by concepts from the social sciences.

The following three articles examine marketing from the macro or societal viewpoint. Cox discusses the role of marketing in efficiently bridging the gap between production and consumption to provide consumer convenience. Drucker concentrates on the importance of marketing to economic development in terms of raising living standards and promoting individual freedom. Beckman's article summarizes marketing's contribution to economic want satisfaction by the creation of time, place, and possession utility, and suggests that this contribution can be measured by the value-added concept.

The remaining three articles in this section on marketing philosophy present the micro or individual firm view of the marketing function. Verdoorn presents the underlying economic theory of micro-marketing in terms of realizing certain objectives (primarily profits) by utilizing certain instruments (the marketing mix) within certain environmental conditions. McKitterick discusses the ascendency of the marketing function and its increasing consumer-orientation as a result of historical development and changing management perspective. Keith's chronicle of the development of the marketing function at Pillsbury illustrates the process described by McKitterick.

1. THE ANALYTICAL FRAMEWORK FOR MARKETING*

Wroe Alderson

My assignment is to discuss the analytical framework for marketing. Since our general purpose here is to consider the improvement of the marketing curriculum, I assume that the paper I have been asked to present might serve two functions. The first is to present a perspective of marketing which might be the basis of a marketing course at either elementary or advanced levels. The other is to provide some clue as to the foundations in the social sciences upon which an analytical framework for marketing may be built.

Economics has some legitimate claim to being the original science of markets. Received economic theory provides a framework for the analysis of marketing functions which certainly merits the attention of marketing teachers and practitioners. It is of little importance whether the point of view I am about to present is a version of economics, a hybrid of economics and sociology, or the application of a new emergent general science of human behavior to marketing problems. The analytical framework which I find congenial at least reflects some general knowledge of the social sciences as well as long experience in marketing analysis. In the time available I can do no more than present this view in outline or skeleton form and leave you to determine how to classify it or whether you can use it.

An advantageous place to start for the analytical treatment of marketing is with the radical heterogeneity of markets. Heterogeneity is inherent on both the demand and the supply sides. The homogeneity which the economist assumes for certain purposes is not an an-

*Reprinted from Delbert Duncan (ed.), *Proceedings: Conference of Marketing Teachers from Far Western States* (Berkeley: University of California, 1958), pp. 15–28.

tecedent condition for marketing. Insofar as it is ever realized, it emerges out of the marketing process itself.

The materials which are useful to man occur in nature in heterogeneous mixtures which might be called conglomerations since these mixtures have only a random relationship to human needs and activities. The collection of goods in the possession of a household or an individual also constitutes a heterogeneous supply, but it might be called an assortment since it is related to anticipated patterns of future behavior. The whole economic process may be described as a series of transformations from meaningless to meaningful heterogeneity. Marketing produces as much homogeneity as may be needed to facilitate some of the intermediate economic processes but homogeneity has limited significance or utility for consumer behavior or expectations.

The marketing process matches materials found in nature or goods fabricated from these materials against the needs of households or individuals. Since the consuming unit has a complex pattern of needs, the matching of these needs creates an assortment of goods in the hands of the ultimate consumer. Actually the marketing process builds up assortments at many stages along the way, each appropriate to the activities taking place at that point. Materials or goods are associated in one way for manufacturing, in another way for wholesale distribution, and in still another for retail display and selling. In between the various types of heterogeneous collections relatively homogeneous supplies are accumulated through the process of grading, refining, chemical reduction and fabrication.

Marketing brings about the necessary transformations in heterogeneous supplies through a multiphase process of sorting. Matching of every individual need would be impossible if the consumer had to search out each item required or the producer had to find the users of a product one by one. It is only the ingenious use of intermediate sorts which make it possible for a vast array of diversified products to enter into the ultimate consumer assortments as needed. Marketing makes mass production possible first by providing the assortment of supplies needed in manufacturing and then taking over the successive transformations which ultimately produce the assortment in the hands of consuming units.

To some who have heard this doctrine expounded, the concept of sorting seems empty, lacking in specific behavioral content, and hence unsatisfactory as a root idea for marketing. One answer is that sorting is a more general and embracing concept than allocation which many economists regard as the root idea of their science. Allocation is only one of the four basic types of sorting, all of which are involved in marketing. Among these four, allocation is certainly no more significant than assorting, one being the breaking down of a homogeneous supply and the other the building up of a heterogeneous supply. Assorting, in fact, gives more direct expression to the final aim of marketing but allocation performs a major function along the way.

There are several basic advantages in taking sorting as a central concept. It leads directly to a fundamental explanation of the contribution of marketing to the overall economy of human effort in producing and distributing goods. It provides a key to the unending search for efficiency in the marketing function itself. Finally, sorting as the root idea of marketing is consistent with the assumption that heterogeneity is radically and inherently present on both sides of the market and that the aim of marketing is to cope with the heterogeneity of both needs and resources.

At this stage of the discussion it is the relative emphasis on assorting as contrasted with allocation which distinguishes marketing theory from at least some versions of economic theory. This emphasis arises naturally from the preoccupation of the market analyst with consumer behavior. One of the most fruitful approaches to understanding what the consumer is doing is the idea that she is engaged in building an assortment, in replenishing or extending an inventory of goods for use by herself and her family. As evidence that this paper is not an attempt to set up a theory in opposition to economics it is acknowledged that the germ of this conception of consumer behavior was first presented some eighty years ago by the Austrian economist Boehm-Bawerk.

The present view is distinguished from that of Boehm Bawerk in its greater emphasis on the probabilistic approach to the study of market behavior. In considering items for inclusion in her assortment the consumer must make judgments concerning the relative probabilities of future occasions for use. A product in the assortment is intended to provide for some aspect of future behavior. Each such occasion for use carries a rating which is a product of two factors, one a judgment as to the probability of its incidence and the other a measure of the urgency of the need in case it should arise. Consumer goods vary with respect to both measures. One extreme might be illustrated by cigarettes with a probability of use approaching certainty but with relatively small urgency or penalty for deprivation on the particular occasion for use. At the other end of the scale would be a home fire extinguisher with low probability but high urgency attaching to the expected occasion of use.

All of this means that the consumer buyer enters the market as a problem-solver. Solving a problem, either on behalf of a household or on behalf of a marketing organization means reaching a decision in the face of uncertainty. The consumer buyer and the marketing executive are opposite numbers in the double search which pervades marketing; one looking for the goods required to complete an assortment, the other looking for the buyers who are uniquely qualified to use his goods. This is not to say that the behavior of either consumers or executives can be completely characterized as rational problem-solvers. The intention rather is to assert that problem-solving on either side of the market involves a probabilistic approach to heterogeneity on the other side. In order to solve his own problems arising from the heterogeneous demand, the marketing executive should understand the processes of consumer decisions in coping with heterogeneous supplies.

The viewpoint adopted here with respect to the competition among sellers is essentially that which is associated in economics with such names as Schumpetor, Chamberlin and J. M. Clark and with the emphasis on innovative competition, product differentiation and differential advantage. The basic assumption is that every firm occupies a position which is in some respects unique, being differentiated from all others by characteristics of its products, its services, its geographic location or its specific combination of these features. The survival of a firm requires that for some group of buyers it should enjoy a differential advantage over all other suppliers. The sales of any active marketing organization come from a core market made up of buyers with a preference for this source and a fringe market which finds the source acceptable, at least for occasional purchases.

In the case of the supplier of relatively undifferentiated products or services such as the wheat farmer, differential advantage may pertain more to the producing region than to the individual producer. This more diffused type of differential advantage often becomes effective in the market through such agencies as the marketing cooperative. Even the individual producer of raw materials, however, occupies a position in the sense that one market or buyer provides the customary outlet for his product rather than another. The essential point for the present argument is that buyer and seller are not paired at random even in the marketing of relatively homogeneous products but are related to some scale of preference or priority.

Competition for differential advantage implied goals of survival and growth for the marketing organization. The firm is perennially seeking a favorable place to stand and not merely immediate profits from its operations. Differential advantage is subject to change and neutralization by competitors. In dynamic markets differential advantage can only be preserved through continuous innovation. Thus competition presents an analogy to a succession of military campaigns rather than to the pressures and attrition of a single battle. A competitor may gain ground through a successful campaign based on new product features or merchandising ideas. It may lose ground or be forced to fall back on its core position because of the successful campaigns of others. The existence of the core position helps to explain the paradox of survival in the face of the destructive onslaughts of innovative competition.

Buyers and sellers meet in market transactions each side having tentatively identified the other as an answer to its problem. The market transaction consumes much of the time and effort of all buyers and sellers. The market which operates through a network of costless transactions is only a convenient fiction which economists adopt for certain analytical purposes. Potentially the cost of transactions is so high that controlling or reducing this cost is a major objective in market analysis and executive action. Among economists John R. Commons has given the greatest attention to the transaction as the unit of collective action. He drew a basic distinction between strategic and routine transactions which for present purposes may best be paraphrased as fully negotiated and routine transactions.

The fully negotiated transaction is the prototype of all exchange transactions. It represents a matching of supply and demand after canvassing all of the factors which might affect the decision on either side. The routine transaction proceeds under a set of rules and assumptions established by previous negotiation or as the result of techniques of pre-selling which take the place of negotiation. Transactions on commodity and stock exchanges are carried out at high speed and low cost but only because of carefully established rules governing all aspects of trading. The economical routines of self-service in a super market are possible because the individual items on display have been pre-sold. The routine transaction is the end-result of previous marketing effort and ingenious organization of institutions and processes. Negotiation is implicit in all routine transactions. Good routines induce both parties to save time and cost by foregoing explicit negotiation.

The negotiated transaction is the indicated point of departure for the study of exchange values in heterogeneous markets. Many considerations enter into the decision to trade or not to trade on either side of the market. Price is the final balancing or integrating factor which permits the deal to be made. The seller may accept a lower price if relieved from onerous requirements. The buyer may pay a higher price if provided with specified services. The integrating price is one that assures an orderly flow of goods so long as the balance of other considerations remains essentially unchanged. Some economists are uneasy about the role of the negotiated transaction in value determination since bargaining power may be controlling within wide bargaining limits. These limits as analyzed by Commons are set by reference to the best alternatives available to either partner rather than by the automatic control of atomistic competition. This analysis overlooks a major constraint on bargaining in modern markets. Each side has a major stake in a deal that the other side can live with. Only in this way can a stable supply relationship be established so as to achieve the economics of transactional routines. Negotiation is not a zero sum game since the effort to get the best of the other party transaction by transaction may result in a loss to both sides in terms of mounting transactional cost.

In heterogeneous markets price plays an important role in matching a segment of supply with the appropriate segment of demand. The seller frequently has the option of producing a stream-lined product at a low price, a deluxe product at a high price or selecting a price-quality combination somewhere in between. There are considerations which exert a strong influence on the seller toward choosing the price line or lines which will yield the greatest dollar volume of sales. Assuming that various classes of consumers have conflicting claims on the productive capacity of the supplier, it might be argued that the price-quality combination which maximized gross revenue represented the most constructive compromise among these claims. There are parallel considerations with respect to the claims of various participants in the firm's activities on its operating revenue. These claimants include labor, management, suppliers of raw materials and stockholders. Assuming a perfectly fluid situation with respect to bargaining among these claimants, the best chance for a satisfactory solution is at the level of maximum gross revenue. The argument becomes more complicated when the claims of stockholders are given priority, but the goal would still be maximum gross revenue as suggested in a recent paper by William J. Baumol. My own intuition and experience lead me to believe that the maximization of gross revenue is a valid goal of marketing management in heterogeneous markets and adherence to this norm appears to be widely prevalent in actual practice.

What has been said so far is doubtless within the scope of economics or perhaps constitutes a sketch of how some aspects of economic theory might be reconstructed on the assumption of heterogeneity rather than homogeneity as the normal and prevailing condition of the market. But there are issues raised by such notions as enterprise survival, expectations, and consumer behavior, which in my opinion cannot be resolved within the present boundaries of economic science. Here marketing must not hesitate to draw upon the concepts and techniques of the social sciences for the enrichment of its perspective and for the advancement of marketing as an empirical science.

The general economist has his own justifications for regarding the exchange process as a smoothly functioning mechanism which operates in actual markets or which should be taken as the norm and standard to be enforced by government regulation. For the marketing man, whether teacher or practitioner, this Olympian view is untenable. Marketing is concerned with those who are obliged to enter the market to solve their problems imperfect as the market may be. The persistent and rational action of these participants is the main hope for eliminating or moderating some of these imperfections so that the operation of the market mechanism may approximate that of the theoretical model.

To understand market behavior the marketing man takes a closer look at the nature of the participants. Thus he is obliged, in my opinion, to come to grips with the organized behavior system. Market behavior is primarily group behavior. Individual action in the market is most characteristically action on behalf of some group in which the individual holds membership. The organized behavior system is related to the going concern of John R. Commons but with a deeper interest in what keeps it going. The organized behavior system is also a much broader concept including the more tightly organized groups acting in the market such as business firms and households and loosely connected systems such as the trade center and the marketing channel.

The marketing man needs some rationale for group behavior, some general explanation for the formation and persistence of organized behavior systems. He finds this explanation in the concept of expectations. Insofar as conscious choice is involved, individuals operate in groups because of their expectations of incremental satisfactions as compared to what they could obtain operating alone. The expected satisfactions are of many kinds, direct and indirect. In a group that is productive activity is held together because of an expected surplus over individual output. Other groups such as households and purely social organizations expect direct satisfactions from group association and activities. They also expect satisfactions from future activities facilitated by the assortment of goods held in common. Whatever the character of the system, its vitality arises from the expectations of the individual members and the vigor of their efforts to achieve them through group action. While the existence of the group is entirely derivative, it is capable of operating as if it had a life of its own and was pursuing goals of survival and growth.

Every organized behavior system exhibits a structure related to the functions it performs. Even in the simplest behavior system there must be some mechanism for decision and coordination of effort if the system is to provide incremental satisfaction. Leadership emerges at an early stage to perform such functions as directing the defense of the group. Also quite early is the recognition of the rationing function by which the leader allocates the available goods or satisfactions among the members of the group.

As groups grow in size and their functions become more complex functional specialization increases. The collection of individuals forming a group with their diversified skills and capabilities is a meaningful heterogeneous ensemble vaguely analogous to the assortment of goods which facilitates the activities of the group. The group, however, is held together directly by the generalized expectations of its members. The assortment is held together by a relatively weak or derivative bond. An item "belongs" to the assortment only so long as it has some probability of satisfying the expectations of those who possess it.

This outline began with an attempt to live within the framework of economics or at least within an economic framework amplified to give fuller recognition to heterogeneity on both sides of the market. We have now plunged into sociology in order to deal more effectively with the organized behavior system. Meanwhile we attempt to preserve the line of communication to our origins by basing the explanations of group behavior on the quasi-economic concept of expectations.

The initial plunge into sociology is only the beginning since the marketing man must go considerably further in examining the functions and structure of organized behavior systems. An operating group has a power structure, a communication structure and an operating structure. At each stage an effort should be made to employ the intellectual strategy which has already been suggested. That is, to relate sociological notions to the groundwork of marketing economics through the medium of such concepts as expectations and the processes of matching and sorting.

All members of an organized behavior system occupy some position or status within its power structure. There is a valid analogy between the status of an individual or operating unit within the system and the market position of the firm as an entity. The individual struggles for status within the system having first attained the goal of membership.

For most individuals in an industrial society, status in some operating system is a prerequisite for satisfying his expectations. Given the minimal share in the power of the organization inherent in membership, vigorous individuals may aspire to the more ample share of power enjoyed by leadership. Power in the generalized sense referred to here is an underlying objective on which the attainment of all other objectives depends. This aspect of organized behavior has been formulated as the power principle, namely, "The rational individual will act in such a way to promote the power to act." The word "promote" deliberately glosses over an ambivalent attitude toward power, some individuals striving for enhancement and others being content to preserve the power they have.

Any discussion which embraces power as a fundamental concept creates uneasiness for some students on both analytical and ethical ground. My own answer to the analytical problem is to define it as control over expectations. In these terms it is theoretically possible to measure and evaluate power, perhaps even to set a price on it. Certainly it enters into the network of imputations in a business enterprise. Management allocates or rations status and recognition as well as or in lieu of material rewards. As for the ethical problem, it does not arise unless the power principle is substituted for ethics as with Macchiavelli. Admitting that the power principle is the essence of expediency, the ethical choice of values and objectives is a different issue. Whatever his specific objectives, the rational individual will wish to serve them expediently.

If any of this discussion of power seems remote from marketing let it be remembered that major preoccupation of the marketing executive, as pointed out by Oswald Knauth, is with the creation or the activation of organized behavior systems such as marketing channels and sales organizations. No one can be effective in building or using such systems if he ignores the fundamental nature of the power structure.

The communication structure serves the group in various ways. It promotes the survival of the system by reinforcing the individual's sense of belonging. It transmits instructions and operating commands or signals to facilitate coordinated effort. It is related to expectations through the communication of explicit or implied commitments. Negotiations between suppliers and customers and much that goes on in the internal management of a marketing organization can best be understood as a two-way exchange of commitments. A division sales manager, for example, may commit himself to produce a specified volume of sales. His superior in turn may commit certain company resources to support his efforts and make further commitments as to added rewards as an incentive to outstanding performance.

For some purposes it is useful to regard marketing processes as a flow of goods and a parallel flow of informative and persuasive messages. In these terms the design of communication facilities and channels becomes a major aspect of the creation of marketing systems. Marketing has yet to digest and apply the insights of the rapidly developing field of communication theory which in turn has drawn freely from both engineering and biological and social sciences. One stimulating idea expounded by Norbert Wiener and others is that of the feedback of information in a control system. Marketing and advertising research are only well started on the task of installing adequate feedback circuits for controlling the deployment of marketing effort.

Social psychology is concerned with some problems of communication which are often encountered in marketing systems. For example, there are the characteristic difficulties of vertical communication which might be compared to the transmission of telephone messages along a power line. Subordinates often hesitate to report bad news to their superiors fearing to take the brunt of emotional reactions. Superiors learn to be cautious in any discussion of the subordinate's status for fear that a casual comment will be interpreted as a commitment. There is often a question as to when a subordinate should act and report and when he should refer a matter for decision upstream. Progress in efficiency, which is a major goal in marketing, depends in substantial part on technological improvement in communication facilities and organizational skill in using them.

The third aspect of structure involved in the study of marketing systems is operating structure. Effective specialization within an organization requires that activities which are functionally similar be placed together but properly coordinated with other activities. Billing by wholesaler grocers, for example, has long been routinized in a separate billing department. In more recent years the advances in mechanical equipment have made it possible to coordinate inventory control with billing, using the same set of punch cards for both functions. Designing an operating structure is a special application of sorting. As in the sorting of goods to facilitate handling, there are generally several alternative schemes for classifying activities presenting problems of choice to the market planner.

Functional specialization and the design of appropriate operating structures is a constant problem in the effective use of marketing channels. Some functions can be performed at either of two or more stages.

One stage may be the best choice in terms of economy or effectiveness Decision on the placement of a function may have to be reviewed periodically since channels do not remain static. Similar considerations arise in the choice of channels. Some types of distributors or dealers may be equipped to perform a desired service while others may not. Often two or more channels with somewhat specialized roles are required to move a product to the consumer. The product's sponsor can maintain perspective in balancing out these various facilities by thinking in terms of a total operating system including his own sales organization and the marketing channels employed.

The dynamics of market organization pose basic problems for the marketing student and the marketing executive in a free enterprise economy. Reference has already been made to the competitive pursuit of differential advantage. One way in which a firm can gain differential advantage is by organizing the market in a way that is favorable to its own operations. This is something else than the attainment of a monopolistic position in relation to current or potential competitors. It means creating a pattern for dealing with customers or suppliers which persists because there are advantages on both sides. Offering guarantees against price declines on floor stocks is one example of market organization by the seller. Attempts to systematize the flow of orders may range from various services offered to customers or suppliers all the way to complete vertical integration. Another dynamic factor affecting the structure of markets may be generalized under the term "closure." It frequently happens that some marketing system is incomplete or out of balance in some direction. The act of supplying the missing element constitutes closure, enabling the system to handle a greater output or to operate at a new level of efficiency. The incomplete system in effect cries out for closure. To observe this need is to recognize a form of market opportunity. This is one of the primary ways in which new enterprises develop, since there may be good reasons why the missing service cannot be performed by the existing organizations which need the service. A food broker, for example, can cover a market for several accounts of moderate size in a way that the individual manufacturer would not be able to cover it for himself.

There is a certain compensating effect between closure as performed by new or supplementary marketing enterprises and changes in market organization brought about by the initiative of existing firms in the pursuit of differential advantage. The pursuit of a given form of advantage, in fact, may carry the total marketing economy out of balance in a given direction creating the need and opportunity for closure. Such an economy could never be expected to reach a state of equilibrium, although the tendency toward structural balance is one of the factors in its dynamics. Trade regulation may be embraced within this dynamic pattern as an attempt of certain groups to organize the market to their own advantage through political means. Entering into this political struggle to determine the structure of markets are some political leaders and some administrative officials who regard themselves as representing the consumer's interests. It seems reasonable to believe that the increasing sophistication and buying skill of consumers is one of the primary forces offsetting the tendency of the free market economy to turn into something else through the working out of its inherent dynamic forces. This was the destiny foreseen for the capitalistic system by Schumpeter, even though he was one of its staunchest advocates.

The household as an organized behavior system must be given special attention in creating an analytical framework for marketing. The household is an operating entity with an assortment of goods and assets and with economic functions to perform. Once a primary production unit, the household has lost a large part of these activities to manufacturing and service enterprises. Today its economic operations are chiefly expressed through earning and spending. In the typical household there is some specialization between the husband as primary earner and the wife as chief purchasing agent for the household. It may be assumed that she becomes increasingly competent in buying as she surrenders her production activities such as canning, baking and dressmaking, and devotes more of her time and attention to shopping. She is a rational problem solver as she samples what the market has to offer in her effort to maintain a balanced inventory or assortment of goods to meet expected occasions of use. This is not an attempt to substitute Economic Woman for the discredited fiction of Economic Man. It is only intended to assert that the decision structure of consumer buying is similar to that for industrial buying. Both business executive and housewife enter the market as rational problem solvers, even though there are other aspects of personality in either case.

An adequate perspective on the household for marketing purposes must recognize several facets of its activities. It is an organized behavior system with its aspects of power, communication, and operating structure. It is the locus of forms of behavior other than instrumental or goal-seeking activities. A convenient three-way division, derived from the social sciences, recognizes instrumental, congenial, and symptomatic behavior. Congenial behavior is that kind of activity engaged in for its own sake and presumably yielding direct satisfactions. It is exemplified by the act of consumption as compared to all of the instrumental activities which prepare the way for consumption. Symptomatic behavior reflects maladjustment and is neither pleasure-giving in itself nor an efficient pursuit of goals. Symptomatic behavior is functional only to the extent that it serves as a signal to others that the individual needs help.

Some studies of consumer motivation have given increasing attention to symptomatic behavior or to the projection of symptoms of personality adjustment which might affect consumer buying. The present view is that the effort to classify individuals by personality types is less urgent for marketing than the classification of families. Four family types with characteristically different buying behavior have been suggested growing out of the distinction between the instrumental and congenial aspects of normal behavior. Even individuals who are fairly well adjusted in themselves will form a less than perfect family if not fully adapted to each other.

On the instrumental side of household behavior it would seem to be desirable that the members be well coordinated as in any other operating system. If not, they will not deliver the maximum impact in pursuit of family goals. On the congenial side it would appear desirable for the members of a household to be compatible. That means enjoying the same things, cherishing the same goals, preferring joint activities to solitary pursuits or the company of others. These two distinctions yield an obvious four-way classification. The ideal is the family that is coordinated in its instrumental activities and compatible in its congenial activities. A rather joyless household which might nevertheless be well managed and prosperous in material terms is the coordinated but incompatible household. The compatible but uncoordinated family would tend to be happy-go-lucky and irresponsible with obvious consequences for buying behavior. The household which was both uncoordinated and incompatible would usually be tottering on the brink of dissolution. It might be held together formally by scruples against divorce, by concern for children, or by the dominant power of one member over the others. This symptomology of families does not exclude an interest in the readjustment of individuals exhibiting symptomatic behavior. Such remedial action lies in the sphere of the psychiatrist and the social worker, whereas the marketer is chiefly engaged in supplying goods to families which are still functioning as operating units.

All of the discussion of consumers so far limits itself to the activities of the household purchasing agent. Actually the term consumption as it appears in marketing and economic literature nearly always means consumer buying. Some day marketing may need to look beyond the act of purchasing to a study of consumption proper. The occasion for such studies will arise out of the problems of inducing consumers to accept innovations or the further proliferation of products to be included in the household assortment. Marketing studies at this depth will not only borrow from the social sciences but move into the realm of esthetic and ethical values. What is the use of a plethora of goods unless the buyer derives genuine satisfaction from them? What is the justification of surfeit if the acquisition of goods serves as a distraction from activities which are essential to the preservation of our culture and of the integrity of our personalities?

It has been suggested that a study of consumption might begin with the problem of choice in the presence of abundance. The scarce element then is the time or capacity for enjoyment. The bookworm confronted with the thousands of volumes available in a great library must choose in the face of this type of limitation.

The name hedonomics would appear to be appropriate for this field of study suggesting the management of the capacity to enjoy. Among the problems for hedonomics is the pleasure derived from the repetition of a familiar experience as compared with the enjoyment of a novel experience or an old experience with some novel element. Another is the problem of direct experience versus symbolic experience, with the advantages of intensity on the one hand and on the other the possibility of embracing a greater range of possible ideas and sensations by relying on symbolic representations. Extensive basic research will probably be necessary before hedonomics can be put to work in marketing or for the enrichment of human life through other channels.

This paper barely suffices to sketch the analytical framework for marketing. It leaves out much of the area of executive decision-making in marketing on such matters as the weighing of uncertainties and the acceptance of risk in the commitment of resources. It leaves out market planning which is rapidly becoming a systematic discipline centering in the possibilities for economizing time and space as well as resources. It leaves out all but the most casual references to advertising and demand formation. Advertising is certainly one of the most difficult of marketing functions to embrace within a single analytical framework. It largely ignores the developing technology of physical distribution. Hopefully what it does accomplish is to show how the essentially economic problems of marketing may yield to a more comprehensive approach drawing on the basic social sciences for techniques and enriched perspective.

2. CONSUMER CONVENIENCE AND THE RETAIL STRUCTURE OF CITIES*

Reavis Cox

Although marketing men say a great deal about consumption, they really know surprisingly little about it.

This statement may seem paradoxical, even nonsensical, when one considers how enormous a volume of research has been carried out by investigators in this area. They have assembled masses of data about the number of consumers, how old they are, where they are, and how they have moved about geographically in recent years. Thanks to them, analysts have detailed information as to where consumers work, sleep, and go to church; how much money they have; where they spend it; what they buy with it; and how much debt they have accumulated or paid off in any given year. They have told us a great deal about what consumers read, hear over the radio, or see on television, and how they respond to editorial matter and advertising.

To the shrill alarm of some critics (and the derision of others) they have even begun to probe around in levels of the human personality that lie below the conscious, looking for clues that will let them explain, if not control, what consumers do.

In the face of this staggering accumulation of facts, how can one say seriously that we really know very little about consumption?

These words have been chosen very carefully. What marketing men have studied most assiduously is the consumer-buyer; and a little reflection will make it clear that the consumer-buyer can by no means be considered identical with the consumer.

*Reprinted from the *Journal of Marketing*, national quarterly publication of the American Marketing Association (April, 1959), pp. 355–362.

BOUNDARIES OF THE "ECONOMY"

By a long-standing convention economists and others tend to draw a sharp line between what lies within and what lies without the "economy" on the consumer's side of the field. Goods cross the boundary and "move out of the economy" when ever some ultimate consumer or his representative buys them from a consumer service agency, such as a retail store. For analytical and statistical purposes consumption takes place at the time and place of this final sale. What happens thereafter is no doubt interesting and may be important; but it is not "economics."

The boundary thus set up is, of course, strictly arbitrary. The fiction that it exists is harmless enough when recognized for what it is. It can even be helpful in some kinds of formal research, since it makes acts of consumption identifiable, observable, and countable. But it becomes increasingly hard for marketing men to accept with a straight face as a valid description of reality. Too much evidence is accumulating that what goes on "outside the economy" both before and after the final sale has extremely important effects upon marketing.

Consider, for example, what happens as consumers accumulate ever-increasing inventories of houses and consumer durables. These inventories inevitably exert powerful influences upon their behavior as buyers. Furthermore, difficulties arise because goods that have "disappeared" into consumption through a retail sale commonly reappear a little later as trade-ins offered in part payment for new merchandise. Statisticians who would measure the flow of goods into, through, and out of the economy find that they must treat consumers as extractive agencies who feed into the system each year billions of dollars worth of raw or partly processed materials. Especially important in this regard are houses and automobiles.

So, paradoxically, "production" and "consumption" get all mixed up with each other. The economic universe is not really a flat plate from which people and things vanish forever when they fall over the edge. Correspondingly, consumers do not really crawl up over the edge out of a vacuum when they become buyers.

Important reasons impel marketing to rescue from oblivion many things that go on outside the conventional economy. Consumers present themselves repeatedly at the boundary as consumer-buyers. What sorts of problems do they face in planning for this journey? What difficulties do they overcome in making it? What remains for them to do after they have made a purchase? What, if anything, have they done to organize effective procedures for the handling of these problems? A consideration of such matters is very important for marketing men, and particularly for retailers, who are the agents through whom consumers make many of their contacts with the economy.

DELIVERING A STANDARD OF LIVING

What is ordinarily said about the American consumer by marketing men might lead one to believe that he is a child upon whom the sun of fortune has shone so benignly that he has no problems at all. It has become almost mandatory, in talking about him, to point to a wonderful fact: as a daily matter of course our marvelously productive economy provides him with a level of living that once would have excited the envy of kings.

This statement contains a large element of truth, but its constant reiteration has become wearing. Such boasting is hardly designed to strengthen American prestige in a world where bitter dislike, probably based in part upon envy, stands ready to boil up at slight provocation from under a thin veneer of official courtesy. Even in our own country, too many people still do not have equitable shares in this copious stream of goods. And many of those who have moved into what their ancestors would have called a utopia are finding that high-level consumption brings with it ills as well as blessings.

Although Americans would thus do well to tone down their loud expressions of self-satisfaction, the fact remains that year after year their economy does turn over to the mass of its people, at the boundary where it comes into contact with them as consumers, a stupendous mass of goods and services. Even in a year of business depression, such as 1957 or 1958, they found themselves depressed at a high level indeed. What they accomplished can be described only as fantastic.

The accomplishment depends upon carrying through successfully what has been described as a vast exercise in logistics. Participating in this exercise are an enormous number of economic entities. They include over 175 million people, each of whom must be connected with a multitude of others upon whom he has to draw for goods and services. Not all these people come directly to the boundary line that connects consumption with the economy. Many of them—being too young, or too old, or too ill, or too irresponsible, or too busy—have others who buy for them. They come to market through a family or some other type of consumer-buying unit, of which the nation has something on the order of fifty million. The organization and management of these consumer units is one of the formidable accomplishments within the field of consumption about which almost nothing is known.

Dealing with the horde of consumer-buyers, directly or through intermediaries, are at least ten million producers and distributors of goods—nearly five million farms, well over four million business firms (half of these wholesale and retail merchants—the rest manufacturers, builders, extractors, and providers of a wide range of services), at least 150 thousand government agencies that have the power to buy and sell, and an unknown but very large number of individuals who provide professional services, run one-man businesses, or do part-time retailing and the like.

These are not isolated entities, but parts of channel structures. Every time he buys something, and more particularly every time he buys some material good, the consumer finds himself standing at the end point in a long assembly line. This line comprises an assortment and a sequence of agencies. It may be a very short line, consisting of only one or two firms. More commonly it will be a long one made up of several different kinds of firms in a good many different places. Frequently it will be both long and intricate, with sub-assemblies feeding into the main line.

Although channels can be classified into types and generalizations made about each type, every time a consumer buys something he is served by a particular combination of specific firms that may never have been put together before and may never be put together again.

The number of possible combinations and permutations of the agencies available to serve him is so great that, for many goods, it would be an extraordinary circumstance if he were ever served twice by any one combination and sequence of agencies. The oranges, the suits, the automobiles delivered to him thus reach him through an ever-changing assortment of firms. But the organization of the economy is such that he can confidently count on having available for him almost anything he wants whenever and wherever he wants it if he has the money to pay for it.

COLLECTING A STANDARD OF LIVING

Is there any analogous task that must be performed on the consumer's side of the boundary? Students sometimes call what business does, in Paul Mazur's striking phrase, the delivery of a standard of living. It is an intricate, difficult, and costly task. Are there corresponding difficulties and costs on the other side of the boundary, where the consumer works for himself?

Quite obviously there are; and these difficulties have an important bearing both upon the management of retailing and upon the operation of our cities. What Mazur called delivery of his standard of living to the consumer is more properly to be called delivery to the consumer-buyer. One can never fully understand marketing or control it well in the interest of efficiency unless he learns that the consumer proper does not receive his share of the economy's output passively and without effort. He has to decide what he wants, go out and collect it, and use it after he has received it.

An observer can very easily overlook the amount of work these three aspects of consumption impose upon consumers in this country's affluent economy. Conventional ways of thinking carry with them a conviction that consumption is always and endlessly a positive pleasure —rewarding, enjoyable, and effortless. There simply cannot be too much of it.

This may seem like a truism. Yet many consumers, as the economy pours out its flood of goods upon them, must wonder now and then how consumption has got to be so much work and whether it is really worth all that it takes out of them. They must find it very strange indeed to be told now and again that consumption is no longer a pleasure or a privilege, but a duty—that one must keep on buying and consuming, not because he wants to but because if he lets up ever so briefly he is likely to bring a depression crashing down about his ears.

It would be rewarding to wander down the byway such thoughts open to view; but it is a byway. The task here is to explore the main road. A moment's reflection will make it evident that, even after the assembly lines have done their work for him, the consumer still faces a considerable task of assembling and collecting for himself. The number of times he must present himself personally somewhere or other in order to receive a good or a service obviously is large, even though no one knows exactly how large because the matter has been so little studied.

As a start toward building up knowledge in this area Professor Charles S. Goodman, of the University of Pennsylvania, recently undertook to work out an estimate of the number of times consumers buy something or other during the course of a year. (His estimates are being prepared for publication.) He found nineteen lines of retail trade for which he could come up with tolerably acceptable figures covering the year 1954. In these nineteen trades, consumers and their representatives made approximately 69 billion purchases, an average of more than 400 per person, or nearly 1,700 for a family of four.

This total does not include transactions in many retail trades for which no usable estimates could be made. It omits purchases of services offered by such organizations as the post office, transportation agencies, telephone companies, and other utilities, banks, theaters, hospitals, and professional men. It passes over the large number of occasions when the consumer presents himself in person at a church, a park, a school or a college, or before a television set to receive a service for which he pays no formal price but which enters into both his real cost and his real income. Clearly the places to which a typical consumer must go physically as a consumer or send someone to represent him add up to very large numbers over any one year, and to a prodigious total in the course of a lifetime.

CLUSTERING AND CONVENIENCE IN MARKETING

Owing to the size of this burden, the consumer must resort to what may be called the practice of "clustering" his purchases. In less developed economies, where a very large number of people engage in petty trade, at least as a supplement to their other activities, sellers and buyers spend many hours marketing a few handfuls of this or that commodity.

In our economy, neither buyers nor sellers can do this and get around to the full budget of business that must be done. On the contrary, sellers are under heavy pressure to minimize real-unit costs. Buyers also must economize by organizing their purchases into clusters through the device of multi-purpose shopping trips that reduce the time and effort required for individual transactions. Or they cluster their purchasing geographically by going to stores and shopping centers where they can find a wide variety of goods or services within small areas. We know from common knowledge that this happens; but we have nothing remotely approaching an accurate count or an adequate quantitative measure of the consequences.

Consideration of the nature and purpose of clustering means a new look at the old idea that *convenience* is one of the services some types of retail stores provide for their customers. But convenience is a much more complex concept than marketing men used to think. The familiar classification of goods and stores into such categories as convenience, shopping, and specialty does not stand up under analysis. In a real sense every store has to offer convenience to its customers. It would be foolhardy for any merchant deliberately to select a location that he can label inconvenient.

The differences among locations lie rather in what they make convenient—picking up a staple of low price with a minimum of effort, fitting a new purchase into some household's existent or planned assortment of clothing or furniture, comparing what competing merchants have to offer, minimizing the time required to buy a week's supply of groceries, and so on. Furthermore, what the consumer finds it convenient to do is profoundly affected by what he gains from the effort. A substantial price cut can compensate for a great deal of inconvenience in location, and in other aspects of a transaction, as the discount houses have made so abundantly clear.

Eugene J. Kelley has pointed out that when consumers shop, they must achieve an acceptable balance between what he calls "commodity costs" and what he calls "convenience costs."[1] Commodity costs are the sums of money paid to a seller for any goods purchased. Convenience costs are the sums of money paid to agencies other than the seller as an incident to the purchase (for example, train or car fares, payments for gasoline, parking fees, telephone tolls, postage, delivery charges, and financing charges) plus the time and energy used by the consumer in shopping, buying, and carrying the transaction into effect. Kelley also offers a number of new insights into the nature and complexity of the concept of convenience.

What marketing men seem to have in mind when they speak of consumer convenience in marketing relates to the physical aspects of the problem of clustering. But convenience relates to a consumer's whole structure of living, not to isolated bits and pieces such as purchases of particular units of goods. The consumer buys many items, not one. What he should and presumably does do is to economize as best he can the cost or effort he expends in acquiring a varied assortment of goods and services over a long period, not the cost or effort expended on individual units.

AGGREGATE CONVENIENCE

This can be put another way by saying that the consumer seeks aggregate convenience. He is best served when the agencies to which

[1]Eugene J. Kelley, "The Importance of Convenience in Consumer Purchasing," *The Journal of Marketing*, Vol. 23 (July, 1958), pp. 32–38.

he goes as a consumer-buyer are arranged into clusters that help him to minimize the aggregate effort he spends in collecting and using his whole standard of living. Or it can be put the other way around, by saying that he endeavors to maximize the return he receives in all forms from devoting a given budget of time, or effort, or money to shopping.

Although aggregate convenience will not be easy to measure, it is important because even as an abstract concept it throws new light upon the services marketing performs. The ramifications of this idea could be traced out in many directions. The present article confines itself to only one—the function of the city as a means of maximizing aggregate convenience for consumers.

Nothing is more astonishing about modern man's way of life than the extremes to which he has carried the process of jamming himself down into a few densely crowded cities. We have heard much about the so-called "explosion" of cities over the last few years, as people have poured out from central cities and covered the surrounding countryside with continually expanding suburbs. But, even after we allow for this trend, the bulk of our people live on an astonishingly small fraction of our land area.

Why, in the face of the fact that so much can be said against cities as dwelling places, do people crowd about each other so densely? The answer is complex. Numerous, varied, and little understood forces enter into the result. Very important among them, however, are the economies that cities make possible in marketing; and one important economizing influence they exert upon marketing is the aid they give consumers through maximizing aggregate convenience. They make it possible for consumers to come into physical contact easily and in rapid succession with the large number of places at which they collect the goods and services delivered to them by the economy's assembly lines. Any particular place can be reached quickly in case of need and, over a period, large numbers of different places can be touched, as consumers collect their total budgets of goods and services.

Although empirical studies of movement by people and goods within cities are few and fragmentary, one thing seems clear. The principal characteristic the consumer seeks in his city for purposes of collecting his share of the level of the living is easy accessibility to a large number of places, any one or any combination of which he can reach quickly as his wants dictate. It is also clear that the principal devices used to establish aggregate convenience are two: (1) well located bases of operation for the consumer himself, connected with each other by effective transportation of goods and people;[2] (2) easy communication (notably radio, television, newspapers, the postal system, and the telephone).

Effective transportation makes it possible for people to go quickly and easily where they need to go and so to meet at the end points of assembly lines the goods and services they seek from the economy. Effective communication makes it possible for people to inform and do business with each other quickly and easily without coming close together physically, whenever physical contact is not required to get the transaction done.

THE PRINCIPLE OF EFFICIENT CONGESTION

The significance of traffic congestion in cities is made somewhat clearer by this sort of analysis. It has long been one of the paradoxes of cities that people crowd into them until they create atrocious traffic jams.

Why do they do this? Even more important, why are the jams so persistent? This is another way of asking why people continue to subject themselves to this kind of congestion when they know it exists.

The answer seems to be that congestion means contacts, and contacts are what people seek when they crowd into the city in the first place. Retailers have long done all they could to encourage traffic because traffic means business.

This suggests another principle that should be followed in trying to solve the traffic problems of cities—the principle of efficient congestion. There are no more efficient markets in the world than the exchanges that conduct trading in stocks or in commodity futures. Yet in an important sense these are extremely congested markets, because the trading interests of the whole world in some group of securities or some class of commodities are concentrated in them. Their congestion is efficient because they engage only in the bare essentials of their business. They confine themselves strictly to buying and selling, and concentrate these activities in the hands of a few floor traders who can do all the trading required expeditiously.

Those who would improve our cities as marketing institutions need to show a comparable degree of imagination in learning how to

[2]For a more detailed consideration of what is meant by "bases of operation" for city people and how such bases are linked together, see Robert B. Mitchell and Chester Rapkin, *Urban Traffic: A Function of Land Use* (New York: Columbia University Press, 1954), especially Chapter 4.

concentrate within them those aspects of marketing that need congestion, while sluffing off traffic that merely impedes the business at hand without being really necessary.

These thoughts about the nature of the city as a marketing institution also suggest what it is that the automobile has done to and for it. In order to establish an efficient clustering of activities as they move about, consumers must balance as best they can ease of movement, speed of movement, and flexibility as to direction in movement.

When city dwellers had to depend upon walking wherever they went, they had extreme flexibility as to direction, but also slowness of movement and the need to expend considerable effort if they went anywhere. So their movements were narrowly restricted. Mass transportation in its successive forms reduced the effort expended and increased speed, thus making it easy to travel relatively long distances; but it severely restricted direction of movement to a few set lines. The automobile has retained speed and entails very little effort. It also has reintroduced a large degree of flexibility as to direction. The full effect upon the structure of cities has not yet worked itself out.

Thus far, people have "exploded" into the suburbs, taking with them shopping-center "clusters" to accommodate much of what they used to find in the city center. Behind them they have left varying degrees of confusion and blight.

As to what will eventually become of the central business districts, no one has yet worked out a clear picture. Similarly, the ultimate structure of suburban retailing has not yet become evident. What seems probable is that spreading networks of improved highways around at least the large cities will permit consumers to take still more advantage of the flexibility in direction of travel possible with automobiles.

If this happens, it may well be that consumers will find it about as easy to shop stores in several shopping centers on one expedition, moving from place to place by car, as their grandparents found it to shop several stores in one center, moving from place to place on foot or by public transit. Under such conditions, if they develop, what is convenient for consumers will again have changed. The resultant effects upon the structure of retailing are likely to be drastic.

3. MARKETING AND ECONOMIC DEVELOPMENT*

Peter F. Drucker

MARKETING AS A BUSINESS DISCIPLINE

The distinguished pioneer of marketing, whose memory we honor today, was largely instrumental in developing marketing as a systematic business discipline—in teaching us how to go about, in an orderly, purposeful and planned way to find and create customers; to identify and define markets; to create new ones and promote them; to integrate customers' needs, wants, and preferences, and the intellectual and creative capacity and skills of an industrial society, toward the design of new and better products and of new distributive concepts and processes.

On this contribution and similar ones of other Founding Fathers of marketing during the last half century rests the rapid emergence of marketing as perhaps the most advanced, certainly the most "scientific" of all functional business disciplines.

But Charles Coolidge Parlin also contributed as a Founding Father toward the development of marketing as a *social discipline.* He helped give us the awareness, the concepts, and the tools that make us understand marketing as a dynamic process of society through which business enterprise is integrated productively with society's purposes and human values. It is in marketing, as we now understand it, that we satisfy individual and social values, needs, and wants—be it through producing goods, supplying services, fostering innovation, or creating

*Reprinted from the *Journal of Marketing*, national quarterly publication of the American Marketing Association (January, 1958), pp. 252–259.

satisfaction. Marketing, as we have come to understand it, has its focus on the customer, that is, on the individual making decisions within a social structure and within a personal and social value system. Marketing is thus the process through which economy is integrated into society to serve human needs.

I am not competent to speak about marketing in the first sense, marketing as a functional discipline of business. I am indeed greatly concerned with marketing in this meaning. One could not be concerned, as I am, with the basic institutions of industrial society in general and with the management of business enterprise in particular, without a deep and direct concern with marketing. But in this field I am a consumer of marketing alone—albeit a heavy one. I am not capable of making a contribution. I would indeed be able to talk about the wants and needs I have which I, as a consumer of marketing, hope that you, the men of marketing, will soon supply:—a theory of pricing, for instance, that can serve, as true theories should, as the foundation for actual pricing decisions and for an understanding of price behavior; or a consumer-focused concept and theory of competition. But I could not produce any of these "new products" of marketing which we want. I cannot contribute myself. To use marketing language, I am not even "effective demand," in these fields as yet.

THE ROLE OF MARKETING

I shall today in my remarks confine myself to the second meaning in which marketing has become a discipline: The role of marketing in economy and society. And I shall single out as my focus the role of marketing in the economic development, especially of underdeveloped "growth" countries.

My thesis is very briefly as follows. Marketing occupies a critical role in respect to the development of such "growth" areas. Indeed marketing is the most important "multiplier" of such development. It is in itself in every one of these areas the least developed, the most backward part of the economic system. Its development, above all others, makes possible economic integration and the fullest utilization of whatever assets and productive capacity an economy already possesses. It mobilizes latent economic energy. It contributes to the greatest needs: that for the rapid development of enterpreneurs and managers, and at the same time it may be the easiest area of managerial work to get going. The reason is that, thanks to men like Charles Coolidge Parlin, it is the most systematized and, therefore, the most learnable and the most teachable of all areas of business management and enterpreneurship.

INTERNATIONAL AND INTERRACIAL INEQUALITY

Looking at this world of ours, we see some essentially new facts.

For the first time in man's history the whole world is united and unified. This may seem a strange statement in view of the conflicts and threats of suicidal wars that scream at us from every headline. But conflict has always been with us. What is new is that today all of mankind shares the same vision, the same objective, the same goal, the same hope, and believes in the same tools. This vision might, in gross over-simplification, be called "industrialization."

It is the belief that it is possible for man to improve his economic lot through systematic, purposeful, and directed effort—individually as well as for an entire society. It is the belief that we have the tools at our disposal—the technological, the conceptual, and the social tools—to enable man to raise himself, through his own efforts, at least to a level that we in this country would consider poverty, but which for most of our world would be almost unbelievable luxury.

And this is an irreversible new fact. It has been made so by these true agents of revolution in our times: the new tools of communication—the dirt road, the truck, and the radio, which have penetrated even the furthest, most isolated and most primitive community.

This is new, and cannot be emphasized too much and too often. It is both a tremendous vision and a tremendous danger in that catastrophe must result if it cannot be satisfied, at least to a modest degree.

But at the same time we have a new, unprecedented danger, that of international and interracial inequality. We on the North American continent are a mere tenth of the world population, including our Canadian friends and neighbors But we have at least 75 per cent of the world income. And the 75 per cent of the world population whose income is below $100 per capita a year receive together perhaps no more than 10 per cent of the world's income. This is inequality of income, as great as anything the world has ever seen. It is accompanied by very high equality of income in the developed countries, especially in ours where we are in the process of proving that an industrial society does not have to live in extreme tension between the few very rich and the many very poor as lived all earlier societies of man. But what used to be national inequality and economic tension is now rapidly becoming international (and unfortunately also interracial) inequality and tension.

This is also brand new. In the past there were tremendous differences between societies and cultures: in their beliefs, their concepts, their ways of life, and their knowledge. The Frankish knight who went on Crusade was an ignorant and illiterate boor, according to the standards of the polished courtiers of Constantinople or of his Moslem enemies. But economically his society and theirs were exactly alike. They had the same sources of income, the same productivity of labor, the same forms and channels of investment, the same economic institutions, and the same distribution of income and wealth. Economically the Frankish knight, however much a barbarian he appeared, was at home in the societies of the East; and so was his serf. Both fitted in immediately and without any difficulty.

And this has been the case of all societies that went above the level of purely primitive tribe.

The inequality in our world today, however, between nations and races, is therefore a new—and a tremendously dangerous—phenomenon.

What we are engaged in today is essentially a race between the promise of economic development and the threat of international worldwide class war. The economic development is the opportunity of this age. The class war is the danger. Both are new. Both are indeed so new that most of us do not even see them as yet. But they are the essential economic realities of this industrial age of ours. And whether we shall realize the opportunity or succumb to danger will largely decide not only the economic future of this world—it may largely decide its spiritual, its intellectual, its political, and its social future.

SIGNIFICANCE OF MARKETING

Marketing is central in this new situation. For marketing is one of our most potent levers to convert the danger into the opportunity.

To understand this we must ask: What do we mean by "underdeveloped"?

The first answer is, of course, that we mean areas of very low income. But income is, after all, a result. It is a result first of extreme agricultural over-population in which the great bulk of the people have to find a living on the land which, as a result, cannot even produce enough food to feed them, let alone produce a surplus. It is certainly a result of low productivity. And both, in a vicious circle, mean that there is not enough capital for investment, and very low productivity of what is being invested—owing largely to misdirection of investment into unessential and unproductive channels.

All this we know today and understand. Indeed we have learned during the last few years a very great deal both about the structure of an under-developed economy and about the theory and dynamics of economic development.

What we tend to forget, however, is that the essential aspect of an "underdeveloped" economy and the factor the absence of which keeps it "under-developed," is the inability to organize economic efforts and energies, to bring together resources, wants, and capacities, and so to convert a self-limiting static system into creative, self-generating organic growth.

And this is where marketing comes in.

Lack of Development in "Under-developed" Countries

First, in every "under-developed" country I know of, marketing is the most under-developed—or the least developed—part of the economy, if only because of the strong, pervasive prejudice against the "middleman."

As a result, these countries are stunted by inability to make effective use of the little they have. Marketing might by itself go far toward changing the entire economic tone of the existing system—without any change in methods of production, distribution of population, or of income.

It would make the producers capable of producing marketable products by providing them with standards, with quality demands, and with specifications for their product. It would make the product capable of being brought to markets instead of perishing on the way. And it would make the consumer capable of discrimination, that is, of obtaining the greatest value for his very limited purchasing power.

In every one of these countries, marketing profits are characteristically low. Indeed the people engaged in marketing barely eke out a subsistence living. And "mark-ups" are minute by our standards. But marketing costs are outrageously high. The waste in distribution and marketing, if only from spoilage or from the accumulation of unsalable inventories that clog the shelves for years, has to be seen to be believed. And marketing service is by and large all but non-existent.

What is needed in any "growth" country to make economic development realistic, and at the same time produce a vivid demonstration of what economic development can produce, is a marketing system:—a system of physical distribution, a financial system to make possible the distribution of goods, and finally actual marketing, that is, an actual system of integrating wants, needs, and purchasing power of the consumer with capacity and resources of production.

This need is largely masked today because marketing is so often confused with the traditional "trader and merchant" of which every one of these countries has more than enough. It would be one of our most important contributions to the development of "under-developed" countries to get across the fact that marketing is something quite different.

It would be basic to get across the triple function of marketing the function of crystallizing and directing demand for maximum productive effectiveness and efficiency; the function of guiding production purposefully toward maximum consumer satisfaction and consumer value; the function of creating discrimination that then gives rewards to those who really contribute excellence, and that then also penalize the monopolist, the slothful, or those who only want to take but do not want to contribute or to risk.

Utilization by the Entrepreneur

Marketing is also the most easily accessible "multiplier" of managers and entrepreneurs in an "under-developed" growth area. And managers and entrepreneurs are the foremost need of these countries. In the first place, "economic development" is not a force of nature. It is the result of the action, the purposeful, responsible, risk-taking action, of men as entrepreneurs and managers.

Certainly it is the entrepreneur and manager who alone can convey to the people of these countries an understanding of what economic development means and how it can be achieved.

Marketing can convert latent demand into effective demand. It cannot, by itself, create purchasing power. But it can uncover and channel all purchasing power that exists. It can, therefore, create rapidly the conditions for a much higher level of economic activity than existed before, can create the opportunities for the entrepreneur.

It then can create the stimulus for the development of modern, responsible, professional management by creating opportunity for the producer who knows how to plan, how to organize, how to lead people, how to innovate.

In most of these countries markets are of necessity very small. They are too small to make it possible to organize distribution for a single-product line in any effective manner. As a result, without a marketing organization, many products for which there is an adequate demand at a reasonable price cannot be distributed; or worse, they can be produced and distributed only under monopoly conditions. A marketing system is needed which serves as the joint and common channel for many producers if any of them is to be able to come into existence and to stay in existence.

This means in effect that a marketing system in the "under-developed" countries is the *creator of small business*, is the only way in which a man of vision and daring can become a businessman and an entrepreneur himself. This is thereby also the only way in which a true middle class can develop in the countries in which the habit of investment in productive enterprise has still to be created.

Developer of Standards

Marketing in an "under-developed" country is the developer of standards—of standards for product and service as well as of standards of conduct, of integrity, of reliability, of foresight, and of concern for the basic long-range impact of decisions on the customer, the supplier, the economy, and the society.

Rather than go on making theoretical statements let me point to one illustration: The impact Sears Roebuck has had on several countries of Latin America. To be sure, the countries of Latin America in which Sears operates—Mexico, Brazil, Cuba, Venezuela, Colombia, and Peru—are not "under-developed" in the same sense in which Indonesia or the Congo are "under-developed." Their average income, although very low by our standards, is at least two times, perhaps as much as four or five times, that of the truly "under-developed" countries in which the bulk of mankind still live. Still in every respect except income level these Latin American countries are at best "developing." And they have all the problems of economic development—perhaps even in more acute form than the countries of Asia and Africa, precisely because their development has been so fast during the last ten years.

It is also true that Sears in these countries is not a "low-price" merchandiser. It caters to the middle class in the richer of these countries, and to the upper middle class in the poorest of these countries. Incidentally, the income level of these groups is still lower than that of the worker in the industrial sector of our economy.

Still Sears is a mass-marketer even in Colombia or Peru. What is perhaps even more important, it is applying in these "under-developed" countries exactly the same policies and principles it applies in this country, carries substantially the same merchandise (although most of it produced in the countries themselves), and applies the same concepts of marketing it uses in Indianapolis or Philadelphia. Its impact and experience are, therefore, a fair test of what marketing principles, marketing knowledge, and marketing techniques can achieve.

The impact of this one American business which does not have more than a mere handful of stores in these countries and handles no more than a small fraction of the total retail business of these countries is truly amazing. In the first place, Sears' latent purchasing power has fast become actual purchasing power. Or, to put it less theoretically, people have begun to organize their buying and to go out for value in what they do buy.

Secondly, by the very fact that it builds one store in one city, Sears forces a revolution in retailing throughout the whole surrounding area. It forces store modernization. It forces consumer credit. It forces a different attitude toward the customer, toward the store clerk, toward the supplier, and toward the merchandise itself. It forces other retailers to adopt modern methods of pricing, of inventory control, of training, of window display, and what have you.

The greatest impact Sears has had, however, is the multiplication of new industrial business for which Sears creates a marketing channel. Because it has had to sell goods manufactured in these countries rather than import them (if only because of foreign exchange restrictions), Sears has been instrumental in getting established literally hundreds of new manufacturers making goods which, a few years ago, could not be made in the country, let alone be sold in adequate quantity. Simply to satisfy its own marketing needs, Sears has had to insist on standards of workmanship, quality, and delivery—that is, on standards of production management, of technical management, and above all of the management of people—which, in a few short years, have advanced the art and science of management in these countries by at least a generation.

I hardly need to add that Sears is not in Latin America for reasons of philanthropy, but because it is good and profitable business with extraordinary growth potential. In other words, Sears is in Latin America because marketing is the major opportunity in a "growth economy"—precisely because its absence is a major economic gap and the greatest need.

The Discipline of Marketing

Finally, marketing is critical in economic development because marketing has become so largely systematized, so largely both learnable and teachable. It is the discipline among all our business disciplines that has advanced the furthest.

I do not forget for a moment how much we still have to learn in marketing. But we should also not forget that most of what we have learned so far we have learned in a form in which we can express it in general concepts, in valid principles and, to a substantial degree, in quantifiable measurements. This, above all others, was the achievement of that generation to whom Charles Coolidge Parlin was leader and inspiration.

A critical factor in this world of ours is the learnability and teachability of what it means to be an entrepreneur and manager. For it is the entrepreneur and the manager who alone can cause economic development to happen. The world needs them, therefore, in very large numbers; and it needs them fast.

Obviously this need cannot be supplied by our supplying entrepreneurs and managers, quite apart from the fact that we hardly have the surplus. Money we can supply. Technical assistance we can supply, and should supply more. But the supply of men we can offer to the people in the "under-developed" countries is of necessity a very small one.

The demand is also much too urgent for it to be supplied by slow evolution through experience, or through dependence on the emergence of "naturals." The danger that lies in the inequality today between the few countries that have and the great many countries that have not is much too great to permit a wait of centuries. Yet it takes centuries if we depend on experience and slow evolution for the supply of entrepreneurs and managers adequate to the needs of a modern society.

There is only one way in which man has ever been able to short-cut experience, to telescope development, in other words, to *learn something*. That way is to have available the distillate of experience and skill in the form of knowledge, of concepts, of generalization, of measurement—in the form of *discipline*, in other words.

THE DISCIPLINE OF ENTREPRENEURSHIP

Many of us today are working on the fashioning of such a discipline of entrepreneurship and management. Maybe we are further along than most of us realize.

Certainly in what has come to be called "Operation Research and Synthesis" we have the first beginnings of a systematic approach to the entrepreneurial task of purposeful risk-taking and innovation—so far only an approach, but a most promising one, unless indeed we become so enamored with the gadgets and techniques as to forget purpose and aim.

We are at the beginning perhaps also of an understanding of the basic problems of organizing people of diversified and highly advanced skill and judgment together in one effective organization, although again no one so far would, I am convinced, claim more for us than that we have begun at last to ask intelligent questions.

But marketing, although it only covers one functional area in the field, has something that can be called a discipline. It has developed general concepts, that is, theories that explain a multitude of phenomena in simple statements. It even has measurements that record "facts" rather than opinions. In marketing, therefore, we already possess a learnable and teachable approach to this basic and central problem not only of the "under-developed" countries but of all countries. All of us have today the same survival stake in economic development. The risk and danger of international and interracial inequality are simply too great.

Marketing is obviously not a cure-all, not a paradox. It is only one thing we need. But it answers a critical need. At the same time marketing is most highly developed.

Indeed without marketing as the hinge on which to turn, economic development will almost have to take the totalitarian form. A totalitarian system can be defined economically as one in which economic development is being attempted without marketing, indeed as one in which marketing is suppressed. Precisely because it first looks at the values and wants of the individual, and because it then develops people to act purposefully and responsibly—that is, because of its effectiveness in developing a free economy—marketing is suppressed in a totalitarian system. If we want economic development in freedom and responsibility, we have to build it on the development of marketing.

In the new and unprecedented world we live in, a world which knows both a new unity of vision and growth and a new and most dangerous cleavage, marketing has a special and central role to play. This role goes beyond "getting the stuff out the back door," beyond "getting the most sales with the least cost," beyond "the optimal integration of our values and wants as customers, citizens, and persons, with our productive resources and intellectual achievements"—the role marketing plays in a developed society.

In a developing economy, marketing is, of course, all of this. But in addition, in an economy that is striving to break the age-old bondage of man to misery, want, and destitution, marketing is also the catalyst for the transmutation of latent resources into actual resources, of desires into accomplishments, and the development of responsible economic leaders and informed economic citizens.

4. THE VALUE ADDED CONCEPT AS A MEASUREMENT OF OUTPUT*

Theodore N. Beckman

In a very broad sense the term "management" has at times been used to refer to the control of activities, whatever their nature. Thus, we often hear complaints that a certain person cannot even "manage" his own affairs—business or personal—let alone those of others. We even speak occasionally of "self-management," thus using the term in a strictly subjective manner. In the most accepted sense, however, the term management is used to cover the planning, organizing, and controlling of the activities of an *organization.*

WHY OUTPUT IS A BASIC MEASUREMENT OF MANAGEMENT

Essentially, management has to do with the most effective and economical use of all factors of production and their component parts in the accomplishment of the organization's objectives, the main one of which is that of producing a desired output. This output may be in the form of goods extracted, manufactured, and/or marketed, or in services rendered. To this end it becomes necessary to establish standards of performance and then to measure actual performance against these standards for a proper evaluation of what has been accomplished and as a means of obtaining enhanced efficiency in the future.

Because a defined and desired output is the principal aim and purpose of an organization, and because each of the factors of production or components thereof must necessarily be related to it, output becomes the basic measurement of management. It is, therefore, of

*Reprinted from *Advanced Management* (April, 1957), pp. 6–9.

utmost importance, first, that we have a correct conception of the output that is to be measured and, second, that such output be properly measured. It makes a lot of difference, for example, whether we are to conceive of output as that of a business enterprise, a business establishment, or a business function. It is even of greater importance to distinguish between what output was created or added to by the given enterprise, establishment, or function and what was created previously by other enterprises or establishments.

INADEQUACY OF CURRENT MEASUREMENTS OF OUTPUT

In general, output of business enterprises is now measured in terms of production, shipments, sales, or receipts. Receipts are invariably expressed in values, which are subject to fluctuations in the purchasing power of the dollar, and are not especially applicable to other than service concerns. When production, shipments, or sales (gross or net) are expressed in values, they suffer from the same shortcoming as receipts, (as is, unfortunately, also true of value added). When expressed in terms of so-called physical volume, they are in reality nothing but values in constant dollars. Even when production, shipments, or sales are measured in physical units, the results may be of little value in measuring output, except perhaps in such commodities as steel or cement, because the units do not remain unchanged over any extended period of time. A 1957 model of a given make of automobile is certainly a different product even from the same make of car of an earlier vintage. The same thing is true of tires, batteries, and the vast majority of products in use today.

However, the most important weakness in all these measurements of output is that they all involve considerable duplication. Thus, in the production, shipments, or sales of a manufacturer, no matter how expressed, are included the costs of materials and supplies and purchased parts that were produced by others, in addition to what was added by the manufacturer in question. Moreover, this sort of duplication varies substantially from enterprise to enterprise. For example, one manufacturer might conceivably make a finished product in a completely integrated operation from the raw materials on. In such an instance the duplication would be insignificant or nonexistent. At the other extreme, a manufacturer may merely assemble a finished product from parts and supplies made by others, in which instance the duplication would be several times the contribution made by such a manufacturer. Between these two extremes, there are all sorts of gradations and variations in this regard. This at once exaggerates the contribution of some, understates that of others, and in all cases makes comparison futile and misleading.

What has just been stated should not be taken to imply any lack of value in data on production, shipments, sales, or receipts. Such data are still important for purposes of planning; budgeting; setting quotas; determination of rental values: figuring commissions, other operating expenses, gross and net profits; and for many other uses. What it does mean is that they are found wanting as measurements of output for basic management purposes and especially for determining the real contribution made by the business unit or function that is the subject of measurement.

VALUE ADDED AFFORDS BEST MEASUREMENT OF OUTPUT

It is believed that value added best measures the output of an establishment, an enterprise, an industry, or any other segment or sector of our economy. In time, this concept may also be used to measure the output that may be attributed to a given business function or process. In any event, it can be used in that manner internally by a business establishment or enterprise.

At present the use of value added is more or less restricted to the field of manufacturing and even there it is not as widely used outside the Census of Manufactures and other governmental agencies as is warranted. What is needed is wide application of this concept to all phases of the economy and strong attempts to do so are now being made by a number of potent organizations and others interested in progress in economic thought.

NATURE OF VALUE ADDED CONCEPT AS USED BY CENSUS OF MANUFACTURES

The value added concept has been used by the Bureau of the Census in connection with its censuses of manufactures for over a quarter of a century. As stated in its various appropriate publications, "Value added by manufacture is calculated by subtracting the cost of materials, supplies, and containers, fuel, purchased electric energy, and contract work from the total value of shipments." It thus represents the difference between the selling value of products shipped or delivered and the cost of materials, supplies, and containers, plus the cost of fuel, purchased electric energy, and contract work. Basically, then, the difference represents the net value of the operations of the reporting establishment itself without any admixtures of the labors or operations of other establishments and this is presumed to measure the value added by the process of manufacture. It is a measure of the net output of the establishment, industry, industry group, or all manufacturing industries, as the case may be. Even then it is subject to certain limitations.

REASONS FOR CENSUS USE OF VALUE ADDED BY MANUFACTURE

For some years there has been a tendency for the Census of Manufactures to shift emphasis more and more from value of products shipped to value added by manufacturer as a measure of the contribution to the economy of the manufacturing sector and parts thereof. As a matter of fact, in its annual surveys of manufactures value added by manufacture has completely replaced the value of production or shipments, although, as previously indicated, there are still some very important uses to data on the latter. Among the major reasons for this shift in emphasis was a desire to avoid duplication. This is clearly expressed in the following excerpts from the Bureau's publications:

> "The value of products is not a satisfactory measure of the importance of a given industry, because only part of this value is actually created within the industry. Another part and often a much larger one, is contributed by the value of the materials used. The aggregates for cost of materials and value of products include large amounts of duplication due to the use of the products of some industries as materials by others." . . . "Statistics of 'value added by manufacture' are almost entirely free from the duplication which is a factor in the total value of products." . . .[1]

Another reason was the Bureau's conviction that value added by manufacture is a fairly accurate measure of what is accomplished or created by a given industry and affords the best means for comparison of the economic contribution of one industry with that of another. This

[1]Fifteenth Census of the United States. Manufactures: 1929, Volume I, United States Government Printing Office, Washington: 1933, pages 6 and 8. In approximately identical phrasing the same substance is expressed on page 18 of Volume II of Census of Manufactures: 1947, U.S.G.P.O.: 1949.

can be clearly discerned from the following excerpt in one of its publications:

> "'Value added by manufacture' measures the approximate value created in the process of manufacture. It, therefore, provides the most satisfactory census measure of the relative importance of given industries for the United States as a whole or for geographic areas."[2]

ESSENCE OF THE VALUE ADDED CONCEPT AS NOW USED

Theoretically, the treatment of the value added concept by the Census of Manufactures is functional in character, since it is presumed to measure the contribution made by the *process* of manufacture as contrasted with the process of marketing or any other process. That is certainly the avowed purpose repeatedly stated in appropriate census publications. Actually, however, the concept is treated institutionally, in that the value added by manufacture is computed on an establishment basis and thus covers *all* activities performed by the manufacturing establishment including those of distribution or marketing. This would seem to be inevitable under existing conditions of gathering such information on a broad scale by a government agency or by a trade association, because of the current state of the arts in accounting, at least in practical application. This means that for practical reasons the measurement of value added must for the present be on an institutional rather than a functional basis, except for more detailed internal operation analysis within an enterprise.

Again, the word "value" as part of value added is used in the same practical sense as it is used in connection with value of products or value of shipments. To be sure, value is fundamentally a subjective quality involving the satisfactions to human beings mainly as consumers and can be truly known only to the human being involved, assuming full consciousness on his part of such satisfactions. Certainly, there is no way of practically measuring such satisfactions and their differing intensities except through expressions in the market place in the form of prices. It is in this latter sense that the term value is used. It is assumed that the price a person will pay for a product or service is in general a reasonable measure of its value to him. Without at this

[2]Annual Survey of Manufactures: 1949 and 1950, U. S. Government Printing Office, Washington: 1952, p. 8.

time going into further theoretical discussions of the nature of economic value, suffice it to say that there are other good reasons for treating it in the common sense and practical way in which it is used in connection with the value added concept.

Finally, the term value added is used in the same sense as value created or value produced. This is in line with the best current economic thinking that production is the creation of economic values and that such values are created through the addition of utilities, which are capacities in goods or services to satisfy human wants. Essentially, there are four types of classes of utilities: form, place, time, and possession. *Form* utility is created in any extracting, processing, or manufacturing operation which converts or *transforms* scarce resources such as raw materials or semi-manufactures to increasingly satisfying states. An automobile manufacturer who assembled a completed product from various parts and supplies purchased by him creates form utility, just as does a canner who processes the raw tomatoes by canning *Place* utility is created when a product or service is made available where the customer wants it. For this purpose, goods must be *transferred* from where they are first available to the next place and on until they reach their final destination in business or for ultimate consumer use. *Time* utility is created when the product or service is made available to the customer when he wants it. *Possession* utility is created when the product or service is at the user's command, i.e., in his possession, legally and physically, as through the transfer of title to goods.

It is now generally recognized among economists and other students of the subject that the creation of these utilities spells the creation of economic values and that this is the essence of production. This means that whoever creates these utilities is engaged in production, so that a wholesaler or a retailer who normally creates place, time, and possession utilities is as much a producer as is a processor who changes a product from one form to another. It also means that all who are engaged in the creation of utilities or economic values are productive and, by their work, add value and make a contribution to our economy.

ADVANTAGES FROM USE OF VALUE ADDED CONCEPT THROUGHOUT THE ECONOMY

It stands to reason that the adoption of the value added concept in the measurement of output in all sectors of the economy including farming, mining, and distribution, would have the same advantages as those derived from its use in connection with manufacturing. In the first place, it is the best reasonably available *absolute* measure of the value created in the process of whatever part of the economy is being measured. It measures, without any duplication, what the activities in question have actually contributed to our society in terms of enhanced value of goods and services through the creation of utilities.

Second, value added is the best reasonably available *relative* measure of value created that can be used for proper and fairly accurate comparison with anything else similarly measured. In this manner, it will be possible for the first time to make proper comparison between the economic contribution made, for example, by farming, manufacturing, mining, marketing, and certain services. Also, it would make possible a proper comparison of one segment of, say, distribution like wholesaling with another like retailing or of one type or of wholesaling or retailing with another.

Third, use of the concept will help to view costs in their proper perpective. While cost is a measure of *input* or of what a business spends or puts into its activities, value added is a measure of the *output* produced by such costs. Value added is thus really the value received for the costs incurred or for the input in terms of labor, entrepreneurial management, capital, and other factors of production. Not only is it essential that the two should not be confused or used interchangeably except from a strictly social viewpoint according to which income and outgo must necessarily balance, but it is also essential that costs should not be viewed by themselves without relation to value added. To look at costs by themselves, without knowing what was gotten for them is hardly scientific and, in fact, quite misleading.

Fourth, application of the value added concept to any part of the economy would necessarily result in improved public relations. As in manufacturing, where it has been used for some time, it would tend to shift emphasis from costs and wastes to value added and from a negative to a positive and constructive approach to the problems involved.

A PREREQUISITE TO MEASUREMENT OF PRODUCTIVITY

As may be surmised from what has already been stated, value added is not in itself a measurement of productivity. It merely measures production, i.e., the result of productive activity involved in the creation of economic values, not the rate at which such production has proceeded with reference to some factor of production or a part thereof. Unfortunately, it is a common error to confuse production with productivity. For example, it is often publicized that in this country we have a productivity at the rate of 3% per year. What it really means, assuming the percentage to be correct, is that our production or total output such as gross national product has been increasing at the rate indicated, but it does not measure the productivity or degree of efficiency of our labor force, capital resources, or any other factor of production. In fact, it may well be that productivity has actually declined at certain times, when the increase in the labor force, accumulated capital, and in other factors of production are considered.

Properly used, productivity is a ratio or relationship between output on the one hand and resources expended to produce that output on the other. Usually, an attempt is made to relate output to a factor of production deemed essentially or principally responsible for it. This has generally resulted in measuring productivity in terms of output per unit of direct labor such as a man-hour. It is obvious that when this is done, value added more nearly represents the contribution made by a unit of labor than do sales, products, or shipments.

At this juncture it may not be inappropriate to point out the fallacy in using solely man-hours of direct labor in computations of productivity, for it has led many to believe that all increases in productivity are attributable to this type of labor. The truth of the matter is that supervisory or indirect labor may have had as much or more to do with enhancing productivity as did direct labor. Moreover, increased productivity may frequently be caused far more by greater capital investment per unit of product or per unit of labor than by increased skill of or application by labor. For this reason, productivity may well take the form of a ratio of output to investment in capital goods or to machine hours of operation.

Again, management may be chiefly responsible for enhanced productivity. A case in point is the redesigning and rearrangement by management of a production line for a given product in the electrical field with the result that five men on a line could produce more than twice the physical volume formerly produced by seven men. Labor had nothing to do with this increase in productivity, as the type and skill of labor used on the lines remained unchanged.

Finally, land as a factor of productivity may be the factor that enhances productivity in a given situation. It is well known that a proper location of a business may have much to do with the amount of output produced, whether it be in terms of sales or value added.

It is, therefore, believed that much progress can be made in the measurement of productivity, if the output in terms of value added would be related to the various factors of production and not to labor alone. The difficulty of developing such measurements is no more of an excuse for not doing the job than the difficulty of complying with a law is an excuse for violating it. Besides, I am of the conviction that the job can be done and that it may be possible to determine just what factor of production is responsible for enhanced productivity and to what approximate degree.

A PREREQUISITE TO MEASUREMENT OF OVERALL EFFICIENCY

Similarly, value added is not in itself a measurement of efficiency, but merely the proper output figure to be used in such a measurement. Especially in the measurement of overall efficiency, value added is the best numerator to be related to a denominator of total costs or any of its components and to net profits. It follows, therefore, that it would be erroneous to conclude that output viewed as value added would cause us to be concerned about ways and means of increasing it for its own sake, just as it would be erroneous to assume that input viewed in terms of costs would cause us to be concerned with ways and means of reducing it for its own sake and without due regard to the values obtained for such cost.

EMPHASIS ON PRODUCTIVE CHARACTER OF ALL ECONOMIC ACTIVITY

One of the most significant benefits to be derived from the use of value added as a measurement of output is the emphasis it gives to the productive character of whatever economic activity it measures. This approach to economic analysis inevitably leads to the conclusion that economic values are created by all segments of the economy and by all persons making up the labor force and, consequently, all of them are engaged in productive work.

The significance of this becomes apparent upon a brief review of a few highlights in the development of economic thought in this regard through the centuries. For example, as great a philosopher as Aristotle deemed money to be unproductive, on the ground that a piece of money cannot beget another piece of money. Such unsound thinking held sway in most parts of the world until the 14th century. During the periods of both Greek and Roman civilizations agriculture was considered the only productive economic activity. Even as late as the middle of the 18th century there arose a school of French economists, known as the Physiocrats, who believed and taught that agriculture was the only honorable industry and that land was the only real factor of production and possibly also the labor working upon it. Manufacturing and commerce were considered by them as unproductive and, in fact, all trade was deemed vulgar as was all mechanical labor. Strange as it may seem, there are still people amongst our governmental and political leaders today whose thinking harks back to the physiocratic school of economics, as when they bemoan the allegedly small share of the consumer's dollar received by the farmer compared with the much larger share retained in the form of "spread" by middlemen amongst whom are included manufacturers, processors, and transportation agencies. Even Adam Smith, the father of classical economics considered as productive only that part of labor which was bestowed on salable goods. He specifically regarded all menial servants, professional men, and public officials as unproductive. Some of his followers similarly referred to soldiers, servants, and other *unproductive* laborers.

It was not until the beginning of this century that economists generally accepted four factors of production, when to the familiar trinity of land, labor, and capital was added that of enterprise or of entrepreneurial management. In common parlance, however, and among business men generally we still speak of production as having to do with the change in form of products in the extractive and manufacturing industries and look down upon all other types of economic activity as possibly something to be tolerated but to be eliminated or reduced in importance at every opportunity.

It is high time that we all get in line with sound economic thinking and stop the silly argument as to who or what part of our labor force is or is not productive and whether one type of labor is engaged in production and another is not. If the classical concept of the terms production or productive were to be applied today, it would be found that only a little over two-fifths of our labor force would be engaged in production, while nearly three-fifths would be considered sterile or unproductive. This is silly on the very face of it. This means that we must stop treating persons engaged in certain economic activities like marketing or the services and professions as second-class citizens or no citizens at all in our economic life. The truth of the matter is that they are all creating values and are therefore part of the production process engaged in productive activity.

CONCLUSION

The value added concept as a measurement of output, in my judgment, presents a challenge to all persons concerned with creative thinking in the field of management. It calls for study and reflection, for a reappraisal of the traditional approach to the problem, and for some hard thinking along perhaps new and unconventional lines. It calls for a realistic treatment of our economic environment, for adventure in the realm of economic thought, and for a generous share of iconoclasticism. It is hoped that the necessary data will soon be made available to do all that in the scientific way to which leaders in management have become accustomed.

5. MARKETING FROM THE PRODUCER'S POINT OF VIEW*

P. J. Verdoorn

THEORY AND POLICY

In recent years a number of discussions have been devoted to the scientific status of *marketing*.[1] To the not-directly-interested outsider, the most conspicuous aspect of these discussions is the clearly demonstrated lack of a general method of approach to marketing problems. This has prevented a logical "hierarchy" among the different problems of marketing and the integration of the relevant theories. As a result, the subject still consists of a number of mutually unrelated fields of study. True, each of these by itself has been elaborated in a scientific manner; but we still lack a general framework in which the various aspects of marketing are related to one another and which, at the same time, shows their delimitation with respect to other fields of study.

The object of a theory of marketing is to explain the activities of the policy makers who ". . . direct the flow of goods and services from producer to consumer or user." Therefore, the student of these essentially economic problems, if he wishes to arrive at a general system of approach, must turn for guidance to economic theory—in particular, to the theory of the firm.

As will be shown in what follows, the modern theory of the "policy maker," as put forward by Frisch and Tinbergen,[2] provides an ade-

*Reprinted from the *Journal of Marketing*, national quarterly publication of the American Marketing Association (January, 1956), pp. 221–235.

[1]Cf., for a concise survey of older contributions, K. D. Hutchinson, "Marketing As a Science, An Appraisal," the *Journal of Marketing*, January 1952, pp. 286–93. Also, J. E. Jeuck, "Marketing Research—Milestone or Millstone?," *Ibid.*, April 1953, pp. 382–84; and Edmund D. McGarry, "Some Viewpoints in Marketing," *Ibid.*, July 1953, pp. 33–41.

[2]Cf. J. Tinbergen, *On the Theory of Economic Policy* (Amsterdam: North-Holland Publishing Company, 1952) and *Centralization and Decentralization in Economic Policy* (Amsterdam: North-Holland Publishing Company, 1954).

quate basis for a general method of approach sufficiently flexible to be applied to the various subject matters of marketing. If we regard the various interested parties in the marketing process as so many "policy makers," then it is obvious that each of them will want to realize certain *objectives*. To this end he utilizes certain *instruments* available to him; in this, however, he is bound to a large number of circumstances that have to be accepted as *data*.

Each of these parties—be it the producer, the distributor, the consumer, or the government—will thus be regarded as a policy maker. For each of these policy makers—interested either in purchasing or marketing the product, or in both—a formal theory for either activity can be devised. By combining the theories of purchasing and marketing with respect to a given link in the distributive channel, it is possible to arrive at a single theory for that link as such (for example, the wholesaler or the broker).

It is obvious that the character of the objectives, instruments, and data changes with that of the successive groups of policy makers. For instance, the manner in which one policy maker manipulates his instruments will have to be accepted as a datum by the other policy makers. Thus, the price quoted by the producer means a datum for the wholesaler. By studying the influence of one and the same phenomenon (price, advertising, etc.) on the purchase and marketing policies of the successive groups of policy makers, it is also possible to arrive at a complete theory covering the phenomenon in question (say, price formation or advertising). Finally, conditional upon the part played by the several objectives, data, and instruments in the case of a particular product, it will be possible to elaborate a specific theory covering the product's channel of distribution as a whole.

By working along these lines, one may ultimately obtain a logical hierarchy among the different sets of problems in the widely ramifying field of marketing.

As a tentative beginning of such a working method, the following pages aim at presenting an elaboration, along general lines, of a theory of marketing by the producer as the first and most important link in the marketing channel.

BASIC CONSIDERATIONS

Requirements as to Theory

The requirements of a theory of marketing may be regarded as threefold.

(i) First, it should indicate the way in which the marketing instruments should be utilized in principle if the objectives of the firm are to be realized as well as possible, given the possibilities at its disposal.

(ii) This fundamental theory should allow for a systematic approach to actual problems of marketing having both theoretical validity and practical value.

(iii) The theory must be fit to serve as a starting point for the explanation of actual marketing policy, as observed in a given concrete situation.

Factors Relevant to Policy

In deciding upon marketing policy for a given period, a great multiplicity of factors must be taken into consideration. These factors may be split into three groups:

First, of the concrete *possibilities* available to the enterprise, the following different subdivisions, among others, suggest themselves from a sales-policy angle.

(i) *technical capacity* (that is, the possibility of producing certain combinations of products up to certain quantities);

(ii) availability of *manpower* and *raw materials*;

(iii) *organizational possibilities* (that is, the ability to meet organizational requirements or to effect changes in the field of management); and

(iv) the *financial position* (that is, the possibility of financing new investments or increasing the working capital, either by the firm itself or by third parties).

While these factors may be regarded as "data," as possibilities affecting the firm's marketing policy they are all frequently subject to "limitations." For example, the firm may be able to produce, say, one million units of product per year but not more than one million. Changes in organization too are subject to limitations if a definite time limit is considered. Finally, the financial position of the enterprise sets certain limitations, both to the increase of production and to any new investments that can be effected within a given period. In this latter case, the limits are mutually dependent: liquid assets intended for investment cannot serve to increase the working capital and vice versa. Limits of this kind will, in the following, be indicated by the term *boundary conditions* which marketing policy has to satisfy.

The second group is the *objectives* of the enterprise, in which marketing policies must be regarded as merely one part of the managerial policy responsible for the implementation of these objectives. In a theory of marketing, therefore, all other parts of the managerial policy must be accepted as *data.* In fact, the possibilities described above depend, in part, upon these other managerial activities. As two of the most obvious objectives of an enterprise, we may mention, for instance, making the highest possible profits and retaining one's share of the market.

The *instruments* available to the firm's marketing policy are the third group. As such, we may reckon, for example, the price, the firm's product line, and its sales organization (salesmen, distributors, etc.). It is obvious that the manner in which these instruments are combined must be the deciding factor in the success or failure of a marketing policy. We may also put it this way: that the price of the products, their quality, the product line as a whole, etc. are the "unknowns" in the problem.

Policy Formulation

Logically speaking, therefore, in formulating a marketing policy, the part played by the possibilities, objectives, and instruments described above is this: the entrepreneur, after allowing for the limitations inherent in the possibilities of his enterprise, shall try to choose his marketing instruments in such a way that his objectives will be realized as satisfactorily as possible. Representing this schematically, we have:

A *Limitations*	B *Objectives*	C *Instruments*
a_1	x_1	y_1
a_2	x_2	y_2
a_3	x_3	y_3
•	•	•
•	•	•
•	•	•
a_k	x_m	y_n

in which $a_1, \ldots, a_n$ and $x_1, \ldots, x_n$ represent the equations or inequalities which sales policy has to satisfy if its limitations are to be taken into account and its objectives realized.

In order to arrive at a workable marketing theory, we must first of all ascertain what relationships exist between the various limitations, objectives, and instruments. And this should be done both for the different factors between category and category and among the factors within one and the same category.

We shall find, of course, that the nature of the limitations varies considerably as between one enterprise and another. But—although the theory must take into account the existence of a variety of limitations imposed upon the possibilities and must show in what way they should be taken into account—the actual, concrete nature of the limitations (since they will function as data) is nevertheless of merely secondary importance for the theory. Obviously, the same does not apply to the instruments nor to the objectives. For this reason, the separate factors of these latter two categories must be more closely examined.

THE OBJECTIVES OF THE ENTERPRISE

The Profit Goal

The ultimate objective of any enterprise is, naturally, to make a profit. Traditional economic theory asserts, moreover, that managerial policy should be such as to ensure the maximum profits. On a very long-term view, this hypothesis is, for the majority of enterprises, sufficiently realistic to serve as a basis for a theory of marketing.

On a short-term view, however, this hypothesis is too narrow to be realistic. For, the entrepreneur not only looks to this year's profits but also to that of next and subsequent years. It would hardly be rational to maximize this year's profits at the expense of the firm's future earnings.

Secondary Objectives

If future profits are not to be unduly jeopardized, managerial policy must from year to year take into account a number of factors which, on a short-term view, assume the character of *secondary objectives*. It should be observed that it is immaterial for the theory of marketing as such whether these secondary objectives are regarded as desirable for their own sake, or whether they are merely intermediary objectives set to obviate endangering future profits in an irresponsible way.

In practice, we find as secondary objectives in formulating a marketing policy:

(i) The wish to ensure the *subsistence* of the enterprise under all circumstances. Very often, this amounts to the requirement that the firm's share in the market must not shrink but, if possible, expand. This is the reason why—particularly in the United States—the loss of part of the market is often regarded as a calamity of the same order of magnitude as the reversal of profits into losses.

(ii) Closely bound up with the striving after the highest possible profits is the requirement that *potential competitors ought to be discouraged*. This implies, *inter alia*, that, with an eye to aspiring competitors, prices should be fixed at not too high a level. Dean here uses the term "stay-out pricing."[3]

(iii) A very important practical point is the wish to maintain *"undiluted control,"* that is, to refrain from granting outside groups a say in the management. This implies that in financial matters risk taking should be avoided as much as possible. For, a lack of liquid assets will necessitate financial assistance from outside sources, with the danger that the management is no longer free in its direction of affairs. This situation frequently causes a certain tension between the preference for liquidity and the requirements of profit maximization.[4]

(iv) For the purpose of retaining, consolidating, and, if possible, developing along healthy lines the firm's share in the market, it is essential to avoid provoking any resistance among those groups upon which the enterprise depends for carrying on its business (customers, suppliers, shareholders, personnel, official authorities, the general public, and others). This aspect of the enterprise is generally indicated by the term *"public relations."* All according to the nature of the enterprise, these public relations will give rise to a number of independent objectives of managerial policy, which, in their turn, represent as many guiding lines for the marketing policy. One may here think, for example, of the role of the government with respect to price agreements among manufacturers; the public's attitude with regard to the quality of the products; or the requirement, from the point of view of satisfactory personnel relations, of ensuring steady sales in order to maintain employment in the enterprise itself.

[3]J. Dean, *Managerial Economics* (New York: Prentice-Hall, Inc., 1951), p. 30.

[4]W. Fellner, *Competition Among the Few* (New York: A. A. Knopf, 1949), p. 146 et seq.; W. W. Cooper, "Revisions to the Theory of the Firm," *American Economic Review*, December 1949, p. 1204 et seq.; Dean, *op. cit.*, p. 32.

(v) Quite apart from these auxiliary objectives, every branch of industry or business has certain *ethical "codes,"* and every management maintains for itself a certain standard of ethics which will check unbridled profit maximization. These codes and ethical standards are to a large extent identical with what would be considered "sound business" from the public relations angle.

Present Value of Future Profits

In all of this there still remains a somewhat vague concept—namely, that of the maximization of future profits—which lends the auxiliary objectives mentioned above their significance. A relatively realistic definition, however, is possible here by assuming as a hypothesis that the entrepreneur will strive after the highest possible present value of future profits.[5] This hypothesis leaves sufficient room to allow for differences in mentality or, as the case may be, technical and institutional circumstances governing the enterprise. All according to whether the management's "horizon" is either close by or more distant, future profits will be weighted low or high as compared with present profits. Correspondingly, also, the said auxiliary objectives will then weigh either light or heavy, unless, as happens very often, they are striven after for their own sake.

Boundary Conditions

If we disregard this latter point, we shall be able to formalize the total picture still further. We then get the case that present profits must be maximized, but under the side condition that the present value of all future profits shall not be impaired. This side condition is satisfied so long as the intermediary objectives, a few examples of which were given above, are being realized. It is evident that each of these intermediary objectives constitutes another limit which must not be exceeded by the marketing policy.

Technically speaking, therefore, we get this situation: the intermediary objectives represent as many *boundary conditions* that must not be exceeded in maximizing present profits. Providing these boundary conditions are observed, the net value of future profits will not be impaired.

[5]Fellner, *op. cit.*, p. 158 et seq.; H. Brems, *Product Equilibrium Under Monopolistic Competition* (Cambridge: Harvard University Press, 1951), Chapter 8; Dean, *op. cit.*, p. 29.

The term "boundary conditions" clearly expresses the typical character of the intermediary objectives: if potential competition is to be discouraged, then any price is permissible from this point of view, providing it does not exceed a certain level, say, $1.00 per unit. With that, the figure of $1.00 sets a limit to the pricing policy; any price is acceptable, providing it does not exceed one dollar. In this way, a maximum condition for the pricing policy is found. In exactly the same way, the demand that the existing share in the market must be retained implies a minimum condition for projected sales. Again, from the angle of public relations or codes of ethics, we shall find a minimum condition with respect to quality or a maximum condition with respect to price.

In the latter case, therefore, the *boundary conditions are interdependent*: the lower the price has been fixed, the more justified one will be to lower one's demands as to quality. We already came across a similar phenomenon when discussing financial liquidity. If this is to be maintained, we find a boundary condition both with respect to total "out-of-pocket expenses" and with respect to investments—and, with that to maximum output. The consequences of this interdependence have been dealt with by Cooper.[6]

THE INSTRUMENTS OF MARKETING POLICY

Available Instruments

A policy is implemented by utilizing certain instruments. In the case of marketing policy, the enterprise has at its disposal five groups of instruments, namely:

(i) *The price.* A distinction should be made as to the factory price, the price charged to the ultimate consumer or user, and the successive trade-channel discounts.
(ii) *The quality of the product.*
(iii) *Promotional effort.* This term should cover all activities intended to be directly instrumental in effecting sales and including, as the most important items, the activities of the sales force and advertising.
(iv) *The distribution channels.*
(v) *The firm's product line.*

[6]Cooper, *op. cit.*

Substitutability of Instruments

An important feature of these instruments is that they allow for a certain degree of substitution among themselves. This is very clearly seen in the case of the triad: price, quality, and advertising. The same applies to the triad: sales force, distribution, and advertising. In other words, it is, in principle, quite possible that a large number of different combinations of the instruments would produce the same net profits.

A given combination of instruments, for example, a price x with a quality y and an advertising budget at a level z, etc., is indicated by the term "marketing mix."[7] Now it is obvious that one particular "mix" may yield higher profits than any other. But it does not, *a priori*, follow from this that maximum profits can only be realized by one, and no more than one, "marketing mix." What is certain, however, is that there may be considerable differences in the net profits obtained as between one combination and another. The fact alone that a certain possibility of substitution exists in the use of the different instruments will lead one to assume that any striving after perfectionism with respect to one particular instrument, coupled with the neglect of the possibilities afforded by other instruments, may lead to unfavorable results.

Costs of Instruments

Another important aspect is the part played by *costs*. For, the use of a given instrument invariably entails a financial sacrifice for the firm. This may either take the form of a sacrifice as to *price*—that is, in the case of price reduction—or it may consist of an increase in *costs*. From the viewpoint of marketing policy, there is no essential difference between the two. Each instrument, therefore, may be regarded as a "center of costs." All according to whether a given instrument is manipulated more intensively, net profits per unit of product, *ceteris paribus*, fall.

The form of these sacrifices differs as between one instrument and another. In the case of the price, it occurs in the form of either a positive or a negative sacrifice of gross revenue; in the case of an alteration in the quality of the product, there is a change in the actual cost of production. This latter change may affect both constant and

[7]N. H. Borden, *Advertising, Text and Cases* (Chicago: Richard D. Irwin, Inc., 1950), pp. 164–66.

variable costs. In the case of promotional effort, the usual thing that happens is a change in constant costs per unit of time (advertising, sales force). An exception to this, however, is the compensation of salesmen insofar as they work on a commission basis.

A change in the choice of distribution channels leads to a positive or negative change in gross revenue as a result of the concomitant alteration of the discount structure. With respect to the firm's product line, the situation is more complicated. When an item in the program is either added or scrapped, the quality costs of the items maintained may be subject to change. In addition, changes in both the costs and the efficiency of the other instruments are to be expected.

THE THEORY OF MARKETING

Summary Statement

Summarizing, it may be said that an enterprise has at its disposal certain possibilities, each of which, however, is subject to certain limitations. In addition, the enterprise strives for a plurality of objectives, the most important of which is the maximization of present profits. In this, the other objectives act as so many side conditions. Both the possibilities and these side conditions represent certain boundary conditions which, in the process of maximizing present profits, must not be exceeded. Finally, with regard to its marketing policy, the enterprise can utilize a number of instruments for the purpose of realizing both its main and its auxiliary objectives.

The central problem of marketing theory, therefore, is how to combine the five instruments constituting the "marketing mix" in such a way as to ensure the highest possible present profits, taking into account the various boundary conditions such as concern for future profits and limitation of available means. As already stated above, the objections against the present state of the theory of marketing are, first, that the method of treatment of the different subjects is often too isolated and, second, that it is not related closely enough to the theory of the firm as such. Using the terminology developed in the preceding paragraphs, a theory of marketing will accordingly have to allow for a symmetrical method of dealing simultaneously with the several instruments and the boundary conditions arising as a result of the limited possibilities and the auxiliary objectives of the enterprise.

Diminishing Returns

Leaving these boundary conditions provisionally out of consideration, we get the picture of an enterprise with unlimited productive and financial possibilities. This enterprise knows only one objective: maximization of present profits. Taking the existing demand structure as given, the firm will then be subject to only one group of limitations, namely, those resulting from the sales potential of its market.

With respect to each of the instruments, it then follows that, beyond a certain limit, it will be subject to diminishing returns. This applies to price reductions, improvements of quality, the activity of the sales force, trade-channel discounts, advertising, and in certain cases to the extent of the product line.

Maximization Rule

If only one instrument is changed, the others remaining unchanged, the following *maximum rule* applies:

> It is irrational to raise the costs of an instrument if the increase in gross revenue does not offset the extra costs of the instrument itself plus the additional costs of producing the additional volume of sales.

The term "costs" has here been used in its wider meaning so that it covers also the sacrifice of gross revenue in case of a price reduction or a rise in the middlemen's discounts. Gross proceeds must then obviously be measured in constant prices.

Rule of Choice

The fact that a given instrument has not exceeded this limit does not necessarily imply that it has been used rationally. Thus, if the salesmen's organization is inadequately developed, an irrationally great deal of advertising will be necessary to realize a given marketing objective, etc.

A correct combination in the *relative* use of the several instruments, however, may be achieved by applying a variant of the rule that weighted marginal revenues should be equated.[8] In its modified form, it may be called the *rule of choice*:

[8]*Vide*, for example, A. L. Bowley, *The Mathematical Groundwork of Economics* (Oxford: Clarendon Press, 1924), p. 29.

> A rise in the unit cost of a given instrument by one cent is to be preferred to that of other instruments, as long as it enables a greater increase of the quantity sold than would result either from lowering the price by one cent or from raising the unit costs of the other instruments by one cent.

The accuracy of this rule may be tested by comparing two alternative cases, in one of which the unit price is lowered by $1.00, advertising costs in the other case being raised by $1.00. Both measures are assumed to result in a 50-per-cent increase of sales. According to the "rule of choice," therefore, an equal change in business results may be expected in both cases. This, in fact, is seen to be so in Table I.

TABLE I

RULE OF CHOICE: EXAMPLE OF LOWERED PRICE VERSUS INCREASED ADVERTISING

	Situation without price reduction or increased advertising	*Price reduction*	*Increased advertising*
Quantity sold	100,000	150,000	150,000
Price	$ 10.00	$ 9.00	$ 10.00
Advertising cost per unit	—	—	1.00
Variable costs per unit	5.00	5.00	5.00
Proceeds	1,000,000	1,350,000	1,500,000
Variable costs	500,000	750,000	750,000
Advertising	—	—	175,000
Constant costs	500,000	500,000	500,000
Net profit	—	100,000	100,000

GENERAL RULE

In the absence of boundary conditions, we finally get as a general rule for the optimal composition of the marketing mix:[9]

> Optimal combination of instruments has been attained when improvement in the net profit is not possible either by a change in one of the instruments or by another combination.

Each of the instruments then satisfies the maximum rule given above.

FORMAL PRINCIPLES

Viewed purely formally, the basic principles of marketing policy do not deviate from the laws governing production. For total production

[9]Cf. J. R. Hicks, *Value and Capital* (Oxford: Clarendon Press, 1939), p. 86.

should be increased to the point where marginal cost equals marginal revenue. In a material respect, however, there exists a quite definite difference. This is clear when the factors are considered that are decisive for marginal cost: If only production costs are taken into account, while the cost of marketing is left out of consideration, these factors are: the prices of the production factors and what one might call the "technical coefficients" of the manufacturing process.

Where marketing costs are also reckoned with, the "demand coefficients" of the market form an additional element in the problem. For an increase of sales by one unit of product not only requires additional production costs but also extra costs of marketing. The sum of these two has to satisfy the condition that it shall be a minimum. In other words, the point at issue is not marginal cost if all the factors of production and marketing instruments are changed proportionally but minimum marginal cost if every possible combination of factors of production and marketing instruments is taken into account. The question on which instruments the marginal cost of marketing will bear and the size of the total amount is decided by the sensitiveness of demand with respect to quality improvement, advertising, salesmen's activity, etc.[10]

Complicating Factors

Once these demand coefficients are known, the application of the rules given above no longer presents any difficulties. In order, however, to arrive at a realistic theory, it is necessary to recognize four complications which were neglected above.

(i) The existence of *boundary conditions*, which have been explicitly left out of consideration in the beginning of this paragraph.

(ii) The fact that not all instruments are amenable to infinitesimal variations. This applies, first and foremost, to the quality of the product. An automobile, for example, may have either "rocket" drive or not. Something similar applies with respect to the distribution channels and, in practice, also to the other instruments. Generally, the problem of *noncontinuous substitution* arises as soon as qualitative criteria are changed.

(iii) The fact that certain marketing costs should be considered as *investments*. This occurs, among other things, in the case

[10] R. M. Shone, "Selling Costs," *Review of Economic Studies II*, 1935, pp. 225–31. Cf. especially Brems, *op. cit.*, Chapter 5, Paragraph 44.

of advertising. There, the influence of marketing costs often will show a "distributed lag." Expenses incurred in the present period partly influence future profits.

(iv) The fact that more than one product is marketed; that is, the problems connected with the fifth instrument, the firm's *product line*.

The theoretical aspects of the latter two complications touch upon the theory of production at least as much as upon the theory of marketing.[11] Let us, therefore, confine ourselves to the two first mentioned.

The problem of the boundary conditions can, in principle, be solved either mathematically or graphically. For the mathematical method, reference should be made to Tinbergen's treatment of the problem of government economic policy.[12] The graphic method, however, is to be preferred for the marketing policy because it is easier to follow for the nonmathematical reader. In addition to this, it allows for the second complication, namely, noncontinuous substitution possibilities.

GRAPHIC METHOD OF APPROACH

Quality, Sales Promotion, and Distribution Channels as Variables

The complications of the product line and the existence of time lags have already been disregarded. Besides, the problem may be simplified even further by assuming the retail price to be given. Distribution-channel discounts will be considered as costs—which is, moreover, the most practical way of looking at it from the producer's point of view. Let us, to start with, also leave the boundary conditions out of consideration.

By simplifying the problem in this way, only three instruments remain to be dealt with: quality, sales promotion, and the choice of distribution channels. The question then is, how these three instruments can be combined into the marketing mix that will ensure the maximum profit at the given retail price.

Let us now represent the situation graphically. The quantities to be marketed are plotted on the horizontal axis; gross revenue and total

[11]Cf. Brems, *op. cit.*, Chapter 8. With regard to the product line: R. Dorfman, *Applications of Linear Programming to the Theory of the Firm* (Berkeley: University of California Press, 1951).

[12]Cf. the two publications cited in footnote 2 above.

cost corresponding to these quantities, on the vertical axis. Revenue may then be represented, in Figure 1, by the straight line R going through the origin. For, the price being given, revenue varies proportionately to total sales.

Total cost, however, is not only dependent upon the quantity sold but also on the composition of the marketing mix with the aid of which those quantities were sold.

As already remarked, the instruments cannot in many cases be subjected to infinitesimal changes. But not more than one quantity sold and only one level of total cost correspond to a specific combination of instruments. In other words, any imaginable marketing mix can be represented by a single point in the diagram. This makes it possible to examine and find out—for example, on the basis of a given quality—the extent to which sales and total cost may vary when changes occur in the activities of salesmen, in promotion, and/or in the choice of distribution channels. Admittedly, quality, too, is a variable; but the same procedure may be followed with respect to the different qualities that are within the scope of the firm's technical possibilities.

Figure 1 gives a picture of a case in which three different qualities have been studied, shown respectively by squares, circles, and triangles. For each quality, a number of realistic alternative suppositions have been made with respect to sales promotion and distribution channels and the consequences with respect to marketing possibilities and total cost have been examined.

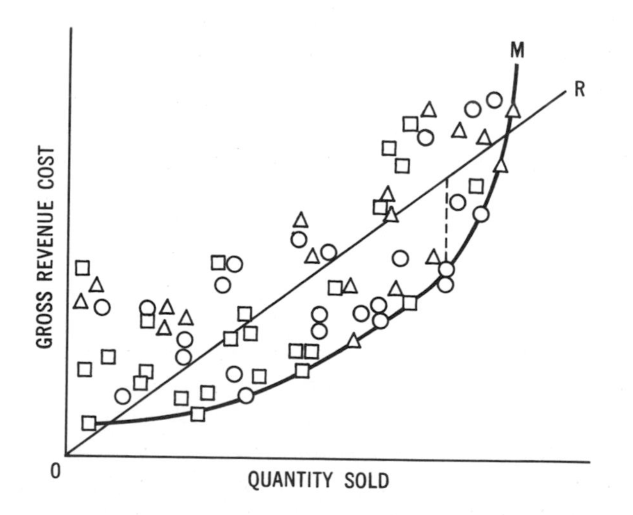

FIGURE 1. Determination of Most Profitable Marketing Mix at a Given Price

If this diagram is filled in as completely as possible—that is, for all possible qualities and the corresponding combinations of sales promotion and distribution channels—it will obviously contain a much larger number of points. But, since we are dealing in principle with noncontinuous phenomena, a good many open places will nevertheless remain in the diagram. This means that in practice no marketing mix corresponds to the combination of sales and costs in question. For this reason, Brems—who has developed this method of graphic representation—calls this diagram the "oasis and desert map," the filled-in dots representing as many cases in the desert of technical and practical impossibilities.[13]

The advantage of this method is that it enables one to determine very realistically the *minimum-cost curve*, that is, the curve showing minimum cost for each volume of sales at a given unit price. It is subject to the conditions that, going from left to right,

(i) none of the points must appear below the curve; and
(ii) the successive combinations forming part of the curve must show a continuous rising line of marginal cost.

This minimum-cost curve is shown as the broken line (M). It differs from the traditional cost curve in that

(i) it is discontinuous; and
(ii) it allows for the fact that the volume of sales is dependent upon the composition of production as well as of marketing cost.

The marketing mix with which, at the given price, profits will be maximal is found by seeking the combination in which the distance between total cost and the gross revenue curve is greatest. If the minimum-cost curve had been continuous, marginal cost would at this point equal price. The optimal marketing mix, at a given price, therefore, is determined in the same way as in the case of perfect competition.

Price Variable

To ascertain the influence of price changes, the "oasis and desert map" should be constructed for several prices. For each price, too, the corresponding minimum-cost curve can be determined. These minimum-cost curves can be incorporated within a recapitulation diagram, as shown in Figure 2. The difference between this and the original

[13]Brems, *op. cit.*, Chapter 5.

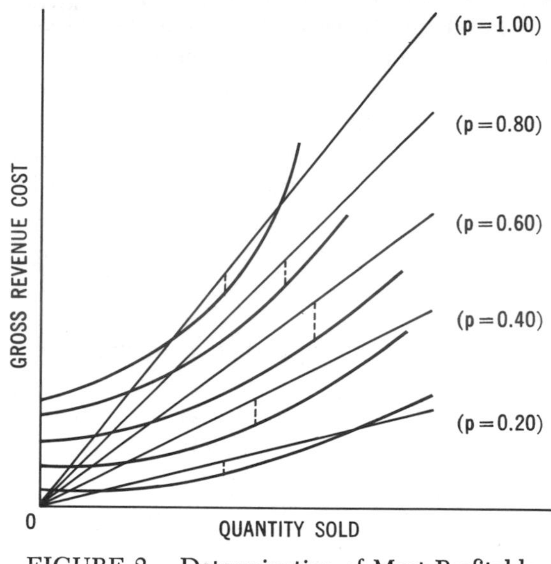

FIGURE 2. Determination of Most Profitable Marketing Mix; Price (p) as Variable

"oasis and desert map" is that in Figure 2 *each point already shows the minimal combination of cost at which a given quantity can be sold at a given price.* For each minimum-cost curve, the "mix" that will yield the largest profit is known. The best "mix" of all minimum-cost curves, therefore, may be found quite simply by comparing for the different curves the distances between the best "mix" and the corresponding points on the gross-revenue lines.

Introduction of Boundary Conditions

In this recapitulation diagram, it is also possible to represent the influence of the most important boundary conditions. If, for instance, the share in the market is required to increase by a given percentage, then this means that sales must increase from, say, 100 to at least 110. This desideratum can be expressed graphically in Figure 3 by the line v_1 drawn perpendicularly on the abscissa at a sales figure of 110. All combinations to the left of this line then fail to satisfy the condition that sales shall increase to 110 and can therefore be discarded.

If it is considered undesirable—from a competitive point of view—that the price should rise above, say, 0.80, then the combinations corresponding to the minimum-cost curve at a price of 0.80 also constitute a boundary. All combinations at a higher level then become unacceptable. For this reason, the minimum curve 0.80 is shown in the diagram as a heavy curve. (*P*).

As we have already seen, the maintenance of liquidity gives rise to two boundary conditions, namely, one with respect to investments and one with respect to working capital. The former is the simpler of the two; it sets a limit to total sales. It is represented by the line v_2. The second boundary condition is more complicated. As long, however, as fixed cost remains unchanged, there is in every enterprise a definite relation between total cost and the need for working capital. It is obvious that this relation may be changed by modifying the composition of total cost, that is, by a different choice of "marketing mix." It nevertheless appears plausible that, as soon as the figure of investment and, with that, the amount of working capital available are known, a ceiling figure for total cost can be calculated, at least tentatively. In the short run, this ceiling is dependent upon the possibility of raising short-term credits and, to a lesser degree, upon "plowing back" and, consequently, primarily upon total revenue. The maximum limit of total cost (the line *L*) will, therefore, show an upward slope.[14] It is

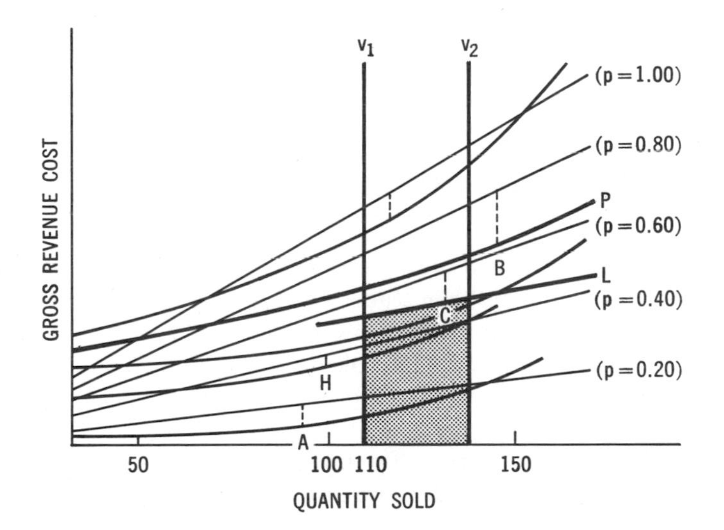

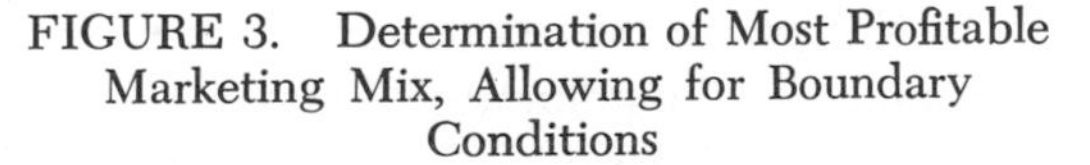
FIGURE 3. Determination of Most Profitable Marketing Mix, Allowing for Boundary Conditions

[14]Since the slope of the total-revenue curve varies proportionately with prices, the exact representation of liquidity as a limiting factor would be a bundle of rays.

important to note, however, that the two boundary conditions are interdependent: if v^2 is set higher, L will be lower, and vice versa.

Taking the boundary conditions into account, therefore, considerably limits the possibility of choice from all imaginable combinations—in fact, to the small shaded area in Figure 3.

Assume H to represent the marketing mix that has been used by the firm up to the present moment. Then it is clear that its position might be improved considerably by switching the mix to B. B, in fact, represents the *maximum maximorum* of profits. But then, it lies outside the possibilities of our firm. Although the required price is still within its reach—since B is situated exactly on the boundary condition P—two other boundary conditions originating from requirements of liquidity (v_2 and L) are violated. Neither is the combination A admissible. True, it guarantees a larger net profit than that of the past period, namely, that corresponding to the "mix" H, but the sales of combination A fail to reach the required level v_1.

In order to reckon with all the side conditions set by the intermediary objectives of management, the choice of the mix is restricted to the points within the shaded area. Out of all these points, C guarantees the highest level of present profits. At the same time, since no boundary conditions are violated, it is compatible with the intermediary objectives; that is, future profits will not be impaired unduly by a change from H to C.

EFFICIENCY OF THE INSTRUMENTS

The procedure described above will require modification according to the character of the problem studied and the nature of the accepted boundary conditions. In principle, however, it would seem to provide a practical starting point for a theory of marketing by the producer. It is especially important to note that the two demands formulated in the summary statement above are satisfied, since the method allows for a symmetrical and simultaneous treatment of the instruments while taking into account the most frequently occurring boundary conditions.

However, up to this point, the method of treatment has remained purely formal inasmuch as the influence of a given "marketing mix" on sales and total cost has been assumed to be known. *But if a theory of marketing is to claim completeness, it must also provide a theoretical basis upon which to judge the efficiency of each of the instruments.*

SUPPLEMENTARY THEORIES

In assessing this efficiency, both the general aspects of the instruments and the particular ones that are bound up with the specific nature of the firm which is being investigated enter into consideration. These particular aspects cannot, as such, form part of the theory. We may, however, expect the theory to indicate the general relationship between the particular aspects of the instruments and the specific nature of an enterprise.

If, therefore, the empty boxes still left by the formal approach are to be filled up, the latter must be supplemented with three specific theories, covering:

(i) the efficiency of each of the instruments as such, when considered as a tool for a certain link in the marketing channel;
(ii) the interdependence of the efficiency of the different instruments; and
(iii) the interaction between the specific character and the general situation of the firm and the efficiency of its marketing instruments.

With regard to the first two points, particularly point (i), a large amount of material has already been published both in the scientific and in the more practically oriented literature. Thus, the factor quality has been dealt with in Brems' excellent monograph. An almost complete theory of salesmen's activities is well under way.[15] Advertising, too, has been thoroughly investigated both from the theoretical and from the practical angle.[16] As to the marketing channels, the publication prepared under the sponsorship of the American Marketing Association[17] presents a real gold mine of theoretical and factual

[15]Very useful theoretical approaches have recently been published in The Netherlands: H. Ferro, "Taakstelling en Taakberekening Voor Vertegenwoordigers," *Organisatie en Efficiency*, October/November 1946, pp. 239–47; and L. Meertens, *De Organisatie van de Verkoop* (Leiden: Stenfert Kroese, 1954), Chapter VI (both in Dutch). On the practical level: J. H. Davis, *Increasing Wholesale Drug Salesmen's Effectiveness* (Columbus: Ohio State University Press, 1948); N. Hall, "Setting Standards to Improve Sales Performance," *American Management Association Marketing Series No. 84*, 1952, pp. 28–36.

[16]N. S. Buchanan, "Advertising Expenditures; A Suggested Treatment," *The Journal of Political Economy*, August 1942, pp. 539–55; B. Barfod, "The Theory of Advertising," *Econometrica* 8, July 1940, pp. 279–81; A. Rasmussen, "The Determination of Advertising Expenditure," *The Journal of Marketing*, April 1952, pp. 439–47.

[17]American Marketing Association, *Marketing Channels for Manufactured Products*, ed. Richard M. Clewett (Homewood: Richard D. Irwin, Inc., 1954).

material. Finally, the product line has in recent years been given the attention it deserves.[18] For the interdependence of the efficiency of the different instruments, the reader is referred to Dorfman and Steiner's recent contribution, which is still exclusively on the theoretical level.[19]

The time now seems ripe, therefore, not only for a general, formal theory such as proposed in the above but also for the relevant specialized theories bearing on each of the instruments separately. These specialized theories, however, should in this case remain ancillary to the general theory of the link in the marketing channel that is being investigated. In other words, the instrument in question must be analyzed with respect to its efficiency as an instrument for the link in question. Quite definitely, the solution of the present problem is in no way enhanced by any theory of advertising, of salesmen, or of the retail trade for their own sake. For, the neglect of the instrumental character of the instrument would allow it an existence of its own, with the result that the organic bond with the theory of the firm is lost again.

ADAPTING THE INSTRUMENTS TO THE FUNCTIONAL POSITION OF THE FIRM

There remains—as a third desideratum—the solution of the problem of adapting the instruments to the specific circumstances of the firm. This is a problem of great practical importance. For, in principle, there are a very large number of points in the "oasis and desert map," but only a small proportion of these—that is, those within the boundary conditions—are relevant. From the combinations corresponding to these points, those must then be selected which shall be as efficient as possible, that is, guarantee the highest possible net profit.

In practice, therefore, instead of studying all possible combinations, only the most efficient ones will be examined. Now, in what way can the concretely given situation in which the enterprise finds itself be taken as a compass for an efficient use of the instruments?

The logical link between the two is formed by the *functional position* of the enterprise on the market. In this, differences between the function performed by the enterprise and those performed by its

[18] Dean, *op. cit.*, Chapter 3; D. M. Phelps, *Planning the Product* (Chicago: Richard D. Irwin, Inc., 1949), pp. 41–76. Cf., for an approach with the aid of "linear programming," the source cited in footnote 11.

[19] R. Dorfman and P. O. Steiner, "Optimal Advertising and Optimal Quality," *American Economic Review XLIV*, 5, December 1954, pp. 826–37.

immediate competitors are particularly important. For the fact that a given amount of orders is being booked proves the existence of a certain preference on the part of customers for the product of the firm in question. This, again, shows that the function performed by the firm differs to a certain extent from that of its competitors.[20] Since, apart from location, the relation of firm to customer is governed almost exclusively by the use of the marketing instruments, it is clear that these functional differences are based, in their turn, on a different use of the instruments.

It stands to reason that the "marketing mix," as between one producer and another, may show a large number of differences, even with respect to similar products. The question is only, to which of these differences must the client's preference be attributed? In other words, from this point of view, we may *a priori* expect both relevant and nonrelevant differences.

Now whenever a difference in the use of an instrument or a combination of instruments is found to have a positive influence, this may be regarded as representative of an ultimate "asset"—for example, technical know-how, good public relations, effectiveness of an advertising message, the fact that it is possible to sell at relatively low prices, the right choice of retailers, etc.[21] It should be noted, however, that the question of whether a given use of an instrument does or does not represent an "asset" to the firm's sales policy depends entirely on the structure of its "own" market as it exists at a given moment. Thus, a low price may be in some cases considered a plus, and in other cases a minus, item.

Summarizing, the determinants of the firm's functional position may be set out schematically as follows:

[20] A more systematic treatment of the problem of the firm's functional position is given in the present writer's *De Eigen Markt der Onderneming* (Leiden: Stenfert Kroese, 1952), pp. 9–12 (in Dutch).

[21] In this, the line of thought is the reverse of the customary one where customers' preference or the firm's good will is itself considered an asset. Cf., for example, L. Hurwicz, "Theory of the Firm and Investment," *Econometrica 14*, April 2, 1946, pp. 109–37.

The question as to how a given combination of instruments can be most effectually manipulated is governed—so far as the marketing aspect of the problem is concerned—by two "poles":

(i) existing or potential preference on the part of the customer and

(ii) the firm's ultimate assets (from the marketing point of view).

If a firm decides upon a certain functional position or, as the case may be, wants to utilize its existing position to its fullest extent, then clearly the thing to do when choosing an instrument is to take full advantage of the already available marketing assets. Conversely, if we wish to judge the efficacy of a given marketing mix, the crucial question is, whether the available assets are adequately utilized with respect to the requirements of the existing functional position of the firm.

Here we have, therefore, a criterion—quite practical for purposes of marketing research—to decide in the first instance upon the relative merits of a given marketing mix.

SYSTEMATIC CONTROL BY MEANS OF THE "MARKETING AUDIT"

In the preceding paragraph, however, the full emphasis is on the term "in the first instance." For, not only the marketing aspect of the problem but also the firm's objectives and possibilities determine the extent to which the marketing mix is really efficient in the sense of being optimal. In addition to the functional position, therefore, the cost of production and the boundary conditions, as given by the limited possibilities and auxiliary objectives of the enterprise, should be taken into account.

As was shown in the graphic analysis, the problem thereby assumes a somewhat complicated character. In practical cases, therefore, its solution requires a more systematic method of investigation than that provided by the traditional procedures of market research.

This largely explains the need felt for a systematic marketing audit and the work started by some research agencies along these lines.[22] The most important aspect of this systematic audit of all marketing

[22]The author is indebted to Mr. Wroe Alderson of Alderson & Sessions and to Mr. Donald F. Blankertz of the Wharton School of Finance and Commerce for the information concerning the marketing audit.

activities is not so much its being some novel technique of market research. It is rather in the systematic set-up of the entire investigation, in which account is taken not only of the existing and expected possibilities of the market but also, and simultaneously, of the objectives and possibilities of the firm itself.

6. WHAT IS THE MARKETING MANAGEMENT CONCEPT?*

J. B. McKitterick

The papers presented here provide intensive discussion of the implications of the marketing concept to top management decisions, to organization structure and to market strategy. From this one would infer that the marketing concept itself is an unequivocal thing, certainly as explicit as the turbo aire ride, the filter that leaves the taste in and the woman who is every inch a female—to mention three of its most recent manifestations. Yet one of the most charming attributes of this tireless conference subject is its study resistance to onslaughts of definition and prescription. Indeed, to be asked to define the marketing concept can almost be accepted in the spirit of a challenge—because it is probably impossible—or if you have already tried and know it is impossible, then such a request can be passed off as spoken in jest—or more morbidly, considered as an insult. In view of the great amount of attention already being given to the definitions of the marketing concept, it seems to me that it would be timely to look into the general economic developments that have accompanied this heightened interest in marketing. So rather than present the views of General Electric on this subject, it is my intention to speak somewhat more freely about the relationship between the evolution of business philosophy and the style of competition that characterizes modern markets. If in this manner we can develop a clearer understanding of why we are increasingly formulating business policy in terms of market considerations, we will have a better starting point for this discussion of means of implementation.

Anyone who gets a new idea bearing on business philosophy and who then takes the trouble to scan corresponding utterances of preced-

*Reprinted from Frank M. Bass (ed.), *The Frontiers of Marketing Thought and Science* (Chicago: American Marketing Association, 1957), pp. 71–81.

ing generations will return to this thought with increased awareness of its apparent lack of originality. In an attempt to locate the historic significance of this marketing concept that we are going to discuss today, I started reading the 1930 and 1940 issues of the *Journal of Marketing* and the *Harvard Business Review.* To my surprise, I found that many of the viewpoints expressed and the stances advocated on business philosophy bear striking resemblance to current writings. Indeed, what really seems to have changed are the phenomena—the goings on—that the authors cite to validate the importance and rationale of their message. So we have here a not unfamiliar problem in the social sciences; namely that words change their meaning much more slowly than the things to which they refer. This is particularly true of concepts such as profit, overhead, productivity and marketing orientation—which deal not so much with things that happen as with ways of thinking about them.

In order to map changing meanings, it frequently is helpful to superimpose on a history of thought some crude scheme of classification which takes its definitions from the present. If we do this in the case of the marketing concept, we will notice that over the last thirty years the preoccupation of businessmen with the customer increasingly has been formulated in terms of an end rather than in terms of a means. Correspondingly, the conception of profit as the end objective in business seems to have declined, with a tendency to view it more as a basic condition that must be satisfied. To be sure, thirty years ago businessmen admonished each other to keep the customer's interests in mind, but they usually connected this focus merely with their own need to adjust prices and volume of production to what the market would accept. Indeed, if we read between the lines, we find that the customer used to be the chap that you sent the bill to—frequently a distributor, agent or dealer, but very rarely the actual end user. And sales tactics were conceived in terms of exploiting some scheme that would permit dealing with these trade institutions on a semi-exclusive basis. There was almost no mention of the idea that the manufacturer should focus his attention on the end user, and base his competitive footing on some superiority of value that matched with the needs of a particular group of these users. And it was obvious that few manufacturers felt that they had ability to look at the trade structure as a group of institutions for hire, to be selected and employed to perform specific functions that this end user needed. On the contrary, the trade structure was regarded as an impenetrable barrier—it *was* the market, and this fellow we have been calling the end user was the exclusive problem of the dealer, and no concern of the manufacturer.

Occasionally someone like Oswald Knauth, who has always been a bit ahead of his time, would remind the manufacturer that packaging and product styling had better be customer oriented. But by comparison to these occasional warnings to the man at the helm to keep his eye on what the customer was doing, there were urgent exhortations to the man in the engine room to get more output with less input. Indeed, the problem of winning out over competition seemed to be conceived essentially in terms of subtracting from the costs of production, and delivering an equivalent product at a lower price. So it was quite fitting that in the 1930's manufacturers studied the economics of scale, economists explored marginal concepts for setting the volume of production, and the government tried to prevent the large and efficient firm from sinking its smaller adversaries with the torpedo of lower price. In a short body of remarks it is out of scale to put a generalization such as this to adequate test, yet I cannot entirely resist some elaboration, because the social implications of what we call the marketing concept in the end are going to be of much greater importance than its bearing on management theory.

If we examine the 1920–1940 period, we find that it witnessed great gains in productivity, but not all of these gains were distributed to the labor force. The installed horsepower per production worker almost doubled, and the output per worker more than doubled. However, the average hourly wage in these twenty years increased only from 50¢ to 66¢—not quite a third, and the number of production workers stayed almost constant at around 8½ million members in a population that actually grew by over 20%. So, with rising productivity only to a limited degree passed on to the static body of production workers in the form of wage increases, consumer prices fell steadily until in 1940 they were only 70% of the 1920 level, and unemployment in a growing population was a serious and long continuing problem. During this same period, the design and manner of use of most products changed only slowly, and the gross national product increased a scant 14%.

To sum it up, the business ideology of producing the same product for less cost scarcely turned out to be an adequate driving force for economic growth. While a great deal of criticism was directed at the imperfections of markets organized around administered prices, subsequent events suggest that the real trouble was that most consumers had inadequate income and inadequate reason to buy. In short, productivity gains unevenly accompanied by innovation of new products and broad distribution of purchasing power resulted in a condition of chronic underconsumption.

Starting around 1940, the threat of war and the sponsorship of government combined to introduce a basic transformation in the business process which has had far reaching consequences. In a nutshell, business discovered research. On the eve of this revolution the total research outlay of businessmen stood at perhaps 100 million dollars. Today, these outlays are somewhere around four billions, and for the first time over 50% of all the research done in this country is being paid for by industry out of its own pocket. If we throw in the defense effort which the government pays for, the total research outlay rises to about 7½ billions. However, our interest here is not so much in the growth of this new industry or the sheer size of its burden, which seems likely to surpass the total cost of all advertising; rather we are concerned to learn what research did to the growth of the economy and to the problems of designing and managing an enterprise.

Where the pre-1940 period was preoccupied with trying to make the same product cheaper, the postwar period saw a new dimension added to competition, in which the focus was to try and make the old product better, or even more bold, to try and launch a new product. And as the research-equipped manufacturer looked around for applications for his new found creative power, he frequently discovered them in markets that he heretofore had not entered. The petroleum refinery began to turn out chemicals; the rubber plant, plastics; new alloys challenged older metals; electronics cast its shadows over hydraulics; and soon, everyone's research and competitive endeavor was attacking someone else's status quo. Established concepts of industry alignment began to obliterate, schemes narrowly conceived to defend market position in terms of price advantage proved inadequate; and managements began to contend with problems of uncertainty that had multiple dimensions. A labor plentiful economy overnight became a labor short economy, and even though the number of employee and production workers had grown 50% since 1940, and their productivity probably another 50%, still the demand for their services has grown even faster, and wages have gone up some 70% in constant dollars. So here we had a reversal of the conditions of the preceding 20 years; worker income rose more rapidly than productivity, competition was focused on using research to obsolete old ways of doing things, a flood of new products poured forth to meet the rising discretionary spending power, and we became so impressed with the results of focusing on what would be better for the customer rather than merely cheaper that we invented a now familiar phrase—"the marketing concept"—to describe this triumph of innovation over productive capacity.

If we look back on these basic changes in the economy, we find clues to many of the problems which have concerned management science over the last ten years. I refer especially to the constant search for means of planning and control that can contend with these rapidly changing marketing conditions. For example, many businessmen have complained that the problem of predicting the customer's behavior has been greatly complicated both by his rapidly rising discretionary income and by his growing control over the use of leisure time. Mink coats and motor cars, buying things and buying experiences all have begun to interact, and the passing fad and the more slowly changing style of life of which it is a part have become very difficult to diagnose and distinguish. And as we already have noted, the industrial customer with his multiple raw material and process alternatives, and his possibilities of sub-contracting entire operations, swimming all the while in his own competitive sea of changing functions and market alignments, presents an equally fickle target for prediction.

At the same time both the need for and difficulty of business planning have been heightened by technological trends in the production and distribution process. The long term commitments required by automated plants, guaranteed wages, basic research, and multi-million dollar national promotions imply not only irreversible decisions, but also greater lead time, because the assumptions in planning have to hold good over a longer and longer period as the separation between decision and implementation grows apace. The annual budget in many companies has been supplemented with the five year and even the twenty year plan. The very considerable risks entailed in these large resource commitments, combined with the increasing hazards posed by the caprice of the customer and the research efforts of an undefined arena of prospective competitors, have resulted in a powerful urge for diversification. Few businesses today seem to be able to undertake the risk of staying in a single market with a single product. Indeed, observing the pell-mell flight to add new products and markets, one might say that the most characteristic response of modern corporations to uncertainty is to refuse to choose. As new product applications emerge, as new categories of customers come into the market, as new technologies compete to answer the old need, the corporation is inclined to embrace each in turn, forfeiting no opportunity, straddling all risks.

In due course, the organization structure begins to grow like a Christmas tree as the work of decision making is subdivided to take advantage of the specialized information and skills required. The sales executive is joined by the service manager, the product development manager, the advertising manager, the distribution planning manager, the market research director, and the whole team is duplicated anew as further lines are added. Many decisions become difficult to deal with in such a structure because they straddle the responsibilities of individuals. And when it comes to prepare purposive plans, the business is troubled by its inability to bring its own identity into view—to see entirely its unique resources, skills and commitments, and the whole market environment of which they are a part.

Finally, in analyzing this planning problem and its bearing on the marketing concept, something probably should be said about the decline of the owner-manager. The great size of modern enterprise, the progressive tax structures, and the new found affluence of even the most lowly worker all have combined to lessen the inclination and ability of individuals to undertake an entrepreneurial role in many markets. Fortunately, the very economic growth which rules out individual enterprise in one area opens up an opportunity for it somewhere else—as in the service industries. But it is my impression that the passing of the entrepreneur, where it has occurred, has removed an important element in the planning process, because he supplied the reason for planning in the sense that he specified the objectives to be attained. Indeed, this enterpreneur made planning easy—if at the same time fickle—by telling people what he wanted to accomplish, and the whole matter was scarcely less personal or more complicated than his choice of a necktie for the day. In the modern corporation we have replaced the owner-manager with a hired management accountable in concept to a diffuse and rapidly changing body of shareholders, but actually in performance quite sensitive to the appraisal of multiple audiences among customers, suppliers, labor, financial institutions, government and the public at large. By degrees, therefore, the decline of perfect competition and the decline of the entrepreneur with his simple conception of objectives are not unrelated events. Today's complex markets with many dimensions of competition have been accompanied by a corresponding multiplication of the values to be reconciled in the policies of modern enterprises.

So to summarize, business management has very difficult planning decisions to make, requiring that it foresee and analyze many alternate developments relating to its customers, competitors, and its own resources, and management must get these decisions made by people who are organized in an enormously complex structure, in which they are aware of the interrelationships of their part and the business, but unable to adequately see the whole business and its environment, and the ends to be served by all these forecasts and decisions are becoming increasingly diffuse and uncertain. It is in this sort of setting that the marketing concept was born, and it is my belief, after reflecting both on the background of the movement and the many statements of the case which businessmen have set forth, that what this really represents is a search for a management philosophy—a primacy of decision values—that can restore order and manageability out of what threatens to seem like chaos. Indeed, at the risk of introducing controversy, I would speculate that looking back on this development twenty years hence, the marketing concept belatedly will be recognized as an appropriate voicing of the basic purpose of corporate institutions grown too large to be adequately guided by the profit interests of a single compact group of owners. Certainly, anyone who carefully subtracts out of the total expenses of a modern business all of the sums expended on preparation for the future—ranging from research and advertising to new plant and training of personnel—is bound to discover that profit is a feeble measure of the current day's battle with competition, and is certainly meaningless if not considered with reference to accompanying changes in market position. With many companies today operating in conditions of oligopoly, it is small wonder that enlargement of the market and competitive share held in that market have become matters of management concern at least equal if not prerequisite to profit.

Now I want to turn from the general economic conditions and management problems which accompanied the emergency of the marketing concept to a discussion of its implications for business practices. Necessarily, this will be a highly personal statement because it is next to impossible to synthesize into a single theme what others have already set forth on this subject. It does seem to me, however, that the real distinction of the marketing concept which leads to the conclusion "this company has it" or "this one doesn't," is not so much a matter of organization structure or day-to-day tactics as it is a matter of what the management is trying to accomplish.

A moment ago I referred to the shifting focus of objectives that has characterized the evolution of modern business enterprise—first, from a focus on profit for the owner to a striving for market position and success against competition, and most recently to a focus on growth in which there is a continuing planned effort to enlarge the size of the market. It seems to me that the crux of the marketing concept is expressed in the latter orientation. When a company sets out to increase its sales, not by depriving its historic competitors of the market position which they already have captured, but by the application of research and insight to the task of creating new markets—indeed, new businesses—then we know that we are dealing with a management that has fully embraced the marketing concept. To be sure, as already has been brought out rather fully, any such endeavor is not without its economic repercussions in other markets and industries, but the very extent of these effects, reaching as they do to far and foreign places, confirms that something more than a minor improvement in the lot of the customer must have occurred. So to say it precisely, a company committed to the marketing concept focuses its major innovative effort on enlarging the size of the market in which it participates by introducing new generic products and services, by promoting new applications for existing products, and by seeking out new classes of customers who heretofore have not used the existing products.

In all cases the word "new" means more then just new to the company in question. It means "new," period. This is a somewhat more rigorous definition than to merely say that the business must constantly think of the customers' best interests or put supremacy in marketing functions foremost. And I might add that the rigor is deliberate, because only thinking of the customer and mere technical proficiency in marketing both turn out to be inferior hands when played against the company that couples its thoughts with action and actually comes to market with a successful innovation. To be sure, the business that seeks to apply its research and mass production and national promotion prowess to such ambitious notions as doing really new things is going to have to be knowledgeably benign with respect to the customer, and it certainly will reduce its risks to the degree that it is experienced and skillful in its marketing organization. But if the product and the service and the way they are sold are fundamentally in the customer's best interests, a great deal of amateurism in marketing tactics can be tolerated without serious consequences. Turning the issue around, if business enterprises are to compete successfully in the quicksilver of modern markets, something more than sophistication in means of doing marketing work is going to be required. Indeed, to plan at all, and think adequately of what competition might do and its possible effects before committing multi-million dollar resources, requires knowledge of the customer which penetrates to the level of theory. *So the principal task of the marketing function in a management concept is not so much to be skillful in making the customer do what suits the interests of the business as to be skillful in conceiving and then making the business do what suits the interests of the customer.* As Frank Knight observed some years ago, in conditions of real uncertainty, the outcome of a venture will be controlled much more by the entrepreneurial decision on what major course of action to undertake than by expert practice in implementation.[1] Thus, the central

[1]Frank H. Knight—*Risk, Uncertainty, and Profit* (Boston: Houghton Mifflin Company, 1921).

meaning of the marketing concept to the decision structure of a business in that the major purpose of the venture is taken from the need to solve some problem in the outer environment—some betterment for the customer—and all subsidiary decisions dealing with the acquisition and allocation of resources within the business are bent to that objective. In this light, certain tests can be applied to our daily business practices which sharpen the distinction between the marketing concept and the mere awareness in management that superiority in the marketing function is beginning to be of greater strategic importance than superiority in the production function.

For example, we might ask, is the service of customers or defense against competition the main focus of the creative search for better courses of action? Is the business in the habit of undertaking tactics which pay their way in added sales volume, but which in prompt imitation by competition fail to add to profit? If so, is the overall marketing effort really adding consumable value for the customer, or only adding cost—as for instance, advertising expenditures which seek to make like products seem unlike, and product redesign which attempts to produce obsolescence without adding to the functions performed by the product? Is the business constantly exhausting itself, trying to hold back changes introduced by its competitors—as when it refuses to recognize a new product technology, a new service, or a new sales channel which the customer seems to prefer? Is foolish pride—as the songwriter puts it—causing the management to reject the verdict of the marketplace? Is the business trying to be all things to all customers when their requirements and interests in the product are so fragmenting that some forfeiture of clientele and specialization of customer alignment obviously are needed? Is what the business considers a good salesman essentially a customer oriented man or is he a loyal "company" man, intent on making the customer understand his employer's policies? And finally, is the business using its resources and ability to innovate on tasks that smaller competitors with less overhead can handle better, or is it taxing its capacities to the fullest in undertakings that really challenge it?

These are fairly direct questions, but the answers turn on rather subtle differences in the marketing posture of a company. By and large, it is my observation that concerns which are in an active growth phase will pass this sort of test; those that have slowed down and see themselves as digging in for a defense against younger, more vigorous competitors in time will fail the test. Certainly, anyone who examines the turnover in rankings of the hundred largest corporations, or the turnover in the leadership position in even the smallest markets, cannot fail to see that the graveyards of business are full of those who conceived their obligations to the customer too narrowly.

Now, one might ask, how can the active growth phase of a company be infinitely prolonged? In the end, will not the constant adding of new products, new applications and new users lead to a loss of identity and a nomad-like wandering over the entire market terrain? And how does a company so oriented—or disoriented—respond to the attack of competition? Must every action pass the test of what is truly in the customer's interests? To be sure, these are important questions. But much of the difficulty is removed if we remember that it often is in the interests of both the customer and the company that it abandon a market, that it forego an existing product line and forfeit some present clientele to competition.

Where two groups of product users have different requirements in either the product or the services that go with it, the constant temptation is to suppress these differences, to force homogenization of the requirements, and we all are familiar with examples of the skillful use of price policy, engineering standards, advertising, and product design to such ends. Yet when such an unnatural marriage is challenged by a competitor who selects only one of the two user groups as his intended clientele, a competitor who aligns all his decisions in the interests of that single group and who brings to it a specially designed product, then the profit position of the company that is straddling the issue is likely to become quite untenable. In the same way, a company may choose to deal with two unrelated markets in a manner that is dictated by the desire to apply some common technology or shared resource of production or distribution. The endeavor in each market being limited by the requirements of the opposite market, this company, too, is vulnerable to a competitor that specializes in only one of these undertakings. So I submit, it is no prescription of dogma but the hard facts of competition that argue for coupling a program of innovation and growth with a sharp pruning knife to cut out the commitments that threaten to compromise the marketing concept. If we all freely admitted our mistakes and were prompt in forfeiting a losing battle to competition, a great deal of pointless advertising could be turned into profit, and a substantial improvement could be worked in sales to other markets where efforts have been less than customer oriented due to the conflicts that have been baked in. Indeed, it is precisely because of this constant need for pruning that companies which were guided by pre-war notions of production efficiency, and which grew along lines of by-product diversification and vertical integration are in the gravest sort of difficulty today. Hence the most cogent argument for designing an industrial enterprise from the customer backward into the factory, rather than from the production process forward, so to speak, is that the success of the venture is becoming much less dependent on its production efficiency and much more dependent on its flexibility in adjusting to the risks posed by the changing requirements of its customers.

7. THE MARKETING REVOLUTION*

Robert J. Keith

The consumer, not the company, is in the middle.

In today's economy the consumer, the man or woman who buys the product, is at the absolute dead center of the business universe. Companies revolve around the customer, not the other way around.

Growing acceptance of this consumer concept has had, and will have, far-reaching implications for business, achieving a virtual revolution in economic thinking. As the concept gains ever greater acceptance, marketing is emerging as the most important single function in business.

A REVOLUTION IN SCIENCE

A very apt analogy can be drawn with another revolution, one that goes back to the sixteenth century. At that time astronomers had great difficulty predicting the movements of the heavenly bodies. Their charts and computations and celestial calendars enabled them to estimate the approximate positions of the planets on any given date. But their calculations were never exact—there was always a variance.

Then a Polish scientist named Nicolaus Copernicus proposed a very simple answer to the problem. If, he proposed, we assume that the sun, and not the earth, is at the center of our system, and that the earth moves around the sun instead of the sun moving around the earth, all our calculations will prove correct.

The Pole's idea raised a storm of controversy. The earth, everyone knew, was at the center of the universe. But another scientist named Galileo put the theory to test—and it worked. The result was a complete upheaval in scientific and philosophic thought. The effects of Copernicus' revolutionary idea are still being felt today.

*Reprinted from the *Journal of Marketing*, national quarterly publication of the American Marketing Association (January, 1960), pp. 35–38.

A REVOLUTION IN MARKETING

In much the same way American business in general—and Pillsbury in particular—is undergoing a revolution of its own today: a marketing revolution.

This revolution stems from the same idea stated in the opening sentence of this article. No longer is the company at the center of the business universe. Today the customer is at the center.

Our attention has shifted from problems of production to problems of marketing, from the product we *can* make to the product the consumer *wants* us to make, from the company itself to the market place.

The marketing revolution has only begun. It is reasonable to expect that its implications will grow in the years to come, and that lingering effects will be felt a century, or more than one century, from today.

So far the theory has only been advanced, tested, and generally proved correct. As more and more businessmen grasp the concept, and put it to work, our economy will become more truly marketing oriented.

PILLSBURY'S PATTERN: FOUR ERAS

Here is the way the marketing revolution came about at Pillsbury. The experience of this company has followed a typical pattern. There has been nothing unique, and each step in the evolution of the marketing concept has been taken in a way that is more meaningful because the steps are, in fact, typical.

Today in our company the marketing concept finds expression in the simple statement, "Nothing happens at Pillsbury until a sale is made." This statement represents basic reorientation on the part of our management. For, not too many years ago, the ordering of functions in our business placed finance first, production second, and sales last.

How did we arrive at our present point of view? Pillsbury's progress in the marketing revolution divides neatly into four separate eras—eras which parallel rather closely the classic pattern of development in the marketing revolution.

1st ERA—PRODUCTION ORIENTED

First came the era of manufacturing. It began with the formation of the company in 1869 and continued into the 1930s. It is significant that the *idea* for the formation of our company came from the *availability* of high-quality wheat and the *proximity* of water power—and not from the availability and proximity of growing major market areas, or the demand for better, less expensive, more convenient flour products.

Of course, these elements were potentially present. But the two major elements which fused in the mind of Charles A. Pillsbury and prompted him to invest his modest capital in a flour mill were, on the one hand, wheat, and, on the other hand, water power. His principal concern was with production, not marketing.

His thought and judgment were typical of the business thinking of his day. And such thinking was adequate and proper for the times.

Our company philosophy in this era might have been stated this way: "We are professional flour millers. Blessed with a supply of the finest North American wheat, plenty of water power, and excellent milling machinery, we produce flour of the highest quality. Our basic function is to mill high-quality flour, and of course (and almost incidentally) we must hire salesmen to sell it, just as we hire accountants to keep our books."

The young company's first new product reveals an interesting example of the thinking of this era. The product was middlings, the bran left over after milling. Millfeed, as the product came to be known, proved a valuable product because it was an excellent nutrient for cattle. But the impetus to launch the new product came not from a consideration of the nutritional needs of cattle or a marketing analysis. It came primarily from the desire to dispose of a by-product! The new product decision was production oriented, not marketing oriented.

2nd ERA—SALES ORIENTED

In the 1930s Pillsbury moved into its second era of development as a marketing company. This was the era of sales. For the first time we began to be highly conscious of the consumer, her wants, and her prejudices, as a key factor in the business equation. We established a commercial research department to provide us with facts about the market.

We also became more aware of the importance of our dealers, the wholesale and retail grocers who provided a vital link in our chain of distribution from the mill to the home. Knowing that consumers and dealers as well were vital to the company's success, we could no longer simply mark them down as unknowns in our figuring. With this realization, we took the first step along the road to becoming a marketing company.

Pillsbury's thinking in this second era could be summed up like this: "We are a flour-milling company, manufacturing a number of products for the consumer market. We must have a first-rate sales organization which can dispose of all the products we can make at a favorable price. We must back up this sales force with consumer advertising and market intelligence. We want our salesmen and our dealers to have all the tools they need for moving the output of our plants to the consumer."

Still not a marketing philosophy, but we were getting closer.

3rd ERA—MARKETING ORIENTED

It was at the start of the present decade that Pillsbury entered the marketing era. The amazing growth of our consumer business as the result of introducing baking mixes provided the immediate impetus. But the groundwork had been laid by key men who developed our sales concepts in the middle forties.

With the new cake mixes, products of our research program, ringing up sales on the cash register, and with the realization that research and production could produce literally hundreds of new and different products, we faced for the first time the necessity for selecting the best new products. We needed a set of criteria for selecting the kind of products we would manufacture. We needed an organization to establish and maintain these criteria, and for attaining maximum sale of the products we did select.

We needed, in fact, to build into our company a new management function which would direct and control all the other corporate functions from procurement to production to advertising to sales. This function was marketing. Our solution was to establish the present marketing department.

This department developed the criteria which we would use in determining which products to market. *And these criteria were, and are, nothing more nor less than those of the consumer herself.* We moved the mountain out to find out what Mahomet, and Mrs. Mahomet, wanted. The company's purpose was no longer to mill flour, nor to manufacture a wide variety of products, but to satisfy the needs and desires, both actual and potential, of our customers.

If we were to restate our philosophy during the past decade as simply as possible, it would read: "We make and sell products for consumers."

The business universe, we realized, did not have room at the center for Pillsbury or any other company or groups of companies. It was already occupied by the customers.

This is the concept at the core of the marketing revolution. How did we put it to work for Pillsbury?

The Brand-Manager Concept

The first move was to transform our small advertising department into a marketing department. The move involved far more than changing the name on organizational charts. It required the introduction of a new, and vitally important, organizational concept—the brand-manager concept.

The brand-manager idea is the very backbone of marketing at Pillsbury. The man who bears the title, brand manager, has total accountability for results. He directs the marketing of his product as if it were his own business. Production does its job, and finance keeps the profit figures. Otherwise, the brand manager has total responsibility for marketing his product. This responsibility encompasses pricing, commercial research, competitive activity, home service and publicity coordination, legal details, budgets, advertising plans, sales promotion, and execution of plans. The brand manager must think first, last, and always of his sales target, the consumer.

Marketing permeates the entire organization. Marketing plans and executes the sale—all the way from the inception of the product idea, through its development and distribution, to the customer purchase. Marketing begins and ends with the consumer. New product ideas are conceived after careful study of her wants and needs, her likes and dislikes. Then marketing takes the idea and marshals all the forces of the corporation to translate the idea into product and the product into sales.

In the early days of the company, consumer orientation did not seem so important. The company made flour, and flour was a staple—no one would question the availability of a market. Today we must determine whether the American housewife will buy lemon pudding cake in preference to orange angel food. The variables in the equation have multiplied, just as the number of products on the grocers' shelves have multiplied from a hundred or so into many thousands.

When we first began operating under this new marketing concept, we encountered the problems which always accompany any major reorientation. Our people were young and frankly immature in some areas of business; but they were men possessed of an idea and they fought for it. The idea was almost too powerful. The marketing concept proved its worth in sales, but it upset many of the internal balances of the corporation. Marketing-oriented decisions resulted in peaks and valleys in production, schedules, labor, and inventories. But the system worked. It worked better and better as maverick marketing men became motivated toward tonnage and profit.

4th ERA—MARKETING CONTROL

Today marketing is coming into its own. Pillsbury stands on the brink of its fourth major era in the marketing revolution.

Basically, the philosophy of this fourth era can be summarized this way: "We are moving from a company which has the marketing concept to a marketing company."

Marketing today sets company operating policy short-term. It will come to influence long-range policy more and more. Where today consumer research, technical research, procurement, production, advertising, and sales swing into action under the broad canopy established by marketing, tomorrow capital and financial planning, ten-year volume and profit goals will also come under the aegis of marketing. More than any other function, marketing must be tied to top management.

Today our marketing people know more about inventories than anyone in top management. Tomorrow's marketing man must know capital financing and the implications of marketing planning on long-range profit forecasting.

Today technical research receives almost all of its guidance and direction from marketing. Tomorrow marketing will assume a more creative function in the advertising area, both in terms of ideas and media selection.

Changes in the Future

The marketing revolution has only begun. There are still those who resist its basic idea, just as there are always those who will resist change in business, government, or any other form of human institution.

As the marketing revolution gains momentum, there will be more changes. The concept of the customer at the center will remain valid; but business must adjust to the shifting tastes and likes and desires and needs which have always characterized the American consumer.

For many years the geographical center of the United States lay in a small Kansas town. Then a new state, Alaska, came along, and the center shifted to the north and west. Hawaii was admitted to the Union and the geographical mid-point took another jump to the west. In very much the same way, modern business must anticipate the restless shifting of buying attitudes, as customer preferences move north, south, east, or west from a liquid center. There is nothing static about the marketing revolution, and that is part of its fascination. The old order has changed, yielding place to the new—but the new order will have its quota of changes, too.

At Pillsbury, as our fourth era progresses, marketing will become the basic motivating force for the entire corporation. Soon it will be true that every activity of the corporation—from finance to sales to production—is aimed at satisfying the needs and desires of the consumer. When that stage of development is reached, the marketing revolution will be complete.

II

Consumer Analysis

The marketing objective of any firm is to identify potential customers and convince them that the firm's product will satisfy their needs. [illegible] objective implies an understanding of human behavior, es[illegible] behavioral role of "consumer." The articles in this section [illegible] the most significant attempts to analyze consumer behavior.

The normative framework for analyzing the consumer is provided by economic theory. Katona has led the movement to integrate economic theory and the behavioral sciences to provide a sound theory of rational economic behavior. Bayton's work is an excellent overview of the usefulness of certain psychological concepts in understanding consumer behavior. Each of the following three articles focuses in greater depth on one of the concepts discussed by Bayton: Bauer on consumer motivation as a function of perceived risk; Festinger's concept of cognitive dissonance; and Kuehn's learning model. These articles have inspired considerable subsequent research. Haire's work with projective techniques is one of the pioneering efforts in applying scientific research methodology to consumer analysis.

The remaining four articles in this section examine the influence of interpersonal relationships on consumer behavior. The general theory of group influence is given in the paper by the Foundation for Research on Human Behavior. Katz reports on the nature of the communications process and the effect of communications on behavior. Martineau concentrates on social class differences as determinants of behavioral patterns. The Foundation for Research on Human Behavior then provides a classificatory system that distinguishes among consumers on the basis of adoption rate of new products.

8. RATIONAL BEHAVIOR AND ECONOMIC BEHAVIOR*

George Katona

While attempts to penetrate the boundary lines between psychology and sociology have been rather frequent during the last few decades, psychologists have paid little attention to the problems with which another sister discipline, economics, is concerned. One purpose of this paper is to arouse interest among psychologists in studies of economic behavior. For that purpose it will be shown that psychological principles may be of great value in clarifying basic questions of economics and that the psychology of habit formation, of motivation, and of group belonging may profit from studies of economic behavior.

A variety of significant problems, such as those of the business cycle or inflation, of consumer saving or business investment, could be chosen for the purpose of such demonstration. This paper, however, will be concerned with the most fundamental assumption of economics, the principle of rationality. In order to clarify the problems involved in this principle, which have been neglected by contemporary psychologists, it will be necessary to contrast the most common forms of methodology used in economics with those employed in psychology and to discuss the role of empirical research in the social sciences.

THEORY AND HYPOTHESES

Economic theory represents one of the oldest and most elaborate theoretical structures in the social sciences. However, dissatisfaction with the achievements and uses of economic theory has grown considerably during the past few decades on the part of economists who are

*Reprinted from *Psychological Review* (September, 1953), pp. 307–318.

interested in what actually goes on in economic life. And yet leading sociologists and psychologists have recently declared "Economics is today, in a theoretical sense, probably the most highly elaborated, sophisticated, and refined of the disciplines dealing with action."[1]

To understand the scientific approach of economic theorists, we may divide them into two groups. Some develop an a priori system from which they deduce propositions about how people *should* act under certain assumptions. Assuming that the sole aim of businessmen is profit maximization, these theorists deduce propositions about marginal revenues and marginal costs, for example, that are not meant to be suited for testing. In developing formal logics of economic action, one of the main considerations is elegance of the deductive system, based on the law of parsimony. A wide gap separates these theorists from economic research of an empirical-statistical type which registers what they call aberrations or deviations, due to human frailty, from the norm set by theory.

A second group of economic theorists adheres to the proposition that it is the main purpose of theory to provide hypotheses that can be tested. This group acknowledges that prediction of future events represents the most stringent test of theory. They argue, however, that reality is so complex that it is necessary to begin with simplified propositions and models which are known to be unreal and not testable.[2] Basic among these propositions are the following three which traditionally have served to characterize the economic man or the rational man:

1. The principle of complete information and foresight. Economic conditions—demand, supply, prices, etc.—are not only given but also known to the rational man. This applies as well to future conditions about which there exists no uncertainty, so that rational choice can always be made. (In place of the assumption of certainty of future developments, we find nowadays more frequently the assumption that risks prevail but the probability of occurrence of different alternatives is known; this does not constitute a basic difference.)
2. The principle of complete mobility. There are no institutional

[1] T. Parsons and E. A. Shils, (Editors), *Toward a General Theory of Action* (Cambridge, Mass.: Harvard University Press, 1951).

[2] A variety of methods used in economic research differ, of course, from those employed by the two groups of economic theorists. Some research is motivated by dissatisfaction with the traditional economic theory; some is grounded in a systematization greatly different from traditional theory (the most important example of such systematization is national income accounting); some research is not clearly based on any theory; finally, some research has great affinity with psychological and sociological studies.

or psychological factors which make it impossible, or expensive, or slow, to translate the rational choice into action.

3. The principle of pure competition. Individual action has no great influence on prices because each man's choice is independent from any other person's choice and because there are no "large" sellers or buyers. Action is the result of individual choice and is not group-determined.

Economic theory is developed first under these assumptions. The theorists then introduce changes in the assumptions so that the theory may approach reality. One such step consists, for instance, of introducing large-scale producers, monopolists, and oligopolists, another of introducing time lags, and still another of introducing uncertainty about the probability distribution of future events. The question raised in each case is this: Which of the original propositions needs to be changed, and in what way, in view of the new assumptions?

The fact that up to now the procedure of gradual approximation to reality has not been completely successful does not invalidate the method. It must also be acknowledged that propositions were frequently derived from unrealistic economic models which were susceptible to testing and stimulated empirical research. In this paper we shall point to a great drawback of this method of starting out with a simplified a priori system and making it gradually more complex and more real—by proceeding in this way one tends to lose sight of important problems and to disregard them.

The methods most commonly used in psychology may appear at first sight to be quite similar to the methods of economics which have just been described. Psychologists often start with casual observations, derive from them hypotheses, test those through more systematic observations, reformulate and revise their hypotheses accordingly, and test them again. The process of hypotheses-observations-hypotheses-observations often goes on with no end in sight. Differences from the approach of economic theory may be found in the absence in psychological research of detailed systematic elaboration prior to any observation. Also, in psychological research, findings and generalizations in one field of behavior are often considered as hypotheses in another field of behavior. Accordingly, in analyzing economic behavior[3] and trying to understand rationality, psychologists can draw on (*a*) the theory of learning and thinking, (*b*) the theory of group belonging, and (*c*) the theory of motivation. This will be done in this paper.

[3]The expression "economic behavior" is used in this paper to mean behavior concerning economic matters (spending, saving, investing, pricing, etc.). Some economic theorists use the expression to mean the behavior of the "economic man," that is, the behavior postulated in their theory of rationality.

HABITUAL BEHAVIOR AND GENUINE DECISION MAKING

In trying to give noneconomic examples of "rational calculus," economic theorists have often referred to gambling. From some textbooks one might conclude that the most rational place in the world is the Casino in Monte Carlo where odds and probabilities can be calculated exactly. In contrast, some mathematicians and psychologists have considered scientific discovery and the thought processes of scientists as the best examples of rational or intelligent behavior.[4] An inquiry about the possible contributions of psychology to the analysis of rationality may then begin with a formulation of the differences between (*a*) associative learning and habit formation and (*b*) problem solving and thinking.

The basic principle of the first form of behavior is repetition. Here the argument of Guthrie holds: "The most certain and dependable information concerning what a man will do in any situation is information concerning what he did in that situation on its last occurrence."[5] This form of behavior depends upon the frequency of repetition as well as on its recency and on the success of past performances. The origins of habit formation have been demonstrated by experiments about learning nonsense syllables, lists of words, mazes, and conditioned responses. Habits thus formed are to some extent automatic and inflexible.

In contrast, problem-solving behavior has been characterized by the arousal of a problem or question, by deliberation that involves reorganization and "direction," by understanding of the requirements of the situation, by weighing of alternatives and taking their consequences into consideration and, finally, by choosing among alternative courses of action.[6] Scientific discovery is not the only example of such

[4]Reference should be made first of all to Max Wertheimer who in his book *Productive Thinking* uses the terms "sensible" and "intelligent" rather than "rational." Since we are mainly interested here in deriving conclusions from the psychology of thinking, the discussion of psychological principles will be kept extremely brief. See M. Wertheimer, *Productive Thinking* (New York: Harper, 1945); G. Katona, *Organizing and Memorizing* (New York: Columbia University Press, 1940); and G. Katona, *Psychological Analysis of Economic Behavior* (New York: McGraw-Hill, 1951), especially Chapters 3 and 4.

[5]E. R. Guthrie, *Psychology of Learning* (New York: Harper, 1935), p. 228.

[6]Cf. the following statement by a leading psychoanalyst: "Rational behavior is behavior that is effectively guided by an understanding of the situation to which one is reacting." French adds two steps that follow the choice between alternative goals, namely, commitment to a goal and commitment to a plan to reach a goal. See T. M. French, *The Integration of Behavior* (Chicago: University of Chicago Press, 1952).

procedures; they have been demonstrated in the psychological laboratory as well as in a variety of real-life situations. Problem solving results in action which is new rather than repetitive; the actor may have never behaved in the same way before and may not have learned of any others having behaved in the same way.

Some of the above terms, defined and analyzed by psychologists, are also being used by economists in their discussion of rational behavior. In discussing, for example, a manufacturer's choice between erecting or not erecting a new factory, or raising or not raising his prices or output, reference is usually made to deliberation and to taking the consequences of alternative choices into consideration. Nevertheless, it is not justified to identify problem-solving behavior with rational behavior. From the point of view of an outside observer, habitual behavior may prove to be fully rational or the most appropriate way of action under certain circumstances. All that is claimed here is that the analysis of two forms of behavior—habitual versus genuine decision making—may serve to clarify problems of rationality. We shall proceed therefore by deriving six propositions from the psychological principles. To some extent, or in certain fields of behavior, these are findings or empirical generalizations; to some extent, or in other fields of behavior, they are hypotheses.

1. Problem-solving behavior is a relatively rare occurrence. It would be incorrect to assume that everyday behavior consistently manifests such features as arousal of a problem, deliberation, or taking consequences of the action into consideration. Behavior which does not manifest these characteristics predominates in everyday life and in economic activities as well.
2. The main alternative to problem-solving behavior is not whimsical or impulsive behavior (which was considered the major example of "irrational" behavior by nineteenth-century philosophers). When genuine decision making does not take place, habitual behavior is the most usual occurrence: people act as they have acted before under similar circumstances, without deliberating and choosing.
3. Problem-solving behavior is recognized most commonly as a deviation from habitual behavior. Observance of the established routine is abandoned when in driving home from my office, for example, I learn that there is a parade in town and choose a different route, instead of automatically taking the usual one. Or, to mention an example of economic behavior: Many businessmen have rules of thumb concerning the timing for reorders of merchandise; yet sometimes they decide to place new orders even though their inventories have not

reached the usual level of depletion (for instance, because they anticipate price increases), or not to order merchandise even though that level has been reached (because they expect a slump in sales).

4. Strong motivational forces—stronger than those which elicit habitual behavior—must be present to call forth problem-solving behavior. Being in a "crossroad situation," facing "choice points," or perceiving that something new has occurred are typical instances in which we are motivated to deliberate and choose. Pearl Harbor and the Korean aggression are extreme examples of "new" events; economic behavior of the problem-solving type was found to have prevailed widely after these events.
5. Group belonging and group reinforcement play a substantial role in changes of behavior due to problem solving. Many people become aware of the same events at the same time; our mass media provide the same information and often the same interpretation of events to groups of people (to businessmen, trade union members, sometimes to all Americans). Changes in behavior resulting from new events may therefore occur among very many people at the same time. Some economists[7] argued that consumer optimism and pessimism are unimportant because usually they will cancel out; in the light of sociopsychological principles, however, it is probable, and has been confirmed by recent surveys, that a change from optimistic to pessimistic attitudes, or vice versa, sometimes occurs among millions of people at the same time.
6. Changes in behavior due to genuine decision making will tend to be substantial and abrupt, rather than small and gradual. Typical examples of action that results from genuine decisions are cessation of purchases or buying waves, the shutting down of plants or the building of new plants, rather than an increase or decrease of production by 5 or 10 per cent.[8]

Because of the preponderance of individual psychological assumptions in classical economics and the emphasis placed on group behavior in this discussion, the change in underlying conditions which has occurred during the last century may be illustrated by a further example. It is related—the author does not know whether the story is

[7] J. M. Keynes, *The General Theory of Employment, Interest and Money* (New York: Harcourt, Brace, 1936), p. 95.

[8] Some empirical evidence supporting these six propositions in the area of economic behavior has been assembled by the Survey Research Center of the University of Michigan. See G. Katona, "Psychological Analysis of Business Decisions and Expectations," *American Economic Review* (1946), pp. 44–63.

true or fictitious—that the banking house of the Rothschilds, still in its infancy at that time, was one of the suppliers of the armies of Lord Wellington in 1815. Nathan Mayer Rothschild accompanied the armies and was present at the Battle of Waterloo. When he became convinced that Napoleon was decisively defeated, he released carrier pigeons so as to transmit the news to his associates in London and reverse the commodity position of his bank. The carrier pigeons arrived in London before the news of the victory became public knowledge. The profits thus reaped laid, according to the story, the foundation to the outstanding position of the House of Rothschild in the following decades.

The decision to embark on a new course of action because of new events was then made by one individual for his own profit. At present, news of a battle, or of change of government, or of rearmament programs, is transmitted in short order by press and radio to the public at large. Businessmen—the manufacturers or retailers of steel or clothing, for instance—usually receive the same news about changes in the price of raw materials or in demand, and often consult with each other. Belonging to the same group means being subject to similar stimuli and reinforcing one another in making decisions. Acting in the same way as other members of one's group or of a reference group have acted under similar circumstances may also occur without deliberation and choice. New action by a few manufacturers will, then, frequently or even usually not be compensated by reverse action on the part of others. Rather the direction in which the economy of an entire country moves—and often the world economy as well—will tend to be subject to the same influences.

After having indicated some of the contributions which the application of certain psychological principles to economic behavior may make, we turn to contrasting that approach with the traditional theory of rationality. Instead of referring to the formulations of nineteenth-century economists, we shall quote from a modern version of the classical trend of thought. The title of a section in a recent article by Kenneth J. Arrow is "The Principle of Rationality." He describes one of the criteria of rationality as follows: "We can imagine the individual as listing, once and for all, all conceivable consequences of his actions in order of his preference for them."[9] We are first concerned with the expression "all conceivable consequences." This expression seems to contradict the principle of selectivity of human behavior. Yet habitual behavior is highly selective since it is based on

[9]K. J. Arrow, "Mathematical Models in the Social Sciences", in D. Lerner and H. D. Lasswell, (Editors), *The Policy Sciences* (Stanford: Stanford University Press, 1951), p. 135.

(repeated) past experience, and problem-solving behavior likewise is highly selective since reorganization is subject to a certain direction instead of consisting of trial (and error) regarding all possible avenues of action.

Secondly, Arrow appears to identify rationality with consistency in the sense of repetition of the same choice. It is part and parcel of rational behavior, according to Arrow, that an individual "makes the same choice each time he is confronted with the same set of alternatives."[10] Proceeding in the same way on successive occasions appears, however, a characteristic of habitual behavior. Problem-solving behavior, on the other hand, is flexible. Rationality may be said to reflect adaptability and ability to act in a new way when circumstances demand it, rather than to consist of rigid or repetitive behavior.

Thirdly, it is important to realize the differences between the concepts, action, decision, and choice. It is an essential feature of the approach derived from considering problem-solving behavior that there is action without deliberate decision and choice. It then becomes one of the most important problems of research to determine under what conditions genuine decision and choice occur prior to an action. The three concepts are, however, used without differentiation in the classical theory of rationality and also, most recently, by Parsons and Shils. According to the theory of these authors, there are "five discrete choices (explicit or implicit) which every actor makes before he can act;" before there is action "a decision must always be made (explicitly or implicitly, consciously or unconsciously)."[11]

There exists, no doubt, a difference in terminology, which may be clarified by mentioning a simple case: Suppose my telephone rings: I lift the receiver with my left hand and say, "Hello." Should we then argue that I made several choices, for instance, that I decided not to lift the receiver with my right hand and not to say "Mr. Katona speaking"? According to our use of the terms decision and choice, my action was habitual and did not involve "taking consequences into consideration."[12] Parsons and Shils use the terms decision and choice in a

[10]In his recent book Arrow adds after stating that the economic man "will make the same decision each time he is faced with the same range of alternatives": "The ability to make consistent decisions is one of the symptoms of an integrated personality." See K. J. Arrow, *Social Choice and Individual Values* (New York: Wiley, 1951), p. 2.

[11]T. Parsons and E. A. Shils, *op. cit.*

[12]If I have reason not to make known that I am at home, I may react to the ringing of the telephone by fright, indecision, and deliberation (should I lift the receiver or let the telephone ring?) instead of reacting in the habitual way. This is an example of problem-solving behavior characterized as deviating from habitual behavior. The only example of action mentioned by Parsons and Shils, "a man driving his automobile to a lake to go fishing," may be habitual or may be an instance of genuine decision making.

different sense, and Arrow may use the terms "all conceivable consequences" and "same set of alternatives" in a different sense from the one employed in this paper. But the difference between the two approaches appears to be more far-reaching. By using the terminology of the authors quoted, and by constructing a theory of rational action on the basis of this terminology, fundamental problems are disregarded. If every action by definition presupposes decision making, and if the malleability of human behavior is not taken into consideration, a one-sided theory of rationality is developed and empirical research is confined to testing a theory which covers only some of the aspects of rationality.

This was the case recently in experiments devised by Mosteller and Nogee. These authors attempt to test basic assumptions of economic theory, such as the rational choice among alternatives, by placing their subjects in a gambling situation (a variation of poker dice) and compelling them to make a decision, namely, to play or not to play against the experimenter. Through their experiments the authors prove that "it is feasible to measure utility experimentally,"[13] but they do not shed light on the conditions under which rational behavior occurs or on the inherent features of rational behavior. Experiments in which making a choice among known alternatives is prescribed do not test the realism of economic theory.

MAXIMIZATION

Up to now we have discussed only one central aspect of rationality—means rather than ends. The end of rational behavior, according to economic theory, is maximization of profits in the base of business firms and maximization of utility in the case of people in general.

A few words, first, on maximizing profits. This is usually considered the simpler case because it is widely held (*a*) that business firms are in business to make profits and (*b*) that profits, more so than utility, are a quantitative, measurable concept.

When empirical research, most commonly in the form of case studies, showed that businessmen frequently strove for many things in addition to profits or in place of profits, most theorists were content with small changes in their systems. They redefined profits so as to include long-range profits and what has been called nonpecuniary or psychic profits. Striving for security or for power was identified with striving for profits in the more distant future; purchasing goods from a

[13] F. Mosteller and P. Nogee, "An Experimental Measurement of Utility," *Journal of Political Economy* (1951), pp. 371–405.

high bidder who was a member of the same fraternity as the purchaser, rather than from the lowest bidder—to cite an example often used in textbooks—was thought to be maximizing of nonpecuniary profits. Dissatisfaction with this type of theory construction is rather widespread. For example, a leading theorist wrote recently:

> If *whatever* a business man does is explained by the principle of profit maximization—because he does what he likes to do, and he likes to do what maximizes the sum of his pecuniary and nonpecuniary profits—the analysis acquires the character of a system of definitions and tautologies, and loses much of its value as an explanation of reality.[14]

The same problem is encountered regarding maximization of utility. Arrow defines rational behavior as follows: ". . . among all the combinations of commodities an individual can afford, he chooses that combination which maximizes his utility or satisfaction"[15] and speaks of the "traditional identification of rationality with maximization of some sort."[16] An economic theorist has recently characterized this type of definition as follows:

> The statement that a person seeks to maximize utility is (in many versions) a tautology: it is impossible to conceive of an observational phenomenon that contradicts it. . . . What if the theorem is contradicted by observation: Samuelson says it would not matter much in the case of utility theory; I would say that it would not make the slightest difference. For there is a free variable in his system: the tastes of consumers. . . . Any contradiction of a theorem derived from utility theory can always be attributed to a change of tastes, rather than to an error in the postulates or logic of the theory.[17]

What is the way out of this difficulty? Can psychology, and specifically the psychology of motivation, help? We may begin by characterizing the prevailing economic theory as a single-motive theory and contrast it with a theory of multiple motives. Even in case of a single decision of one individual, multiplicity of motives (or of vectors or forces in the field), some reinforcing one another and some conflicting with one another, is the rule rather than the exception. The motiva-

[14]F. Machlup, "Marginal Analysis and Empirical Research," *American Economic Review* (1946), p. 526.

[15]K. J. Arrow, *op. cit.*

[16]K. J. Arrow, *Social Choice and Individual Values* (New York: Wiley, 1951). The quotation refers specifically to Samuelson's definition but also applies to that of Arrow.

[17]G. J. Stigler, "Review of P. A. Samuelson's Foundations of Economic Analysis," *Journal of American Statistical Association* (1948), p. 603.

tional patterns prevailing among different individuals making the same decision need not be the same; the motives of the same individual who is in the same external situation at different times may likewise differ. This approach opens the way (*a*) for a study of the relation of different motives to different forms of behavior and (*b* for an investigation of changes in motives. Both problems are disregarded by postulating a single-motive theory and by restricting empirical studies to attempts to confirm or contradict that theory.

The fruitfulness of the psychological approach may be illustrated first by a brief reference to business motivation. We may rank the diverse motivational patterns of businessmen by placing the striving for high immediate profits (maximization of short-run profits, to use economic terminology; charging whatever the market can bear, to use a popular expression) at one extreme of the scale. At the other extreme we place the striving for prestige or power. In between we discern striving for security, for larger business volume, or for profits in the more distant future. Under what kinds of business conditions will motivational patterns tend to conform with the one or the other end of the scale? Preliminary studies would seem to indicate that the worse the business situation is, the more frequent is striving for high immediate profits, and the better the business situation is, the more frequent is striving for nonpecuniary goals.[18]

Next we shall refer to one of the most important problems of consumer economics as well as of business-cycle studies, the deliberate choice between saving and spending. Suppose a college professor receives a raise in his salary or makes a few hundred extra dollars through a publication. Suppose, furthermore, that he suggests thereupon to his wife that they should buy a television set while the wife argues that the money should be put in the bank as a reserve against a "rainy day." Whatever the final decision may be, traditional economic theory would hold that the action which gives the greater satisfaction was chosen. This way of theorizing is of little value. Under what conditions will one type of behavior (spending) and under what conditions will another type of behavior (saving) be more frequent? Psychological hypotheses according to which the strength of vectors is related to the immediacy of needs have been put to a test through nationwide surveys over the past six years.[19] On the basis of survey

[18]G. Katona, *Psychological Analysis of Economic Behavior* (New York: McGraw-Hill, 1951), pp. 193–213.

[19]In the Surveys of Consumer Finances, conducted annually since 1946 by the Survey Research Center of the University of Michigan for the Federal Reserve Board and reported in the *Federal Reserve Bulletin*. See a forthcoming publication of the Survey Research Center on consumer buying and inflation during 1950–52.

findings the following tentative generalization was established: Pessimism, insecurity, expectation of income declines or bad times in the near future promote saving (putting the extra money in the bank), while optimism, feeling of security, expectation of income increases, or good times promote spending (buying the television set, for instance).

Psychological hypotheses, based on a theory of motivational patterns which change with circumstances and influence behavior, thus stimulated empirical studies. These studies, in turn, yielded a better understanding of past developments and also, we may add, better predictions of forthcoming trends than did studies based on the classical theory. On the other hand, when conclusions about utility or rationality were made on an a priori basis, researchers lost sight of important problems.[20]

DIMINISHING UTILITY, SATURATION, AND ASPIRATION

Among the problems to which the identification of maximizing utility with rationality gave rise, the measurability of utility has been prominent. At present the position of most economists appears to be that while interpersonal comparison of several consumers' utilities is not possible, and while cardinal measures cannot be attached to the utilities of one particular consumer, ordinal ranking of the utilities of each individual can be made. It is asserted that I can always say either that I prefer *A* to *B*, or that I am indifferent to having *A* or *B*, or that I prefer *B* to *A*. The theory of indifference curves is based on this assumption.

In elaborating the theory further, it is asserted that rational behavior consists not only of preferring more of the same goods to less ($2 real wages to $1, or two packages of cigarettes to one package, for the same service performed) but also of deriving diminishing increments of satisfaction from successive units of a commodity.[21] In terms of an old textbook example, one drink of water has tremendous value to a thirsty traveler in a desert; a second, third, or fourth drink may still have some

[20]It should not be implied that the concepts of utility and maximization are of no value for empirical research. Comparison between maximum utility as determined from the vantage point of an observer with the pattern of goals actually chosen (the "subjective maximum"), which is based on insufficient information, may be useful. Similar considerations apply to such newer concepts as "minimizing regrets" and the "minimax."

[21]This principle of diminishing utility was called a "fundamental tendency of human nature" by the great nineteenth century economist, Alfred Marshall.

value but less and less so; an *n*th drink (which he is unable to carry along) has no value at all. A generalization derived from this principle is that the more of a commodity or the more money a person has, the smaller are his needs for that commodity or for money, and the smaller his incentives to add to what he has.

In addition to using this principle of saturation to describe the behavior of the rational man, modern economists applied it to one of the most pressing problems of contemporary American economy. Prior to World War II the American people (not counting business firms) owned about 45 billion dollars in liquid assets (currency, bank deposits, government bonds) and these funds were highly concentrated among relatively few families; most individual families held no liquid assets at all (except for small amounts of currency). By the end of the year 1945, however, the personal liquid-asset holdings had risen to about 140 billion dollars and four out of every five families owned some bank deposits or war bonds. What is the effect of this great change on spending and saving? This question has been answered by several leading economists in terms of the saturation principle presented above. "The rate of saving is . . . a diminishing function of the wealth the individual holds"[22] because "the availability of liquid assets raises consumption generally by reducing the impulse to save."[23] More specifically: a person who owns nothing or very little will exert himself greatly to acquire some reserve funds, while a person who owns much will have much smaller incentives to save. Similarly, incentives to increase one's income are said to weaken with the amount of income. In other words, the strength of motivation is inversely correlated with the level of achievement.

In view of the lack of contact between economists and psychologists, it is hardly surprising that economists failed to see the relevance for their postulates of the extensive experimental work performed by psychologists on the problem of levels of aspiration. It is not necessary in this paper to describe these studies in detail. It may suffice to formulate three generalizations as established in numerous studies of goal-striving behavior:[24]

1. Aspirations are not static, they are not established once for all time.

[22]G. Haberler, *Prosperity and Depression, 3rd ed.* (Geneva: League of Nations, 1941), p. 199.

[23]The last quotation is from the publication of the U. S. Department of Commerce, *Survey of Current Business*, May 1950, p. 10.

[24]K. Lewin, et al., "Level of Aspiration," in J. Hunt (Editor), *Personality and the Behavior Disorders* (New York: Ronald, 1944).

2. Aspirations tend to grow with achievement and decline with failure.
3. Aspirations are influenced by the performance of other members of the group to which one belongs and by that of reference groups.

From these generalizations hypotheses were derived about the influence of assets on saving which differed from the postulates of the saturation theory. This is not the place to describe the extensive empirical work undertaken to test the hypotheses. But it may be reported that the saturation theory was not confirmed; the level-of-aspiration theory likewise did not suffice to explain the findings. In addition to the variable "size of liquid-asset holdings," the studies had to consider such variables as income level, income change, and savings habits. (Holders of large liquid assets are primarily people who have saved a high proportion of their income in the past!)[25]

The necessity of studying the interaction of a great number of variables and the change of choices over time leads to doubts regarding the universal validity of a one-dimensional ordering of all alternatives. The theory of measurement of utilities remains an empty frame unless people's established preferences of *A* over *B* and of *B* over *C* provide indications about their probable future behavior. Under what conditions do people's preferences give us such clues, and under what conditions do they not? If at different times *A* and *B* are seen in different contexts—because of changed external conditions or the acquisition of new experiences—we may have to distinguish among several dimensions.

The problem may be illustrated by an analogy. Classic economic theory postulates a one-dimensional ordering of all alternatives; Gallup asserts that answers to questions of choice can always be ordered on a yes—uncertain (don't know)—no continuum; are both arguments subject to the same reservations? Specifically, if two persons give the same answer to a poll question (e.g., both say "Yes, I am for sending American troops to Europe" or "Yes, I am for the Taft-Hartley Act") may they mean different things so that their identical answers do not permit any conclusions about the similarity of their other attitudes and their behavior? Methodologically it follows from the last argument that yes-no questions need to be supplemented by open-ended questions to discern differences in people's level of information and motivation. It also follows that attitudes and preferences should be ascertained

[25]The empirical work was part of the economic behavior program of the Survey Research Center under the direction of the author.

through a multi-question approach (or scaling) which serves to determine whether one or several dimensions prevail.

ON THEORY CONSTRUCTION

In attempting to summarize our conclusions about the respective merits of different scientific approaches, we might quote the conclusions of Arrow which he formulated for social science in general rather than for economics:

> To the extent that formal theoretical structures in the social sciences have not been based on the hypothesis of rational behavior, their postulates have been developed in a manner which we may term *ad hoc*. Such propositions . . . depend, of course, on the investigator's intuition and common sense.[26]

The last sentence seems strange indeed. One may argue the other way around and point out that such propositions as "the purpose of business is to make profits" or "the best businessman is the one who maximizes profits" are based on intuition or supposed common sense, rather than on controlled observation. The main problem raised by the quotation concerns the function of empirical research. There exists an alternative to developing an axiomatic system into a full-fledged theoretical model in advance of testing the theory through observations. Controlled observations should be based on hypotheses, and the formulation of an integrated theory need not be delayed until all observations are completed. Yet theory construction is part of the process of hypothesis-observation-revised hypothesis and prediction-observation, and systematization should rely on some empirical research. The proximate aim of scientific research is a body of empirically validated generalizations and not a theory that is valid under any and all circumstances.

The dictum that "theoretical structures in the social sciences must be based on the hypothesis of rational behavior" presupposes that it is established what rational behavior is. Yet, instead of establishing the characteristics of rational behavior a priori, we must first determine the conditions a_1, b_1, c_1 under which behavior of the type x_1, y_1, z_1 and the conditions a_2, b_2, c_2 under which behavior of the type x_2,

[26]K. J. Arrow, "Mathematical Models in the Social Sciences," in D. Lerner and H. D. Lasswell, (Editors), *The Policy Sciences* (Stanford: Stanford University Press, 1951), p. 137.

y_2, z_2 is likely to occur. Then, if we wish, we may designate one of the forms of behavior as rational. The contributions of psychology to this process are not solely methodological; findings and principles about noneconomic behavior provide hypotheses for the study of economic behavior. Likewise, psychology can profit from the study of economic behavior because many aspects of behavior, and among them the problems of rationality, may be studied most fruitfully in the economic field.

This paper was meant to indicate some promising leads for a study of rationality, not to carry such study to its completion. Among the problems that were not considered adequately were the philosophical ones (rationality viewed as a value concept), the psychoanalytic ones (the relationships between rational and conscious, and between irrational and unconscious), and those relating to personality theory and the roots of rationality. The emphasis was placed here on the possibility and fruitfulness of studying forms of rational behavior, rather than the characteristics of *the* rational man. Motives and goals that change with and are adapted to circumstances, and the relatively rare but highly significant cases of our becoming aware of problems and attempting to solve them, were found to be related to behavior that may be called truly rational.

9. MOTIVATION, COGNITION, LEARNING—BASIC FACTORS IN CONSUMER BEHAVIOR*

James A. Bayton

MOTIVATION, COGNITION, LEARNING

The analysis of consumer behavior presented here is derived from diverse concepts of several schools of psychology—from psychoanalysis to reinforcement theory.

Human behavior can be grouped into three categories—motivation, cognition, and learning. Motivation refers to the drives, urges, wishes, or desires which initiate the sequence of events known as "behavior." Cognition is the area in which all of the mental phenomena (perception, memory, judging, thinking, etc.) are grouped. Learning refers to those changes in behavior which occur through time relative to external stimulus conditions.

Each broad area is pertinent to particular problems of consumer behavior. All three together are pertinent to a comprehensive understanding of consumer behavior.

MOTIVATION

Human Needs

Behavior is initiated through needs. Some psychologists claim that words such as "motives," "needs," "wishes," and "drives" should not be used as synonyms; others are content to use them interchangeably. There is one virtue in the term "drive" in that it carries the connotation of a force pushing the individual into action.

*Reprinted from the *Journal of Marketing*, national quarterly publication of the American Marketing Association (January, 1958), pp. 282–289.

Motivation arises out of tension-systems which create a state of disequilibrium for the individual. This triggers a sequence of psychological events directed toward the selection of a goal which the individual *anticipates* will bring about release from the tensions and the selection of patterns of action which he *anticipates* will bring him to the goal.

One problem in motivation theory is deriving a basic list of the human needs. Psychologists agree that needs fall into two general categories—those arising from tension-systems physiological in nature (biogenic needs such as hunger, thirst, and sex), and those based upon tension-systems existing in the individual's subjective psychological state and in his relations with others (psychogenic needs).

Although there is not much disagreement as to the list of specific biogenic needs, there is considerable difference of opinion as to the list of specific psychogenic needs. However, the various lists of psychogenic needs can be grouped into three broad categories:

1. *Affectional needs*—the needs to form and maintain warm, harmonious, and emotionally satisfying relations with others.
2. *Ego-bolstering needs*—the needs to enhance or promote the personality; to achieve; to gain prestige and recognition; to satisfy the ego through domination of others.
3. *Ego-defensive needs*—the needs to protect the personality; to avoid physical and psychological harm; to avoid ridicule and "loss of face"; to prevent loss of prestige; to avoid or to obtain relief from anxiety.

One pitfall in the analysis of motivation is the assumption that a particular situation involves just one specific need. In most instances the individual is driven by a combination of needs. It seems likely that "love" brings into play a combination of affectional, ego-bolstering, and ego-defensive needs as well as biogenic needs. Within the combination some needs will be relatively strong, others relatively weak. The strongest need within the combination can be called the "prepotent" need. A given consumer product can be defined in terms of the specific need-combination involved and the relative strengths of these needs.

Another pitfall is the assumption that identical behaviors have identical motivational backgrounds. This pitfall is present whether we are thinking of two different individuals or the same individual at two different points in time. John and Harry can be different in the motivational patterns leading to the purchase of their suits. Each could have one motivational pattern influencing such a purchase at age twenty and another at age forty.

Ego-Involvement

One important dimension of motivation is the degree of ego-involvement. The various specific need-patterns are not equal in significance to the individual. Some are superficial in meaning; others represent (for the individual) tremendous challenges to the very essence of existence. There is some evidence that one of the positive correlates of degree of ego-involvement is the amount of cognitive activity (judging, thinking, etc.) involved. This means that consumer goods which tap low degrees of ego-involvement will be purchased with a relatively lower degree of conscious decision-making activity than goods which tap higher degrees of ego-involvement. Such a factor must be considered when decisions are made on advertising and marketing tactics.

At times the ego-involvement factor is a source of conflict between client and researcher. This can occur when research reveals that the product taps a low degree of ego-involvement within consumers. The result is difficult for a client to accept; because *he* is ego-involved and, therefore, cognitively active about his product, consumers must certainly be also. It is hard for such a client to believe that consumers simply do not engage in a great deal of cognitive activity when they make purchases within his product class. One way to ease this particular client-researcher conflict would be for the researcher to point out this implication of the ego-involvement dimension.

"True" and Rationalized Motives

A particular difficulty in the study of motivation is the possibility that there can be a difference between "true" motives and rationalized motives. Individuals sometimes are unaware of the exact nature of drives initiating their behavior patterns. When this occurs, they attempt to account for their behavior through "rationalization by assigning motivations to their behavior which are acceptable to their personality structures. They may do this with no awareness that they are rationalizing. There can be other instances, however, in which individuals are keenly aware of their motivations, but feel it would be harmful or socially unacceptable to reveal them. When this is the case, they deliberately conceal their motivations.

These possibilities create a problem for the researcher. Must he assume that every behavior pattern is based upon unconscious motivation? If not, what criteria are to be used in deciding whether to be alert to unconscious motivation for this behavior pattern and not that one? What is the relative importance of unconscious motives, if present, and rationalized motives? Should rationalized motives be ignored? After all, rationalized motives have a certain validity for the individual—they are the "real" motives insofar as he is aware of the situation.

The situation is even more complicated than this—what about the dissembler? When the individual actually is dissembling, the researcher must attempt to determine the true motives. But, how shall we determine whether we are faced with a situation where the respondent is rationalizing or dissembling? In a given case, did a projective technique reveal an unconscious motive or the true motive of a dissembler? Conceptually, rationalized motives and dissembled motives are not equal in psychological implication; but it is rare, if ever, that one finds attempts to segregate the two in consumer research directed toward the analysis of motivation. This failure is understandable, to some extent, because of the lack of valid criteria upon which to base the distinction.

COGNITION

Need-Arousal

Motivation, thus, refers to a state of need-arousal—a condition exerting "push" on the individual to engage in those activities which he anticipates will have the highest probability of bringing him gratification of a particular need-pattern. Whether gratification actually will be attained or not is a matter of future events. Central to the psychological activities which now must be considered in the sequence are the complex of "mental" operations and forces known as the cognitive process. We can view these cognitive processes as being *purposive* in that they serve the individual in his attempts to achieve satisfaction of his needs. These cognitive processes are *regulatory* in that they determine in large measure the direction and particular steps taken in his attempt to attain satisfaction of the initiating needs.

The Ego-Superego Concept

The ego-superego concept is pertinent to a discussion of cognitive activities which have been triggered by needs. Discussions of the ego-superego concept usually come under the heading of motivation as an aspect of personality. It is our feeling that motivation and the consequences of motivation should be kept systematically "clean." In the broadest sense, ego and superego are mental entities in that they involve memory, perceiving, judging, and thinking.

The Ego. The ego is the "executive," determining how the individual shall seek satisfaction of his needs. Through perception, memory, judging, and thinking the ego attempts to integrate the needs, on the one hand, and the conditions of the external world, on the other, in such manner that needs can be satisfied without danger or harm to the individual. Often this means that gratification must be postponed until a situation has developed, or has been encountered, which does not contain harm or danger. The turnpike driver who does not exceed the speed limit because he sees signs saying there are radar checks is under the influence of the ego. So is the driver who sees no cars on a straight stretch and takes the opportunity to drive at excessive speed.

The Superego. The superego involves the ego-ideal and conscience. The ego-ideal represents the positive standards of ethical and moral conduct the individual has developed for himself. Conscience is, in a sense, the "judge," evaluating the ethics and morality of behavior and, through guilt-feelings, administering punishment when these are violated. If a driver obeys the speed limit because he would feel guilty in doing otherwise, he is under the influence of the superego. (The first driver above is under the influence of the ego because he is avoiding a fine, not guilt feelings.)

Specific Examples

Credit is a form of economic behavior based to some extent upon ego-superego considerations. It is generally felt that one cause of consumer-credit expansion has been a shift away from the superego's role in attitudes toward credit. The past ego-ideal was to build savings; debt was immoral—something to feel guilty about, to avoid, to hide. These two superego influences restrained the use of credit. For some cultural reason, credit and debt have shifted away from the superego dominance and are now more under the control of the ego—the primary concern now seems to be how much of it can be used without risking financial danger.

The purchasing of specific consumer goods can be considered from the point of view of these two influences. Certain goods (necessities, perhaps) carry little superego influence, and the individual is psychologically free to try to maximize the probability of obtaining satisfaction of his needs while minimizing the probability of encountering harm in so doing. Other goods, however, tap the superego. When a product represents an aspect of the ego-ideal there is a strong positive force to possess it. Conversely, when a product involves violation of the conscience, a strong negative force is generated against its purchase.

Let us assume that, when the need-push asserts itself, a variety of goal-objects come into awareness as potential sources of gratification. In consumer behavior these goal-objects may be different brand names. The fact that a particular set of goal-objects come into awareness indicates the generic character of this stage in the cognitive process—a class of goal-objects is seen as containing the possible satisfier. What the class of goal-objects and the specific goal-objects within the class "promise" in terms of gratification are known as "expectations."

There are, then, two orders of expectation: generic expectancies, and object-expectancies. Suppose the needs were such that the individual "thought" of brands of frozen orange juice. Some of the generic expectations for frozen orange juice are a certain taste, quality, source of vitamin C, protection against colds, and ease of preparation. The particular brands carry expectations specifically associated with one brand as against another. The expectation might be that brand A has a more refreshing taste than brand B.

In many instances, cognitive competition occurs between two or more generic categories before it does between goal-objects within a generic category. Much consumer-behavior research is directed toward the investigation of generic categories—tires, automobiles, appliances, etc. But perhaps not enough attention has been given to the psychological analysis of cognitive competition between generic categories. An example of a problem being studied is the competition between television viewing, movie going, and magazine reading. For a particular producer, cognitive competition within the pertinent generic category is usually of more concern than cognitive competition between his generic category and others. The producer usually wants only an intensive analysis of consumer psychology with respect to the particular generic category of which his product is a member.

Let us now assume that under need-push four alternative goal-objects (brands A, B, C, and D) came into awareness. Why these particular brands and not others? Why are brands E and F absent? An obvious reason for brand E's absence might be that the individual had never been exposed to the fact that brand E exists. He had been exposed to brand F, however. Why is it absent? The problem here is one of memory—a key cognitive process. The producers of brands E and F obviously are faced with different problems.

Two sets of circumstances contain the independent variables that determine whether a given item will be remembered. One is the nature of the experience resulting from actual consumption or utilization of the goal-object. This will be discussed later when we come to the reinforcement theory of learning. The other is the circumstances present on what might be called vicarious exposures to the goal-object—vicarious in that at the time of exposure actual consumption or utilization of the goal-object does not occur. The most obvious example would be an advertisement of the goal-object. Of course, the essential purpose of an advertisement is to expose the individual to the goal-object in such a manner that at some subsequent time it will be remembered readily. The search for the most effective methods of doing this by manipulation of the physical aspects of the advertisement and the appeals used in it is a continuing effort in consumer-behavior research. Finally, for many consumers these two sets of circumstances will be jointly operative. Experiences with the goal-object and subsequent vicarious exposures can coalesce to heighten the memory potential for them.

Making a Choice

With, say, four brands in awareness, the individual must now make a choice. What psychological factors underlie this choice? The four brands could be in awareness due to the memory factor because they are immediately present in the environment; or some because they are in the environment, and the others because of memory.

The first problem is the extent to which the items are differentiated. The various goal objects have attributes which permit the individual to differentiate between them. The brand name is one attribute; package another; design still another. These differentiating attributes (from the point of view of the consumer's perceptions) can be called signs or cues. All such signs are not equally important in consumer decisions. Certain of them are depended upon much more than others. For example, in a study of how housewives select fresh oranges, the critical or key signs were thickness of skin, color of skin, firmness of the orange, and presence or absence of "spots" on the skin.

The signs have expectancies associated with them. Package (a sign) can carry the expectancy of quality. Thinskin oranges carry the expectancy of juice; spots carry the expectancy of poor taste quality and insufficient amount of juice. Often sign-expectancies determined through consumer research are irrelevant or invalid. Signs are irrelevant when they do not represent a critical differentiating attribute of a goal-object. Certain discolorations on oranges have nothing to do with their intrinsic quality. Expectancies are invalid when they refer to qualities that do not in fact exist in association with a particular sign.

The different goal-objects in awareness can be assessed in terms of the extent to which they arouse similar expectancies. This phenomenon of similarity of expectations within a set of different goal-objects is known as generalization. One goal-object (brand A, perhaps), because of its associated expectancies, can be assumed to have maximum appeal within the set of alternative goal-objects. The alternates then can be ordered in terms of how their associated expectancies approximate those of brand A. Is this ordering and the psychological distances between the items of the nature of:

Brand A		Brand A
Brand B		
	or	
		Brand B
Brand C		Brand C

These differences in ordering and psychological distance are referred to as generalization gradients. In the first case, the expectancies associated with brand B are quite similar to those of brand A, but are not quite as powerful in appeal. Brand C has relatively little of this. In the second case, the generalization gradient is of a different form, showing that brand B offers relatively little psychological competition to brand A. (There will also be generalization gradients with respect to cognitive competition between generic categories.) In addition to the individual producer being concerned about the memory potential of his particular brand, he needs to determine the nature of the generalization gradient for his product and the products of his competitors. Mere ordering is not enough—the "psychological distances" between positions must be determined, also, and the factor determining these distances is similarity and expectancy.

The discussion above was concerned with cognitive processes as they relate to mental representation of goal-objects under the instigation of need-arousal. The items brought into awareness, the differentiating sign-expectancies, and the generalization gradient are the central factors in the particular cognitive field aroused under a given "need-push." One important dimension has not yet been mentioned—instrumental acts. These are acts necessary in obtaining the goal-object and the acts involved in consuming or utilizing it. Examples are: "going downtown" to get to a department store, squeezing the orange to get its juice, ease of entry into service stations, and the operations involved in do-it-yourself house painting.

Instrumental acts can have positive or negative value for the individual. One who makes fewer shopping trips to downtown stores because of traffic and parking conditions displays an instrumental act with negative value. Frozen foods are products for which much of the appeal lies in the area of instrumental acts. The development of automatic transmissions and of power-steering automobiles are examples of product changes concerned with instrumental acts. The point is that concentration upon cognitive reactions to the goal-object, *per se*, could be masking critical aspects of the situation based upon cognitive reactions to the instrumental acts involved in obtaining or utilizing the goal-object.

LEARNING

Goal-Object

Starting with need-arousal, continuing under the influence of cognitive processes, and engaging in the necessary action, the individual arrives at consumption or utilization of a goal-object. Using our consumer-behavior illustration, let us say that the consumer bought brand A and is now in the process of consuming or utilizing it. We have now arrived at one of the most critical aspects of the entire psychological sequence. It is with use of the goal-object that degree of gratification of the initial needs will occur.

Reinforcement

When consumption or utilization of the goal-object leads to gratification of the initiating needs there is "reinforcement." If at some later date the same needs are aroused, the individual will tend to repeat the process of selecting and getting to the same goal-object. If brand A yields a high degree of gratification, then at some subsequent time, when the same needs arise, the consumer will have an increased tendency to select brand A once again. Each succeeding time that brand A brings gratification, further reinforcement occurs, thus further increasing the likelihood that in the future, with the given needs, brand A will be selected.

This type of behavioral change—increasing likelihood that an act will be repeated—is learning; and reinforcement is necessary for learning to take place. Continued reinforcement will influence the cognitive processes. Memory of the goal-object will be increasingly enhanced; particular sign-expectancies will be more and more firmly established; and the generalization gradient will be changed in that the psychological distance on this gradient between brand A and the competing brands will be increased.

Habit

One of the most important consequences of continued reinforcement is the influence this has on the extent to which cognitive processes enter the picture at the times of subsequent need-arousal. With continued reinforcement, the amount of cognitive activity decreases; the individual engages less and less in decision-making mental activities. This can continue until, upon need-arousal, the goal-obtaining activities are practically automatic. At this stage there is a habit.

Note this use of the term "habit." One frequently hears that a person does certain things by "*force* of habit," that habit is an initiator of behavioral sequences. Actually habits are not initiating forces in themselves; habits are repeated response patterns accompanied by a minimum of cognitive activity. There must be some condition of need-arousal before the habit-type response occurs. This has serious implications in the field of consumer behavior. The promotional and marketing problems faced by a competitor of brand A will be of one type if purchase behavior for brand A is habitual, of another if this is not true. If the purchase is largely a habit, there is little cognitive activity available for the competitor to "work on."

Frequency of repeating a response is not a valid criterion for determining whether or not a habit exists. An act repeated once a week can be just as much a habit as one repeated several times a day. The frequency of a response is but an index of the frequency with which the particular need-patterns are aroused. Frequency of response also is often used as a measure of the *strength* of a habit. The test of the strength of a habit is the extent to which an individual will persist in an act after it has ceased providing need gratification. The greater this persistence, the stronger was the habit in the first place.

PROBLEM—CONCEPT—RESEARCH

The above views integrate concepts in contemporary psychology which seem necessary for a comprehensive explanation of human behavior, and apply these concepts to the analysis of consumer behavior. Each psychological process touched upon contains areas for further analysis and specification.

Some type of comprehensive theory of human behavior is necessary as a *working tool* to avoid a lack of discipline in attacking problems in consumer behavior. Too frequently a client with a practical problem approaches a researcher with an indication that all that is needed is a certain methodology—depth interviewing, scaling, or projective devices, for example.

The first step should be to take the practical problem and translate it into its pertinent conceptual entities. This phase of the problem raises the question of motivations. Here is a question involving relevance and validity of sign-expectancies. There is a question dealing with a generalization gradient, etc. Once the pertinent conceptual entities have been identified, and only then, we arrive at the stage of hypothesis formulation. Within each conceptual entity, a relationship between independent and dependent variables is established as a hypothesis to be tested.

Often the relation between conceptual entities must be investigated. For example, what is the effect of continuing reinforcement on a specific generalization gradient? Within the same research project, one psychological entity can be a dependent variable at one phase of the research and an independent variable at another. At one time we might be concerned with establishing the factors associated with differential memory of sign-expectancies. At another time we could be concerned with the influence of remembered sign-expectancies upon subsequent purchase-behavior.

Discipline requires that one turn to methodology only when the pertinent conceptual entities have been identified and the relationships between independent and dependent variables have been expressed in the form of hypotheses. Fundamentally this sequence in the analysis of a problem serves to delimit the methodological possibilities. In any event, the methodologies demanded are those which will produce unambigious tests of each particular hypothesis put forth. Finally, the results must be translated into the terms of the original practical problem.

We have used the term "discipline" in this phase of our discussion.

The researcher must discipline himself to follow the above steps. Some find this a difficult thing to do and inevitably their data become ambigious. They must resort to improvisation in order to make sense of the results *after* the project is completed. A research project is truly a work of art when the conceptual analysis, the determination of the hypotheses, and the methodologies have been developed in such an "air-tight" sequence that practically all that is necessary is to let the facts speak for themselves.

10. CONSUMER BEHAVIOR AS RISK TAKING*

Raymond A. Bauer

One of the fads in discussions of marketing research is to say that the field of marketing research has been marked by fads. Thus, we have become accustomed to the statement: "Last year it was Motivation Research, this year it's Operations Research; I wonder what it will be next year." Seldom is any such new emphasis a radical departure from the past. At least there is always a handful of protesting orthodox practitioners to exclaim: "But we've been doing it all along." Operations Research, properly speaking, probably should be considered as concerned with simulation as much as with experimentation. But most of the operations research work I have seen in market research uses experimentation rather than simulation, and in this is continuous with traditional, albeit rare, well-executed experiments in marketing research. These new approaches are characterized by a distinctive concentration of attention on particular variables, concepts or techniques. After their potential has been pretty well explored and developed they get absorbed into the general body of research knowledge and technique, usually after having generated a few healthy antibodies.

I make these general remarks about fads in marketing research because I am about to make a modest effort to start a new one. However, if I am to be as modest as my effort I should also state that I have neither confidence nor anxiety that my proposal will cause any major stir. At most, it is to be hoped that it will attract the attention of a few researchers and practitioners and at least survive through infancy. The proposal is that we look at consumer behavior as an instance of risk taking.

We are accustomed to use the term "consumer decision making."

*Reprinted from Robert Hancock (ed.), *Dynamic Marketing for a Changing World* (Chicago: American Marketing Association, 1960), pp. 389–398.

Yet, there has been little concentration of research on the element of risk taking that is as characteristic of consumer behavior as it is of all decision-making. A conspicuous exception is the work of Katona and Mueller on prepurchase deliberation. They found, when buying durable goods, that middle-income people deliberated more than either lower- or upper-income people. When buying sport shirts, lower-income people deliberated most.

Consumer behavior involves risk in the sense that any action of a consumer will produce consequences which he cannot anticipate with anything approximating certainty, and some of which at least are likely to be unpleasant. At the very least, any one purchase competes for the consumer's financial resources with a vast array of alternate uses of that money. The man who buys a pint of whiskey today does not know to what degree he prejudices his son's college education 20 years hence. But, he risks more than alternate purchases. Unfortunate consumer decisions have cost men frustration and blisters, their self-esteem and the esteem of others, their wives, their jobs, and even their lives. Nor is the problem of calculation of consequences a trivial one. It is inconceivable that the consumer can consider more than a few of the possible consequences of his actions, and it is seldom that he can anticipate even these few consequences with a high degree of certainty. When it comes to the purchase of large ticket items the perception of risk can become traumatic. Paul Lazarsfeld tells me that certain unpublished data show that the prospective automobile buyer often goes into a state of virtual panic as he reaches the point of decision, and rushes into his purchase as an escape from the enormity of the problem.

If I may now anticipate what is on your minds, I suspect that about at this point you are saying to yourselves that I have painted an unrealistic picture of the consumer. He simply does not in most instances stand about trying to calculate probabilities and consequences nor is he overtaken by anxiety. True, these things happen on occasion, and particularly on big ticket items, but only in rare instances does the consumer appear to tackle these problems as "risk taking."

If these objections are on your mind, I agree with them. The consumer who consistently tried to act like the classical "rational man" would quickly sink into inaction. This, in fact, is precisely what I would like to stress. Consumers characteristically develop decision strategies and ways of reducing risk that enable them to act with relative confidence and ease in situations where their information is inadequate and the consequences of their actions are in some meaningful sense incalculable. (When I say "in some meaningful sense incalculable," I mean that not only can the outcomes not be anticipated reliably, but the consequences may be drastic.)

Up to now, what I have to say has been abstract and general. Therefore, for the next few minutes I would like to move back to familiar ground and argue that many of the phenomena with which we habitually deal have a strong bearing on the problem of "risk taking." I am not going to contend that risk taking is the only thing involved in these phenomena, but rather that it is a common thread which runs through them and is worth pulling out for inspection.

One of our traditional problems is that of brand loyalty. Brand loyalty may involve a number of considerations. In recent years we have heard stressed the compatibility of the brand image with one's self-image, or with the norms of one's reference group. Brand loyalty is also seen as a means of economizing of decision effort by substituting habit for repeated, deliberate, decisions. Without for a moment minimizing such considerations, I would like to reintroduce the old-fashioned concept of "reliability." Much brand loyalty is a device for reducing the risks of consumer decisions. I am told that sugar is one product for which it has traditionally been difficult to develop brand loyalty. But my friend Edward Bursk tells me that when he was a salesman in Lancaster, Pennsylvania, there was a strong loyalty to a particular brand of sugar. The Pennsylvania Dutch housewives of that area are avid and proud bakers and there is more risk involved in making a cake than in sweetening a cup of coffee or a bowl of cereal. Suppose we were to limit ourselves to small ticket items, and to interview a sample of housewives as to the risks—that is a combination of uncertainty plus seriousness of outcome involved—associated with each category of product. I would predict a strong correlation between degree of risk and brand loyalty.

The recently popular phrase that advertising gives "added value" to a product also bears on the question of risk taking. The "added value" of advertising has usually been discussed in terms of the satisfaction of consumer motives that extend beyond the primary function of the product. It is perhaps worth recalling that one of the customer's motives is to have a feeling of confidence in the product he buys. Some, but not all, consumers are willing to pay added money for added confidence. Others prefer to read "Consumers Reports" in the hope that some obscure, unadvertised, low-priced brand will be rated a best buy. And, it is worth recalling, there are still other consumers in whom advertising does not generate confidence but rather the suspicion that it is added, worthless cost.

Now, relating the questions of brand loyalty and the "added

value" of advertising to risk taking, or its reciprocal "confidence," is scarcely a radical departure from tradition. This must be the working assumption of every competent marketing practitioner. It is instructive, however, to note how little this relationship has been exploited as a research problem. We know that some people are inclined to favor advertised brands in some categories, and that other people will consistently buy the cheapest product in these same categories. This is about the level on which our knowledge rests. It is my suspicion that our recent concern with the prestige element of advertising and well known brands has deflected our attention from the problem of risk taking even when it was right under our nose.

Another recently popular area of concern where the problem of risk taking has been obscured is the phenomenon known as "personal influence." There are exceptions to what I am about to say, but *in general* discussions of personal influence on consumer behavior have been couched in terms that suggest only that opinion leaders are followed because they are style setters and that the follower wants to accrue to himself the prestige of behaving like the pace setters. Seldom is the fact made explicit that one of the very important functions of opinion leaders is to reduce the perceived risk of the behavior in question.

The work of Katz, Menzel, and Coleman on physicians' adoption of a new drug is very pertinent. They found that the doctors they studied tended to follow the lead of respected colleagues *early* in the life history of the drug when adequate information was lacking. Once the drug became sufficiently well established, personal influence no longer played a role. The period of risk was passed.

I have seen data on related products that reenforce the notion that the Katz, Menzel, Coleman findings are related to risk taking. We studied two types of products in the same general product category. We were interested in whether the probability of trial of a product and subsequent preference for that product was influenced by preference for one or another of the companies, or by preference for the salesmen of the various companies. For these particular types of products we confirmed the findings of the drug studies. Both company and salesman preference were more strongly correlated with product trial and preference in the newer products in the general line. That is to say, apparently both company *and* salesmen preference had more influence when product was new and relatively unknown.

However, if I may be permitted some freedom of assumptions and inference, and a certain amount of liberty in filtering out the noise in the data, there were some findings that bore in a more interesting fashion on the problem of personal influence and risk taking. Let me start with some assumptions about the difference between company preference and salesman preference. Relative to each other, company preference is more associated with risk reduction, and salesman preference more with personal influence in the sense of "compliance," of one person "going along" with someone whom he likes. The company is a relatively impersonal entity, and the main function of its reputation is in this instance to guarantee the quality of the product. The salesman, to some extent, also guarantees quality. However, he also exploits his strictly personal relationships to the buyer. Thus we have personal influence operating in two ways, to produce compliance, and to reduce risk. Compliance is relatively more associated with salesman preference, and risk reduction with company preference.

If you accept the above assumptions as reasonable, then certain findings are quite interesting. You will remember that I said we studied two product types. These product types differed as to the degree of risk associated with them. Product type A was by common consent risky. Product type B was safe. In the case of product type A, the risky type of product, the relationship of company preference to product preference was twice as strong as the "effect" (in quotes) of salesman preference. In the case of product type B, the "effect" of company and salesman preference was just about equal. My interpretation of these findings is that when risk was high, the risk relevant factor of company image was the dominant source of influence, and that when risk was low, "personal influence" in the sense of compliance played a relatively more prominent role.

In addition to "personal influence" we have recently been concerned with the effect of "group influence" on consumer behavior. We have heard a great deal in the past few years about the fact that consumers judge their behavior by the standards of groups with whom they identify themselves, or—although this is seldom dealt with—from whom they dissociate themselves. This has been treated predominantly like the classical "keeping up with the Jones." The consumer looks to his reference groups for cues as to the type of consumption that is valued by people whose esteem he in turn values. "But, dahling, everybody, but everybody, knows Wente Brothers' chablis is the best California chablis!"

In his recent work, "Sociological Reflection on Business," Paul Lazarsfeld suggests that group influence will be stronger in those instances in which the wisdom of one's decision is difficult to assess. Interpreted in one way, this suggestion could lead us to the popular notion that when the primary functions of a product are hard to assess, or when all products in a category work equally well, then "secondary attributes" such as group approval come to the fore. Under this interpretation the influence of the group is to get the consumer to pay attention to different attributes of the product. It is equally plausible that in many instances the function of group influence is to reduce perceived risk by confirming the wisdom of the choice. That is to say, the individual may already share the values of his group and agree on the desirability of a given type of purchase but look to the group for guidance as to what is a wise purchase. By a "wise" purchase, I mean one that is likely to satisfy the values for which it is made. In other words, we not only look to our reference groups for standards of values, but on occasion we also use the judgment of the people around us as an informal "Consumer Report." This is what the psychological student of cognition would call "consensual validation." Lacking any sound basis of judgment, we accept the judgment of others.

A final traditional problem worth considering in terms of risk taking is impulse buying, or perhaps we might prefer the label of "prepurchase deliberation." A simple economic approach to impulse buying would suggest that it should increase as a function of the discretionary funds available to the consumer. This would be consistent with Katona and Mueller's finding that the amount of deliberation involved in buying sport shirts was inverse to the consumer's income. Yet, a number of studies show that in many instances the middle-class consumer is more given to deliberation than is the lower-class consumer. When we compare the middle- and lower-class consumers something more than economics simply considered seems to be involved. We speak of the tendency of the middle-class person to plan over a longer period and of various other aspects of middle-class and lower-class culture. Not for a moment would I want to underplay the importance of such cultural factors. However, it is worth while to think of the fact that the middle-class person has both a greater possibility of planning and a greater reason to plan. He has more of an investment in career, reputation, and accumulated property to risk if he gets into serious financial difficulty. The lower-class person has less to risk in terms of such long-run investments. Perhaps more pertinently it is more difficult for him to calculate the consequences of his actions because among other things he is likely to have less information. He is also less likely to have time for deliberation, because, as Katona and Mueller found with respect to durable goods, people of lower income are more likely to make a purchase in a situation where the product to be replaced has already broken down.

So that I may not seem to be arguing against a cultural interpretation, let me say simply that the lower-class consumer seems more prone to a decision strategy based on the assumption that the consequences of one's behavior are essentially incalculable in any event, so one may as well take a plunge and do what seems immediately desirable.

My argument to this point has been that the issue of risk taking is readily seen as an integral part of many familiar phenomena of consumer behavior. This is by no means surprising, and is probably novel only in the degree that I have stressed the fact of risk taking. What will be of more interest will be to understand with more elaboration the devices through which consumers handle the problem of risk. In effect I have suggested mainly one device, namely reliance on some outside source for guidance, whether that outside source be the reputation of the manufacturer of product, an opinion leader or a reference group. This can scarcely exhaust the means that consumers employ to reduce perceived risk, nor does it tell us how the consumer decides where to place his confidence. The discussion of lower- *v.* middle-class deliberation in purchases of durable goods suggests an additional mechanism of reducing perceived risk, namely, to suppress the possible consequences from consciousness and rush through the process with rapidity. This is no more than a caricature of what we all do at times.

It should be noted that I have carefully said "perceived risk" whenever I referred to risk reduction. This is because the individual can respond to and deal with risk only as he perceives it subjectively. If risk exists in the "real world" and the individual does not perceive it, he cannot be influenced by it. On the other hand, he may reduce "perceived risk" by means which have no effect on affairs in the real world. Thus, if he reads advertisements favoring an automobile he has just bought, he may console himself on the wisdom of his action, but he does not reduce the objective probability of the muffler falling off.

Close study will probably reveal a wide range of decision rules which consumers invoke with regularity to reduce the perceived uncertainty involved in the outcome of their decisions. We are not totally oblivious to the existence of such rules. For example, there is a dying race of Americans who abide by the decision rule of not buying anything for which they cannot pay cash. A recent study shows that this is still a dominant decision rule for eating in restaurants. A majority of respondents thought it was improper to use credit cards for eating out, because "you should not eat out when you cannot afford it."[1] Other persons will buy products with plain and sensible design,

[1]Study by Benson and Benson reported in *Wall Street Journal*, May 12, 1960.

fearing that surface aesthetics are designed to cover up bad workmanship and material. Some others will buy the most expensive product, and still others the cheapest product when both have equal amounts of money at their disposal. Such persons, for reasons about which we can only speculate, vary in the extent to which they are willing to pay money to minimize the risk of being disappointed in a product. There may be others who expect a certain rate of product failure as assurance that they are not wasting money on overly-engineered and constructed products. It is doubtful that they will be joyful over the failure of any individual product, but they may persist in patronizing an outlet that features low prices and poor service. The shabbyness of the store and the rudeness of sales personnel may give further reassurance that one is not paying too much for what he buys.

A long list of such decision rules could probably be produced by the reader. However, I suspect that as ingenious as we all are, it is still worth turning to actual consumers to find out from them what their operating decision rules are. We may be in for some surprises. It is of course difficult for a consumer to articulate a notion such as a "decision rule." In an effort to get at such difficult-to-articulate notions, Donald Cox, one of our doctoral students, interviewed two consumers at very great length—an hour or two a week for several months—on their shopping habits. Many of the decision rules reported by these respondents were ones familiar to us. The following two, I suspect, are not entirely familiar. One of the respondents favored shopping in small shops because she saw the proprietor or buyer as having reduced her range of decision by having reduced the number of brands among which he had to choose, and also as having weeded out the least preferable lines. The same consumer would look about to see if a store carried advertised brands. She used this as a means of legitimizing *the store*. Once having satisfied herself on this score she was willing to buy off-brands from this same store. The novelty of individual decision rules is not so important as the fact that the decision rules of each of these subjects appeared to form coherent but contrasting strategies for stabilizing the uncertain world of shopping. Both of these young women could be characterized as highly conscious of the risk involved in shopping. But one regularly relied on external sources of reassurance, while the other was extremely energetic in seeking out information and attempting to achieve the guise of rationality. We plan to continue such exploratory work with consumers. But in the meantime the problem of decision-making has been tackled in other quarters.

There has been a good deal of research on decision-making under conditions of uncertainty, but not much of this work can at this point be translated into terms useful for students of consumer behavior. The students of statistical decision theory have concentrated on how decisions *ought* to be made. That is to say that the decision theorists have been concerned with the calculation of an optimum decision within the framework of an explicitly defined limited set of conditions, rather than with how people habitually *do* make decisions in the real world. Experimental psychological research on decision-making, on the other hand, has studied how people *do* make restricted types of decisions in a laboratory situation. Such research shows minimally that problems of risk and uncertainty are handled variously by different people and under different conditions. Even though it is doubtful that any of these findings are directly applicable in the field of marketing, they have an important general implication for us by demonstrating that people do in fact evolve preferred decision rules even in situations much less complicated than that faced by the consumer on a day-to-day basis.

One body of work deserves our attention. Most of it is reported in Leon Festinger's book called *A Theory of Cognitive Dissonance*. Festinger and his associates have concentrated on the ways in which people reduce perceived risk *after* decisions are made. People will seek out information that confirms the wisdom of their decisions. Thus, people who have just bought an automobile tend preferentially to read ads in favor of the automobile they have bought. People will also perceive information in a way to reenforce their decision; smokers are less likely than non-smokers to believe that cigarettes cause lung cancer, and this relationship holds even after those people who stopped smoking, because they believed in this relationship, were eliminated from the sample. People, finally, change their own attitudes to bolster their perception of the desirability of their actions. They have more favorable attitudes toward products after they have selected them than before they made the decision. Festinger has amassed considerable data to demonstrate that people do employ devices to reduce the perceived risk associated with consumer-type behavior.

Certain psychological research on problems of cognition also promises to be helpful. The book of Bruner, Goodnow, and Austin, *A Study of Thinking*, for example, deals with the way in which people develop decision strategies in handling situations of incomplete information.

The major reason for my remarks on the importance of the risk taking in consumer decision making is my conviction, frankly still in a somewhat less clear state than I would wish, that this is a fruitful area of research. It is my hope that others will suggest leads of which I am ignorant.

11. COGNITIVE DISSONANCE*

Leon Festinger

There is an experiment in psychology that you can perform easily in your own home if you have a child three or four years old. Buy two toys that you are fairly sure will be equally attractive to the child. Show them both to him and say: "Here are two nice toys. This one is for you to keep. The other I must give back to the store." You then hand the child the toy that is his to keep and ask: "Which of the two toys do you like better?" Studies have shown that in such a situation most children will tell you they prefer the toy they are to keep.

This response of children seems to conflict with the old saying that the grass is always greener on the other side of the fence. Do adults respond in the same way under similar circumstances or does the adage indeed become true as we grow older? The question is of considerable interest because the adult world is filled with choices and alternative courses of action that are often about equally attractive. When they make a choice of a college or a car or a spouse or a home or a political candidate, do most people remain satisfied with their choice or do they tend to wish they had made a different one? Naturally any choice may turn out to be a bad one on the basis of some objective measurement, but the question is: Does some psychological process come into play immediately after the making of a choice that colors one's attitude, either favorably or unfavorably, toward the decision?

To illuminate this question there is another experiment one can do at home, this time using an adult as a subject rather than a child. Buy two presents for your wife, again choosing things you are reasonably sure she will find about equally attractive. Find some plausible excuse for having both of them in your possession, show them to your wife and ask her to tell you how attractive each one is to her. After you

*Reprinted from *Scientific American* (October, 1962), pp. 93–102. © 1962 by Scientific American, Inc.

have obtained a good measurement of attractiveness, tell her that she can have one of them, whichever she chooses. The other you will return to the store. After she has made her choice, ask her once more to evaluate the attractiveness of each of them. If you compare the evaluations of attractiveness before and after the choice, you will probably find that the chosen present has increased in attractiveness and the rejected one decreased.

Such behavior can be explained by a new theory concerning "cognitive dissonance." This theory centers around the idea that if a person knows various things that are not psychologically consistent with one another, he will, in a variety of ways, try to make them more consistent. Two items of information that psychologically do not fit together are said to be in a dissonant relation to each other. The items of information may be about behavior, feelings, opinions, things in the environment and so on. The word "cognitive" simply emphasizes that the theory deals with relations among items of information.

Such items can of course be changed. A person can change his opinion; he can change his behavior, thereby changing the information he has about it; he can even distort his perception and his information about the world around him. Changes in items of information that produce or restore consistency are referred to as dissonance-reducing changes.

Cognitive dissonance is a motivating state of affairs. Just as hunger impels a person to eat so does dissonance impel a person to change his opinions or his behavior. The world, however, is much more effectively arranged for hunger reduction than it is for dissonance reduction. It is almost always possible to find something to eat. It is not always easy to reduce dissonance. Sometimes it may be very difficult or even impossible to change behavior or opinions that are involved in dissonant relations. Consequently there are circumstances in which appreciable dissonance may persist for long periods.

To understand cognitive dissonance as a motivating state, it is necessary to have a clearer conception of the conditions that produce it. The simplest definition of dissonance can, perhaps, be given in terms of a person's expectations. In the course of our lives we have all accumulated a large number of expectations about what things go together and what things do not. When such an expectation is not fulfilled, dissonance occurs.

For example, a person standing unprotected in the rain would expect to get wet. If he found himself in the rain and he was not getting wet, there would exist dissonance between these two pieces of information. This unlikely example is one where the expectations of different people would all be uniform. There are obviously many instances where different people would not share the same expectations. Someone who is very self-confident might expect to succeed at whatever he tried, whereas someone who had a low opinion of himself might normally expect to fail. Under these circumstances what would produce dissonance for one person might produce consonance for another. In experimental investigations, of course, an effort is made to provide situations in which expectations are rather uniform.

Perhaps the best way to explain the theory of cognitive dissonance is to show its application to specific situations. The rest of this article, therefore, will be devoted to a discussion of three examples of cognitive dissonance. I shall discuss the effects of making a decision, of lying and of temptation. These three examples by no means cover all the situations in which dissonance can be created. Indeed, it seldom happens that everything a person knows about an action he has taken is perfectly consistent with his having taken it. The three examples, however, may serve to illustrate the range of situations in which dissonance can be expected to occur. They will also serve to show the kinds of dissonance-reduction effects that are obtained under a special circumstance: when dissonance involves the person's behavior and the action in question is difficult to change.

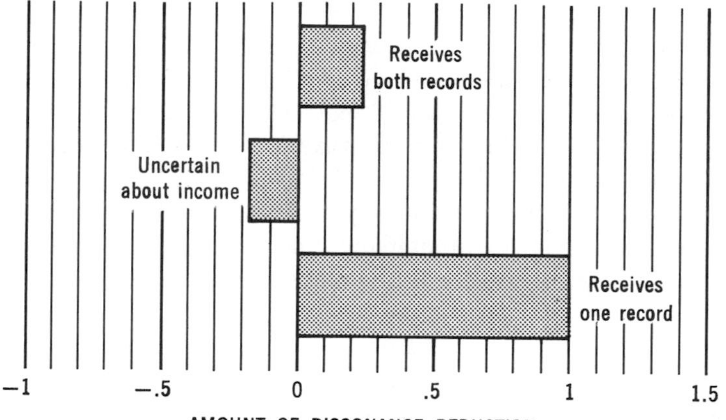

FIGURE 1. Dissonance reduction is a psychological phenomenon found to occur after a person has made a choice between two approximately equal alternatives. The effect of the phenomenon is to enhance the attractiveness of the chosen object or chosen course of action. The chart summarizes the results of an experiment in which high school girls rated the attractiveness of 12 "hit" records before and after choosing one of them as a gift. Substantial dissonance reduction occurred under only one of three experimental conditions described in the text. Under two other conditions no systematic reduction was observed.

Let us consider first the consequences of making a decision. Imagine the situation of a person who has carefully weighed two reasonably attractive alternatives and then chosen one of them—a decision that, for our purposes, can be regarded as irrevocable. All the information this person has concerning the attractive features of the rejected alternative (and the possible unattractive features of the chosen alternative) are now inconsistent, or dissonant, with the knowledge that he has made the given choice. It is true that the person also knows many things that are consistent or consonant with the choice he has made, which is to say all the attractive features of the chosen alternative and unattractive features of the rejected one. Nevertheless, some dissonance exists and after the decision the individual will try to reduce the dissonance.

There are two major ways in which the individual can reduce dissonance in this situation. He can persuade himself that the attractive features of the rejected alternative are not really so attractive as he had originally thought, and that the unattractive features of the chosen alternative are not really unattractive. He can also provide additional justification for his choice by exaggerating the attractive features of the chosen alternative and the unattractive features of the rejected alternative. In other words, according to the theory the process of dissonance reduction should lead, after the decision, to an increase in the desirability of the chosen alternative and a decrease in the desirability of the rejected alternative.

This phenomenon has been demonstrated in a variety of experiments. A brief description of one of these will suffice to illustrate the precise nature of the effect. In an experiment performed by Jon Jecker of Stanford University, high school girls were asked to rate the attractiveness of each of 12 "hit" records. For each girl two records that she had rated as being only moderately attractive were selected and she was asked which of the two she would like as a gift. After having made her choice, the girl again rated the attractiveness of all the records. The dissonance created by the decision could be reduced by increasing the attractiveness of the chosen record and decreasing the attractiveness of the rejected record. Consequently a measurement of dissonance reduction could be obtained by summing both of these kinds of changes in ratings made before and after the decision.

Different experimental variations were employed in this experiment in order to examine the dynamics of the process of dissonance reduction. Let us look at three of these experimental variations. In all three conditions the girls, when they were making their choice, were given to understand there was a slight possibility that they might actually be given both records. In one condition they were asked to rerate the records after they had made their choice but before they knew definitely whether they would receive both records or only the one they chose. The results for this condition should indicate whether dissonance reduction begins with having made the choice or whether it is suspended until uncertainty is resolved. In a second condition the girls were actually given both records after their choice and were then asked to rerate all the records. Since they have received both records and therefore no dissonance existed following the decision, there should be no evidence of dissonance reduction in this condition. In a third condition the girls were given only the record they chose and were then asked to do the rerating. This, of course, resembles the normal outcome of a decision and the usual dissonance reduction should occur.

The chart on page 130 shows the results for these three conditions When the girls are uncertain as to the outcome, or when they receive both records, there is no dissonance reduction—that is, no systematic change in attractiveness of the chosen and rejected records. The results in both conditions are very close to zero—one slightly positive, the other slightly negative. When they receive only the record they chose, however, there is a large systematic change in rating to reduce dissonance. Since dissonance reduction is only observed in this last experimental condition, it is evident that dissonance reduction does

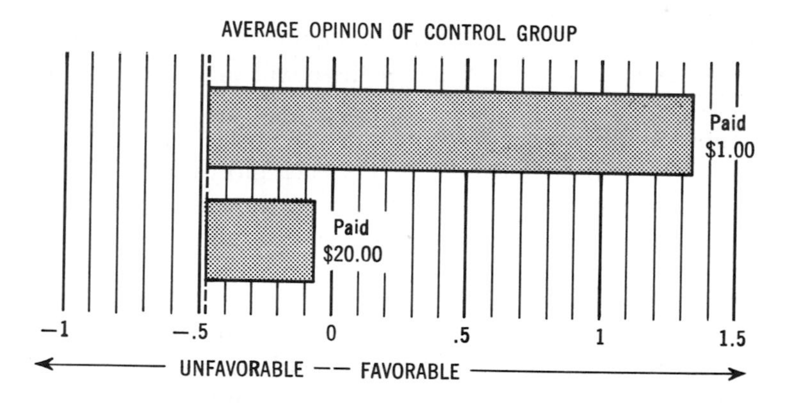

FIGURE 2. Consequences of lying are found to vary, depending on whether the justification for the lie is large or small. In this experiment students were persuaded to tell others that a boring experience was really fun. Those in one group were paid only $1 for their cooperation; in the second group, $20. The low-paid students, having least justification for lying, experienced most dissonance and reduced it by coming to regard the experience favorably.

not occur during the process of making a decision but only after the decision is made and the outcome is clear.

Let us turn now to the consequences of lying. There are many circumstances in which, for one reason or another, an individual publicly states something that is at variance with his private belief. Here again one can expect dissonance to arise. There is an inconsistency between knowing that one really believes one thing and knowing that one has publicly stated something quite different. Again, to be sure, the individual knows things that are consonant with his overt, public behavior. All the reasons that induced him to make the public statement are consonant with his having made it and provide him with some justification for his behavior. Nevertheless, some dissonance exists and, according to the theory, there will be attempts to reduce it. The degree to which the dissonance is bothersome for the individual will depend on two things. The more deviant his public statement is from his private belief, the greater will be the dissonance. The greater the amount of justification the person has for having made the public statement, the less bothersome the dissonance will be.

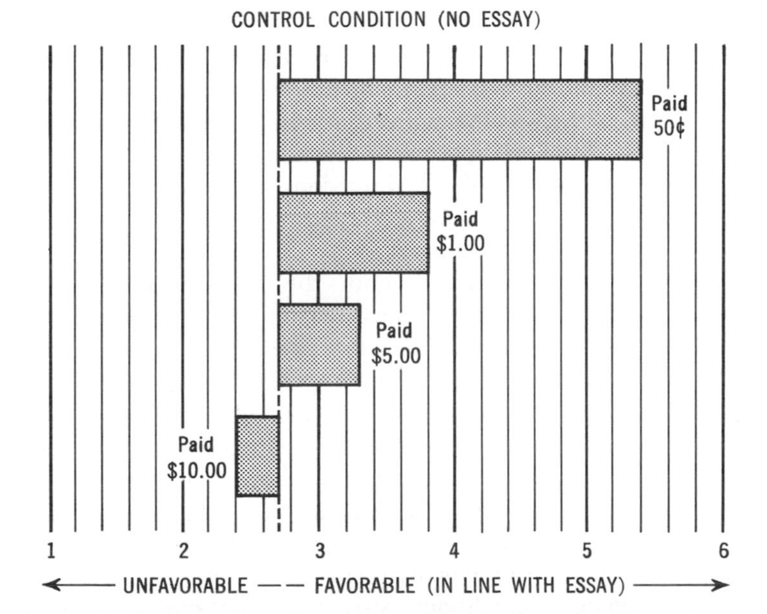

FIGURE 3. Graded change of opinion was produced by paying subjects various sums for writing essays advocating opinions contrary to their beliefs. When examined later, students paid the least had changed their opinion the most to agree with what they had written. Only the highest paid group held to their original opinion more strongly than did a control group.

How can the dissonance be reduced? One method is obvious. The individual can remove the dissonance by retracting his public statement. But let us consider only those instances in which the public statement, once made, cannot be changed or withdrawn; in other words, in which the behavior is irrevocable. Under such circumstances the major avenue for reduction of the dissonance is change of private opinion. That is, if the private opinion were changed so that it agreed with what was publicly stated, obviously the dissonance would be gone. The theory thus leads us to expect that after having made an irrevocable public statement at variance with his private belief, a person will tend to change his private belief to bring it into line with his public statement. Furthermore, the degree to which he changes his private belief will depend on the amount of justification or the amount of pressure for making the public statement initially. The less the original justification or pressure, the greater the dissonance and the more the person's private belief can be expected to change.

An experiment recently conducted at Stanford University by James M. Carlsmith and me illustrates the nature of this effect. In the experiment, college students were induced to make a statement at variance with their own belief. It was done by using students who had volunteered to participate in an experiment to measure "motor performance." The purported experiment lasted an hour and was a boring and fatiguing session. At the end of the hour the experimenter thanked the subject for his participation, indicating that the experiment was over. The real purpose of the hour-long session, however, was to provide each subject with an identical experience about which he would have an unfavorable opinion.

At the end of the fatiguing hour the experimenter enlisted the subject's aid in preparing the next person for the experiment. The subject was led to believe that, for experimental purposes, the next person was supposed to be given the impression that the hour's session was going to be very interesting and lots of fun. The subject was persuaded to help in this deception by telling the next subject, who was waiting in an adjoining room, that he himself had just finished the hour and that it had indeed been very interesting and lots of fun. The first subject was then interviewed by someone else to determine his actual private opinion of the experiment.

Two experimental conditions were run that differed only in the amount of pressure, or justification given the subject for stating a public opinion at variance with his private belief. All subjects, of course, had the justification of helping to conduct a scientific experiment. In addition to this, half of the subjects were paid $1 for their help—a relatively small amount of money; the other subjects were paid $20—a rather large sum for the work involved. From the theory we would expect that the subjects who were paid only $1, having less justification for their action, would have more dissonance and would change their private beliefs more in order to reduce the dissonance. In other words, we would expect the greatest change in private opinion among the subjects given the least tangible incentive for changing.

The illustration on page 132 shows the results of the experiment The broken line in the chart shows the results for a control group of subjects. These subjects participated in the hour-long session and then were asked to give their private opinion of it. Their generally unfavorable views are to be expected when no dissonance is induced between private belief and public statement. It is clear from the chart that introducing such dissonance produced a change of opinion so that the subjects who were asked to take part in a deception finally came to think better of the session than did the control subjects. It is also clear that only in the condition where they were paid a dollar is this opinion change appreciable. When they were paid a lot of money, the justification for misrepresenting private belief is high and there is correspondingly less change of opinion to reduce dissonance.

Another way to summarize the result is to say that those who are highly rewarded for doing something that involves dissonance change their opinion less in the direction of agreeing with what they did than those who are given very little reward. This result may seem surprising, since we are used to thinking that reward is effective in creating change. It must be remembered, however, that the critical factor here is that the reward is being used to induce a behavior that is dissonant with private opinion.

To show that this result is valid and not just a function of the particular situation or the particular sums of money used for reward, Arthur R. Cohen of New York University conducted a similar experiment in a different context. Cohen paid subjects to write essays advocating an opinion contrary to what they really believed. Subjects were paid either $10, $5, $1 or 50 cents to do this. To measure the extent to which dissonance was reduced by their changing their opinion, each subject was then given a questionnaire, which he left unsigned, to determine his private opinion on the issue. The extent to which the subjects reduced dissonance by changing their opinion to agree with what they wrote in the essay is shown in the illustration on page 133. Once again it is clear that the smaller the original justification for engaging in the dissonance-producing action, the greater the change in private opinion to bring it into line with the action.

The final set of experiments I shall discuss deals with the consequences of resisting temptation. What happens when a person wants something and discovers he cannot have it? Does he now want it even more or does he persuade himself that it is really not worth having? Sometimes our common general understanding of human behavior can provide at least crude answers to such questions. In this case, however, our common understanding is ambiguous, because it supplies two contradictory answers. Everyone knows the meaning of the term "sour grapes"; it is the attitude taken by a person who persuades himself that he really does not want what he cannot have. But we are also familiar with the opposite reaction. The child who is not allowed to eat candy and hence loves candy passionately; the woman who adores expensive clothes even though she cannot afford to own them; the man who has a hopeless obsession for a woman who spurns his attentions. Everyone "understands" the behavior of the person who longs for what he cannot have.

Obviously one cannot say one of these reactions is wrong and the other is right; they both occur. One might at least, however, try to answer the question: Under what circumstances does one reaction take place and not the other? If we examine the question from the point of view of the theory of dissonance, a partial answer begins to emerge.

Imagine the psychological situation that exists for an individual who is tempted to engage in a certain action but for one reason or another refrains. An analysis of the situation here reveals its similarity to the other dissonance-producing situations. An individual's knowledge concerning the attractive aspects of the activity toward which he was tempted is dissonant with the knowledge that he has refrained from engaging in the activity. Once more, of course, the individual has some knowledge that is consonant with his behavior in the situation. All the pressures, reasons and justifications for refraining are consonant with his actual behavior. Nevertheless, the dissonance does exist, and there will be psychological activity oriented toward reducing this dissonance.

As we have already seen in connection with other illustrations, one major way to reduce dissonance is to change one's opinions and evaluations in order to bring them closer in line with one's actual behavior. Therefore when there is dissonance produced by resisting temptation, it can be reduced by derogating or devaluing the activity toward which one was tempted. This derivation from the theory clearly implies the sour-grapes attitude, but both theory and experiment tell us that such dissonance-reducing effects will occur only when there was insufficient original justification for the behavior.

Where the original justification for refraining from the action was great, little dissonance would have occurred and there would have been correspondingly little change of opinion in order to reduce dissonance. Therefore one might expect that if a person had resisted temptation in a situation of strong prohibition or strong threatened punishment, little dissonance would have been created and one would not observe the sour-grapes effect. One would expect this effect only if the person resisted temptation under conditions of weak deterrent.

This line of reasoning leaves open the question of when the reverse effect occurs—that is, the situation in which desire for the "unattainable" object is increased. Experimentally it is possible to look at both effects. This was done by Elliot Aronson and J. M. Carlsmith, at Stanford University, in an experiment that sheds considerable light on the problem. The experiment was performed with children who were about four years old. Each child was individually brought into a large playroom in which there were five toys on a table. After the child had had an opportunity to play briefly with each toy, he was asked to rank the five in order of attractiveness. The toy that the child liked second best was then left on the table and the other four toys were spread around on the floor. The experimenter told the child that he had to leave for a few minutes to do an errand but would be back soon. The experimenter then left the room for 10 minutes. Various techniques were employed to "prohibit" the child from playing with the particular toy he liked second best while the experimenter was out of the room.

For different children this prohibition was instituted in three different ways. In one condition there was no temptation at all; the experimenter told the child he could play with any of the toys in the room and then took the second-best toy with him when he left. In the other two conditions temptation was present: the second-best toy was left on the table in the experimenter's absence. The children were told they could play with any of the toys in the room except the one on the table. The children in one group were threatened with mild punishment if they violated the prohibition, whereas those in the other group were threatened with more severe punishment. (The actual nature of the punishment was left unspecified.)

During his absence from the room the experimenter observed each child through a one-way mirror. None of the children in the temptation conditions played with the prohibited toy. After 10 minutes were up the experimenter returned to the playroom and each child was again allowed to play briefly with each of the five toys. The attractiveness of each toy for the child was again measured. By comparing the before and after measurements of the attractiveness of the toy the child originally liked second best, one can assess the effects of the prohibition. The results are shown in the chart below.

When there was no temptation—that is, when the prohibited toy was not physically present—there was of course no dissonance, and the preponderant result is an increase in the attractiveness of the prohibited toy. When the temptation is present but the prohibition is enforced by means of a severe threat of punishment, there is likewise little dissonance created by refraining, and again the preponderant result is an increase in the attractiveness of the prohibited toy. In other words, it seems clear that a prohibition that is enforced in such a way

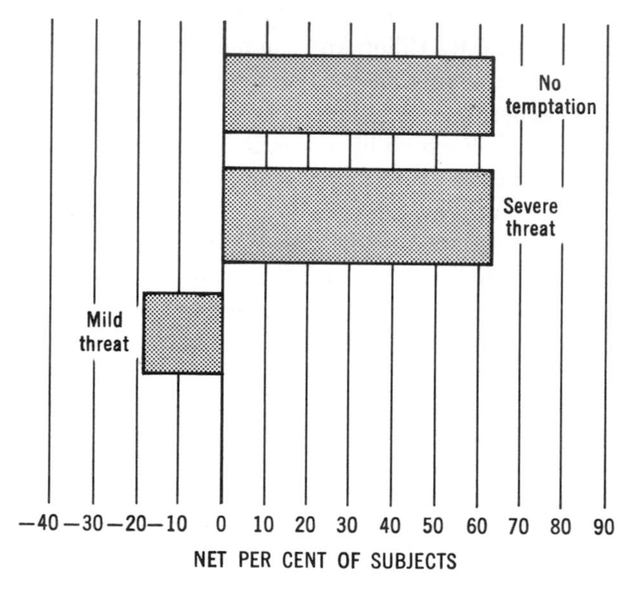

FIGURE 4. Consequences of temptation were explored by prohibiting children from playing with a desirable toy. Later the children were asked to re-evaluate the attractiveness of the forbidden toy. In one case the prohibition was enforced by removing the toy from the child's presence. In the second case the prohibition took the form of a threat of severe punishment; in the third case, a threat of mild punishment. The chart shows the net per cent of children who thought the forbidden toy more attractive after the experiment than before. ("Net per cent" means the per cent who found the toy more attractive minus the per cent who found it less so.) Evidently only those threatened mildly experienced much dissonance, and they reduced it by downgrading the toy's desirability. Others thought the toy more desirable.

as not to introduce dissonance results in a greater desire for the prohibited activity.

The results are quite different, however, when the prohibition is enforced by only a mild threat of punishment. Here we see the result to be expected from the theory of dissonance. Because the justification for refraining from playing with the toy is relatively weak, there is appreciable dissonance between the child's knowledge that the toy is attractive and his actual behavior. The tendency to reduce this dissonance is strong enough to more than overcome the effect apparent in the other two conditions. Here, as a result of dissonance reduction, we see an appreciable sour-grapes phenomenon.

The theory of cognitive dissonance obviously has many applications for everyday life. In addition to throwing light on one's own behavior, it would seem to carry useful lessons for everyone concerned with understanding human behavior in a world where everything is not black and white.

12. CONSUMER BRAND CHOICE—A LEARNING PROCESS?*

Alfred A. Kuehn

The phenomenon of consumer brand shifting is a central element underlying the dynamics of the marketplace. To understand and describe market trends adequately, we must first establish the nature of the influences on consumer choice with respect to products and brands. Research directed at establishing the conditions under which consumers will shift from one brand to another offers hope of providing a framework within which to evaluate the influence of price, advertising, distribution and shelf space, and various types of sales promotion.

What do we know about brand choice? What behavioral mechanisms appear to underlie this phenomenon? Is such behavior habitual? Is learning involved? Does repeated purchasing of a brand reinforce the brand choice response? What is the relationship between consumer purchase frequencies and brand shifting behavior? These questions will be discussed in the light of available empirical data and a model which appears to describe them.

A MODEL OF CONSUMER BRAND SHIFTING

A model equivalent to a generalized form of the Estes[1] and Bush-Mosteller[2] stochastic (probabilistic) learning models appears to de-

*Reprinted from *Journal of Advertising Research,* © Advertising Research Foundation, Inc. (January, 1962), pp. 10–17.

[1] William K. Estes, "Individual Behavior in Uncertain Situations: An Interpretation in Terms of Statistical Association Theory," in Thrall, R. M., C. H. Coombs, and R. L. Davis (eds.), *Decision Processes* (New York: John Wiley & Sons, Inc., 1954).

[2] Robert R. Bush and Frederick Mosteller, *Stochastic Models for Learning* (New York: John Wiley & Sons, Inc., 1955).

scribe consumer brand shifting quite well. To illustrate how this brand shifting model describes changes in the consumer's probability of purchasing any given brand as a result of his purchases of that brand (for example, Brand A) and competing brands (for example, Brand X), let us examine the effect of the four-purchase sequence XAAX upon a consumer with initial probability $P_{A,1}$ by referring to Figure 1.

The model is described or defined in terms of four parameters, namely, the intercepts and slopes of the two lines referred to in Figure 1 as the Purchase Operator and the Rejection Operator. If the brand in question is purchased by the consumer on a given buying occasion, the consumer's probability of again buying the same brand the next time that type product is purchased is read from the Purchase Operator. If the brand is rejected by the consumer on a given buying occasion, the consumer's probability of buying that brand when he next buys that type product is read from the Rejection Operator. Thus, note in Figure 1 that our hypothetical consumer begins on trial 1 with the probability $P_{A,1}$ of buying Brand A. The consumer chooses some other brand (X) on trial 1, however, and thus his probability of buying Brand A on trial 2 ($P_{A,2}$) is obtained from the Rejection Operator, resulting in a slight reduction in the probability of purchasing A on the next trial. On trial 2, however, the consumer does purchase Brand A and thus increases

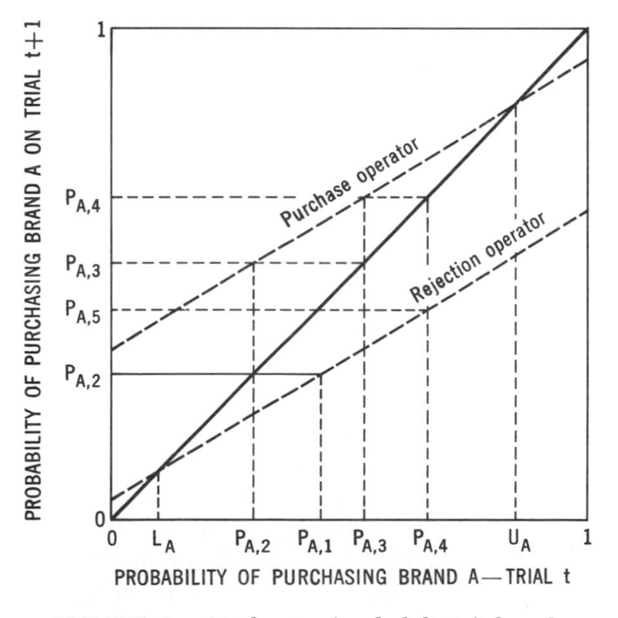

FIGURE 1. Stochastic (probabilistic) brand shifting model.

the likelihood of his again buying the brand on the next occasion (trial 3) to $P_{A,3}$. Continuing in this fashion, the consumer again buys A on trial 3, thereby increasing his probability of purchasing Brand A on trial 4 to $P_{A,4}$. He again rejects A on trial 4, however, decreasing his probability of buying A on trial 5 to $P_{A,5}$.

Two characteristics of the model should be noted: (1) The probability $P_{A,t}$ approaches but never exceeds the upper limit U_A with repeated purchasing of the brand, and (2) the probability $P_{A,t}$ approaches but never drops below the lower limit L_A with continued rejection of the brand. Using Bush and Mosteller's terminology, this would be referred to as an incomplete learning, incomplete extinction model insofar as U_A is less than 1 and L_A is greater than 0. This is equivalent to saying that consumers will generally not develop such strong brand loyalties (or buying habits) as to insure either the rejection or purchase of a given brand.

It should also be pointed out that the Purchase and Rejection Operators are functions of the time elapsed between the consumer's t^{th} and $t + 1^{st}$ purchases and the merchandising activities of competitors. The time effect can be illustrated by three sets of operators shown for high, medium, and very low frequency purchasers of a rapidly consumed, nondurable consumer product (see Figure 2). Note that the slopes of the Purchase and Rejection Operators decrease and that the upper and lower limits approach each other as the time between purchases increases.

At the one limit (Δ time between purchases approaching 0) the Purchase and Rejection Operators approach the diagonal, L approaches 0, and U approaches 1. At the other limit (Δ time between purchases approaching ∞), L and U approach each other and the Purchase and Rejection Operators approach a slope equal to 0.

The main problem that remains in making use of the model is then the estimation of the four parameters defining the Purchase and Rejection Operators as a function of the time between purchases. If this could be done a priori, the model might be of value to marketing management for use in forecasting. At present, however, the model's primary use is in evaluating the effects of past and current competitive marketing activity. Thus, the parameters of the model are estimated for short time periods and related to the actions of all competitors in the market. Since the path of aggregate consumer purchasing behavior could be established for any given set of parameter values, it follows that the parameter estimates obtained from fitting the model can provide a means for evaluating the influence of the market conditions prevailing during the period in which the sequential purchase data are collected.

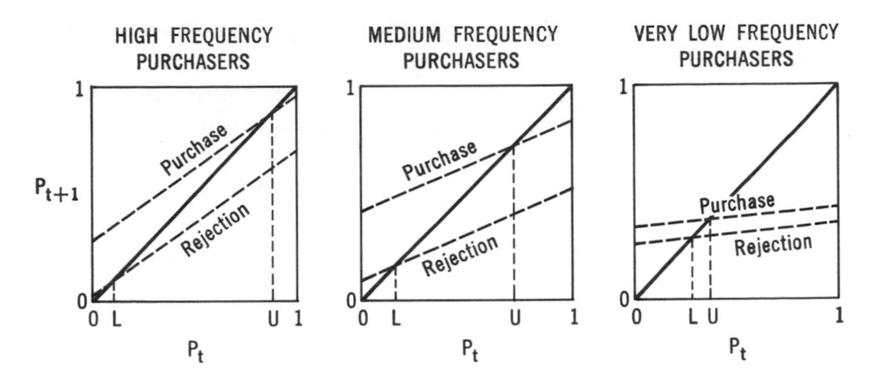

FIGURE 2. Effect of time between purchases upon purchase and rejection operators.

An efficient method has been developed to estimate these brand shifting parameters (maximum likelihood estimates) on the basis of sequences of two to four purchases. This makes it feasible to relate this model to consumer purchasing behavior observed during relatively short periods of time. This is a must if the technique is to be useful, since merchandising conditions do not remain constant for long periods of time—products are modified, advertising themes and budgets are altered, special promotions are generally temporary in nature, and price levels may change from time to time. The technique used to estimate the brand shifting parameters will be outlined in the near future as a working paper in the Carnegie Tech (GSIA) Research in Marketing Project series. The Bush-Mosteller approach to estimating the parameters of their stochastic learning model cannot, in its current state of development, be applied to the brand shifting model since (1) techniques have not been developed to estimate simultaneously the four basic parameters of the model, and (2) the methods outlined require a long history or records of trials (and, therefore, data collected over a long period of time during which there is stability in merchandising activity) from which to develop parameter estimates.

EMPIRICAL BRAND SHIFTING RESEARCH

What evidence is there in support of the model? Three types of empirical studies have led to the formulation and continued development of the above model:[3]

[3]The first two of the following three studies are reported in detail in Alfred A. Kuehn, "An Analysis of the Dynamics of Consumer Behavior and Its Implications for Marketing Management" (unpublished Ph.D. dissertation, Graduate School of Industrial Administration, Carnegie Institute of Technology, 1958).

1. Analysis of 3, 4, 5, and 6 purchase sequences of consumer brand purchases.
2. Analysis of effects of time between consumer purchases upon a consumer's probability of purchasing individual brands of product.
3. Simulation of consumer brand choice behavior.

Each of these three studies is discussed briefly below.

ANALYSIS OF BRAND PURCHASE SEQUENCES

Sequential purchase data can provide some insight into consumer brand switching. The data analyzed below represent the frozen orange juice purchases of approximately 600 Chicago families in the three years 1950 to 1952. More than 15,000 individual purchases of frozen orange juice were collected in monthly diaries by the *Chicago Tribune* Consumer Panel during this period. Data were analyzed as sequences of five purchases by means of a factorial analysis to determine the influence of the consumer's first four brand choices within each sequence upon his choice of a brand on the next (fifth in the sequence) buying occasion. The data and analysis prepared for the Snow Crop brand are summarized in Table 1.

In column 1, the letter "S" is used to represent a purchase of the Snow Crop brand, the letter "O" to represent the purchase of any brand of frozen orange juice *other* than Snow Crop. Thus the sequence SSSS indicates a sequence of four purchases of Snow Crop. The sequences OSSS represents one purchase of some brand other than Snow Crop followed by three purchases of Snow Crop.

Column 2 tabulates the sample sizes from which the observed and predicted probabilities of purchasing Snow Crop on the subsequent buying occasion (fifth purchase in the sequence) were calculated.

Column 3 is computed on the basis of the observed frequencies of the five-purchase sequences. Thus, there were 296 sequences exhibiting the pattern SSSO in the first four positions of the sequence. Snow Crop was purchased on the fifth buying occasion in 144 of these sequences. The best estimate of the observed probability of buying Snow Crop given the past purchase record of SSSO is therefore $144/296 = 0.486$.

The predicted column is based upon the results of the previously referred to factorial analysis of past purchase effects. Each of the four past brand purchases were examined with respect to their individual (primary) effects and the effects of their interactions with each other.

TABLE 1

COMPARISON OF OBSERVED AND PREDICTED PROBABILITY OF PURCHASING SNOW CROP GIVEN THE FOUR PREVIOUS BRAND PURCHASES

Previous Purchase Pattern (1)	*Sample Size (2)*	*Observed Probability of Purchase (3)*	*Predicted Probability of Purchase (4)*	*Deviation of Predictions (5)*
SSSS	1,047	0.806	0.832	+0.026
OSSS	277	0.690	0.691	+0.001
SOSS	206	0.665	0.705	+0.040
SSOS	222	0.595	0.634	+0.039
SSSO	296	0.486	0.511	+0.025
OOSS	248	0.552	0.564	+0.012
SOOS	138	0.565	0.507	−0.058
OSOS	149	0.497	0.493	−0.004
SOSO	163	0.405	0.384	−0.021
OSSO	181	0.414	0.370	−0.044
SSOO	256	0.305	0.313	+0.008
OOOS	500	0.330	0.366	+0.033
OOSO	404	0.191	0.243	+0.052
OSOO	433	0.129	0.172	+0.043
SOOO	557	0.154	0.186	+0.032
OOOO	8,442	0.048	0.045	−0.003

The individual effects of the past four purchase positions were highly significant but the interaction effects were not significantly different from 0 to 5 percent level at the significance (that is, there was greater than 5 percent probability of results as extreme as those observed arising by chance if there were in fact no interaction effects).

There is close agreement between the observed and predicted probabilities in view of the limited sample size. There appear, however, to be systematic deviations on the high side when Snow Crop is purchased either one or three times (also predictions are generally low given two purchases) during the last four buying occasions. Subsequent analysis indicated that these systematic deviations were reduced or eliminated when a record of the fifth past brand purchase was included in the analysis.

Casual inspection of Table 1 suggests that the most recent purchase of the consumer is not the only one influencing his brand choice. This finding raises some question about the uses currently being made of purchase-to-purchase Markov Chain Analyses which assume that only the most recent purchase of the consumer is influential. The analysis of "primary" effects referred to above showed that the purchase of Snow Crop on the most recent buying occasion added 0.321 to the probability of the consumer buying Snow Crop on his next purchase. Similarly, the second most recent purchase added 0.198, the third 0.127 and the fourth 0.141.[4]

Note that the first three purchase effects decline roughly exponentially. That is, the ratio of the importance of the first purchase to that of the second is approximately equal to the ratio of the second to the third. The fourth, however, increases rather than decreases! This reversal has been traced to the fact that past purchases beyond the fourth most recent purchase were excluded from the analysis. The increased importance attached to the fourth most recent purchase for purposes of prediction reflects its high correlation with the fifth and earlier past purchases not incorporated in the study. When these same data were re-analyzed using six-purchase sequences, the exponential relationship of declining primary purchase effects fit the first through fourth past purchases. As would be expected, however, the fifth past purchase effect was larger than the fourth because of its higher correlation with the consumer's sixth and even earlier past purchases.

Observation of the exponentially declining effects of past purchases led to the testing of the brand shifting model outlined in Figure 1 since that model has the characteristic of weighting the influence of past brand choices exponentially when the slopes of the Purchase and Rejection operators are identical. Subsequent research with products other than frozen orange juice has tended to confirm the exponential weighting of past brand purchases by consumers for predictive purposes. The exponential weights vary substantially, however, among product classes. Products such as toilet soap, cereals, and toothpaste were found to have substantially lower rates of decline in weights as one goes back into the purchase history as a result of the tendency of purchasing families to use some mix of brands on a routine basis to satisfy different uses, desires for variety, and differences in preference of individual family members. To be sure, this brand-mix effect is operative even in the case of frozen orange juice but for quite a different reason. Many families use a mix of brands of frozen orange juice because of the lack of availability of individual brands of product in all of the stores among which the consumer shifts in the course of his week-to-week shopping trips.

[4]To illustrate the computation of the predicted probabilities in column 4, Table 1, the probability of a Snow Crop purchase given the history SOOO is 0.045 (the probability of purchase given OOOO) plus 0.141 or 0.186, the probability given SOOS is 0.045 + 0.141 + 0.321 = 0.507 and the predicted probability given OSSS is 0.045 + 0.127 + 0.198 + 0.321 = 0.691.

Effect of Consumer Purchase Frequencies

Let us consider the effect of time between purchases upon the consumer's probability of repurchasing the same brand. In Figure 3 we observe the probability of a consumer's buying the same brand on two consecutive purchases of the product decreasing to the share of market of the brand as time between purchases increases. Whenever a great amount of time has elapsed since the consumer's last purchase of the product, the brand he last bought has little influence upon his choice of a brand—the probability of his buying any given brand in this case is approximately equal to the share of market of that brand. It should be noted that the probability of repurchase decreases at a constant rate with the passing of time; this characteristic, which we shall refer to as the "time rate of decay of purchase probability," is significant since it provides a simple framework within which to incorporate the effects of time into a procedure for forecasting consumer purchase probabilities.

Let us now expand our view of the effects of time upon repurchase probability in terms of the time period required for the consumer to make N individual purchases of frozen orange juice concentrate. Note that the curve in Figure 4 labeled $N = 1$ is the same curve as in Figure 3.

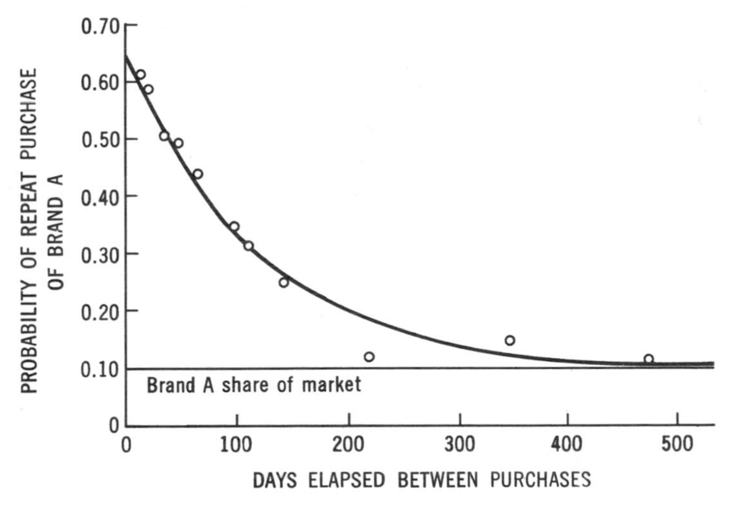

FIGURE 3. The probability of a consumer's buying the same brand on two consecutive purchases of frozen orange juice decreases exponentially with an increase in time between those purchases.

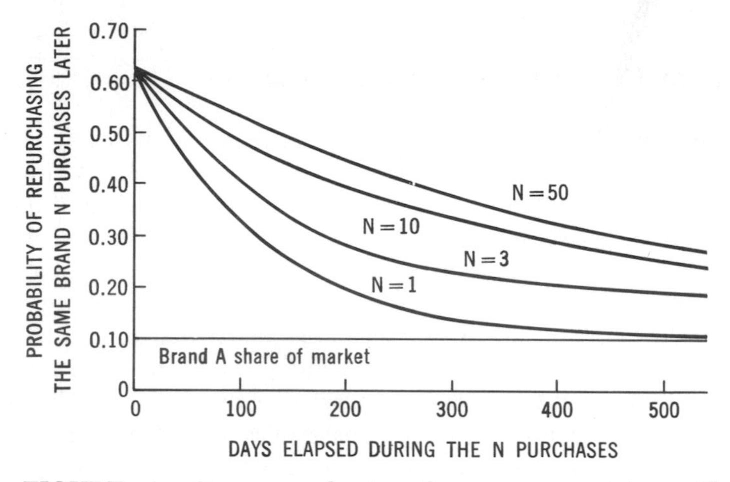

FIGURE 4. Consumers buying frozen orange juice with greatest frequency have the highest probability of continuing to buy the same brand.

Observe also that the probability of repurchasing the same brand at any given time in the future, without regard to the brands chosen in the interim, increases as we go up from $N = 1$ to $N = 3$, $N = 10$, and $N = 50$. Thus, on the average, a consumer who makes his fiftieth purchase of frozen orange juice 300 days after some arbitrary purchase of a given brand has a much higher probability of again choosing that brand than does the consumer who makes only 1, 3, or 10 purchases in that interval of time.

Figure 5 illustrates the relationship between the rates of decay of purchase probability associated with the curves in Figure 4 and the average time elapsed between purchases. The rate of decay of $N = 1$ in Figure 4 is 0.01298 per day. The rate of decay of $N = 50$ is 0.00282. Here again we find a relationship which, because of its simplicity, can after some manipulation be conveniently incorporated into a model forecasting consumer brand choice probabilities. The rate of decay increases linearly with an increase in the average time between purchases. The data points plotted in Figure 5 represent the rates of decay computed for 10 values of N, four of which were illustrated by the curves in Figure 4.

Simulation of Consumer Brand Choice

The brand shifting model outlined in Figure 1 earlier in this paper has been tested by computing the predicted purchase probabilities of consumers on each of approximately 13,000 occasions of purchase of frozen orange juice and comparing aggregates of these predictions with recorded brand purchases. The procedure followed was to first divide the probability space, zero to one, into 76 probability ranges. Then, whenever the computer programed model predicted a certain probability for a given family buying a given brand on a given buying occasion, the results of that purchase were recorded in the computer storage location representing the corresponding probability range. Thus, it was possible to compare within each of the 76 probability cells the average predicted probability of purchasing individual brands with the observed proportion of trials on which the brand was in fact purchased. The predicted and observed probabilities and numbers of purchases were then compared individually and simultaneously for all 76 cells with respect to the binomial and χ^2 distributions that would be expected if the model were perfect. The 76 normal deviates, referred to here by "t," computed for the individual cells with respect to the Snow Crop predictions were approximately normally distributed, 50 lying within 1 standard deviation, 71 lying within 2 standard deviations, and 76 falling within 3 standard deviations. The

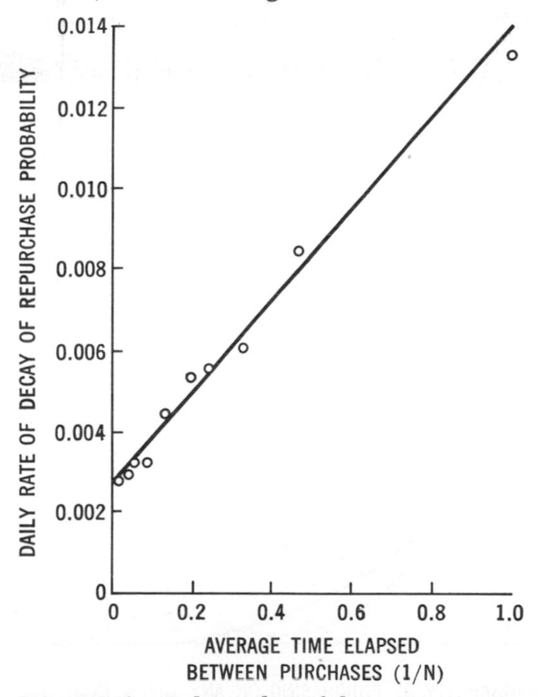

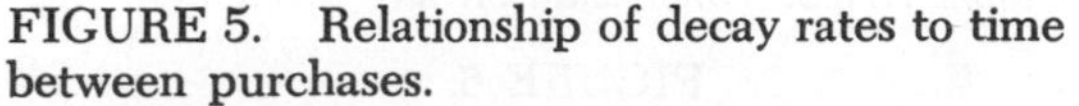
FIGURE 5. Relationship of decay rates to time between purchases.

χ^2 value indicated no significant deviation at the 10 percent level. Similar results were obtained in an analysis of predictions for the Minute Maid brand, 53 "t" values lying within one standard deviation, 70 lying within two standard deviations and all 76 cases falling within three standard deviations.

The above results suggest that the model offers promise for use in describing consumer behavior in probabilistic terms. The model was not tested with respect to individual families, the number of purchases being made by most individual families being considered as providing too small a sample to yield a reasonably powerful test of the predictions of the model. In other words, since rejection is unlikely given a small sample size per family, acceptance does not carry much weight with respect to an evaluation of the model. In the aggregate, the model stood up surprisingly well given the over-all test sample size of approximately 13,000 purchase predictions. (Interestingly enough, when the lower limit L was held at zero in certain tests designed to determine its importance in the model, the "t" values associated with certain low probability cells ranged from 40 to 65 standard deviations.) Of course, if the sample size were to be increased substantially, significant deviations would have been obtained since the model is not a perfect representation of the brand purchase sequences of consumers.

The predictions of the model were also used to obtain a frequency distribution of consumers throughout the three-year time period ac-

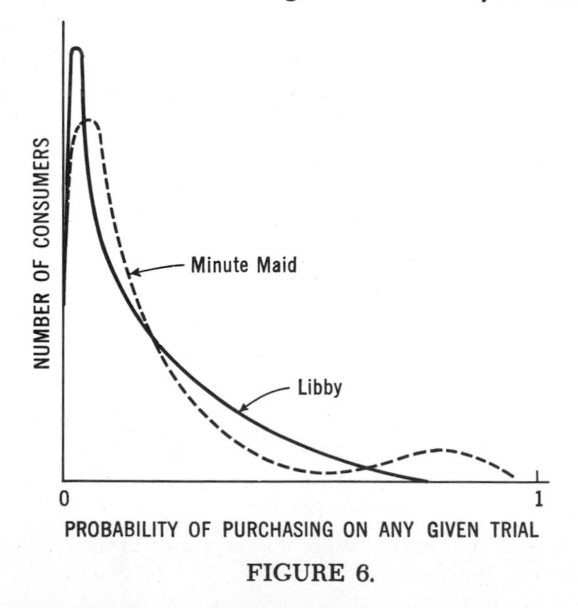

FIGURE 6.

cording to their probability of buying specific brands of product. Figure 6 provides a comparison of the profiles (smoothed) for Libby and Minute Maid frozen orange juice. As might be expected, most consumers have a low probability of buying any specific brand. Those consumers who have a high probability of buying one brand must necessarily have a low probability of buying several other brands. Minute Maid was in the enviable position of having a small group of customers with a very high probability of buying the brand. Libby did not have such a following. The fact that Minute Maid developed frozen orange juice and was the first brand available to consumers probably helped the firm develop the group of loyal (or habitual) customers, a sizable portion of which it had been able to retain in the face of growing competition. As the innovator of frozen orange juice, Minute Maid also developed a pre-eminent market position in terms of retail availability, a factor which undoubtedly helped the firm maintain a sales advantage relative to competition.

ADAPTIVE BEHAVIOR OR SPURIOUS RESULTS?

In a paper titled "Brand Choice as a Probability Process,"[5] Ronald Frank reports that certain results he has observed with respect to repeat purchase probabilities as a function of a brand's run length are similar in appearance to what would be expected with associative learning under conditions of reward. He then notes, in a footnote, that my data also seem to suggest this interpretation, a point on which there is agreement.[6] The balance of Frank's article is then directed at demonstrating that:

1. Purchase sequence data generated by families for a given brand using a Monte Carlo approach on the assumption that each family's probability of purchasing the brand remained constant throughout the time period produced repeat purchase probabilities as a function of run length which closely approximated in the aggregate the actual observed empirical probabilities.
2. The number of runs observed for *most* families is consistent with what might be expected under the assumption that each

[5]Ronald E. Frank, "Brand Choice as a Probability Process," *Journal of Business*, Vol. XXXV (January, 1962), pp. 43–56.

[6]Alfred A. Kuehn, "A Model for Budgeting Advertising," in Bass, *et al.* (ed.), *Mathematical Models and Methods in Marketing* (Homewood, Ill.: Richard D. Irwin, Inc., 1961).

family's probability of purchasing any given brand remained constant throughout the time period.

As a result of his success in generating a relationship in (1) above that has the appearance of actual data. Frank states, "These results cast suspicion on the use of a 'learning' model to describe the observations." In view of this statement, which bears directly upon the work I have outlined earlier in this paper, in my thesis, and elsewhere, some defense appears to be in order.

Frank's observations in no way invalidate the findings outlined earlier in this paper. He has shown that it is inappropriate to attribute to learning *all* of the increase in repeat purchase probability associated with increases in run length, an error which has probably been made by more than a few researchers. This is not, however, the approach outlined here or in my thesis. As a matter of fact, the approach used in my thesis could be applied to Frank's coffee data to test whether the probabilities are in fact constant and, if this is not the case, to estimate the appropriate weightings. If consumers were to have a constant probability of brand choice from trial to trial, the most recent purchase positions would not have a greater primary effect on the predicted purchase probabilities than that of any other purchase position—all of the primary effects would be identical except for sampling variations. Similarly, if the probabilities of brand choice were constant from trial to trial, the Purchase and Rejection Operators in the adaptive brand shifting model outlined at the beginning of this paper would be superimposed on the diagonal (see Figure 1). In other words, the special case considered by Frank can be treated successfully by both of the analytic techniques used in my studies and discussed in this paper. Frank is correct when he states that much of what might appear to be a learning effect on the basis of repeat purchase probabilities as a function of run length is due to the aggregation of consumers having different probabilities (at the start of the run)—this is, however, no problem when one takes into account the effect of all past purchases which have a significant impact upon the consumer's purchase probability, since such an approach does not disregard the information contained in purchases prior to the current run, an important consideration when the run is very short. Since past purchases will, except in highly unusual cases, have decreasing effects (as one goes back in time) upon the consumer's subsequent purchase probability, taking into account all significant past purchases does not generally require the availability of an unduly long record of the consumer's purchase history.

The second point that Frank makes—namely, that most consumers behave as though they had constant purchase probabilities—would appear to represent a misinterpretation of statistical results. Frank sets up his hypothesis, tests it at some level of significance for each of a large number of cases (families), and then interprets the results as though all cases not shown to deviate statistically on an individual basis are consistent with the hypothesis. Actually, the hypothesis was that consumers have a constant probability of purchase, and the results indicated that a larger number of the individual cases tested lay outside the confidence limits than is consistent with the hypothesis, thereby rejecting the hypothesis *in toto*!

To be sure, the hypothesis of constant probability is, in effect, a straw man. It is generally recognized that consumers do change their buying behavior over time. Whether such behavior is called adjustment, adaptation, or learning is unimportant. It should be noted, however, that even though the over-all market for coffee was quite stable in the period studied by Frank, and the sample sizes were limited to 14 months of purchase by each family, the hypothesis was in fact rejected on an over-all basis, the only appropriate way in which to interpret the results of the test. Perhaps, as Frank suggests, some consumers do have constant probabilities of choosing individual brands during certain periods of time. Such a hypothesis cannot be tested, however, unless a procedure independent of the test is available for identifying these consumers and the relevant time periods.

SUMMARY

A model describing brand shifting behavior as a probabilistic process and incorporating the effects of past purchases and time elapsed between purchases has been outlined. A defense of this approach to the study of mechanisms underlying consumer brand choice has also been presented. What has not been discussed is the way in which such merchandising factors as price, advertising, product characteristics, retail availability, and promotions (price off, coupons, merchandise packs, and so on) influence the parameters of the model and the extensions of the model that might be required to incorporate such effects. Some earlier results of research on the influence of these variables have been incorporated into an aggregate "expected value" form of the model presented here. Much work, however, remains to be done.

13. PROJECTIVE TECHNIQUES IN MARKETING RESEARCH*

Mason Haire

It is a well accepted maxim in merchandizing that, in many areas, we are selling the sizzle rather than the steak. Our market research techniques, however, in many of these same areas, are directed toward the steak. The sizzle is the subjective reaction of the consumer; the steak the objective characteristics of the product. The consumer's behavior will be based on the former rather than the latter set of characteristics. How can we come to know them better?

When we approach a consumer directly with questions about his reaction to a product we often get false and misleading answers to our questions. Very often this is because the question which we heard ourselves ask was not the one (or not the only one) that the respondent heard. For example: A brewery made two kinds of beer. To guide their merchandizing techniques they wanted to know what kind of people drank each kind, and particularly, what differences there were between the two groups of consumers. A survey was conducted which led up to the questions "Do you drink —— beer?" (If *yes*) "Do you drink the *Light* or *Regular*?" (These were the two trade names under which the company marketed.) After identifying the consumers of each product it was possible to find out about the characteristics of each group so that appropriate appeals could be used, media chosen, etc.

An interesting anomaly appeared in the survey data, however. The interviewing showed (on a reliable sample) that consumers drank *Light* over *Regular* in the ratio of 3 to 1. The company had been producing and selling Regular over Light for some time in a ratio of 9 to 1. Clearly, the attempt to identify characteristics of the two kinds was a failure. What made them miss so far?

*Reprinted from the *Journal of Marketing*, national quarterly publication of the American Marketing Association (April, 1950), pp. 649–656.

When we say "Do you drink *Light* or *Regular*?" we are at once asking which brand is used, but also, to some extent, saying "Do you drink the regular run-of-the-mill product or do you drink the one that is more refined and shows more discrimination and taste?" The preponderance of "Light" undoubtedly flows from this kind of distortion.

When we ask questions of this sort about the product we are very often asking also about the respondent. Not only do we say "What is ——— product like?" but, indirectly "What are *you* like?" Our responses are often made up of both elements inextricably interwoven. The answers to the second question will carry clichés and stereotypes, blocks, inhibitions, and distortions, whenever we approach an area that challenges the person's idea of himself.

There are many things that we need to know about a consumer's reaction to a product that he can not tell us because they are to some extent socially unacceptable. For instance, the snob appeal of a product vitally influences its sale, but it is a thing that the consumer will not like to discuss explicitly. In other cases the consumer is influenced by motives of which he is, perhaps, vaguely aware, but which he finds difficult to put into words. The interviewer-respondent relationship puts a good deal of pressure on him to reply and to make sense in his reply. Consequently, he gives us stereotypical responses that use clichés which are commonly acceptable but do not necessarily represent the true motives. Many of our motives do not, in fact, "make sense," and are not logical. The question-answer relation demands sense above all. If the response does not represent the true state of affairs the interviewer will never know it. He will go away. If it does not make sense it may represent the truth, but the respondent will feel like a fool and the interviewer will not go away. Much better produce a cliché and be rid of him.

THE NATURE OF PROJECTIVE TESTS

Still other kinds of motives exist of which the respondent may not be explicitly conscious himself. The product may be seen by him as related to things or people or values in his life, or as having a certain role in the scheme of things, and yet he may be quite unable, in response to a direct question, to describe these aspects of the object. Nevertheless, these characteristics may be of great importance as motives. How can we get at them?

Clinical psychologists have long been faced with a parallel set of problems. It is quite usual for a patient to be unable or unwilling to tell the therapist directly what kinds of things are stirring in his motivational pattern. Information about these drives are of vital importance to the process of cure, so a good deal of research has been directed towards the development of techniques to identify and define them. The development of projective techniques as diagnostic tools has provided one of the most useful means to uncover such motivations, and the market-researcher can well afford to borrow their essentials from the therapist.

Basically, a projective test involves presenting the subject with an ambiguous stimulus—one that does not quite make sense in itself—and asking him to make sense of it. The theory is that in order to make it make sense he will have to add to it—to fill out the picture—and in so doing he projects part of himself into it. Since we know what was in the original stimulus we can quite easily identify the parts that were added, and, in this way, painlessly obtain information about the person.

Examples of these tests come readily to hand. Nearly everyone is familiar with the Rorschach Test, in which a subject is shown a series of ink-blots and asked to tell what they look like. Here the stimulus is incomplete in itself, and the interpretation supplied by the patient provides useful information. This test yields fairly general answers about the personality, however, and often we would like to narrow down the area in which the patient is supplying information.

The Thematic Apperception Test offers a good example of this function. Let us suppose that with a particular patient we have reason to suppose that his relation to figures of authority is crucial to his therapeutic problem. We can give him a series of pictures where people are shown, but where the relationship of authority or the characteristics of the authoritarian figure are not complete. He is asked to tell a story about each picture. If in each story the subordinate finally kills the figure of authority we have certain kinds of knowledge; if, on the other hand, he always builds the story so the subordinate figure achieves a secure and comfortable dependence, we have quite different information. It is often quite impossible to get the subject to tell us these things directly. Either he cannot or will not do so. Indirectly, however, he will tell us how he sees authority. Can we get him, similarly, to tell us how a product looks to him in his private view of the world?

APPLICATION OF PROJECTIVE TEST IN MARKET RESEARCH

Let us look at an example of this kind of thing in market research. For the purposes of experiment a conventional survey was made of attitudes toward Nescafé, an instant coffee. The questionnaire included the questions "Do you use instant coffee?" (If *No*) "What do you dislike about it?" The bulk of the unfavorable responses fell into the general area "I don't like the flavor." This is such an easy answer to a complex question that one may suspect it is a stereotype, which at once gives a sensible response to get rid of the interviewer and conceals other motives. How can we get behind this facade?

In this case an indirect approach was used. Two shopping lists were prepared. They were identical in all respects, except that one list specified Nescafé and one Maxwell House Coffee. They were administered to alternate subjects, with no subject knowing of the existence of the other list. The instructions were "Read the shopping list below. Try to project yourself into the situation as far as possible until you can more or less characterize the woman who bought the groceries. Then write a brief description of her personality and character. Wherever possible indicate what factors influenced your judgment."

Shopping List I

Pound and a half of hamburger
2 loaves Wonder bread
bunch of carrots
1 can Rumford's Baking Powder
Nescafé instant coffee
2 cans Del Monte peaches
5 lbs. potatoes

Shopping List II

Pound and a half of hamburger
2 loaves Wonder bread
bunch of carrots
1 can Rumford's Baking Powder
1 lb. Maxwell House Coffee (Drip Ground)
2 cans Del Monte peaches
5 lbs. potatoes

Fifty people responded to each of the two shopping lists given above. The responses to these shopping lists provided some very interesting material. The following main characteristics of their descriptions can be given:

1. 48 per cent of the people described the woman who bought Nescafé as lazy; 4 per cent described the woman who bought Maxwell House as lazy.
2. 48 per cent of the people described the woman who bought Nescafé as failing to plan household purchases and schedules well; 12 per cent described the woman who bought Maxwell House this way.

3. 4 per cent described the Nescafé woman as thrifty; 16 per cent described the Maxwell House woman as thrifty.
   12 per cent described the Nescafé woman as spendthrift; 0 per cent described the Maxwell House woman this way.
4. 16 per cent described the Nescafé woman as not a good wife; 0 per cent described the Maxwell House woman this way.
   4 per cent described the Nescafé woman as a good wife; 16 per cent described the Maxwell House woman as a good wife.

A clear picture begins to form here. Instant coffee represents a departure from "home-made" coffee, and the traditions with respect to caring for one's family. Coffee-making is taken seriously, with vigorous proponents for laborious drip and filter-paper methods, firm believers in coffee boiled in a battered sauce pan, and the like. Coffee drinking is a form of intimacy and relaxation that gives it a special character.

On the one hand, coffee making is an art. It is quite common to hear a woman say, "I can't seem to make good coffee," in the same way that one might say, "I can't learn to play the violin." It is acceptable to confess this inadequacy, for making coffee well is a mysterious touch that belongs, in a shadowy tradition, to the plump, aproned figure who is a little lost outside her kitchen but who has a sure sense in it and among its tools.

On the other hand, coffee has a peculiar role in relation to the household and the home-and-family character. We may well have a picture, in the shadowy past, of a big black range that is always hot with baking and cooking, and has a big enamelled pot of coffee warming at the back. When a neighbor drops in during the morning, a cup of coffee is a medium of hospitality that does somewhat the same thing as cocktails in the late afternoon, but does it in a broader sphere.

These are real and important aspects of coffee. They are not physical characteristics of the product, but they are real values in the consumer's life, and they influence his purchasing. We need to know and assess them. The "labor-saving" aspect of instant coffee, far from being an asset, may be a liability in that it violates these traditions. How often have we heard a wife respond to "This cake is delicious!" with a pretty blush and "Thank you—I made it with such and such a prepared cake mix." This response is so invariable as to seem almost compulsive. It is almost unthinkable to anticipate a reply "Thank you, I made it with Pillsbury's flour, Fleischman's yeast, and Borden's milk." Here the specifications are unnecessary. All that is relevant is the implied "I made it"—the art and the credit are carried directly by the verb that covers the process of mixing and processing the ingredients. In ready-mixed foods there seems to be a compulsive drive to refuse credit for the product, because the accomplishment is not the housewife's but the company's.

In this experiment, as a penalty for using "synthetics" the woman who buys Nescafé pays the price of being seen as lazy, spendthrift, a poor wife, and as failing to plan well for her family. The people who rejected instant coffee in the original direct question blamed its flavor. We may well wonder if their dislike of instant coffee was not to a large extent occasioned by a fear of being seen by one's self and others in the role they projected onto the Nescafé woman in the description. When asked directly, however, it is difficult to respond with this. One can not say, "I don't use Nescafé because people will think I am lazy and not a good wife." Yet we know from these data that the feeling regarding laziness and shiftlessness was there. Later studies (reported below) showed that it determined buying habits, and that something could be done about it.

ANALYSIS OF RESPONSES

Some examples of the type of response received will show the kind of material obtained and how it may be analyzed. Three examples of each group are given below.

Descriptions of a Woman Who Bought, Among Other Things, Maxwell House Coffee

> "I'd say she was a practical, frugal woman. She bought too many potatoes. She must like to cook and bake as she included baking powder. She must not care much about her figure as she does not discriminate about the food she buys."
>
> "The woman is quite influenced by advertising as signified by the specific name brands on her shopping list. She probably is quite set in her ways and accepts no substitutes."
>
> "I have been able to observe several hundred women shoppers who have made very similar purchases to that listed above, and the only clue that I can detect that may have some bearing on her personality is the Del Monte peaches. This item when purchased singly along with the other more staple foods indicates that she may be anxious to please either herself or members of her family with a 'treat.' She is probably a thrifty, sensible housewife."

Descriptions of a Woman Who Bought, Among Other Things, Nescafé Instant Coffee

"This woman appears to be either single or living alone. I would guess that she had an office job. Apparently, she likes to sleep late in the morning, basing my assumption on what she bought such as Instant Coffee which can be made in a hurry. She probably also has can [sic] peaches for breakfast, cans being easy to open. Assuming that she is just average, as opposed to those dazzling natural beauties who do not need much time to make up, she must appear rather sloppy, taking little time to make up in the morning. She is also used to eating supper out, too. Perhaps alone rather than with an escort. An old maid probably."

"She seems to be lazy, because of her purchases of canned peaches and instant coffee. She doesn't seem to think, because she bought two loaves of bread, and then baking powder, unless she's thinking of making cake. She probably just got married."

"I think the woman is the type who never thinks ahead very far—the type who always sends Junior to the store to buy one item at a time. Also she is fundamentally lazy. All the items, with possible exception of the Rumford's, are easily prepared items. The girl may be an office girl who is just living from one day to the next in a sort of haphazard sort of life."

As we read these complete responses we begin to get a feeling for the picture that is created by Nescafé. It is particularly interesting to notice that the Nescafé woman is protected, to some extent, from the opprobrium of being lazy and haphazard by being seen as a single "office girl"—a role that relieves one from guilt for not being interested in the home and food preparation.

The references to peaches are significant. In one case (Maxwell House) they are singled out as a sign that the woman is thoughtfully preparing a "treat" for her family. On the other hand, when the Nescafé woman buys them it is evidence that she is lazy, since their "canned" character is seen as central.

In terms of the sort of results presented above, it may be useful to demonstrate the way these stories are coded. The following items are extracted from the six stories quoted:

Maxwell House	*Nescafé*
1. practical	1. single
frugal	office girl
likes to cook	sloppy
	old maid

2. influenced by advertising
   set in her ways
3. interested in family
   thrifty
   sensible

2. lazy
   does not plan
   newlywed
3. lazy
   does not plan
   office girl

Items such as these are culled from each of the stories. Little by little categories are shaped by the content of the stories themselves. In this way the respondent furnishes the dimensions of analysis as well as the scale values on these dimensions.

Second Test

It is possible to wonder whether it is true that the opprobrium that is heaped on the Nescafé woman comes from her use of a device that represents a short-cut and labor-saver in an area where she is expected to embrace painstaking time-consuming work in a ritualistic way. To test this a variation was introduced into the shopping lists. In a second experiment one hundred and fifty housewives were tested with the form given above, but a sample was added to this group which responded to a slightly different form. If we assume that the rejection in the first experiment came from the presence of a feeling about synthetic shortcuts we might assume also that the addition of one more shortcut to both lists would bring the Maxwell House woman more into line with the Nescafé woman, since the former would now have the same guilt that the Nescafé woman originally had, while the Nescafé woman, already convicted of evading her duties, would be little further injured.

In order to accomplish this a second prepared food was added to both lists. Immediately after the coffee in both lists the fictitious item, "Blueberry Fill Pie Mix" was added. The results are shown in the accompanying table.

Table I. Personality Characteristics Ascribed to Users of Prepared Foods

If They Use	*No Prepared Food (Maxwell House alone)*		*Nescafé (alone)*		*Maxwell House (plus Pie Mix)*		*Nescafé (plus Pie Mix)*	
They are seen as:	*Number*	*Per Cent*	*Number*	*Per Cent*	*Number*	*Per Cent*	*Number*	*Per Cent*
Not Economical	12	17	24	32	6	30	7	35
Lazy	8	11	46	62	5	25	8	40
Poor Personality and Appearance	28	39	39	53	7	35	8	40
N =	72		74		20		20	

It will be seen immediately, in the first two columns, that the group to whom the original form of the list were given showed the same kind of difference as reported above in their estimates of the two women. The group with an additional prepared food, however, brought the Maxwell Coffee woman down until she is virtually undistinguishable from the Nescafé. There seems to be little doubt but that the prepared-food-character, and the stigma of avoiding housewifely duties is responsible for the projected personality characteristics.

Relation to Purchasing

It is still relevant to ask whether the existence of these feelings in a potential consumer is related to purchasing. It is hypothesized that these personality descriptions provide an opportunity for the consumer to project hopes and fears and anxieties that are relevant to the way the product is seen, and that they represent important parts of her motivation in buying or not buying. To test this hypothesis, a small sample of fifty housewives, comparable in every way to the group just referred to, was given the original form of the shopping list (Nescafé only). In addition to obtaining the personality description, the interviewer, on a pretext, obtained permission to look at her pantry shelves

Table II

The woman who buys Nescafé is seen as:	*By Women Who Had Instant Coffee in the House (N = 32)*		*By Women Who Did Not Have Instant Coffee in the House (N = 18)*	
	Number	*Per Cent*	*Number*	*Per Cent*
Economical**	22	70	5	28
Not economical	0	0	2	11
Can not cook or does not like to**	5	16	10	55
Plans balanced meals*	9	29	2	11
Good housewife, plans well, cares about family**	9	29	0	0
Poor housewife, does not plan well, does not care about family*	5	16	7	39
Lazy*	6	19	7	39

*A single asterisk indicates that differences this great would be observed only 5 times out of 100 in repeated samplings of a population whose true difference is zero.

**A double asterisk indicates that the chances are 1 in 100. We are justified in rejecting the hypothesis that there is no difference between the groups.

and determine personally whether or not she had instant coffee of any brand. The results of this investigation are shown in the accompanying table.

The trend of these data shows conclusively that if a respondent sees the woman who buys Nescafé as having undesirable traits, she is not likely to buy instant coffee herself. The projected unacceptable characteristics go with failure to buy, and it does not seem unwarranted to assume that the association is causal.

Furthermore, these projected traits are, to some extent, additive. For instance, if a respondent describes the woman as having one bad trait only, she is about twice as likely not to have instant coffee. However, if she sees her as having two bad traits, and no good ones (e.g., lazy, can not cook), she is about three times as likely not to have instant coffee as she is to have it. On the other hand, if she sees her as having two good traits (e.g., economical, cares for family), she is about six times as likely to have it as not.

It was pointed out earlier that some women felt it necessary to "excuse" the woman who bought Nescafé by suggesting that she lived alone and hence could not be expected to be interested in cooking, or that she had a job and did not have time to shop better. Women who had instant coffee in the house found excuses almost twice as often as those who did not use instant coffee (12 out of 32, or 42 per cent, against 4 out of 18, or 22 per cent). These "excuses" are vitally important for merchandizing. The need for an excuse shows there is a barrier to buying in the consumer's mind. The presence of excuses shows that there is a way around the barrier. The content of the excuses themselves provides valuable clues for directing appeals toward reducing buying resistance.

CONCLUSIONS

There seems to be no question that in the experimental situation described here:

(1) Motives exist which are below the level of verbalization because they are socially unacceptable, difficult to verbalize cogently, or unrecognized.

(2) These motives are intimately related to the decision to purchase or not to purchase, and

(3) It is possible to identify and assess such motives by approaching them indirectly.

Two important general points come out of the work reported. The first is in the statement of the problem. It is necessary for us to see a product in terms of a set of characteristics and attributes which are part of the consumer's "private world," and as such may have no simple relationship to characteristics of the object in the "real" world. Each of us lives in a world which is composed of more than physical things and people. It is made up of goals, paths to goals, barriers, threats, and the like, and an individual's behavior is oriented with respect to these characteristics as much as to the "objective" ones. In the area of merchandizing, a product's character of being seen as a path to a goal is usually very much more important as a determinant of purchasing than its physical dimensions. We have taken advantage of these qualities in advertising and merchandizing for a long time by an intuitive sort of "playing-by-ear" on the subjective aspects of products. It is time for a systematic attack on the problem of the phenomenological description of objects. What kinds of dimensions are relevant to this world of goals and paths and barriers? What kind of terms will fit the phenomenological characteristics of an object in the same sense that the centimetre-gram-second system fits its physical dimensions? We need to know the answers to such questions, and the psychological definitions of valued objects.

The second general point is the methodological one that it is possible, by using appropriate techniques, to find out from the respondent what the phenomenological characteristics of various objects may be. By and large, a direct approach to this problem in terms of straightforward questions will not yield satisfactory answers. It is possible, however, by the use of indirect techniques, to get the consumer to provide, quite unselfconsciously, a description of the value-character of objects in his environment.

14. GROUP INFLUENCE IN MARKETING*

On the common sense level the (reference group) concept says in effect that man's behavior is influenced in different ways and in varying degrees by other people. Comparing one's own success with that of others is a frequent source of satisfaction or disappointment. Similarly, before making a decision one often considers what such and such a person or such and such a group (whose opinion one has *some* reason to follow) would do in these circumstances, or what they would think of one for making a certain decision rather than another. Put in these ways, of course, reference group influence represents an unanalyzed truism which has long been recognized. The problem to which social scientists have been addressing themselves intensively only for the last two decades, however, concerns the refinement of this common sense notion to the end that it might be applied meaningfully to concrete situations.

The real problems are to determine which kinds of groups are likely to be referred to by which kinds of individuals under which kinds of circumstances in the process of making which decisions, and to measure the extent of this reference group influence. Towards this end empirical researches have been conducted in recent years which have at least made a start in the process of refining the reference group concept.

Reference group theory as it has developed has become broad enough to cover a wide range of social phenomena, both with respect to the relation of the individual to the group and with respect to the type of influence exerted upon the individual by the group in question.

*Reprinted from *Group Influence in Marketing and Public Relations* (Ann Arbor: Foundation for Research on Human Behavior, 1956), pp. 1–12.

KINDS OF REFERENCE GROUPS

Reference groups against which an individual evaluates his own status and behavior may be of several kinds.

They may be *membership* groups to which a person actually belongs. There can be small face-to-face groups in which actual association is the rule, such as families or organizations, whether business, social, religious, or political. On the other hand, there can be groups in which actual membership is held but in which personal association is absent. (For example, membership in a political party, none of whose meetings are personally attended.)

Reference groups may be *categories* to which a person automatically belongs by virtue of age, sex, education, marital status and so on. This sort of reference group relationship involves the concept of role. For example, before taking a certain action an individual might consider whether this action would be regarded as appropriate in his role as a man or husband or educated person or older person or a combination of all of these roles. What is involved here is an individual's perception of what society, in general or that part of it with which he has any contact, expects people of his age, or sex, or education or marital status to do under given circumstances.

They may be *anticipatory* rather than actual membership groups. Thus a person who aspires to membership in a group to which he does *not* belong may be more likely to refer to it or compare himself with its standards when making a decision than he is to refer to the standards of the group in which he actually belongs but would like to leave. This involves the concept of upward mobility. When such upward mobility is sought in the social or business world it is ordinarily accompanied by a sensitivity to the attitudes of those in the groups to which one aspires, whether it involves the attitudes of country club members in the eyes of the aspiring non-member or the attitudes of management in the eyes of the ambitious wage earner or junior executive.

There are also negative, *dissociative* reference groups. These constitute the opposite side of the coin from the anticipatory membership groups. Thus an individual sometimes avoids a certain action because it is associated with a group (to which the individual may or may not in fact belong) from which he would like to dissociate himself.

INFLUENCE ON INDIVIDUAL BEHAVIOR

Reference groups influence behavior in two major ways. First, they influence *aspiration levels* and thus play a part in producing satisfaction or frustration. If the other members of one's reference group (for example, the neighbors) are wealthier, more famous, better gardeners, etc., one may be dissatisfied with one's own achievements and may strive to do as well as the others.

Second, reference groups influence *kinds* of behavior. They establish approved patterns of using one's wealth, of wearing one's fame, of designing one's garden. They set tabus too, and may have the power to apply actual sanctions (for example, exclusion from the group). They thus produce *conformity* as well as *contentment* (or discontentment).

These two kinds of influence have, however, a good deal in common. Both imply certain perceptions on the part of the individual, who attributes characteristics to the reference group which it may or may not actually have. Both involve psychological rewards and punishment.

RELATIVE DEPRIVATION—AN EXAMPLE OF REFERENCE GROUP INFLUENCE

As already indicated, one of the chief problems in the field of reference group theory is to identify which of several groups that might serve as a frame or reference under given circumstances actually is invoked by an individual.

This is sometimes difficult to get at directly, as individuals are not always *aware* of which reference groups they are evaluating their behavior against, or may not be anxious to reveal them where they are conscious of such groups.

During World War II the Research Branch of the United States Army was concerned with morale of troops under different circumstances, and the morale often seemed not to reflect objective conditions. Thus, for example, soldiers in the Military Police who had received fewer promotions than their opposite numbers in the Air Force were nevertheless more satisfied with their rank than were the average Air Force men. Many similar phenomena were noted in which the men who were apparently suffering greater hardship on an absolute basis were more satisfied than others apparently suffering less hardship on an absolute basis. In an effort to explain these *apparent* inconsistencies the concept of "relative deprivation" was introduced. It was found that in each case there existed a reference group with which the individual soldier tended to compare his own lot. Only if he felt deprived *relative to this group* did his morale suffer. Two examples should suffice.

Army Promotions The fact that Military Police were often more satisfied with their progress than were the more rapidly promoted Air Force Men was explained as follows: Absolute achieved status evidently was not the key to their feelings but rather the relation of the soldier's status to that of others he regarded as his standard of comparison. Thus the Private First Class in the Military Police may have been more satisfied than the Corporal in the Air Force, because in the Military Police virtually no enlisted man expected to get higher than Private First Class, while in the Air Force soldiers saw sergeants and better all around them.

Negro Troops It was found that the morale of Northern Negroes in southern army camps was higher than that of Northern Negroes in northern camps located in the areas where presumably Negroes in general were accorded better treatment. This apparent incongruity was again explained by identifying the reference group against which the Northern Negro compared himself in each instance. The reference group which turned this apparent inconsistency into a plausible reaction in this case was the Negro civilians whom the soldiers encountered while on pass in neighboring towns. The Negro soldier's pay was the same in the North as it was in the South, but in the North he found Negro civilians making so much money in defense plants that his pay appeared small by comparison. On the other hand, relative to most Negro civilians he saw in southern towns, the Negro soldier had a position of comparative wealth and dignity. Thus the psychological values of Army life to the Negro soldier in the South relative to the Southern Negro civilian greatly exceeded the psychological values of Army life to the Negro soldier in the North relative to the Northern Negro civilian.

THE PRACTICAL VALUE OF THE REFERENCE GROUP CONCEPT IN MARKETING AND PUBLIC RELATIONS

In applying the reference group concept to practical problems in marketing and public relations three basic questions arise:

1. *Reference Group Relevance*—How do you determine whether and to what extent reference group influence is operating in a given situation? The reference group is after all just one of many influences in decision making, varying greatly in prominence from situation to situation.
2. *Reference Group Identification*—How do you identify the particular reference group or groups or individuals who are

most relevant in influencing decisions under given circumstances? This is perhaps the most difficult question to answer in many cases, particularly where multiple reference groups are involved.

3. *Reference Group Identification and Effective Communication* —Once having identified the nature of the group influence operating in a given situation, how do you then make use of this knowledge in achieving the most effective *communication* with the groups or individuals?

The payoff is of course in this area, since the answers to the first two questions are of value only to the extent that they can be translated into more pertinent and effective communications, designed to influence purchasing behavior or the attitudes of various publics towards an organization.

Experimental evidence is now available which sheds light on each of these three questions. From this evidence as well as from the general advancement in the methodology of social research in recent years there have emerged some generalizations, very tentative in nature. These can be applied only with the most careful attention to the special circumstances operating in individual instances, and serve more as guides to fruitful ways of examining problems as they arise than as simple answers to problems.

Whether or not reference group influence is likely to come into play in the decisions of individuals depends on many interrelated factors. For descriptive purposes, however, it is convenient to consider some of these factors under two major headings:

1. *Influence determinants which vary primarily according to the individual making the decision*, such as the feeling of security or insecurity with respect to potential reference groups, the perception of the positions of these groups concerning kinds of behavior expected or stands on specific issues, and the extent of knowledge about the matter on which a decision must be made.
2. *Influence determinants which vary primarily according to the matter to be decided*, such as the attributes of the product, in a marketing situation, or the nature of the organization and issue at state, in a public relations situation.

In marketing, it is rarely practical to utilize information about individual differences (the first class above), because products must be designed and advertised with large groups in mind.[1] In public

[1] An exception to this generalization may be found in the case of personal selling, where knowledge of the individual's specific relation to and perception of certain groups would be highly relevant.

relations, on the other hand, individual differences may be very important. In this area the *general* attention level with respect to a particular issue is often low. Under these circumstances the relevant public may be largely confined to a few individuals, and in such cases knowledge of the relation between these individuals and potential reference groups would certainly be to the point.

A. INDIVIDUAL DIFFERENCES AND REFERENCE GROUP INFLUENCE

1. The Relation of Security Level and Conformity to Reference Group Influence

A tentative generalization which has emerged in this area and which has been supported by some experimental evidence is this:

Individuals enjoying the greatest amount of security by virtue of their prestige and status within a group will generally conform (both publicly and privately) to the standards of that group, but are also freest to deviate from the group norms on occasions when, to their minds, particular circumstances seem to justify such deviations. On the other hand those with lowest feelings of security and least status in a group are most likely *publicly* to conform to its norms on all occasions even though harboring private opposition and resentment. The latter holds, of course, only if there are penalties associated with loss of membership in the particular group. Conformity then serves the purpose of maintaining membership in that group.

The following experiment conducted under laboratory conditions at Yale University lent support to this hypothesis.[2]

Eighteen groups, each composed of six Yale freshmen, were formed for the experiment. They were motivated to cooperate by being told that they would meet for several sessions to work on certain problems and that the best group would win a prize. To promote group cohesion without sacrificing cooperation, each group was told that it would stop from time to time to evaluate its own members and expel any who were seriously interfering with the progress of the group. It was pointed out, however, that such expulsion was not to be taken lightly, as it would carry a considerable stigma and hence was only to be considered under very serious circumstances. The groups were given

[2]J. E. Dittes and H. H. Kelley, "Effects of Different Conditions of Acceptance upon Conformity to Group Norms," *Journal of Abnormal and Social Psychology* (1956).

several problems on which they were asked to come to some agreement. One of these problems was in the area of juvenile delinquency. Each of the 18 groups was presented with some information about two gangs of juvenile delinquents, and asked to decide which of these gangs most deserved help from a social worker. The information was structured in such a way as to make Gang A appear to be the logical candidate for aid from the social worker. As planned by the researchers, the various units deliberated and came to the jointly-arrived-at decision that Gang A most deserved aid. After these group decisions were made, artificial images were set up in the mind of each individual as to how highly he was regarded by the group to which he belonged. This was accomplished by having the group members rate each other, in writing; however, the experiment leader did not use this information but gave each student fictitious information on how he was regarded by other members of his six man group. One person in each group was told that he was very highly regarded, two were told that they had been given an average rating, another two that the group's regard for them was quite low, and finally one member of each group was told that he was on the verge of rejection.

After these varying images of esteem by the particular group had been established (designed to set up feelings ranging all the way from very high to very low sense of security) a new item of information about the juvenile gangs was introduced. This item introduced some counter evidence pointing rather clearly in favor of Gang B as being the logical choice for aid.

After the new evidence was introduced, private and public expressions of conformity to the originally announced judgments of the group were obtained from those of very low, average and high prestige (as artificially manipulated for experimental purposes) with the following results:

1. Men with lowest prestige and security in relation to their group—those who believed they were on the verge of expulsion—were, when queried privately, most willing to deviate from the originally established norm of their group. However, when placed in the position of having to take a public stand these same people were most likely to conform to the originally announced norms of the groups, and least likely to deviate even though their own private inclination on the basis of the facts at hand was to do so.
2. Men with average status and security exhibited considerable conformity, even in their private opinions.
3. Men with highest status and security were found, when

queried privately, to be quite willing to differ from the original group decision and felt the greatest freedom to express their non-conformity publicly.

These relationships may be expressed graphically as follows:

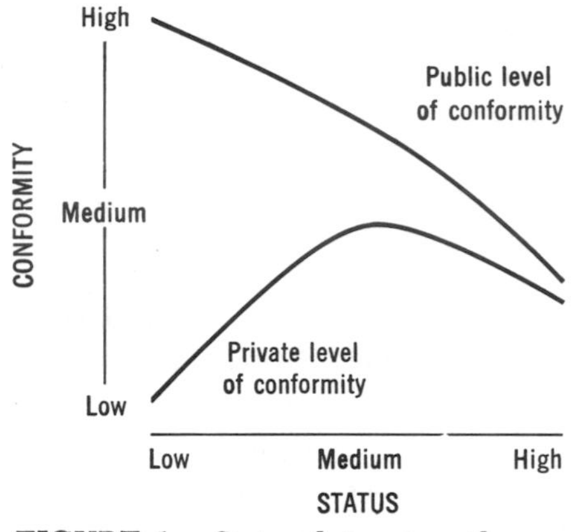

FIGURE 1. Status determines the consistency between public and private conformity.

Practical Implications

If a person has high status and feels very secure relative to a group, he can be appealed to directly on the merits of the case and is in the best position to take the lead in deviating should he so desire, with least risk of losing status with the group he prizes. Seeking to influence such people through reference group appeals, when the merits of the case are inconsistent with the appeals, may have little success.

On the other hand, as suggested by the data just reviewed, those with lesser status in their group and less feeling of security are most likely to be influenced in public or visible actions by appeals involving their reference group. They are more likely to observe the norms of the group than others, even if they privately disagree with its specific position, since they require acceptance from the group for their own security. However, if the reference group influence conflicts with their own judgement or works against their own best interests, they are likely to develop an underlying resistance to the idea. Such resistance may find expression in other ways.

A practical example of the operation of this principle in the field of public relations and specifically in the area of influencing legislation may be drawn from experience in Washington. Particularly on issues where mass public attention and interest is low, considerable effort is concentrated on the most crucial of all publics, Congress itself. A Congressman of course has several reference groups, prominent among which are his constituents and the remainder of Congress. Naturally he greatly values the esteem of both of these groups. His very existence in Congress depends on the former and his self-esteem as well as the degree of cooperation he can depend upon getting for his own projects depends upon the high regard of the latter. The Congressman's status and security with regard to his constituents may be measured by such items as the size of his pluralities and the length of his service. Within Congress his status may be measured by, among other things, such items as seniority and cooperation by other members in the past.

Suppose a group was interested in changing a long standing piece of legislation which appeared to have represented the majority views of Congress for a considerable period of time. Suppose also that there was considerable merit in the proposed change, but that the public was relatively little concerned with this legislation. The Congressman's primary reference groups with respect to this issue is likely, therefore, to be his colleagues in the House. A freshman Congressman with little security and status would not, even though he privately favored this new legislation, be likely to oppose publicly the prevailing reference group position, by introducing the legislation or placing his name on an initial list of sponsors, while a Congressman with security and status might be more willing to do so.

For those outside of Congress interested in seeing the measure passed, winning the support of so-called bellwethers within Congress for this would be a primary objective. Such Congressmen, by virtue of their secure position in Congress, are most free to deviate and take the lead on occasions, where the case merits it. Though they generally show considerable respect for the norms of their "club" they are also in the best position to ignore this reference group when the right occasion arises.

2. The Individual's Perception of Norms of Potential Reference Group

Perhaps one of the more obvious limitations on the relevance of a potential reference group in influencing a decision is an individual's lack of knowledge or incorrect perception of the group's actual position on an issue, even where he values the group's views or at least its acceptance of him. Thus, for example, the American Legion may be an effective reference group for a substantial number of veterans with respect to veterans' legislation. It may be much less so, however, in connection with views on international affairs. The Legion has a position on such matters, but the average veteran is much less likely to know just what that position is. Along this line, a study[3] conducted for a Church Council found issues on which the Church's national policy was not followed by a considerable portion of the Church's members. The study revealed that these differences between Church policy and the opinions of its individual members were not necessarily conscious nonconformity with group norms, but rather in many cases reflected ignorance of what those norms were.

One practical implication from these studies is that the effective influence of a reference group, even one known to command a substantial following, may be increases by giving special publicity to the position of the group on a specific issue.

3. Independent Knowledge About the Matter to be Decided

Experimental evidence has indicated that reference group influence is particularly potent in an informational vacuum. Where the individual has little if any knowledge about the attributes of a product or the issues involved in a public relations campaign, reference group influence is maximized. On the other hand, where the individual has personal knowledge and experience, the reference group influence is likely to be *less* relevant, other things being equal. Thus, for example, in the same study of a Church and its parishioners alluded to above, it was found that uninformed parishioners tended to have the same attitudes on secular issues as did their clergymen, but among those parishioners who were politically informed and had other sources of information on these issues there was a tendency more often to ignore the positions taken by their clergymen.

B. DIFFERENT KINDS OF DECISIONS AND REFERENCE GROUP INFLUENCE

1. Marketing and Reference Group Relevance

As has already been suggested, the reference group constitutes just one of the many influences in buying decisions, and this influence varies from product to product. How then does one determine whether reference group influence is likely to be a factor in buying behavior in

[3]Bureau of Applied Social Research, Columbia University.

connection with a given product or brand? Research has been conducted on the various factors that influence buying behavior with reference to several products, and out of this have emerged some general ideas about how reference group influences may enter into purchasing.

Buying may be a completely individualistic kind of activity or it may be very much socially conditioned. Consumers are often influenced by what others buy, especially those persons with whom they compare themselves, or use as reference groups.

The conspicuousness of a product is perhaps the most general attribute bearing on its susceptibility to reference group influence. There are two aspects to conspicuousness in this particular context that help to determine reference group influence. First the article must be conspicuous in the most obvious sense that it can be seen and identified by others. Secondly it must be conspicuous in the sense of standing out and being noticed. In other words, no matter how visible a product is, if virtually everyone owns it, it is not conspicuous in the second sense of the word. This leads to a further distinction: reference groups may influence either (a) the purchase of a product, or (b) the choice of a particular brand or type, or (c) both.

The possible susceptibility of various product and brand buying to reference group influence is suggested in the following figure:

Reference group influence relatively:	Product: weak −	Product: strong +	Brand or type
strong +	clothing furniture magazines refrigerator (type) toilet soap	cars* cigarettes* beer (prem. vs. reg.)* drugs*	+
weak −	soap canned peaches laundry soap refrigerator (brand) radios	air conditioners* instant coffee* TV (black & white)	−

FIGURE 2. Products and brands of consumer goods may be classified by extent to which reference groups influence their purchase.

*The classification of all starred products is based on actual experimental evidence. Other products in this table are classified speculatively on the basis of generalizations derived from the sum of research in this area and confirmed by the judgment of seminar participants.

According to this classification a particular item might be susceptible to reference group influence in its purchase in three different ways, corresponding to three of the four cells in the above figure. Reference group influence may operate with respect to product alone (Brand + Product —) as in the upper left cell, or it may operate both with respect to brand and product (Brand + Product +) as in the upper right cell, or it may operate with respect to product but not brand (Brand — Product +) as in the lower right cell.

Only the "minus-minus" items of the kind illustrated (Brand — Product —) in the lower left cell are not likely to involve any significant reference group influence in their purchase *at the present time.*

What are some of the characteristics that place an item in a given category, and what significance do such placements have for marketing and advertising policy?

a. "Product-plus, brand-plus" items Autos constitute an article where both the product and the brand are socially conspicuous. Whether or not a person buys a car, and also what particular brand he buys, is likely to be influenced by what others do. This also holds true for cigarettes, for drugs (decisions made by M.D.'s as to what to prescribe) and for beer with respect to type (premium vs. regular) as opposed to brand. Cigarettes and drugs, however, qualify as "plus-plus" items in a manner different from cars.

For example, while the car belongs to a class of products where brand differentiation is based at least substantially on real differences in attributes, the cigarette belongs to a class of product in which it is difficult to differentiate one brand from another by attributes: hence attributes are ascribed largely through reference group appeal built up by advertising. Popular images of the kinds of people who smoke various brands have been created at great cost, and in some cases additional images are being created to broaden a particular brand's market. In the case of drugs, it was found that the reference group influencing *whether* the product was used was different from that influencing the particular *brand* selected. Reference group influence was found to be prominent in determining whether or not beer was purchased at all, and also in determining whether regular or premium beer was selected. It did not appear to influence strongly choice of a particular brand.

b. "Product plus, brand minus" items Instant Coffee is one of the best examples of this class of items. Whether it is served in a household depends in considerable part on whether the housewife, in view of her own reference groups and the image she has of their attitudes towards this product, considers it appropriate to serve it. The brand itself in this instance is not conspicuous or socially important and is a matter largely for individual choice. In the case of air conditioners, it was found that little prestige attached to the particular brand used, and reference group influence related largely to the idea of purchasing the product itself. Analysis in one city revealed that the purchase of this often "visible from the outside" product was concentrated in small neighborhood areas. Clusters of conditioners were frequently located in certain rows and blocks. In many cases clusters did not even cross streets. Immediate neighbors apparently served as a powerfully influential group in the purchase of these appliances. In this general class may also be found the black and white TV set, with its antenna often visible on the outside of the house. As the saturation point in black and white TV set ownership rapidly approaches, however, the influence of reference groups may soon become minor, and the product can then be put in the "brand minus, product minus" quadrant, along with refrigerators. Color TV may remain in the "brand plus, product minus" quadrant, with type (color) rather than brand per se the element which is strongly related to reference groups.

c. "Product minus, brand plus" items This group is made up essentially of products that all people or at least a very high proportion of people use, although differing as to type or brand.

Perhaps the leading example in this field is clothing. There could hardly be a more socially visible product than this, but the fact that everyone in our society wears clothing takes the *product* out of the area of reference group influence. The *type* of clothing purchased is, however, very heavily influenced by reference groups, with each subculture in the population (teenagers, zootsuiters, Ivy League collegians, western collegians, workers, bankers, advertising men, etc.) setting its own standards and often prescribing within fairly narrow limits what those who feel related to these groups can wear. Similarly, though not quite as dramatically, articles like furniture, magazines, refrigerators and toilet soap are seen in almost all homes, causing their purchase in general to fall outside of the orbit of reference group influence. The visibility of these items, however, coupled with the wide variety of styles and types among them make the selection of particular kinds highly susceptible to reference group influence.

d. "Product minus, brand minus" items Purchasing behavior in this class of items is governed largely by product attributes rather than by the nature of the presumed users. In this group neither the products nor the brands tend to be socially conspicuous. This is not to say that personal influence cannot operate with respect to purchasing the kind of items included in this group. As with all products, some people tend to exert personal influence and others tend to be influenced by individual persons. Reference groups as such, however, exert relatively little influence on buying behavior in this class of items. Examples of items in this category are salt, canned peaches, laundry soap and radios. It is apparent that placement in this category is not *necessarily* inherent in the product itself and hence is not a static placement. Items can move in and out of this category.

While it is true that items which are essential socially inconspicuous, like salt and laundry soap, are natural candidates for this category, it is not entirely out of the realm of possibility that through considerable large scale advertising and other promotional efforts images of the kind of people who use certain brands of salt or laundry soap could be built up so as to bring reference group influence into play on such items, much as has been the case with cigarettes. The task here would be more difficult, however, since the cigarette is already socially visible. On the other hand, items such as radios and refrigerators which are conspicuously visible and whose purchase was once subject to considerable reference group influence have now slipped into this category through near saturation in ownership.

Implications of Strong and Weak Reference Group Influence for Advertising and Marketing

It should be stressed again that this scheme of analysis is introduced to show how reference group influence might enter into purchasing behavior in certain cases. It cannot be regarded as generally applicable to marketing problems on all levels. There is still a need to know more precisely where many different products or brands fit into this scheme. Attempts to fit products and brands into the classification above suggest research that needs to be done to obtain more relevant information about each product.

Assuming, however, that a product or brand has been correctly placed with respect to the part played by reference groups in influencing its purchase, how can this help in marketing the product in question?

Where neither product nor brand appear to be associated strongly with reference group influence, advertising should emphasize the product's attributes, intrinsic qualities, price, and advantages over competing products.

Where reference group influence is operative, the advertiser should stress the kinds of people who buy the product, reinforcing and broadening where possible the existing stereotypes of users. This involves learning what the stereotypes are and what specific reference groups enter into the picture, so that appeals can be "tailored" to each major group reached by the different media employed.

Although it is important to see that the "right" kind of people use a product, a crucial problem is to make sure that the popular image of the product's users is as broad as possible without alienating any important part of the product's present or potential market in the process. Creating or reinforcing a stereotype of consumers which is too small and exclusive for a mass-produced item may exclude a significant portion of the potential market. On the other hand, some attempts to appeal to new groups through advertising in mass media have resulted in the loss of existing groups of purchasers whose previous (favorable) image of the product-user was adversely affected. One possible means for increasing the base of the market for a product by enlarging the image of its users is to use separate advertising media through which a new group can be reached without reducing the product's appeal to the original group of users. Another method might be to appeal to a new group through cooperative advertising by a number of companies producing the product, possibly through a trade association. This would minimize the risk to an individual producer who, trying to reach a new group of users through his own advertising (women as opposed to men or wealthy as opposed to average people, for example), might antagonize people who had a strong need to identify with the *original* image of the product's kind of user.

Product Attributes Versus Reference Group Influence

A technique which could serve to assess the relative influence of reference groups, as compared with product attributes, on the purchase of any given product was employed in research on a food product which will be referred to as product "X".

A cross-section of "X" users was asked several questions relating to particular attributes of "X", such as whether it was more harmful or beneficial for one's health, whether or not it was considered fattening, whether it was considered extravagant or economical, whether or not it tasted good, and so on. These same people were also asked a reference group-oriented question about "X", to determine whether or not "X" was popular with most of their friends. It was found that there was usually more "X" eating among people who reacted negatively to "X"'s attributes but admitted to its popularity among most of their friends, than among those who reacted positively to "X" 's attributes but indicated that it was not popular with their friends.

These relationships are shown in Table 1 on the next page.

In this table, the scores in parentheses are those of people whose replies showed both attribute influence and reference group influence exerting pressure in the same direction.

Special attention should be directed towards the other scores. These represent situations in which people are under cross-pressures. For each of the four attributes considered, the reference group influence is stronger than the attribute influence, in the use of "X". This is brought out by the arrows, which point toward the cross-pressure situations where the reference group influence is adverse. In all of these, consumption frequency is less than where attribute influence alone is negative. Or, put another way, positive perception of reference group behavior with respect to the food product ("X" is very popular) coupled with negative perception of its actual attribute value ("X" does more harm than good, is fattening, etc.) leads to more consumption than negative perception of reference group behavior ("X" not very popular) coupled with positive perception of actual attribute value ("X" does more good than harm, not fattening, economical).

As can be seen from the comparisons indicated by the arrows, reference group influence is markedly stronger than attribute influence for three of the four attributes. Only for "taste" does the attribute influence come close to competing with reference group influence in determining consumption of "X".

One implication of this finding would be that advertising by the "X" industry might stress the variables that are related to the products' *social* utility for its consumers, rather than base its advertising solely on the *physical* attributes of the product.

In a study of a beverage, it was found that, of those who drank the beverage in question, 95% claimed that their friends also drank it, while of those who did not drink this beverage 85% also claimed that their friends did *not* drink it.

Some products, then, must be sold to whole social groups rather than primarily to individuals.

TABLE I

RELATION BETWEEN REFERENCE GROUP AND ATTRIBUTE INFLUENCE IN USE OF FOOD PRODUCT "X"

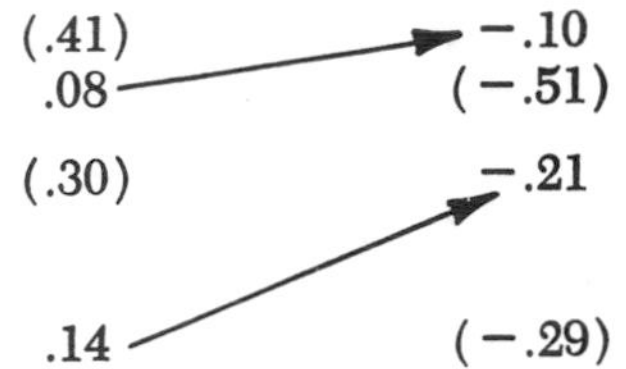

	+ *Reference Group* −	
	With most of respondent's friends "X" is:	
Product Attribute	*Very Popular*	*Not Very Popular*
Effects of "X" on health	Index of Frequency of Eating "X" *	
+ more good than harm	(.41)	−.10
− more harm than good	.08	(−.51)
+ do not avoid fattening food and/or feel "X" is not really or a little fattening	(.30)	−.21
− try to avoid fattening food and feel "X" is really or a little fattening	.14	(−.29)
Economic Value Judgment		
+ fairly economical	(.29)	−.20
− sort of an extravagance	.11	(−.33)
Taste Judgment		
+ tastes good	(.42)	.05
− no reference to good taste**	.09	(−.38)

*All scores in the above table constitute an index of the frequency of "X" eating among respondents falling into the given cell. The scoring procedure used was:

Frequent "X" users—score +1
Medium "X" users—score 0
Occasional "X" users—score −1

The final score is derived by subtracting the number of occasional "X" users in a given cell from the number of frequent users and dividing the remainder by the total number of respondents in the cell.

For example, the index score .41 was obtained as follows:

329 respondents felt that a moderate amount of "X" does more good than harm AND report that "X" is very popular with most of their friends.

Of these 329 respondents 178 are frequent "X" users, 97 are medium "X" users, and 43 are occasional "X" users.

The score: 178 − 43 = 135 The Index value: 135/329 =.41

**"Tastes good" represents the selection of this phrase from a word list of various attributes that might be applied to "X". "No Reference to Good Taste" refers to those respondents who did not select "Tastes Good" from the word list.

Source: Bureau of Applied Social Research, Columbia University

15.

THE TWO-STEP FLOW OF COMMUNICATION: AN UP-TO-DATE REPORT OF AN HYPOTHESIS*[1]

Elihu Katz

The hypothesis that "ideas often flow from radio and print to opinion leaders and from these to the less active sections of the population" has been tested in several successive studies. Each study has attempted a different solution to the problem of how to take account of interpersonal relations in the traditional design of survey research. As a result, the original hypothesis is largely corroborated and considerably refined.

Analysis of the process of decision-making during the course of an election campaign led the authors of *The People's Choice* to suggest that the flow of mass communications may be less direct than was commonly supposed. It may be, they proposed, that influences stemming from the mass media first reach "opinion leaders" who, in turn, pass on what they read and hear to those of their every-day associates for whom they are influential. This hypothesis was called "the two-step flow of communication."[2]

The hypothesis aroused considerable interest. The authors themselves were intrigued by its implications for democratic society. It was a healthy sign, they felt, that people were still most successfully

*Reprinted from *Public Opinion Quarterly* (Spring, 1957), pp. 61–78.

[1]This may be identified as Publication No. A-225 of the Bureau of Applied Social Research, Columbia University. It is an abridged version of a chapter in the author's "Interpersonal Relations and Mass Communications: Studies in the Flow of Influence," unpublished Ph.D. thesis, Columbia University, 1956. The advice and encouragement of Dr. Paul F. Lazarsfeld in the writing of this thesis are gratefully acknowledged. A former staff member of the Bureau of Applied Social Research at Columbia University, the author is now on leave from his post as assistant professor of sociology at the University of Chicago and is currently guest lecturer in sociology at the Hebrew University in Jerusalem.

[2]Paul F. Lazarsfeld, Bernard Berelson, and Hazel Gaudet, *The People's Choice,* 2d ed. (New York: Columbia University Press, 1948), p. 151.

persuaded by give-and-take with other people and that the influence of the mass media was less automatic and less potent than had been assumed. For social theory, and for the design of communications research, the hypothesis suggested that the image of modern urban society needed revision. The image of the audience as a mass of disconnected individuals hooked up to the media but not to each other could not be reconciled with the idea of a two-step flow of communication implying, as it did, networks of interconnected individuals through which mass communications are channeled.

Of all the ideas in *The People's Choice*, however, the two-step flow hypothesis is probably the one that was least well documented by empirical data. And the reason for this is clear: the design of the study did not anticipate the importance which interpersonal relations would assume in the analysis of the data. Given the image of the atomized audience which characterized so much of mass media research, the surprising thing is that interpersonal influence attracted the attention of the researchers at all.[3]

In the almost seventeen years since the voting study was undertaken, several studies at the Bureau of Applied Social Research of Columbia University have attempted to examine the hypothesis and to build upon it. Four such studies will be singled out for review. These are Merton's study of interpersonal influence and communications behavior in Rovere;[4] the Decatur study of decision-making in marketing, fashions, movie-going and public affairs, reported by Katz and Lazarsfeld;[5] the Elmira study of the 1948 election campaign reported by Berelson, Lazarsfeld and McPhee;[6] and, finally, a very recent study by Coleman, Katz, and Menzel on the diffusion of a new drug among doctors.[7]

[3]For the discussion of the image of the atomized audience and the contravening empirical evidence, see Elihu Katz and Paul F. Lazarsfeld, *Personal Influence: The Part Played by People in the Flow of Mass Communications* (Glencoe, Ill.: The Free Press, 1955), pp. 15–42; Eliot Friedson, "Communications Research and the Concept of the Mass," *American Sociological Review*, Vol. 18 (1953), pp. 313–317; and Morris Janowitz, *The Urban Press in a Community Setting* (Glencoe, Ill.: The Free Press, 1952).

[4]Robert K. Merton, "Patterns of Influence: A Study of Interpersonal Influence and Communications Behavior in a Local Community," in Paul F. Lazarsfeld and Frank N. Stanton, eds., *Communications Research, 1948–9* (New York: Harper and Brothers, 1949), pp. 180–219.

[5]Elihu Katz and Paul F. Lazarsfeld, *op. cit.*, Part Two.

[6]Bernard R. Berelson. Paul F. Lazarsfeld, and William N. McPhee, *Voting: A Study of Opinion Formation in a Presidential Campaign* (Chicago: University of Chicago Press, 1954).

[7]A report on the pilot phase of this study is to be found in Herbert Menzel and Elihu Katz, "Social Relations and Innovation in the Medical Profession," *Public Opinion Quarterly*, Vol. 19 (1955), pp. 337–52; a volume and various articles on the full study are now in preparation.

These studies will serve as a framework within which an attempt will be made to report on the present state of the two-step flow hypothesis, to examine the extent to which it has found confirmation and the ways in which it has been extended, contracted and reformulated. More than that, the studies will be drawn upon to highlight the successive strategies which have been developed in attempting to take systematic account of interpersonal relations in the design of communications research, aiming ultimately at a sort of "survey sociometry." Finally, these studies, plus others which will be referred to in passing, will provide an unusual opportunity to reflect upon problems in the continuity of social research.[8]

FINDINGS OF *THE PEOPLE'S CHOICE*

The starting point for this review must be an examination of the evidence in the 1940 voting study which led to the original formulation of the hypothesis. Essentially, three distinct sets of findings seem to have been involved. The first had to do with *the impact of personal influence*. It is reported that people who made up their minds late in the campaign, and those who changed their minds during the course of the campaign, were more likely than other people to mention personal influence as having figured in their decisions. The political pressure brought to bear by everyday groups such as family and friends is illustrated by reference to the political homogeneity which characterizes such groups. What's more, on an average day, a greater number of people reported participating in discussion of

[8]Other authors who have drawn upon the concepts of opinion leadership and the two-step flow of communication, and developed them further, are Matilda and John Riley, "A Sociological Approach to Communications Research," *Public Opinion Quarterly*, Vol. 15 (1951), pp. 445–460; S. N. Eisenstadt, "Communications Processes Among Immigrants in Israel," *Public Opinion Quarterly*, Vol. 16 (1952), pp. 42–58 and "Communication Systems and Social Structure: An Exploratory Study," *Public Opinion Quarterly*, Vol. 19 (1955), pp. 153–167; David Riesman, *The Lonely Crowd* (New Haven: Yale University Press, 1950); Leo A. Handel, *Hollywood Looks at its Audience* (Urbana: University of Illinois Press, 1950). The program of research in international communications at the Bureau of Applied Social Research has given considerable attention to opinion leadership; see Charles Y. Glock, "The Comparative Study of Communications and Opinion Formation," *Public Opinion Quarterly*, Vol. 16 (1952–53), pp. 512–523; J. M. Stycos, "Patterns of Communication in a Rural Greek Village," *Public Opinion Quarterly*, Vol. 16 (1952), pp. 59–70; and the forthcoming book by Daniel Lerner, Paul Berkman, and Lucille Pevsner, *Modernizing the Middle East*. Forthcoming studies by Peter H. Rossi, Robert D. Leigh, and Martin A. Trow are also concerned with the interplay of personal and mass media influences in local communities.

the election than hearing a campaign speech or reading a newspaper editorial. From all of this, the authors conclude that personal contacts appear to have been both more frequent and more effective than the mass media in influencing voting decisions.[9]

The second ingredient that went into the formulation of the hypothesis concerned *the flow of personal influence.* Given the apparent importance of interpersonal influence, the obvious next step was to ask whether some people were more important than others in the transmission of influence. The study sought to single out the "opinion leaders" by two questions: "Have you recently tried to convince anyone of your political ideas?", and "Has anyone recently asked you for your advice on a political question?" Comparing the opinion leaders with others, they found the opinion leaders more interested in the election. And from the almost even distribution of opinion leaders throughout every class and occupation, as well as the frequent mention by decision-makers of the influence of friends, co-workers and relatives, it was concluded that opinion leaders are to be found on every level of society and presumably, therefore, are very much like the people whom they influence.[10]

A further comparison of leaders and others with respect to mass media habits provides the third ingredient: *the opinion leaders and the mass media.* Compared with the rest of the population, opinion leaders were found to be considerably more exposed to the radio, to the newspapers and to magazines, that is, to the formal media of communication.[11]

Now the argument is clear: If word-of-mouth is so important, and if word-of-mouth specialists are widely dispersed, and if these specialists are more exposed to the media than the people whom they influence, then perhaps "ideas often flow from radio and print to opinion leaders and from these to the less active sections of the population."[12]

DESIGN OF THE VOTING STUDY

For studying the flow of influence as it impinges on the making of decisions, the study design of *The People's Choice* had several advantages. Most important was the panel method which made it possible to locate changes almost as soon as they occurred and then to correlate

[9]Lazarsfeld, Berelson, and Gaudet, *op. cit.*, pp. 135–152.
[10]*Ibid.*, pp. 50–51.
[11]*Ibid.*, p. 51.
[12]*Ibid.*, p. 151.

change with the influences reaching the decision-maker. Secondly, the unit of effect, the decision, was a tangible indicator of change which could readily be recorded. But for studying that part of the flow of influence which had to do with contacts among people, the study design fell short, since it called for a random sample of individuals abstracted from their social environments. It is this traditional element in the design of survey research which explains the leap that had to be made from the available data to the hypothesis of the two-step flow of communication.

Because every man in a random sample can speak only for himself, opinion leaders in the 1940 voting study had to be located by self-designation, that is, on the basis of their own answers to the two advice-giving questions cited above.[13] In effect, respondents were simply asked to report whether or not they were opinion leaders. Much more important than the obvious problem of validity posed by this technique is the fact that it does not permit a comparison of leaders with their respective followers, but only of leaders and non-leaders in general. The data, in other words, consist of only two statistical groupings: people who said they were advice-givers and those who did not. Therefore, the fact that leaders were more interested in the election than non-leaders cannot be taken to mean that influence flows from more interested persons to less interested ones. To state the problem drastically, it may even be that the leaders influence only each other, while the uninterested non-leaders stand outside the influence market altogether. Nevertheless, the temptation to assume that the non-leaders are the followers of the leaders is very great, and while *The People's Choice* is quite careful about this, it cannot help but succumb.[14] Thus, from the fact that the opinion leaders were more exposed to the mass media than the non-leaders came the suggestion of the two-step flow of communication; yet, manifestly, it can be true only if the non-leaders are, in fact, followers of the leaders.

The authors themselves point out that a far better method would

[13]Strictly speaking, of course, if a respondent reports whether or not he is a leader he is not speaking for himself but for his followers, real or imagined. Furthermore, it ought to be pointed out for the record that it is sometimes possible for a respondent to speak for others besides himself. The voting studies, for example, ask respondents to report the vote-intentions of other family members, of friends, of co-workers, though this procedure is of undetermined validity.

[14]There is an alternative procedure which is something of an improvement. Respondents can be asked not only whether they have given advice but whether they have taken advice. This was done in the Decatur and Elmira studies which are cited below. Thus the nonleaders can be classified in terms of whether or not they are in the influence market at all, that is, whether or not they are "followers."

have been based on "asking people to whom they turn for advice on the issue at hand and then investigating the interaction between advisers and advisees. But that procedure would be extremely difficult, if not impossible, since few of the related 'leaders' and 'followers' would happen to be included in the sample."[15] As will be shown immediately, this is perhaps the most important problem which succeeding studies have attempted to solve.

DESIGN OF THREE SUBSEQUENT STUDIES

To this point, two aspects of the original statement of the two-step flow hypothesis have been reviewed. First of all, the hypothesis has been shown to have three distinct components, concerning respectively the impact of personal influence; the flow of personal influence; and the relationship of opinion leaders to the mass media. The evidence underlying each has been examined. Secondly, the design of the study has been recalled in order to point up the difficulty that arises from attempting to cope with the fundamentally new problem of incorporating *both* partners to an influence transaction into a cross-sectional study.

From this point forward, the major focus will turn to those studies that have succeeded *The People's Choice*. We will first report the different ways in which three of the four studies selected for review approached the problem of designing research on interpersonal influence.[16] Thereafter, the substantive findings of the several studies will be reviewed and evaluated so as to constitute an up-to-date report on the accumulating evidence for and against the hypothesis of the two-step flow of communication.

1. *The Rovere study*. Undertaken just as the 1940 voting study was being completed, the earliest of the three studies was conducted in a small town in New Jersey. It began by asking a sample of 86 respondents to name the people to whom they turned for information and advice regarding a variety of matters. Hundreds of names were mentioned in response, and those who were designated four times or more were considered opinion leaders. These influentials were then sought out and interviewed.[17]

[15]Lazarsfeld, Berelson, and Gaudet, *op. cit.*, pp. 49–50.

[16]The Elmira study will be omitted at this point because its design is essentially the same as that of the 1940 voting study except for the important fact that it obtained from each respondent considerably more information about the vote-intentions of others in his environment, the kinds of people he talks with, etc., than was done in *The People's Choice*.

[17]Merton, *op. cit.*, pp. 184–185.

Here, then, is the initial attempt, on a pilot scale, to solve the problem of research design posed by *The People's Choice*. To locate influentials, this study suggests, begin by asking somebody, "Who influences you?" and proceed from the persons influenced to those who are designated as influential.

Two important differences between this study and the 1940 voting study must be pointed out. First, there is a difference in the conception of opinion leadership. Whereas the voting study regards any advice-giver as an opinion leader if he influences even one other person (such as a husband telling his wife for whom to vote), the leaders singled out by the criterion employed in Rovere were almost certainly wielders of wider influence.

Secondly, the voting study, at least by implication, was interested in such questions as the extent of the role of interpersonal influence in decision-making and its relative effectiveness compared to the mass media. The Rovere study took for granted the importance of this kind of influence, and proceeded to try to find the people who play key roles in its transmission.

A final point to make in connection with the design of this study is that it makes use of the initial interviews almost exclusively to *locate* opinion leaders and hardly at all to explore the *relationships* between leaders and followers. Once the leaders were designated, almost exclusive attention was given to classifying them into different types, studying the communications behavior of the different types and the interaction among the leaders themselves, but very little attention was given to the interaction between the leaders and the original informants who designated them.

2. *The Decatur study*, carried out in 1945–46, tried to go a step further.[18] Like the voting study, but unlike Rovere, it tried to account for decisions—specific instances in which the effect of various influences could be discerned and assessed. Like Rovere, but unlike the voting study, it provided for interviews with the persons whom individuals in the initial sample had credited as influential in the making of recent decisions (in the realms of marketing, movie-going, and public affairs). The focus of the study this time was not on the opinion leaders alone, but (1) on the relative importance of personal influence and (2) on the person who named the leader as well as the leader—the advisor-advisee dyad.

Ideally, then, this study could ask whether opinion leaders tended to be from the same social class as their followers or whether the tend-

[18]Katz and Lazarsfeld, *op. cit.*, Part Two.

ency was for influence to flow from the upper class downwards. Were members of the dyads likely to be of the same age, the same sex, etc.? Was the leader more interested in the particular sphere of influence than his advisee? Was he more likely to be exposed to the mass media?

Just as the dyad could be constructed by proceeding from an advisee to his adviser, it was also possible to begin the other way around by talking first to a person who claimed to have acted as an adviser, and then locating the person he said he had influenced. The Decatur study tried this too. Using the same kind of self-designating questions employed in the voting study, persons who designated themselves as influential were asked to indicate the names of those whom they had influenced. By "snowballing" to the people thus designated, there arose the opportunity not only to study the interaction between adviser and advisee but also to explore the extent to which people who designated themselves as influential were confirmed in their self-evaluations by those whom they allegedly had influenced. Proceeding in this way, the researchers hoped to be able to say something about the validity of the self-designating technique.[19]

The authors of *The People's Choice* had said that "asking people to whom they turn and then investigating the interaction between advisers and advisees . . . would be extremely difficult if not impossible." And, in fact, it proved to be extremely difficult. Many problems were encountered in the field work, the result of which was that not all the "snowball" interviews could be completed.[20] In many parts of the analysis of the data, therefore, it was necessary to revert to comparisons of leaders and non-leaders, imputing greater influence to groups with higher concentrations of self-designated leadership. Yet, in principle, it was demonstrated that a study design taking account of interpersonal relations was both possible and profitable to execute.

But about the time it became evident that this goal was within reach, the goal itself began to change. It began to seem desirable to take account of chains of influence longer than those involved in the dyad; and hence to view the adviser-advisee dyad as one component of a more elaborately structured social group.

[19]About two-thirds of the alleged influencees confirmed the fact that a conversation had taken place between themselves and the self-designated influential on the subject-matter in question. Of these, about 80 per cent further confirmed that they had received advice. The extent of confirmation is considerably less in the realm of public affairs than it is in marketing or fashion. *Ibid.*, pp. 149–161 and 353–362.

[20]Partly this was due to inability to locate the designated people, but partly, too, to the fact that original respondents did not always know the person who had influenced them as is obvious, for example, in the case of a woman copying another woman's hat style, etc. See *Ibid.*, pp. 362–363.

These changes came about gradually and for a variety of reasons. First of all, findings from the Decatur study and from the later Elmira study revealed that the opinion leaders themselves often reported that their own decisions were influenced by still other people.[21] It began to seem desirable, therefore, to think in terms of the opinion leaders of opinion leaders.[22] Secondly, it became clear that opinion leadership could not be viewed as a "trait" which some people possess and others do not, although the voting study sometimes implied this view. Instead, it seemed quite apparent that the opinion leader is influential at certain times and with respect to certain substantive areas by virtue of the fact that he is "empowered" to be so by other members of his group. Why certain people are chosen must be accounted for not only in demographic terms (social status, sex, age, etc.) but also in terms of the structure and values of the groups of which both adviser and advisee are members. Thus, the unexpected rise of young men to opinion leadership in traditional groups, when these groups faced the new situations of urbanization and industrialization, can be understood only against the background of old and new patterns of social relations within the group and of old and new patterns of orientation to the world outside the group.[23] Reviewing the literature of small group research hastened the formulation of this conception.[24]

One other factor shaped the direction of the new program as well. Reflecting upon the Decatur study, it became clear that while one could talk about the role of various influences in the making of fashion *decisions by individuals*, the study design was not adequate for the study of fashion in the aggregate—*fashion as a process of diffusion*—as long as it did not take account of either the content of the decision or the time factor involved. The decisions of the "fashion changers" studied in Decatur might have cancelled each other out: while Mrs. X reported a change from Fashion A to Fashion B, Mrs. Y might have been reporting a change from B to A. What is true for fashion is true for any other diffusion phenomenon: to study it, one must trace the flow of some specific item over time. Combining this interest in diffusion with that of studying the role of more elaborate social networks of communication gave birth to a new study which focused

[21]*Ibid.*, p. 318; Berelson, Lazarsfeld, and McPhee, *op. cit.*, p. 110.

[22]This was actually tried at one point in the Decatur study. See Katz and Lazarsfeld, *op. cit.*, pp. 283–287.

[23]See, for example, the articles by Eisenstadt, *op. cit.*, and Glock, *op. cit.*; the Rovere study, too, takes careful account of the structure of social relations and values in which influentials are embedded, and discusses the various avenues to influentiality open to different kinds of people.

[24]Reported in Part I of Katz and Lazarsfeld, *op. cit.*

on (1) a specific item, (2) diffusion over time, (3) through the social structure of an entire community.

3. *The drug study.* This study was conducted to determine the way in which doctors make decisions to adopt new drugs. This time, when it came to designing a study which would take account of the possible role of interpersonal influence among physicians, it became clear that there were so few physicians (less than one and one-half per 1000 population) that it was feasible to interview all members of the medical profession in several cities. If all doctors (or all doctors in specialties concerned with the issue at hand) could be interviewed, then there would be no doubt that all adviser-advisee pairs would fall within the sample. All such pairs could then be located within the context of larger social groupings of doctors, which could be measured by sociometric methods.

Doctors in the relevant specialties in four midwestern cities were interviewed. In addition to questions on background, attitudes, drug-use, exposure to various sources of information and influence, and the like, each doctor was also asked to name the three colleagues he saw most often socially, the three colleagues with whom he talked most frequently about cases, and the three colleagues to whom he looked for information and advice.[25]

In addition to the opportunity of mapping the networks of interpersonal relations, the drug study also provided for the two other factors necessary for a true diffusion study: attention to a specific item in the course of gaining acceptance, and a record of this diffusion over time. This was accomplished by means of an audit of prescriptions on file in the local pharmacies of the cities studied, which made it possible to date each doctor's earliest use of a particular new drug—a drug which had gained widespread acceptance a few months before the study had begun. Each doctor could thus be classified in terms of the promptness of his decision to respond to the innovation, and in terms of other information provided by the prescription audit.

Altogether, compared with the earlier studies, the drug study imposes a more objective framework—both psychological and sociological—on the decision. First of all, the decision-maker himself is not the only source of information concerning his decision. Objective data from the prescription record are used as well. Secondly, the role of different influences is assessed not only on the basis of the decision-maker's own reconstruction of the event, but also on the basis of objective correlations from which inferences concerning the flow of

[25]See footnote 7.

influence can be drawn. For example, doctors who adopted the new drug early were more likely to be participants in out-of-town medical specialty meetings than those who adopted it later.

Similarly, it is possible to infer the role of social relations in doctor's decision-making not only from the doctor's own testimony concerning the role of social influences but also from the doctor's "location" in the interpersonal networks mapped by the sociometric questions. Thus, on the basis of sociometric data, it is possible to classify doctors according to their integration into the medical community, or the degree of their influence, as measured by *the number of times* they are named by their colleagues as friends, discussion-partners, and consultants. They can also be classified according to their membership in one or another network of clique, as indicated by *who* names them. Using the first measure makes it possible to investigate whether or not the more influential doctors adopt a drug earlier than those who are less influential. From the second kind of analysis one can learn, for example, whether or not those doctors who belong to the same sub-groups have similar drug-use patterns. In this way, it becomes possible to weave back and forth between the doctor's own testimony about his decisions and the influences involved, on the one hand, and the more objective record of his decisions and of the influences to which he has been exposed, on the other hand.

Note that the networks of social relations in this study are mapped "prior" to the introduction of the new drug being studied, in the sense that friendship, consultation, and so on, are recorded independently of any particular decision the doctor has made. The study is concerned with the potential relevance of various parts of these sociometric structures to the transmission of influence. For example, it is possible to point to the parts of the structure which are "activated" upon the introduction of a new drug, and to describe the sequence of diffusion of the drug as it gains acceptance by individuals and groups in the community. While the Decatur study could hope to examine only the particular face-to-face relationship which had been influential in a given decision, the drug study can locate this relationship against the background of the entire web of *potentially* relevant relationships within which the doctor is embedded.

THE FINDINGS OF STUDIES SUBSEQUENT TO *THE PEOPLES CHOICE*

Having examined the *designs* of these studies, the next step is to explore their *findings* insofar as these are relevant to the hypothesis about the two-step flow of communication. It will be useful to return to the three categories already singled out in discussing *The People's Choice*: (1) the impact of personal influence; (2) the flow of personal influence; and (3) opinion leaders and the mass media. Evidence from the three studies just reported, as well as from the 1948 Elmira study[26] and from others, will be brought together here; but in every case the characteristics of each study's design must be borne in mind in evaluating the evidence presented.

The Impact of Personal Influence

1. *Personal and the mass media influence*. The 1940 study indicated that personal influence affected voting decisions more than the mass media did, particularly in the case of those who changed their minds during the course of the campaign. The Decatur study went on to explore the relative impact of personal influences and the mass media in three other realms: marketing, fashions and movie-going. Basing its conclusions on the testimony of the decision-makers themselves, and using an instrument for evaluating the relative effectiveness of the various media which entered into the decisions, the Decatur study again found that personal influence figured both more frequently and more effectively than any of the mass media.[27]

In the analysis to date, the drug study has not approached the problem of the relative effectiveness of the various media from the point of view of the doctor's own reconstruction of what went into the making of his decision. Comparing mere frequency of mention of different media, it is clear that colleagues are by no means the most frequently mentioned source. Nevertheless, exploration of the factors related to whether the doctor's decision to adopt a drug came early or late indicates that the factor most strongly associated with the time of adoption of the new drug is the extent of the doctor's integration in the medical community. That is, the more frequently a doctor is named by his colleagues as a friend or a discussion partner, the more likely he is to be an innovator with respect to the new drug. Extent of integration proves to be a more important factor than any background factor (such as age, medical school, or income of patients), or any other source of influence (such as readership of medical journals) that was examined.

Investigation of why integration is related to innovation suggests two

[26]Berelson, Lazarsfeld, and McPhee, *op. cit.*
[27]Katz and Lazarsfeld, *op. cit.*, pp. 169–186.

central factors: (1) interpersonal communication—doctors who are integrated are more in touch and more up-to-date; and (2) social support—doctors who are integrated feel more secure when facing the risks of innovation in medicine.[28] Thus the drug study, too, provides evidence of the strong impact of personal relations—even in the making of scientific decisions.

2. *Homogeneity of opinion in primary groups.* The effectiveness of interpersonal influence, as it is revealed in the studies under review, is reflected in the homogeneity of opinions and actions in primary groups. The medium of primary group communication is, by definition, person-to-person. Both of the voting studies indicate the high degree of homogeneity of political opinion among members of the same families, and among co-workers and friends. The effectiveness of such primary groups in pulling potential deviates back into line is demonstrated by the fact that those who changed their vote intentions were largely people who, early in the campaign, had reported that they intended to vote differently from their family or friends.[29]

The drug study, too, was able to examine the extent of homogeneity in the behavior of sociometrically related doctors, and was able to demonstrate that there were situations where similar behavior could be observed. For example, it was found that, when called upon to treat the more puzzling diseases, doctors were likely to prescribe the same drug as their sociometric colleagues. The study also showed that, very early in the history of a new drug, innovating doctors who were sociometrically connected tended to adopt the new drug at virtually the same time. This phenomenon of homogeneity of opinion or behavior among interacting individuals confronting an unclear or uncertain situation which calls for action has often been studied by sociologists and social psychologists.[30]

3. *The various roles of the media.* The 1940 voting study explored some of the reasons why personal influence might be expected to be more influential in changing opinions than the

[28]On the relationship between social integration and self-confidence in a work situation, see Peter M. Blau, *The Dynamics of Bureaucracy* (Chicago: University of Chicago Press, 1955), pp. 126–129.

[29]Lazarsfeld, Berelson, and Gaudet, *op. cit.*, pp. 137–145; Berelson, Lazarsfeld, and McPhee, *op. cit.*, pp. 94–101, 120–122.

[30]That men, faced with an unstructured situation, look to each other to establish a "social reality" in terms of which they act, is a central theme in the work of Durkheim, Kurt Lewin, and his disciples, H. S. Sullivan ("consensual validation"), and in the studies of Sherif, Asch, and others.

mass media: It is often non-purposive; it is flexible; it is trustworthy. It was suggested that the mass media more often play a reinforcing role in the strengthening of predispositions and of decisions already taken. Nevertheless, it was assumed that the various media and personal influence are essentially competitive, in the sense that a given decision is influenced by one *or* the other. The Decatur study tended toward this assumption too, but at one point the study does attempt to show that different media play different parts in the decision-making process and take patterned positions in a sequence of several influences. The drug study elaborates on the roles of the media even further, distinguishing between media that "inform" and media that "legitimate" decisions. Thus in the doctors' decisions, professional media (including colleagues) seem to play a legitimating role, while commercial media play an informing role.

The Flow of Personal Influence

The 1940 voting study found that opinion leaders were not concentrated in the upper brackets of the population but were located in almost equal proportions in every social group and stratum. This finding led to efforts in subsequent studies to establish the extent to which this was true in areas other than election campaigns and also to ascertain what it is that *does* distinguish opinion leaders from those whom they influence.

The first thing that is clear from the series of studies under review is that the subject matter concerning which influence is transmitted has a lot to do with determining who will lead and who follow. Thus, the Rovere study suggests that within the broad sphere of public affairs one set of influentials is occupied with "local" affairs and another with "cosmopolitan" affairs.[31] The Decatur study suggests that in marketing, for example, there is a concentration of opinion leadership among older women with larger families, while in fashions and movie-going it is the young, unmarried girl who has a disproportionate chance of being turned to for advice. There is very little overlap of leadership: a leader in one sphere is not likely to be influential in another unrelated sphere as well.[32]

Yet, even when leadership in one or another sphere is heavily concentrated among the members of a particular group—as was the

[31]Merton, *op. cit.*, pp. 187–188.

[32]For a summary of the Decatur findings on the flow of interpersonal influence, see Katz and Lazarsfeld, *op. cit.*, pp. 327–334.

case with marketing leadership in Decatur—the evidence suggests that people still talk, most of all, to others like themselves. Thus, while the marketing leaders among the older "large-family wives" also influenced other kinds of women, most of their influence was directed to women of their own age with equally large families. In marketing, fashions, and movie-going, furthermore, there was no appreciable concentration of influentials in any of the three socio-economic levels. Only in public affairs was there a concentration of leadership in the highest status, and there was some slight evidence that influence flows from this group to individuals of lower status. The Elmira study also found opinion-leaders in similar proportions on every socio-economic and occupational level and found that conversations concerning the campaign went on, typically, between people of similar age, occupation, and political opinion.

What makes for the concentration of certain kinds of opinion leadership within certain groups? And when influential and influencee are outwardly alike—as they so often seem to be—what, if anything, distinguishes one from the other? Broadly, it appears that influence is related (1) to the *personification of certain values* (who one is); (2) to *competence* (what one knows); and (3) to *strategic social location* (whom one knows). Social location, in turn, divides into whom one knows within a group; and "outside."

Influence is often successfully transmitted because the influencee wants to be as much like the influential as possible.[33] That the young, unmarried girls are fashion leaders can be understood easily in a culture where youth and youthfulness are supreme values. This is an example where "who one is" counts very heavily.

But "what one knows" is no less important.[34] The fact is that older women, by virtue of their greater experience, are looked to as marketing advisers and that specialists in internal medicine—the most "scientific" of the practicing physicians—are the most frequently mentioned opinion leaders among the doctors. The influence of young people in the realm of movie-going can also be understood best in terms of their familiarity with the motion picture world. The Elmira study found slightly greater concentrations of opinion leadership among the more

[33]That leaders are, in a certain sense, the most conformist members of their groups—upholding whatever norms and values are central to the group—is a proposition which further illustrates this point. For an empirical illustration from a highly relevant study, see C. Paul Marsh and A. Lee Coleman, "Farmers' Practice Adoption Rates in Relation to Adoption Rates of Leaders," *Rural Sociology*, Vol. 19 (1954), pp. 180–183.

[34]The distinction between "what" and "whom" one knows is used by Merton, *op. cit.*, p. 197.

educated people on each socio-economic level, again implying the importance of competence. Finally, the influence of the "cosmopolitans" in Rovere rested on the presumption that they had large amounts of information.

It is, however, not enough to be a person whom others want to emulate, or to be competent. One must also be accessible. Thus, the Decatur study finds gregariousness—"whom one knows"—related to every kind of leadership. The Rovere study reports that the leadership of the "local" influentials is based on their central location in the web of interpersonal contacts. Similarly, studies of rumor transmission have singled out those who are "socially active" as agents of rumor.[35]

Of course, the importance of whom one knows is not simply a matter of the number of people with whom an opinion leader is in contact. It is also a question of whether the people with whom he is in touch happen to be interested in the area in which his leadership is likely to be sought. For this reason, it is quite clear that the greater interest of opinion leaders in the subjects over which they exert influence is not a sufficient explanation of their influence. While the voting studies as well as the Decatur study show leaders to be more interested, the Decatur study goes on to show that interest alone is not the determining factor.[36] In fashion, for example, a young unmarried girl is considerably more likely to be influential than a matron with an equally great interest in clothes. The reason, it is suggested, is that a girl who is interested in fashion is much more likely than a matron with an equally high interest to know other people who share her preoccupation, and thus is more likely than the matron to have followers who are interested enough to ask for her advice. In other words, it takes two to be a leader—a leader and a follower.

Finally, there is the second aspect of "whom one knows." An individual may be influential not only because people within his group look to him for advice but also because of whom he knows outside his group.[37] Both the Elmira and Decatur studies found that men are more likely than women to be opinion leaders in the realm of public affairs and this, it is suggested, is because they have more of a chance to get outside the home to meet people and talk politics. Similarly, the Elmira study indicated that opinion leaders belonged to more organi-

[35]Gordon W. Allport and Leo J. Postman, *The Psychology of Rumor* (New York: Henry Holt, 1943), p. 183.

[36]Katz and Lazarsfeld, *op. cit.*, pp. 249–252.

[37]It is interesting that a number of studies have found that the most integrated persons within a group are also likely to have more contacts outside the group than others. One might have expected the more marginal members to have more contacts outside. For example, see Blau, *op. cit.*, p. 128.

zations, more often knew workers for the political parties, and so on, than did others. The drug study found that influential doctors could be characterized in terms of such things as their more frequent attendance at out-of-town meetings and the diversity of places with which they maintained contact, particularly far-away places. It is interesting that a study of the farmer-innovators responsible for the diffusion of hybrid seed-corn in Iowa concluded that these leaders also could be characterized in terms of the relative frequency of their trips out of town.[38]

The Opinion Leaders and the Mass Media

The third aspect of the hypothesis of the two-step flow of communication states that opinion leaders are more exposed to the mass media than are those whom they influence. In *The People's Choice* this is supported by reference to the media behavior of leaders and non-leaders.

The Decatur study corroborated this finding, and went on to explore two additional aspects of the same idea.[39] First of all, it was shown that leaders in a given sphere (fashions, public affairs, etc.) were particularly likely to be exposed to the media appropriate to that sphere. This is essentially a corroboration of the Rovere finding that those who proved influential with regard to "cosmopolitan" matters were more likely to be readers of national news magazines, but that this was not at all the case for those influential with regard to "local" matters. Secondly, the Decatur study shows that at least in the realm of fashions, the leaders are not only more exposed to the mass media, but are also more affected by them in their own decisions. This did not appear to be the case in other realms, where opinion leaders, though more exposed to the media than non-leaders, nevertheless reported personal influence as the major factor in their decisions. This suggests that in some spheres considerably longer chains of person-to-person influence than the dyad may have to be traced back before one encounters any decisive influence by the mass media even though their contributory influence may be perceived at many points. This was

[38]Bryce Ryan and Neal Gross, *Acceptance and Diffusion of Hybrid Seed Corn in Two Iowa Communities* (Ames, Iowa: Iowa State College of Agriculture and Mechanic Arts, Research Bulletin 372), pp. 706–707. For a general summary, see Ryan and Gross, "The Diffusion of Hybrid Seed Corn in Two Iowa Communities," *Rural Sociology*, Vol. 8 (1942), pp. 15–24. An article, now in preparation, will point out some of the parallels in research design and in findings between this study and the drug study.

[39]Katz and Lazarsfeld, *op. cit.*, pp. 309–320.

suggested by the Elmira study too. It found that the leaders, though more exposed to the media, also more often reported that they sought information and advice from other persons.[40]

Similarly, the drug study showed that the influential doctors were more likely to be readers of a large number of professional journals and valued them more highly than did doctors of lesser influence. But at the same time, they were as likely as other doctors to say that local colleagues were an important source of information and advice in their reaching particular decisions.

Finally, the drug study demonstrated that the more influential doctors could be characterized by their greater attention not only to medical journals, but to out-of-town meetings and contacts as well. This finding has already been discussed in the previous section treating the *strategic location* of the opinion leader with respect to "the world outside" his group. Considering it again under the present heading suggests that the greater exposure of the opinion leader to the mass media may only be a special case of the more general proposition that opinion leaders serve to relate their groups to relevant parts of the environment through whatever media happen to be appropriate. This more general statement makes clear the similar functions of big city newspapers for the Decatur fashion leader; of national news magazines for the "cosmopolitan" influentials of Rovere; of out-of-town medical meetings for the influential doctor; and of contact with the city for the farmer-innovator in Iowa[41] as well as for the newly-risen, young opinion leaders in underdeveloped areas throughout the world.[42]

CONCLUSIONS

Despite the diversity of subject matter with which they are concerned, the studies reviewed here constitute an example of continuity and cumulation both in research design and theoretical commitment. Piecing together the findings of the latter-day studies in the light of the original statement of the two-step flow hypothesis suggests the following picture.

Opinion leaders and the people whom they influence are very much alike and typically belong to the same primary groups of family,

[40]Berelson, Lazarsfeld, and McPhee, *op. cit.*, p. 110.

[41]Ryan and Gross, *op. cit.*, choose to explain "trips to the city" as another index of the non-traditional orientation of which innovation itself is also an index.

[42]See the forthcoming book by Lerner, *et. al* cited above.

friends and co-workers. While the opinion leader may be more interested in the particular sphere in which he is influential, it is highly unlikely that the persons influenced will be very far behind the leader in their level of interest. Influentials and influencees may exchange roles in different spheres of influence. Most spheres focus the group's attention on some related part of the world outside the group, and it is the opinion leader's function to bring the group into touch with this relevant part of its environment through whatever media are appropriate. In every case, influentials have been found to be more exposed to these points of contact with the outside world. Nevertheless, it is also true that, despite their greater exposure to the media, most opinion leaders are primarily affected not by the communication media but by still other people.

The main emphasis of the two-step flow hypothesis appears to be on only one aspect of interpersonal relations—interpersonal relations as channels of communication. But from the several studies reviewed, it is clear that these very same interpersonal relations influence the making of decisions in at least two additional ways. In addition to serving as networks of communication, interpersonal relations are also sources of pressure to conform to the group's way of thinking and acting, as well as sources of social support. The workings of group pressure are clearly evident in the homogeneity of opinion and action observed among voters and among doctors in situations of unclarity or uncertainty. The social support that comes from being integrated in the medical community may give a doctor the confidence required to carry out a resolution to adopt a new drug. Thus, interpersonal relations are (1) channels of information, (2) sources of social pressure, and (3) sources of social support, and each relates interpersonal relations to decision-making in a somewhat different way.[43]

The central methodological problem in each of the studies reviewed has been how to take account of interpersonal relations and still preserve the economy and representativeness which the random, cross-sectional sample affords. Answers to this problem range from asking individuals in the sample to describe the others with whom they interacted (Elmira), to conducting "snowball" interviews with influen-

[43]These different dimensions of interpersonal relations can be further illustrated by reference to studies which represent the "pure type" of each dimension. Studies of rumor flow illustrate the "channels" dimension; see, for example, Jacob L. Moreno, *Who Shall Survive* (Beacon, N. Y.: Beacon House, 1953), pp. 440–450. The study by Leon Festinger, Stanley Schachter and Kurt Back, *Social Pressures in Informal Groups* (New York: Harper and Bros., 1950) illustrates the second dimension. Blau, *op. cit.*, pp. 126–129, illustrates the "social support" dimension.

tial-influencee dyads (Decatur), to interviewing an entire community (drug study). Future studies will probably find themselves somewhere in between. For most studies, however, the guiding principle would seem to be to build larger or smaller social molecules around each individual atom in the sample.[44]

[44]Various ways of accomplishing this have been discussed for the past two years in a staff seminar on "relational analysis" at the Bureau of Applied Social Research. The recent study by Seymour M. Lipset, Martin A. Trow, and James S. Coleman, *Union Democracy* (Glencoe, Ill.: The Free Press, 1956) illustrates one approach in its study of printers within the varying social contexts of the shops in which they are employed. The study by Riley and Riley, *op. cit.*, is another good example.

16.

SOCIAL CLASSES AND SPENDING BEHAVIOR*

Pierre Martineau

All societies place emphasis on some one structure which gives form to the total society and integrates all the other structures such as the family, the clique, voluntary association, caste, age, and sex groupings into a social unity.

Social stratification means any system of ranked statuses by which all the members of a society are placed in some kind of a superordinate and subordinate hierarchy. While money and occupation are important in the ranking process, there are many more factors, and these two alone do not establish social position. The concept of social class was designed to include this process of ranking people in superior and inferior social position by any and all factors.

CLASS SYSTEM

It has been argued that there cannot be a class system existent in America when most individuals do not have the slightest idea of its formal structure. Yet in actuality every individual senses that he is more at home with and more acceptable to certain groups than to others. In a study of department stores and shopping behavior, it was found that the Lower-Status woman is completely aware that, if she goes into High-Status department stores, the clerks and the other customers in the store will punish her in various subtle ways.

"The clerks treat you like a crumb," one woman expressed it. After trying vainly to be waited on, another woman bitterly complained that she was loftily told, "We thought you were a clerk."

The woman who is socially mobile gives considerable thought to the external symbols of status, and she frequently tests her status by shopping in department stores which she thinks are commensurate

*Reprinted from the *Journal of Marketing*, national quarterly publication of the American Marketing Association (October, 1958), pp. 121–130.

with her changing position. She knows that, if she does not dress correctly, if she does not behave in a certain manner to the clerks, if she is awkward about the proper cues, then the other customers and the clerks will make it very clear that she does not belong.

In another study, very different attitudes in the purchase of furniture and appliances involving this matter of status were found. Middle-class people had no hesitancy in buying refrigerators and other appliances in discount houses and bargain stores because they felt that they could not "go wrong" with the nationally advertised names. But taste in furniture is much more elusive and subtle because the brand names are not known; and, therefore, one's taste is on trial. Rather than commit a glaring error in taste which would exhibit an ignorance of the correct status symbols, the same individual who buys appliances in a discount house generally retreats to a status store for buying furniture. She needs the support of the store's taste.

In a very real sense, everyone of us in his consumption patterns and style of life shows an awareness that there is some kind of a superiority-inferiority system operating, and that we must observe the symbolic patterns of our own class.

Lloyd Warner and Paul Lunt have described a six-class system: the Upper-Upper, or old families; Lower-Upper, or the newly arrived; Upper-Middle, mostly the professionals and successful businessmen; Lower-Middle, or the white collar salaried class; Upper-Lower, or the wage earner, skilled worker group; and Lower-Lower, or the unskilled labor group.[1] For practical purposes, in order to determine the individual's class position, Warner and his associates worked out a rating index, not based on amount of income but rather on type of income, type of occupation, house type, and place of residence.

Although the Warner thesis has been widely used in sociology, it has not generally been employed in marketing. As a matter of fact, some critics in the social sciences have held that, since Warner's thesis rested essentially on studies of smaller cities in the 10,000-25,000 class, this same system might not exist in the more complex metropolitan centers, or might not be unravelled by the same techniques. Furthermore, many marketers did not see the application of this dimension to the individual's economic behavior, since the studies of Warner and his associates had mostly been concerned with the differences in the broad patterns of living, the moral codes, etc.

[1]W. Lloyd Warner and Paul Lunt, *The Social Life of a Modern Community* (New Haven: Yale University Press, 1950). Also, W. Lloyd Warner, Marchia Meeker, and Kenneth Eells, *Social Class in America* (Chicago: Science Research Associates, 1949).

SOCIAL CLASS IN CHICAGO

Under Warner's guidance, the *Chicago Tribune* has undertaken several extensive studies exploring social class in a metropolitan city, and its manifestations specifically in family buying patterns. The problem was to determine if such a social-class system did exist in metropolitan Chicago, if the dimensions and the relationships were at all similar to the smaller cities which were studied before the far-reaching social changes of the past fifteen years. The studies were undertaken to see if there were any class significances in the individual family's spending-saving patterns, retail store loyalties, and his expressions of taste in typical areas such as automobiles, apparel, furniture, and house types.

It seems that many an economist overlooks the possibility of any psychological differences between individuals resulting from different class membership. It is assumed that a rich man is simply a poor man with more money and that, given the same income, the poor man would behave exactly like the rich man. The *Chicago Tribune* studies crystallize a wealth of evidence from other sources that this is just not so, and that the Lower-Status person is profoundly different in his mode of thinking and his way of handling the world from the Middle-Class individual. Where he buys and what he buys will differ not only by economics but in symbolic value.

It should be understood, of course, that there are no hard and fast lines between the classes. Implicit in the notion of social class in America is the possibility of movement from one class to another. The "office-boy-to-president" saga is a cherished part of the American dream. Bobo Rockefeller illustrates the female counterpart: from coal miner's daughter to socialite. As a corollary of the explorations in class, the study also tried to be definitive about the phenomenon of social mobility—the movement from one class to another.

There are numerous studies of vertical mobility from the level of sociological analysis, mostly by comparing the individual's occupational status to that of his father. There are also studies at the level of psychological analysis. This study attempted to combine the two levels, to observe the individual's progress and also to understand something of the dynamics of the mobile person as compared to the stable individual. The attempt was to look both backward and forward: tracing such factors as occupation, place of residence, and religion back to parents and grandparents, and then where the family expected to be in the next five or ten years, what were the educational plans for each son, each daughter, a discussion of future goals.

Because this article is confined primarily to social class, this section may be concluded by saying that the studies show a very clear relationship between spend-saving aspirations and the factors of mobility-stability.

FRAMEWORK OF STUDY

Following are Warner's hypotheses and assumptions for the study:

I. Assumptions About Symbols and Values and About Saving of Money and Accumulation of Objects

Our society is acquisitive and pecuniary. On the one hand, the values and beliefs of Americans are pulled toward the pole of the accumulation of money by increasing the amount of money income and reducing its outgo. On the other hand, American values emphasize the accumulation of objects and products of technology for display and consumption. The self-regard and self-esteem of a person and his family, as well as the public esteem and respect of a valued social world around the accumulator, are increased or not by such symbols of accumulation and consumption.

The two sets of values, the accumulation of product symbols and the accumulation (saving) of money, may be, and usually are, in opposition.

General working hypotheses stemming from these assumptions were: (1) People are distributed along a range according to the two-value components, running from proportionately high savings, through mixed categories, to proportionately high accumulation of objects. (2) These value variations conform to social and personality factors present in all Americans.

II. Assumptions About Product Symbols, Savers, and Accumulations

American society is also characterized by social change, particularly technological change that moves in the direction of greater and greater production of more kinds and more numerous objects for consumption and accumulation.

Hypothesis: New varieties of objects will be most readily accepted by the accumulators, and most often opposed by the savers.

III. Assumptions About the Social Values of Accumulators and Savers

American society is characterized by basic cultural differences, one of them being social status. Social class levels are occupied by people, some of whom are upward mobile by intent and fact. Others are non-mobile, by intent and fact. The values which dictate judgments about actions, such as the kinds of objects which are consumed and accumulated, will vary by class level and the presence or absence of vertical mobility.

IV. Assumptions About the Personal Values of Accumulators and Savers

The personality components are distributed through the class levels and through the mobility types. By relating the social and personality components, it is possible to state a series of hypotheses about accumulators and savers as they are related to the object world around them, particularly to objects which are new and old to the culture, those which are imposing or not and those which are predominantly for display or for consumption.

At the direct, practical level, all of these theoretical questions can be summarized by one basic question: *What kinds of things are people likely to buy and not buy if they are in given class positions and if they are or are not socially mobile?* In other words, what is the effect on purchasing behavior of being in a particular social class, and being mobile or non-mobile?

If this is the crucial question, theoretically grounded, then a whole series of hypotheses can be laid out concerning values about money and values about buying various kinds of objects for consumption and for display. Some of these are:

1. *There will be a relationship between values held by a particular subject and the extent to which particular products exemplify those values.*
2. *There is a differential hierarchy of things for which it is worth spending money.*
3. *Veblen's theory that conspicuous expenditure is largely applied to the Upper Class is erroneous. It runs all the way through our social system.*

From these statements certain other hypotheses follow:

4. *At different class levels, symbols of mobility will differ.*

There is a differential hierarchy of things on which it is worth spending money. Class and mobility will be two of the dimensions that will differentiate—also personality and cultural background.

5. *The place in the home where these symbols will be displayed will shift at different class levels.*

The underlying assumption here is that there is a hierarchy of importance in the rooms of the house. This hierarchy varies with social class, mobility, age, ethnicity. The studies also revealed clear-cut patterns of taste for lamps, furnishings, house types, etc.

6. *The non-mobile people tend to rationalize purchases in terms of cost or economy.*

In other words, non-mobile people tend to be oriented more toward the pole of the accumulation of money. Purchases, then, are rationalized in terms of the savings involved.

The basic thesis of all the hypotheses on mobility is this: Whereas the stable individual would emphasize saving and security, the behavior of the mobile individual is characterized by spending for various symbols of upward movement. All of the evidence turned up indicates that this difference in values does exist, and furthermore that notable differences in personality dynamics are involved. For instance, the analysis of how families would make investments shows that stable people overwhelmingly prefer insurance, the symbol of security. By contrast, the mobile people at all levels prefer stocks, which are risk-taking. In Warner's words, the mobile individual acts as if he were free, white, and twenty-one, completely able to handle the world, and perfectly willing to gamble on himself as a sure bet to succeed.

Returning to the factor of social class, in this study class placement was based on a multi-state probability area sample of metropolitan Chicago, involving 3,880 households. It was found that the matter of placement could not be done by the relatively simple scoring sufficient for the smaller cities. To secure house typings, it was necessary to provide the field investigators with photographs covering a wide range of dwelling types, all the way from exclusive apartments to rooms over stores. Because of the very complexity of metropolitan life, occupations provided the biggest problem. To solve this operational problem, it was necessary to construct an exhaustive list of occupational types involving degree of responsibility and training required by each. The data finally used to calculate the Index of Status Characteristics (ISC) were:

(weighted by 5) Occupation (from 1 to 7 broad categories)
(weighted by 4) Sources of Income (from 1 to 7 types)
(weighted by 3) Housing Type (from 1 to 7 types)

The sum of the individual's weighted scores was used to predict his social class level as follows:[2]

ISC scores	*Predicted social class placement*
12–21	Upper class
22–37	Upper-middle class
38–51	Lower-middle class
52–66	Upper-lower class
67–84	Lower-lower class

The study very clearly shows that there is a social-class system operative in a metropolitan area which can be delineated. Furthermore, class membership is an important determinant of the individual's economic behavior, even more so than in the smaller city. The one department store in the smaller city may satisfy almost everyone, whereas in the metropolitan city the stores become sharply differentiated.

This is the social-class structure of Metropolitan Chicago, typifying the transformation of the formerly agrarian Midwestern cities from Pittsburgh to Kansas City into a series of big milltowns:

Upper and upper-middle	8.1%
Lower-middle	28.4%
Upper-lower	44.0%
Lower-lower	19.5%

While the Old Families and the Newly Arrived are still recognizable as types, they constitute less than 1 per cent of the population. A similar study in Kansas City turned up so few that they could not be counted at all. On the other hand, we see the emergence of a seventh class, the Upper-Lower "Stars" or Light-Blue Collar Workers. They are the spokesmen of the Upper-Lower Class groups—high income individuals, who have the income for more ostentatious living than the average factory worker but who lack the personal skills or desire for high status by social mobility.

There is certainly a rough correlation between income and social class. But social class is a much richer dimension of meaning. There are so many facets of behavior which are explicable only on a basis of social class dynamics. For instance, this analysis of the purchase of household appliances in Chicago over a four-year period shows a very different picture by income and by class:

[2]Dr. Bevode McCall helped to solve the ISC scoring problem for Metropolitan Chicago.

NINE APPLIANCE TYPES—FOUR-YEAR PERIOD

By Income	
Over $7,000	36.2%
4,000–6,999	46.0%
Under 4,000	17.8%
By Social Class	
Upper and upper-middle	16.6%
Lower-middle	29.2%
Upper-lower	45.7%
Lower-lower	8.5%

Income analysis shows that the lowest income group represents an understandably smaller market, but nevertheless a market. Social-class analysis highlights a fundamental difference in attitudes toward the home between the two lower classes. The Upper-Lower Class man sees his home as his castle, his anchor to the world, and he loads it down with hardware—solid heavy appliances—as his symbols of security. The Lower-Lower Class individual is far less interested in his castle, and is more likely to spend his income for flashy clothes or an automobile. He is less property-minded, and he has less feeling about buying and maintaining a home.

Several *Tribune* studies have explored the way of life and the buying behavior in many new suburbs and communities. All of them quickly become stratified along social-class and mobility dimensions, and, therefore, differ tremendously among themselves. *Fortune* has reported on Park Forest, Illinois, a middle-class suburb of 30,000 and only ten years old. It is characterized by high degrees of both upward and geographical mobility. The people are overwhelmingly those who had moved from other parts of the United States, who had few local roots, and who consequently wanted to integrate themselves in friendship groups. But this was not typical of the new Lower-Status suburbs where the women did relatively little fraternizing. It was not typical of the new Upper-Middle Class mobile suburbs where the people were preoccupied with status symbols, not in submerging themselves in the group.

One new community had crystallized as being for Higher-Status Negroes. This was a resettlement project with relatively high rents for Negroes. Eighty-five per cent of them had come from the South where social class was compressed. But, as soon as they came to Chicago, the class system opened up and they were anxious to establish a social distance between themselves and other Negroes. Almost all of them said they enjoyed the "peace and quiet" of their neighborhood, which was their way of insisting that they were not like the "noisy" lower-class Negroes. They deliberately avoided the stores patronized by other Negroes.

CHOICE OF STORE

All of these studies reveal the close relation between choice of store, patterns of spending, and class membership. In the probability sample delineating social class, such questions were asked in the total metropolitan area as:

> If you were shopping for a good dress, at which store would you be most likely to find what you wanted?
> For an everyday dress?
> For living room furniture?
> At which store do you buy most of your groceries?

To assume that all persons would wish to shop at the glamorous High-Status stores is utterly wrong. People are very realistic in the way they match their values and expectations with the status of the store. The woman shopper has a considerable range of ideas about department stores; but these generally become organized on a scale ranking from very High-Social Status to the Lowest-Status and prestige. The social status of the department store becomes the primary basis for its definition by the shopper. This is also true of men's and women's apparel stores, and furniture stores, on the basis of customer profiles. The shopper is not going to take a chance feeling out of place by going to a store where she might not fit.

No matter what economics are involved, she asks herself who are the other customers in the store, what sort of treatment can she expect at the hands of the clerks, will the merchandise be the best of everything, or lower priced and hence lower quality? Stores are described as being for the rich, for the average ordinary people, or for those who have to stretch their pennies.

The most important function of retail advertising today, when prices and quality have become so standard, is to permit the shopper to make social class identification. This she can do from the tone and physical character of the advertising. Of course, there is also the factor of psychological identification. Two people in the same social class may want different stores. One may prefer a conservative store, one may want the most advanced styling. But neither will go to stores where they do not "fit," in a social-class sense.

In contrast to the independent food retailer, who obviously adapts to the status of the neighborhood, the chain grocers generally invade many income areas with their stores. Nevertheless, customer profiles show that each chain acquires a status definition. The two largest grocery chains in the Chicago area are A&P and Jewel; yet they draw very different customer bodies. A&P is strong with the mass market, whereas Jewel has its strength among the Middle Class.

While the national brand can and often does cut across classes, one can think of many product types and services which do have social class labels. The Upper-Middle Class person rarely travels by motor coach because none of his associates do so, even though there is certainly nothing wrong with this mode of transportation. On the other hand, even with low air-coach fares, one does not see many factory workers or day laborers on vacation around airports. Such sales successes as vodka and tonic water, and men's deodorants and foreign sports cars, were accomplished without benefit of much buying from this part of the market.

COMMUNICATION SKILLS

There is also a relation between class and communication abilities which has significance for marketing. The kind of super-sophisticated and clever advertising which appears in the *New Yorker* and *Esquire* is almost meaningless to Lower-Status people. They cannot comprehend the subtle humor; they are baffled by the bizarre art. They have a different symbol system, a very different approach to humor. In no sense does this imply that they lack intelligence or wit. Rather their communication skills have just been pressed into a different mold.

Here again, style of advertising helps the individual to make class identification. Most of the really big local television success stories in Chicago have been achieved by personalities who radiate to the mass that this is where they belong. These self-made businessmen who do the announcing for their own shows communicate wonderfully well with the mass audience. While many listeners switch off their lengthy and personal commercials, these same mannerisms tell the Lower-Status individual that here is someone just like himself, who understands him.

Social Research, Inc., has frequently discussed the class problem in marketing by dividing the population into Upper-Middle or quality market; the middle majority which combines both the Lower-Middle and Upper-Lower; and then the Lower-Lower. The distinction should be drawn between the Middle Classes and the Lower-Status groups. In several dozen of these store profiles, there is scarcely an instance where a store has appeal to the Lower-Middle and Upper-Lower classes with anything like the same strength.

It would be better to make the break between the Middle Class, representing one-third of the population and the Lower-Status or Working-Class or Wage-Earner group, representing two-thirds of metropolitan Chicago. This permits some psychological distinctions to be drawn between the Middle-Class individual and the individual who is not a part of the Middle-Class system of values. Even though this is the dominant American value system, even though Middle-Class Americans have been taught by their parents that it is the only value system, this Lower-Status individual does not necessarily subscribe to it.

WHO SAVES, WHO SPENDS?

Another important set of behavioral distinctions related to social class position was revealed in the "save-spend aspiration" study. The question was asked: "Suppose your income was doubled for the next ten years, what would you do with the increased income?" This is a fantasy question taken out of the realm of any pressing economic situation to reflect aspirations about money. The coding broke down the answers to this question into five general categories: (1) the mode of saving, (2) the purpose of saving, (3) spending which would consolidate past gains, meet present defensive needs, prepare for future self-advancement, (4) spending which is "self-indulgent-centered," (5) spending which is "house-centered."

Here are some of our findings:[3] The higher the individual's class position, the more likely is he to express some saving aspirations. Conversely, the lower his class position, the more likely is he to mention spending only. Moreover the higher the status, the more likely is the individual to specify *how* he will save his money, which is indicative of the more elaborate financial learning required of higher status.

Proceeding from the more general categories (such as saving versus spending only) to more specific categories (such as non-investment

[3]The saving-spending aspiration analysis was carried out by Roger Coup, graduate student at the University of Chicago.

versus investment saving and the even more specific stock versus real estate investment, etc.) an increasingly sharper class differentiation is found. It is primarily *non-investment* saving which appeals to the Lower-Status person. Investment saving, on the other hand, appeals above all to the Upper-Status person.

Investors almost always specify how they will invest. And here in mode of investment are examples of the most sharply class-differentiated preferences. Intangible forms of investment like stock and insurance are very clearly distinguished as Upper-Status investments. Nearly four times as many Upper-Middles select insurance as would be expected by chance, whereas only one-fifth of the Lower-Lowers select it as would be expected by chance. By contrast, Lower-Status people have far greater preference for tangible investments, specifically ownership of real estate, a farm, or a business.

To sum up, Middle-Class people usually have a place in their aspirations for some form of saving. This saving is most often in the form of investment, where there is a risk, long-term involvement, and the possibility of higher return. Saving, investment saving, and intangible investment saving—successively each of these become for them increasingly symbols of their higher status.

The aspirations of the Lower-Status person are just as often for spending as they are for saving. This saving is usually a non-investment saving where there is almost no risk, funds can be quickly converted to spendable cash, and returns are small. When the Lower-Status person does invest his savings, he will be specific about the mode of investment, and is very likely to prefer something tangible and concrete—something he can point at and readily display.

Turning from mode of saving to purpose of saving, very significant class relationships are likewise evident. Consider the verbalization of saving purpose. Lower-Status people typically explain why one should save—why the very act of saving is important. On the other hand, Middle-Class people do not, as if saving is an end-in-itself, the merits of which are obvious and need not be justified.

Spending is the other side of the coin. Analysis of what people say they will spend for shows similar class-related desires. All classes mention concrete, material artifacts such as a new car, some new appliance. But the Lower-Status people stop here. Their accumulations are artifact-centered, whereas Middle-Class spending-mentions are experience-centered. This is spending where one is left typically with only a memory. It would include hobbies, recreation, self-education and travel. The wish to travel, and particularly foreign travel, is almost totally a Middle-Class aspiration.

Even in their fantasies, people are governed by class membership. In his daydreaming and wishful thinking, the Lower-Status individual will aspire in different patterns from the Middle-Class individual.

PSYCHOLOGICAL DIFFERENCES

This spending-saving analysis has very obvious psychological implications to differentiate between the classes. Saving itself generally suggests foresightedness, the ability to perceive long-term needs and goals. Non-investment saving has the characteristics of little risk-taking and of ready conversion, at no loss, into immediate expenditures—the money can be drawn out of the account whenever the bank is open. Investment spending, on the other hand, has the characteristics of risk-taking (a gamble for greater returns) and of delayed conversion, with possible loss, to expenditures on immediate needs.

Here are some psychological contrasts between two different social groups:

Middle Class

1. Pointed to the future
2. His viewpoint embraces a long expanse of time
3. More urban identification
4. Stresses rationality
5. Has a well-structured sense of the universe
6. Horizons vastly extended or not limited
7. Greater sense of choice-making
8. Self-confident, willing to take risks
9. Immaterial and abstract in his thinking
10. Sees himself tied to national happenings

Lower Status

1. Pointed to the present and past
2. Lives and thinks in a short expanse of time
3. More rural in identification
4. Non-rational essentially
5. Vague and unclear structuring of the world
6. Horizons sharply defined and limited
7. Limited sense of choice-making
8. Very much concerned with security and insecurity
9. Concrete and perceptive in his thinking
10. World revolves around his family and body

CONCLUSIONS

The essential purpose of this article was to develop three basic premises which are highly significant for marketing:

I. *There is a social-class system operative in metropolitan markets, which can be isolated and described.*

II. *It is important to realize that there are far-reaching psychological differences between the various classes.* They do not handle the world in the same fashion. They tend not to think in the same way. As one tries to communicate with the Lower-Status group, it is imperative to sense that their goals and mental processes differ from the Middle-Class group.

III. *Consumption patterns operate as prestige symbols to define class membership, which is a more significant determinant of economic behavior than mere income.* Each major department store, furniture store, and chain-grocery store has a different "pulling power" on different status groups. The usual customers of a store gradually direct the store's merchandising policies into a pattern which works. The interaction between store policy and consumer acceptance results in the elimination of certain customer groups and the attraction of others, with a resulting equilibration around a reasonably stable core of specific customer groups who think of the store as appropriate for them.

Income has always been the marketer's handiest index to family consumption standards. But it is a far from accurate index. For instance, the bulk of the population in a metropolitan market today will fall in the middle-income ranges. This will comprise not only the traditional white collar worker, but the unionized craftsman and the semi-skilled worker with their tremendous income gains of the past decade. Income-wise, they may be in the same category. But their buying behavior, their tastes, their spending-saving aspirations can be poles apart. Social-class position and mobility-stability dimensions will reflect in much greater depth each individual's style of life.

17. THE ADOPTION PROCESS*

For many products, the process of adoption follows a rather uniform pattern, from the time the new product is developed until it is widely accepted by the ultimate consumers. More is known about the adoption of agricultural products and practices than about others. Rural sociologists have been concerned with the introduction of new practices and with new product adoption in agriculture for a number of years, and they have systematically studied the process by which change takes place. In addition, some studies have been made of other kinds of innovation, including the adoption by doctors of new wonder drugs for treatment,[1] the adoption of new educational practices by school systems,[2] and the adoption of color television.[3] The process of adoption in all these cases has been quite similar. There are exceptions to the pattern; for example, black and white television. The general pattern appears so widely, however, that it is the central theme of this report.

Researchers have charted the course of a new product by determining *when* people adopt it. The curve which results is a simple one, the well known probability curve, in cumulative form.[4] A few people adopt a product at first, then a few more, followed by a rather sharp increase and finally a leveling off when most of the potential consumers have adopted the product.

*Reprinted from *The Adoption of New Products* (Ann Arbor: Foundation for Research on Human Behavior, 1959), pp. 1–8.

[1]E. Katz, "The Two-step Flow of Communication: an Up-to-date Report on an Hypothesis," *Public Opinion Quarterly* (1957), pp. 61–78 [see pp. 182–201 of this anthology — eds.]; and H. Menzel and E. Katz, "Social Relations and Innovation in the Medical Profession: The Epidemiology of a New Drug," *Public Opinion Quarterly* (1955–56), pp. 337–352.

[2]P. R. Mort and T. M. Pierce, *A Time Scale for Measuring the Adaptability of School Systems* (New York: Metropolitan School Study Council, 1947).

[3]Batton, Barton, Durstine and Osborn, *Colortown.*

[4]North Central Rural Sociology Committee, *The Diffusion Process* (Ames: Agricultural Extension Service, Iowa State College, Special Report No. 18, 1957).

Such a curve is presented in general form in Figure 1. No scale is given for the time dimension, because this differs from product to product. A number of studies indicate, however, the *form* of the curve remains constant, and therefore that knowledge of the time required for a first relatively small group to adopt a new product will, by establishing the time scale for that product, make possible fairly accurate prediction of the rate of adoption by the rest of the applicable universe.

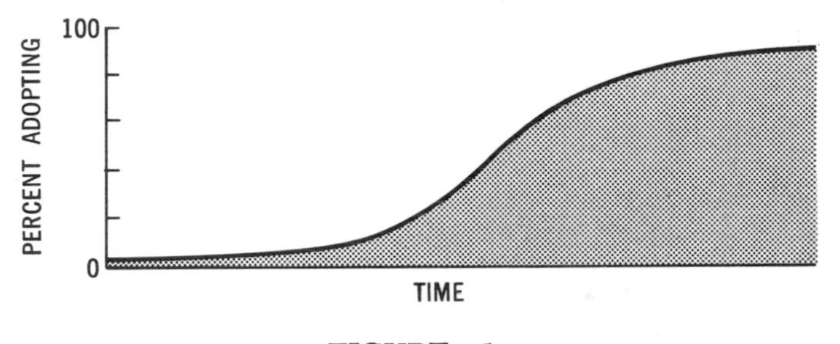

FIGURE 1.

THE KIND OF CHANGE

The time it takes from introduction to wide-spread acceptance depends, in part at least, on the kind of change involved. The adoption of a new product can be viewed as a special case of attitude change. Almost by definition, such a change encounters resistance. The new product or method usually alters or replaces something which is already part of the individual's pattern of thought. If the change under consideration is a really major one, it is quite likely that the attitudes and feelings associated with the old way are strongly held and will account for a great deal of resistance. On the other hand, if the change is trivial, the associated attitudes may be taken on easily. (They may also be cast off easily, of course.) Most new products or practices probably encounter resistance somewhere between these two extremes.

When new products are being adopted, there are different levels of *complexity* of change. The greater the complexity, the more resistance is aroused, and the longer the period required for adoption. Researchers have listed four levels of complexity in the changes usually confronting farmers who are adopting new products or practices.[5] Least

[5]E. A. Wilkening, "The Role of Communicating Agents in Technological Change in Agriculture," *Social Forces* (1956), pp. 361–367.

complex is a simple change in materials or equipment. Such a change might be the decision to try another brand of fertilizer or to increase the amount already being used. A change in technique is slightly more complex. The farmer must learn to use the new method and this may involve more risk. An example might be applying fertilizer along planted rows, instead of broadcast over the field. The third level involves both a change in materials and a change in technique. A farmer who has never used fertilizer faces such a change. He must adopt the new material, acquire the equipment to apply it, and learn how to use the equipment. The most complex change is a change of enterprise; for example, a change from cotton growing to dairying.

Obviously there are shadings in complexity among these four types of change, and other kinds of new products may involve a wider range of complexities than do farming practices. However, the level of complexity is an important factor in determining the time it takes for a new product to be adopted. Fifteen years elapsed between the introduction of hybrid seed corn and its adoption by almost 98 per cent of the farmers.[6] Other changes take longer. The adoption of new educational practices by school systems took 50 years.[7] Some changes take place quickly.

It is not always easy to tell how complex a change is involved in a new product. Hybrid corn is one example. Initially, this seemed like a simple change in materials. Actually, it was a far more complex change. Farmers feared the total reliance on commercial sources for seed corn, something they had previously produced for themselves. Furthermore, many farmers took pride in their ability to select good seed corn from their own crop, and they were accorded status for this skill. The new hybrid corn not only made the farmer feel more dependent, it also did away with an important source of prestige. A large majority of farmers had probably adopted hybrid corn within five years of the initial distribution, but it took fifteen years before almost all farmers were using it. Now, when a new hybrid variety of anything is introduced, it is adopted much more quickly. Examples are hybrid chickens and hybrid hogs.

The complexity of the change is only one important factor in determining the time required for adoption. There are others. For instance, *cost* is important. The more costly the item, the longer it

[6]B. Ryan and N. C. Gross, "The Diffusion of Hybrid Seed Corn in Two Iowa Communities," *Rural Sociology* (1943), pp. 15–24; and B. Ryan and N. C. Gross, *Acceptance and Diffusion of Hybrid Seed Corn in Two Iowa Communities* (Ames: Iowa Agricultural Experiment Station, Research Bulletin 372, 1950).

[7]P. R. Mort and T. M. Pierce, *op. cit.*

takes before it is widely adopted. *Rate of return* and *visibility of return* are also important. A change which has rapid and obvious results is adopted more quickly than a change with slower, less visible results. In the long run, of course, the change which produces slower results may return more, but it still is not adopted as quickly. A new fertilizer is likely to be adopted more quickly, for example, than soil conservation practices.

THE INDIVIDUAL ADOPTION PROCESS

The decision to adopt a new product is not simply a "yes" or "no" decision, nor is it something that happens all at once. When an individual is confronted with the possibility of change, he goes through several mental stages before he finally makes up his mind to adopt or not to adopt. Five stages in the decision-making process may be distinguished. Farmers readily recognized these stages when questioned regarding their decisions to make changes and adopt new products.

Awareness comes first. At this point, the farmer learns about the new product. He knows it exists, but he has only general information about it. The *interest or information* stage follows. If interested, the farmer begins to collect more specific information about the new product. If his interest continues to grow, he wants to know the potentialities of the new product for him; whether or not it will increase his income or contribute to other ends considered by him to be important. The next step is the *mental application or evaluation* stage. The farmer goes through the change mentally and asks himself, "How would I do it? Can I do it? If I do it, will I be better off?" The final stage before adoption is the *trial* stage. At this point the farmer tries the product out on a small scale if this is possible. Many farmers purchased a small can of weed spray and used it on their gardens before they used it on their crops on a large scale. A great many farmers planted six acres of hybrid seed corn the first year, the acreage one bushel of the new seed would sow. Some products cannot be tried out on a small scale, and it seems quite reasonable to expect such products to require a longer adoption time. However, people seem to be quite ingenious at finding ways to try new ideas. Some housewives prepared small amounts of food for freezing, and either rented locker space or used a neighbor's freezer before they gave up traditional canning methods and bought the necessary equipment for themselves. Marketing people have been aware of the value of free trials for many years. The trial stage appears to play a crucial role in the decision-making process. However, the other stages are important too, and probably give meaning to this final step before adoption. They should not be ignored.

The last stage is the *adoption* stage. At this point the farmer decides to adopt the new product and begins using it on a full scale. Presumably he is a "satisfied customer," at least until some other product comes along to replace it and the adoption process starts again.

ADOPTER CATEGORIES

Obviously, not all people adopt a new product at the same time. The adoption curve illustrates this point and suggests that some people arrive at a decision more quickly than others. Some people adopt very quickly. Others wait a long time before they take up the new product, and still others never adopt. There has been a great deal of interest in these individual differences and a great deal of speculation about "innovators," those who are first in a community to adopt a new product. To explore these individual differences, the Iowa State researchers took the data from a number of independent studies of new product adoption by farmers. They divided people into groups according to time of adoption,[8] and then studied each group. Significant differences appeared among them. These were the groups they distinguished and studied:

People Adopting			*Cumulative Total Adopting*
First	2.5%	Innovators	2.5%
Next	13.5%	Early adopters	16.0%
Next	34.0%	Early majority	50.0%
Next	34.0%	Late majority	84.0%
Last	16.0%	Laggards	100.0%

"Innovators" are arbitrarily defined here as the first 2.5 per cent to adopt the new product. Based on the data compiled, these generalizations appear for farm innovators.[9]

[8]For convenience in making comparative studies, researchers used standard deviations of a normal distribution to establish the percentage breaks between categories. People who fall within one standard deviation above the mean are considered in the early majority; people who are between one and two standard deviations above the mean are early adopters. Similarly, people within one standard deviation below the mean are late majority, etc.

[9]North Central Rural Sociology Committee, *How Farm People Accept New Ideas* (Ames: Iowa Agricultural Extension Service, Iowa State College, Special Report No. 15, 1955); and E. M. Rogers, "Categorizing the Adopters of Agricultural Practices," *Rural Sociology* (1943), pp. 15–24.

> They have larger than average farms, are well educated and usually come from well established families. They usually have a relatively high net worth and—probably more important—a large amount of risk capital. They can afford and do take calculated risks on new products. They are respected for being successful, but ordinarily do not enjoy the highest prestige in the community. Because innovators adopt new ideas so much sooner than the average farmer, they are sometimes ridiculed by their conservative neighbors. This neighborhood group pressure is largely ignored by the innovators, however. The innovators are watched by their neighbors, but they are not followed immediately in new practices.
>
> The activities of innovators often transcend local community boundaries. Rural innovators frequently belong to formal organizations at the county, regional, state, or national level. In addition, they are likely to have many informal contacts outside the community; they may visit with others many miles away who are also trying a new technique or product, or who are technical experts.

The "early adopters" are defined as the next 13.5 per cent of the people who adopt the new product. According to the researchers, early adopter farmers have the following characteristics.

> They are younger than the average farmer, but not necessarily younger than the innovators. They also have a higher than average education, and participate more in the formal activities of the community through such organizations as churches, the PTA, and farm organizations. They participate more than the average in agricultural cooperatives and in government agency programs in the community (such as Extension Service or Soil Conservation). In fact, there is some evidence that this group furnishes a disproportionate amount of the formal leadership (elected officers) in the community. The early adopters are also respected as good sources of new farm information by their neighbors.

The third category of adopters is the "early majority," the 34 per cent of people who bring the total adoption to 50 per cent. The number of adoptions increases rapidly after this group begins to adopt.

> The early majority are slightly above average in age, education, and farming experience. They have medium high social and economic status. They are less active in formal groups than innovators or early adopters, but more active than those who

> adopt later. In many cases they are not formal leaders in the community organizations, but they are active members in these organizations. They also attend Extension meetings and farm demonstrations.
>
> The people in this category are most likely to be informal rather than elected leaders. They have a following insofar as people respect their opinions, their "high morality and sound judgment." They are "just like their following, only more so." They must be sure an idea will work before they adopt it. If the informal leader fails two or three times, his following looks elsewhere for information and guidance. Because the informal leader has more limited resources than the early adopters and innovators, he cannot afford to make poor decisions; the social and economic costs are too high.
>
> These people tend to associate mainly in their own community. When people in the community are asked to name neighbors and friends with whom they talk over ideas, these early majority are named disproportionally frequently. On their part, they value highly the opinions their neighbors and friends hold about them, for this is their main source of status and prestige. The early majority may look to the early adopters for their new farm information.

The "late majority" are the fourth category. These are the 34 per cent of farmers who have adopted the new product after the average farmer is already using it.

> Those in this group have less education and are older than the average farmer. While they participate less actively in formal groups, they probably form the bulk of the membership in these formal organizations. Individually they belong to fewer organizations, are less active in organizational work, and take fewer leadership roles than the earlier adopters. They do not participate in as many activities outside the community as do people who adopt earlier.

The last category, the final 16 per cent of those who adopt a new idea, are the "laggards." This group may include the "non-adopters" as well if the new product is not used by everyone.

> They have the least education and are the oldest. They participate least in formal organizations, cooperatives, and government agency programs. They have the smallest farms and the

least capital. Many are suspicious of county Extension agents and agricultural salesmen.

These are some of the important differences among the adopter categories. They may provide useful guidelines for further exploration. For example, each of these categories plays an important role for the others in the adoption process. Innovators are the pioneers, and early adopters wait to see the innovators' results before trying the new product themselves. The early adopters, in turn, often influence the early majority. In addition, each of these categories seems to rely on different sources of information and influence, other than the sources already described.

III

Market Analysis

In addition to understanding consumer behavior, the marketing manager must be cognizant of factors which influence that behavior in particular markets. Consumer purchasing-patterns in a given market are shaped by the dynamic interactions of demand conditions, the institutional arrangement of firms, and the marketing strategies adopted by the firms. Systematic research is necessary to assess the effects of these forces on consumers so that the firm can take advantage of opportunities in the market.

Roberts provides an overview of research methodology and demonstrates the usefulness of the methods of science in market analysis. Lanzillotti's work empirically illustrates the value of scientific inquiry in marketing. His survey of executives of leading business firms provides valuable insights into actual pricing objectives and practices.

The Bucklin paper is a synthesis of product taxonomy. Bucklin reviews Copeland's original classification of goods and subsequent refinements, and he combines these with patronage motives to form a basis for marketing strategy at the retail level. Aspinwall's color spectrum is an alternative classification schema, and he relates the categories to complementary distribution and promotion plans. Pessemier's laboratory experiments suggest a promising means of empirically estimating demand for specific goods. McVey questions the channels concept. In his view, the channel is primarily a historical combination of intermediaries rather than a planned distribution system.

Lavidge and Steiner present a model for assessing the effectiveness of advertising in moving consumers along the continuum from awareness of the product to actual purchase. Forrester approaches this problem in a different way. He suggests the measurement of advertising effectiveness by using his concept of *industrial dynamics,* a total systems approach to examining the firm's performance over time. Hollander is also concerned with marketing change over time. He discusses the dynamic nature of the institutional structure of retailing, using examples from various countries. The articles in this section exemplify the process of market analysis: formulation of a model of market action and validation of the model using empirical data.

18. THE ROLE OF RESEARCH IN MARKETING MANAGEMENT*

Harry V. Roberts

Expansion of marketing research reflects a growing belief that the methods of science are useful in solving the problems of business management. Effective application of marketing research, however, is neither easy nor automatic; and some have even contended that on balance actual applications have been more ineffective than effective.[1] This paper represents an attempt to formulate a framework for analysis of conditions under which marketing research can be expected to be effective and to make incidental suggestions for increasing effectiveness. This framework is founded on *a priori* reasoning and impressionistic evidence; its presentation here is drastically condensed; but it may nonetheless be suggestive both to those who apply research and to those who are intrigued by research for its own sake.

DECISION MAKING

Marketing management can be viewed simply as the continuing attempt to recognize and solve specific marketing problems. A *problem* exists when an objective is desired and there is uncertainty as to how it can best be achieved. A *decision* is the selection of some course of action (or inaction) to attain the objective. There are three imperatives in the process of decision making: (1) possible actions must be recognized; (2) the results of different actions must be predicted; and (3) the order of preference of these predicted results must be assessed. Research is potentially useful for at least the first two of these.

*Reprinted from the *Journal of Marketing*, national quarterly publication of the American Marketing Association (July, 1957), pp. 21–32.

[1]For example, see John E. Jeuck, "Marketing Research—Milestone or Millstone?," *Journal of Marketing*, April 1953, pp. 381–87.

RESEARCH AND INTUITION

"Research" can be contrasted with "intuition" (or "judgment" or "common sense") in the decision-making process.

Research is any relatively systematic, formal, conscious procedure for evolving and testing hypotheses about reality or, in more modern terms, for making decisions. The words "systematic," "formal," and "conscious" differentiate "research" from "intuition." The distinction between research and intuition is not a sharp one, especially since intuition is an essential ingredient of good research, but the major differences of emphasis are these:

(1) While both research and intuition are ultimately oriented toward predictions, intuition is oriented toward narrow and immediate predictions rather than general hypotheses fruitful of many specific predictions.
(2) Intuition is learned, if at all, by experience and demonstration rather than by formal study.
(3) Intuition is seldom subject to logical scrutiny or formal empirical testing.
(4) Research uses such technical tools as mathematics, logic, experimental methods, and statistical inference.

Since research is intuition plus science, it is easy to assume that research can improve upon intuition in the social sciences and business management as well. There is, however, reason to be skeptical of this assumption. A distinguished economist has said,

> We seem to be forced to the conclusion, not that prediction and control are impossible in the field of human phenomena, but that the formal methods of science are of very limited application. Common sense does predict and control, and can be trained to predict and control better; but that does not prove that science can predict and control better than common sense. And it seems very doubtful whether in the majority of social problems the application of logical methods and canons will give as good results as the informal, intuitive process of judgment which, when refined and developed, becomes art.[2]

In order to formulate useful generalizations about the role of research in marketing, two closely related issues must be considered: (1)

[2]Frank H. Knight, *The Ethics of Competition and Other Essays* (London: George Allen and Unwin, Ltd., 1936), pp. 132–33. See also pp. 116–17 and 119.

potential contributions of research to marketing problems and (2) identification of characteristics of marketing problems that make these problems more or less accessible to attack by research.

POTENTIAL CONTRIBUTIONS OF RESEARCH

There are four major kinds of contributions that research can make toward decision making in marketing: (1) systematic description and classification of marketing "facts" as exemplified by the censuses of population and distribution or the data of the Audit Bureau of Circulations; (2) substantive hypotheses that can be used to make predictions; (3) logical and mathematical tools for classifying relevant variables, exploring the logical relationships among hypotheses, and deriving the predictions implied by hypotheses; and (4) the inferential tools of statistics.

Systematic Description and Classification of "Facts"

It is easy to forget and hard to evaluate precisely the contribution of a wealth of descriptive materials to marketing management in America, and indeed these materials are often not even thought of as "marketing research" because of their descriptive rather than analytical orientation. Yet, a little reflection on the pervasive use in marketing, for example, of census materials suggests their indispensable role.

Substantive Hypotheses

In physics the body of substantive hypotheses is large, relatively well articulated by logical connections between individual hypotheses, and well verified by actual testing of the accuracy of predictions derived from hypotheses. In short, one may speak meaningfully of "physical *theory*." By contrast, the so-called "social" or "behavioral" sciences, which have the greatest potential relevance to marketing, *consist largely of apparently unrelated empirical observations with relatively little theory to articulate these observations*. These disciplines rarely contain hypotheses of direct usefulness in solving the specific problems which arise in marketing. Moreover, most current marketing research is *ad hoc* empirical work with little substantive carry-over from one study to another. The so-called "principles" in textbooks rarely yield concrete predictions as to the effect of proposed marketing actions. For example, "principles" of copywriting and advertising format are often listed, but advertising men frequently disagree on the choice of the most effective advertisement.[3]

The main theoretical instrument for potential guidance in marketing is the axiom of rational behavior, which has been applied mainly in economics.[4] Supply and demand theory based on the rationality postulates has some relevance for marketing problems. For example, even without precise quantitative estimates of elasticities of demand for automobiles, this theory will predict the effect of setting the retail list price of cars below the competitive price on (a) the distribution of income between dealers and manufacturers, (b) the rate of production of automobiles, and (c) the rate of sale to consumers of "optional" accessories.[5]

Even though there are few predictive hypotheses in the social sciences, these sciences may often be useful in marketing by suggesting what to look for as opposed to predicting what will be found. Thus, a psychologist might be able to suggest possible advertising appeals that would not occur to a copywriter who lacked a formal background in psychology, even though psychological theory probably could not predict the most effective from a given list of appeals.

Logical and Mathematical Tools

Logical and mathematical tools are essentially languages for the analysis of problems. The concepts of supply and demand schedule, for example, would facilitate the analysis of economic—and some marketing—problems even if they had no predictive value at all. Pure formal logic may also be helpful. For example, there is one advertising "principle" that the advertising message should reach as wide an audience as possible and another that frequent repetitions of the advertising message are desirable. Logic suggests immediately that either "principle" by itself is inadequate and that the real problem is to find some optimal combination of wide coverage and intensive repetition. Similar examples are easy to find; in all of them, logic serves to formulate the real issues and avoid futile talking.

[3]Most textbook principles are really proverbs; for each "principle" there is an equally plausible "principle" stating the opposite. See Herbert A. Simon, *Administrative Behavior* (New York: The Macmillan Company, 1948), pp. 20 ff.

[4]Kenneth J. Arrow, "Mathematical Models in the Social Sciences," *Cowles Commission Papers, New Series, No. 48* (Chicago: Cowles Commission for Research in Economics, 1952), p. 137.

[5]Milton Friedman, "Notes on Lectures in Price Theory" (unpublished manuscript based on notes prepared by David I. Fand and Warren J. Gustus, The University of Chicago Press, 1951), pp. 15–16.

In recent years many new mathematical tools have been made available for possible use in making marketing decisions. For example, various mathematical models have been proposed for problems of strategy, programming, learning, inventory decisions, mass and small group communication, economic forecasting, queuing, capital budgeting, diversification of risk, and so on. Actual applications have undoubtedly lagged behind advance publicity, but enough has been done to suggest exciting developments to come.

Statistical Inference

Statistical inference is potentially useful in marketing as a tool for securing and interpreting empirical observations so that a "rational" decision can be made in the face of uncertainty. In *experimental* applications, managerial actions are actually tried out with the aim of discovering the responses to these actions. All other applications are *nonexperimental* or "*observational.*"

> Evidence cast up by experience is abundant and frequently as conclusive as that from contrived experiments. . . . But such evidence is far more difficult to interpret. It is frequently complex and always indirect and incomplete . . . its interpretation generally requires subtle analysis and involved chains of reasoning, which seldom carry real conviction. . . .[6]

Experimental methods, by contrast, yield evidence free of such difficulties of interpretation so long as: (1) The underlying conditions of the past persist into the future. (2) The experiment is run sufficiently long that responses to experimental stimuli will have time to manifest themselves. (3) The population being studied can be broken down into smaller units (families, stores, sales territories, etc.) for which the experimental stimuli can be measured and for which responses to the stimuli are not "contagious." (4) The experimentor is able to apply or withhold, as *he* chooses, experimental stimuli from any particular unit of the population he is studying. (5) Neither the stimulus nor the response is changed by the fact that an experiment is being conducted. (6) The sample size is large enough to measure important responses to experimental stimuli against the background of uncontrolled sources of variation.

The key to modern statistical design of experiments is withholding experimental stimuli *at random.* To the extent that randomization and

[6]Milton Friedman, *Essays in Positive Economics* (Chicago: The University of Chicago Press, 1953), pp. 10–11.

the other conditions above are met, the responses actually observed will reflect the "true" effects of the stimuli plus random or chance variation. Statistical procedures then need cope only with the interpretation of chance variation. Observational methods must cope both with chance variation and possible systematic error, and systematic error eludes rigorous statistical treatment. For example, one can compare purchases of an advertiser's product between readers and nonreaders of a recent advertisement and try to make statistical allowance for the fact that readers are potentially different from nonreaders in many respects other than the simple fact of seeing or not seeing the advertisement; but after all such allowances, there is no guarantee that systematic differences do not persist. For example, a statistician might make statistical adjustments for factors such as economic status, education, sex, age, etc., that might distinguish readers from nonreaders of the advertisement and then find that the adjusted purchase rate of the product is still higher among readers than non-readers. *Even if* the statistical adjustments have succeeded in making the two groups comparable in respect to *all* variables associated with the tendency to respond to the advertisement's message—and there is never any guarantee in observational studies that this has in fact been achieved—it still may be true that those people who buy the product are more likely to notice and read the advertisement or at least to remember, or say that they remember, having read it.

These fundamental limitations of observational techniques notwithstanding, marketing research has already drawn heavily on them and will do so increasingly in the future. The development of sound methods of sampling of human populations is recent, and advances are still being made. Much of current marketing research has been made possible by this development of sampling theory and practice. Similarly, the development of psychological scaling and factor analysis—which may be viewed as statistical tools—has had a noticeable influence on current practice. Moreover, there are many potentially valuable statistical tools that have not yet been widely applied in marketing research, and others will undoubtedly be developed.

CHARACTERISTICS OF MARKETING PROBLEMS THAT INFLUENCE ATTAINMENT OF AN ECONOMICAL SOLUTION BY RESEARCH

Every marketing problem is different, but certain criteria determine the compatibility of particular problems and methods of research. In the simplest type of problem situation, the proposed actions are given. The response to the actions must be predicted and a decision made in the light of the desired objectives. General economic conditions, actions of competitors, and other actions of the firm are assumed to continue unchanged. Later these assumptions will be relaxed. In each of the criteria listed below, the phrase "other things being equal" should be considered implicit.

The more rapid the response to marketing actions, the easier the problem for research. Often the quality characteristics of manufactured products can be measured only after a long time. Thus, the resistance to weathering of different paints could be tested by (1) actual weathering over five years or (2) accelerated testing in a laboratory. It is well known in product research that accelerated testing is capricious and often perverse.[7] In marketing the shortcomings of accelerated testing are at least as serious but less likely to be discovered, especially for institutional and "indirect-action" advertising and promotion. By contrast, direct-action selling effort such as local and mail-order advertising—for which accelerated testing is unnecessary—has been researched widely with obvious success.[8] In addition to the rapidity of response to direct-action selling effort, there is often a second explanation for success of research: responses are often readily *traceable*. Hence we set down:

The easier it is to trace response to marketing actions, the easier the problem for research. Responses to sales effort are frequently difficult to trace, partly because the many forms of selling effort that impinge on the ultimate consumer are often closely interrelated and many of them are designed to work indirectly. For example, an argument frequently advanced for the use of national advertising to *consumers* is that *dealers* are favorably motivated thereby. Further, consumer buying decisions may be interdependent because of "conspicuous consumption," "word-of-mouth," or "opinion leadership." There are tools for coping with the problem of traceability. Selling stimuli often can be traced to relatively small geographic areas or relatively short time periods. If the buying decisions of consumers are interdependent, the contagion of purchase may be less important between small geographic areas than between individual consumers.

When measurement of the desired responses to marketing actions is impossible or uneconomic, the problem will be easier to the extent that satisfactory substitute responses can be found. If response to sales

[7]Eugene W. Pike, "Testing Components for High-Reliability Systems" (unpublished paper given at the National Meeting on Airborne Electronics of the Institute of Radio Engineers, Dayton, Ohio, May 13, 1953).

[8]For a typical example, see *Printers' Ink*, July 11, 1952, pp. 35 and 110.

stimuli takes too long to manifest itself or is difficult to trace, a substitute response highly correlated with buying responses can be sought. Copy tests, consumer jury ratings, preference studies, and many techniques of questionnaire design and psychological measurement are based upon substitute responses.

In deciding on the validity of proposed substitute responses, there are three closely related approaches: (1) to verify by research that the substitute response is closely correlated with the response of ultimate interest for a class of problems similar to the one being studied, (2) to draw on general theoretical knowledge, and (3) to draw on experience and intuition.

It is hard to find validations of substitute responses in product research. In marketing, there are relatively few documented examples with details of the process of validation. Most of these examples fail to show significant differences for the sales responses but show significant differences for the corresponding substitute responses, usually preference measurements.[9] Here is the dilemma. Should one use preference measurements that show significant differences in response to different selling stimuli but for which results are not related in any known way with sales measurements? Preference measurements may be correlated with sales responses and are perhaps more sensitive. Seymour Banks has suggested that:

> . . . a preferent test can select the best of a series of proposed alternatives, but it cannot tell how much effect the use of this best alternative will have upon sales.[10]

But Banks has also published an excellent counterexample to this speculation.[11] George Brown has suggested in informal discussions that the "chain of causation" from selling stimulus to buying response might be divided into stages: opportunity for exposure to selling effort (for example, read the magazine in which an advertisement appears); actual exposure to selling effort (for example, read the actual advertisement); acquisition of information about or confidence in the product; formation of the intention to buy; and actual purchase. Measure-

[9]See, for example: James H. Lorie and Harry V. Roberts, *Basic Methods of Marketing Research* (New York: McGraw-Hill Book Company, Inc., 1951), pp. 209–11; Seymour Banks, "The Measurement of the Effect of a New Packaging Material upon Preference and Sales," *The Journal of Business*, April 1950, pp. 79ff.; and G. Maxwell Ule, unpublished doctoral dissertation in progress, The University of Chicago, School of Business.

[10]Seymour Banks, *ibid.*, p. 80.

[11]Seymour Banks, "The Prediction of Dress Purchases for a Mail-Order House," *The Journal of Business*, January 1950, pp. 48–57.

ments can be made at any stage of this chain. One might speculate that measurements would be more valid the closer they are to actual purchase, but this is at best only a plausible speculation. In the absence of evidence, speculation is unavoidable; but the search for validation of substitute responses should continue.

To the extent that experimentation is economically feasible, the problem is easier to solve by research. Properly designed experiments are free of many of the limitations of observational studies. Businessmen generally are often better situated to conduct sound experiments than is commonly believed. Actions taken as a result of business decisions represent direct intervention of a kind that is usually impossible in the social sciences. Both "test-tube" experiments as a prelude to final marketing decision and continuing experiments thereafter are often possible and entail little added cost, especially when marketing policies can be introduced piecemeal geographically.

Randomized experimentation is impossible only for "all-or-none" decisions. Major plant construction and advertising in national media are examples. John Jeuck listed major marketing innovations made without research and concluded, ". . . the really significant marketing achievements, the big chance . . . is dependent primarily on imagination and on the skills of management."[12]

Even when randomization through space is precluded, randomization *over time* may be feasible if the full response to selling stimuli—such as special promotions undertaken intermittently at randomly chosen time periods—is rapid and if the statistical behavior of sales in the absence of experimentation is well understood.[13] Unfortunately, the full response may not be manifest sufficiently rapidly. Thus the initial effect of premium offers may be a very substantial increase in the rate of sales followed by a decrease if the premium mainly affects timing of purchases rather than their total amount.

Finally, experimentation may be undesirable if the stimulus or its response is seriously modified by the fact that an experiment is being run.

The success of research in problems that cannot be economically attacked experimentally depends on the adequacy of observational methods. Evaluation of adequacy of observational methods is also frustrated by the absence of evidence, but plausible guides can be offered.

[12]John E. Jeuck, "Marketing Research Today: A Minority Report," *School of Business Publications I*, The University of Chicago, undated, p. 10.

[13]See R. L. Anderson, "Recent Advances in Finding Best Operating Conditions," *Journal of American Statistical Association*, vol. 48, no. 264 (1953), pp. 789–98.

The more adequate the theoretical knowledge, the more adequate are observational methods based on this knowledge. When theoretical knowledge is very good, satisfactory predictions can be made on the basis of existing theory without further recourse to observational study. Bridge building and other feats of engineering construction illustrate this point. More frequently, theory is simply an invaluable aid in the design and interpretation of research, whether observational or experimental. But while experimentation can reach valid results in problems for which theoretical knowledge is wholly or partly lacking, observational studies are seriously weakened when theory is sparse. There is relatively little marketing theory, and intuition must often guide the use of observational techniques. The distinction between "research" and "intuition" therefore becomes very blurred, as in certain areas of medical research in which valid experiments are difficult and theoretical knowledge is meager. In both marketing and medicine, the questions which cannot be subjected to valid experimentation are frequently resolved by the intuition of the practitioner.

Observational techniques may be more adequate to the extent that statistical allowance has been made for disturbing variables that may obscure the relationship being studied. By statistical allowance is meant crossclassification, standardized averages, multiple regression, and related techniques. These techniques are often used in observational studies to answer the question, "what would have happened if certain disturbing variables had not varied?" It seems always prudent to attempt to answer this question within the resources available for research. Except in experimental studies, of course, there is no guarantee that the answers are satisfactory within the usual allowance for chance error.[14]

There are a few special devices, not as widely used as they might be, that may enhance the effectiveness of observational methods in marketing research. (1) Aggregate data can be divided into components, as when sales are studied by territories or families. "Sales analysis," which seems to have lost favor by comparison with survey methods, illustrates the approach. (2) Rates of change through time can be studied instead of absolute levels. While this "before-after" approach is common in sales tests, its use in observational studies is rare, perhaps because of the current emphasis on single surveys. (3) Insightful comparisons can be made such as comparisons of product awareness of advertised and competitive brands during a special campaign or Alfred Politz's comparison of attitudes toward car acceler-

[14]See, for example, W. Allen Wallis and Harry V. Roberts, *Statistics: A New Approach* (Glencoe, Illinois: The Free Press, 1956), ch. 9.

ation with strength of accelerator spring.[15] (4) Different observational methods may be used to attack a single research problem. The degree of convergence of their results may indicate the confidence to be accorded the results of any one of the approaches.

To the extent that changes in present conditions may have to be allowed for, the problem is more difficult for research. Two cases need to be considered: (1) changes that would have occurred anyway; and (2) changes that are, at least in part, responses to the decision in the particular problem.

Changes That Would Have Occurred Anyway The best-known examples are shifts in general business conditions or in demand conditions confronting a whole industry. General economic conditions have such relevance to marketing (and other) problems of the firm that economic and sales forecasting is of great importance. A treatment of the usefulness of research in economic forecasting is beyond our present scope.[16]

As to the modifications of marketing decisions that should be made in the light of predicted changes in economic conditions, economic theory is relatively useful. For example, there is considerable evidence on the difference in response of prices and outputs of durable and nondurable goods or of retail and wholesale prices to changes in economic conditions.

Changes in Part Influenced by the Decision under Consideration The classic illustration analyzed by economic theorists is the situation of duopoly or other small-number competitive situations. The analogue in marketing is easy to find. Suppose, for example, that a company were able by experimental methods to estimate the productivity of its advertising expenditures and that a leading competitor had maintained his advertising unchanged during the period of the experiment. As a result of the experiment, the company might sharply increase its advertising expenditures, making the tacit assumption that

[15]Alfred Politz, "Science and Truth in Marketing Research," *Harvard Business Review*, January–February 1957, pp. 121–22.

[16]See, for example: Harry V. Roberts, "A Method of Improving Sales Forecasts," *Proceedings of Golden Triangle Conference of the American Marketing Association*, 1956 (American Marketing Association, Inc., 1956), pp. 97–102; Robert Ferber, "Sales Forecasting by Correlation Methods," *Journal of Marketing*, January 1954, pp. 219–32; James H. Lorie, "Operations Research and Short-Run Sales Forecasting" (paper delivered before the Second Annual Meeting of the Operations Research Society of America, May 21–22, 1954); Irving Schweiger, "The Contribution of Consumer Anticipations in Forecasting Consumer Demand," in National Bureau of Economic Research, *Short-Term Economic Forecasting*, Studies in Income and Wealth, vol. 17 (Princeton: Princeton University Press, 1955).

the competitor would make no change. The competitor—observing this increase—might increase its advertising, possibly "cancelling out" the effectiveness of the first company's added expenditure and leaving both companies in their original sales position vis-à-vis one another. The experiment would have been entirely adequate in determining what would have happened in the absence of a response by the competitor, but it could lead to a bad decision in the absence of a prediction as to what the competitor would do; how soon he would do it; and what effect, if any, his response would have on the rate of sales of the first company. Competitive responses and interactions also raise serious problems in the interpretation of observational data.

The guessing of competitive reactions may be an art highly dependent on intuition and experience, with formal research perhaps serving chiefly to supply salient background facts. Psychology and social-psychology do not appear to offer useful predictions. Even if the competitive responses could be predicted, their effect on sales could be estimated at best by observational methods.

Finally, the task of research is easier for problems that can be studied and solved independently of other problems because indirect effects do not then have to be considered. One of the key tasks of management—and research—is the fragmentation of the complex of problems facing a company into smaller problems that can be considered relatively independently of other problems.

THE EFFECTIVENESS OF RESEARCH IN THE DISCOVERY OF POSSIBLE NEW ALTERNATIVES FOR ACTION

An essential part of problem solving is the discovery of alternative possibilities for action besides those initially considered or—in alternative terminology—the "identification of problems." This is closely analogous to "formulation of hypotheses" where words like "accident" and "inspiration" readily come to mind. In the context of marketing, John E. Jeuck has said:

> . . . It seems likely that research can do very little in a positive or creative way to lead to those new possibilities that are the essence of creative market development and exploitation. That is simply to say, I suppose, that marketing success depends more upon the imaginative and aggressive personality who may in the process of development make many errors than it does upon the careful coalition of facts and the cautious investigation of alternatives that are the hallmark of research operations.

> In that connection, one must be impressed with how unlikely it would have been for Sears, Roebuck ever to have made a really strong start if Richard Sears had had a clear view of what is usually uncovered in the consumer survey. One wonders how many other companies would have never been started if they had relied upon the typical consumer survey to guide them in their selection of products and policies. . . .[17]

To the extent that Jeuck's comments represent more than a criticism of the frequent use of more or less stereotyped methods in marketing research, they are seriously misleading. Research is probably more effective in unearthing new possibilities for action than in predicting the response to existing ones.[18] Research focuses attention on possible actions that probably would not have been recognized in the absence of research. The new ideas that turn up as an unexpected by-product of research are frequently more valuable than the objectives originally sought. The very discipline of objective recording of data forces people to look at things they would never have looked at otherwise and to question assumptions that would not otherwise have been challenged: research can be a protection against complacency and a stimulus to imagination.

Quality control illustrates a method of research aimed primarily at the discovery of new possibilities for action.[19] The basic idea is that a repetitive process such as a manufacturing or marketing operation is measured at periodic intervals, often by sampling methods. Statistical procedures—"control charts"—have been devised in order to detect systematic changes of the process. The detection of such changes provides a warning that the process should be immediately investigated to see what has happened and to discover "assignable causes." By discovering the "assignable cause," management can either remove a source of trouble or retain and possibly apply more widely an improvement that otherwise might have been lost. Quality control

[17]Jeuck, *op. cit.*, p. 7.

[18]The impressions reported here are based on fairly extensive examination of applications of research in several areas of management. Many of these applications—about 300—were made by students in the 9th, 10th, 11th, and 12th Groups of the Executive Program of the University of Chicago who were given the assignment of applying statistical methods to problems in their own companies. See Harry V. Roberts, "Statistics in Middle Management," *Management Science*, vol. I, nos. 3–4 (1955), pp. 224–32.

[19]The "classic" in this field is Walter A. Shewhart, *Economic Control of Quality of Manufactured Product* (New York: D. Van Nostrand Company, Inc., 1931). A recent text is Eugene L. Grant, *Statistical Quality Control*, revised edition (New York: McGraw-Hill Book Company, Inc., 1952).

methods, then, suggest looking for trouble and therefore opportunity at times and places where the search is likely to be rewarded.

"RESEARCH" VERSUS "INTUITION"

Many problems in business are and should be attacked without the benefit of formal methods of research—especially relatively minor and nonrecurrent problems and those that require very quick decisions. Research would then cost more than its benefits. But though intuition sometimes yields a snap decision without any reflection, it may also involve soul searching and interminable committee meetings, both of which are expensive in terms of executive time.

If the criteria for the applicability of research enumerated above are examined carefully, four seem just as applicable to intuition or informal decision making as to formal methods of research: (1) the more rapid the response to actions, (2) the more easily responses can be traced, (3) the more adequate the substitute responses that can be found, and (4) the fewer the changes in existing conditions that need to be taken into account, the easier is the problem for *either* research or intuition. The criteria that appear to discriminate between research and intuition are the economic feasibility of experimentation and, failing experimentation, the availability of adequate observational tools.

RESEARCH AND THE EXECUTIVE

Many "practical issues" limit the use of research in marketing.

Some managerial problems are really ethical or value problems rather than factual ones. For example, there might be a problem of deciding whether or not to market and promote a cold remedy in the face of good evidence that the remedy had no measurable impact on colds. For such value choices, research or any rational decision-making process is clearly irrelevant. But genuine value problems in marketing probably occur less frequently than generally believed.

"Science" and "research" are very often used as weapons rather than as tools for the analysis of problems. Often research serves to postpone the need for a decision to change policy, to "prove" points, to win arguments, and even to persuade people to buy the product. When research is used predominantly for persuasion, it is almost always used more or less dishonestly. The most subtle form of dishonesty and perhaps the most prevalent is the presentation of only part of the evidence and the suppression of the rest. Such dishonesty is often undetected but nonetheless futile simply because it is a weapon open to all parties. The prevalence of obvious disagreements between experts tends to reduce the layman's respect for research, and the suppression of unfavorable information is likely to become habitual.

Even when intentions are laudable, research is often aimless fact gathering that fails to provide help in making decisions except by accident. Some executives ignore research findings that are inconsistent with conclusions they have already reached; in the name of "evidence," some research men try to persuade executives to make decisions unsupported by the actual research. Perhaps the most revealing symptom of the practical difficulty of using research well is the frequent failure to define adequately the objectives of research. This failure probably stems from a lack of understanding as to what a full statement of objectives really involves and how much hard thinking it demands. Careful formulation of objectives need not and should not preclude the search for the unexpected "by-products" that are often so useful, nor does it preclude the collection of certain basic information—such as the rate of retail sales of one's product—in advance of current problems. But it is only too easy to lapse into the relatively mechanical assembly of information and quietly wander off into irrelevancy so that even useful information may not be properly understood by management even after sustained and aggressive attempts by research men to "sell" their product.

The failure to specify objectives adequately stems in part from human failings but also from the common tendency to regard marketing research as something essentially different from management or as a field for experts who supply the information needed for decisions to executives who then use intuitive judgment in arriving at the final decision. While there are potential advantages to be gained from specialization of functions, the intimate relationship between "research" and "intuition" together with the fact that the final decision rests with management puts on management the primary responsibility of using research well.

Marketing research is only one of the many fields of business in which experts in research aid executives. The executive's task is to use and evaluate the work of the expert without fully understanding the expert's discipline. The dependence on experts, of course, is not unique to business; the most unnerving example for many people is their own dependence on doctors. The executive's dependence on experts has also been recognized and sometimes deplored. The time, ability, and effort required to attain reasonable competence in any field of science ordinarily limits researchers themselves to relatively narrow specialization. Yet, the executive must make good use of the advice of many experts. To say that this task is extremely difficult is only to say that rational or even partly rational decisions are hard to make.

Perhaps the most important potential contribution of "research" in marketing comes from the relatively objective viewpoint that research encourages even among those who do not directly execute it. (The increasing orientation of management toward the "consumer point of view" is probably traceable to marketing research.) One cannot help being impressed by the frequency with which data contradict strongly held beliefs or suggest completely new alternatives for action. However difficult it may be to acquire the needed objectivity, the acquisition is probably not much more difficult for executives than for technically trained research people. In those areas of research where scientific experimentation is seldom used, of which marketing research is one, there are few occasions on which the research man is really "proved wrong," and it is being proved wrong rather than technical training *per se* that probably makes for genuine objectivity. Unfortunately, observational data usually can be interpreted in many plausible ways and frequently fail to convince either research men or executives that their previously held views were wrong.

One can be proved wrong also in the realm of logic, and the importance of sound logic in decision making should not be overlooked. Commonplace examples of importance are easy to find in practice: the assumption that the demand curve is infinitely inelastic for small price rises though not for large ones and the use of full costs rather than marginal costs in making decisions on output. While some errors of logic are extremely subtle and hard to detect, it would not seem unreasonable to expect that executives might learn to avoid the obvious ones. Mistakes of empirical inference also probably turn more frequently on elementary errors than on subtle ones.[20]

Two prerequisites to more effective use of marketing research by executives can be embraced under "objectivity" and some understanding of basic tools of research—particularly logic, economics, and statistics. The fundamental key, however, is the executive's understanding that research, like management itself, must be evaluated ultimately by predictive tests. The single most useful step in fitting research into marketing management would be greater recognition of the fact that

[20]See Wallis and Roberts, *op. cit.*, ch. 3.

the essence of research is neither surveys nor samples but the evolution and testing of hypotheses about marketing by testing the predictions to which they lead.

There is, of course, much more to management than research. There are difficulties in applying research with which we have not attempted to deal, particularly the extent to which the scientific approach to management might dull intuition or lead to overintellectualization that could easily paralyze decisive action. Again, an executive who knows a certain venture to be a long shot may not try nearly so hard to make it succeed as if he believes, erroneously, that it is very likely to be successful. There is little which can be said about these things except to venture the opinion that they are probably overrated in importance. For each man who succeeds in apparently irrational ventures or whose intuition seems to surpass rational calculations, there are many for whom irrationality is the prime cause of failure.

19. PRICING OBJECTIVES IN LARGE COMPANIES*

Robert F. Lanzillotti

The recent sharpened interest of the "Kefauver committee" in administered prices and inflation has focused attention once again on the inadequate state of knowledge of the price-making process.[1] In particular, more empirical information is needed with respect to (a) the motivational hypothesis of the firm, i.e., the specific objectives upon which business firms base pricing decisions, and (b) the mechanics of price formulation. This article is addressed to the first problem; it will present some data on pricing objectives of the firm which have been developed in the course of a general study of pricing policies and practices of large industrial corporations.

I. SCOPE OF PRESENT STUDY

The procedure followed involved the postprandial variety of research. Lengthy interviews were undertaken with officials of twenty companies over periods ranging up to about one week in most cases.[2] A second set of interviews was undertaken several years later to fill in gaps in the data and to ascertain if any changes had been made in

*Reprinted from *American Economic Review* (December, 1958), pp. 921–940.

[1]See *Administered Prices*, Hearings Before the Subcommittee on Antitrust and Monopoly of the Committee on the Judiciary, United States Senate, 85th Cong., 1st Sess., Washington 1958.

[2]The companies were selected from among the largest corporations on the basis of the willingness of management to cooperate by permitting extensive interviews with top company officials: Aluminum Company of America, American Can, A & P Tea Company, du Pont, General Electric, General Foods, General Motors, Goodyear, Gulf, International Harvester, Johns-Manville, Kennecott Copper, Kroger, National Steel, Sears, Standard of Indiana, Standard Oil Company of New Jersey (ESSO), Swift, Union Carbide, and U.S. Steel.

price policy since the original interviews. Pricing obviously being a sensitive area, some officials did not care to discuss their policies except in general terms, but these persons paved the way to individuals who were more willing and, in some cases, more aware of the practices employed and reasons for them.

The questions were designed to elicit information concerning: (1) whether any formal or informal commercial goals had been adopted by the corporation; (2) the procedures employed for implementing and evaluating the goal; (3) the techniques of price determination (i.e., the mechanics of pricing); and (4) the functions of pricing executives (individuals, committees, special divisions, etc.)—including extent of authority on price matters, kinds of materials utilized by them in setting prices, and relative weights given to various price-influencing factors. The portion of the information presented in this paper concerns, for each of the twenty companies, the principal and collateral objectives which are regarded as guiding pricing decisions.

The twenty corporations have one feature in common: each of them is among the 200 largest industrial corporations, and over one-half fall within the 100 largest industrials, in terms of assets. But they differ in a wide variety of ways from each other. Some, like Johns-Manville, U.S. Steel, International Harvester, and Union Carbide, dominate a whole industry and are price leaders. At the other extreme, there are companies like Swift and A & P which face so many competitors of various sizes and abilities that in spite of their absolute size they are very far from being able to make decisions for the market, and do not think of competition in terms of actions of one or a few competitors. The other companies fall between these extremes.

II. COMPANY GOALS: RATIONALIZATIONS OF PRICING METHODS

It is important to recognize at the outset that a company statement of policy is not necessarily an accurate representation of what that policy is.[3] Also, company rationalizations of pricing do not always represent the first step in planning price policy, and not all pricing of a given company is determined by the general company objective.

In a few cases officials insisted that there was little latitude in

[3]The following analysis is based upon the author's interpretations of views expressed orally by officials of the corporations concerned. Of course, neither the companies nor the author wish these views to be interpreted as necessarily the official views of the companies.

selecting a policy. However, for the most part, the prominence of each of the corporations in their respective industries makes most of them masters, to a significant degree, of their fates; hence, they are able to adjust pricing to the company's general goal.

Table 1 presents a summary of the principal and collateral pricing goals of the twenty companies as determined from interviews with their respective officials. The most typical pricing objectives cited were: (1) pricing to achieve a target return on investment; (2) stabilization of price and margin; (3) pricing to realize a target market share; and (4) pricing to meet or prevent competition. In most of the companies, one of the goals predominates, but as the listing of collateral objectives indicates, price-making by any one firm was not always ruled by a single policy objective.[4]

III. PRICING TO ACHIEVE A TARGET RETURN ON INVESTMENT

Target return on investment was perhaps the most frequently mentioned of pricing goals.[5] About one-half of the companies explicitly indicated that their pricing policies were based mainly upon the objective of realizing a particular rate of return on investment, in a

[4]To illustrate, in U.S. Steel, out of a variety of divergent views mentioned, three rationales can be distinguished. (1) The first is the "ideal" price, i.e., pricing that is believed to be "just, fair, and economic," with reference to a general target of about 8 per cent after taxes on stockholders' investment plus long-term debt. This strand is colored by the management's concept of the corporation as the industry leader vested with the responsibilities and subject to the inhibitions of a public utility. In fact, one official said he was "unable to understand or properly describe the Corporation's pricing policy except as something like the approach of the public utilities." (2) The second rationale centers on the difference between the "ideal" system and what officials regard as the "practical exigencies of steel price-making," i.e., limitations imposed upon price policy "by followers who are disloyal and prices of competitive products that get out of hand." (3) A third policy objective is essentially a target market share and is embodied in the motto: "to obtain as a minimum that share of all markets for the products sold, product by product, and territory by territory, to which the corporation's capacity in relation to the industry as the whole entitles it, and to accomplish this participation ratio through the exercise of judgment so as to insure the maximum continuing return on investment to the Corporation."

[5]Target-return pricing is defined as the building up of a price structure designed to provide such a return on capital employed for specific products, product groups, and divisions, as to yield a predetermined corporate average return. In most cases managements referred to stockholders' equity (net worth) plus long-term debt. Usually a standard cost system is used as a means of allocating fixed cost to various product divisions, with the standards premised on an assumed rate of production, typically about 70 per cent to 80 per cent of capacity, and an assumed product-mix as "normal."

TABLE 1. PRICING GOALS OF TWENTY LARGE INDUSTRIAL CORPORATIONS

Company	Principal Pricing Goal	Collateral Pricing Goal	Rate of Return on Investment (After Taxes) 1947–1955[a]		Average Market Share[b]
			Avg.	Range	
Alcoa	20% on investment (before taxes); higher on new products [about 10% effective rate after taxes]	(a) "Promotive" policy on new products (b) Price stabilization	13.8	7.8–18.7	Pig & ingot, 37%; sheet, 46%; other fabrications, 62%[c]
American Can	Maintenance of market share	(a) "Meeting" competition (using cost of substitute product to determine price) (b) Price stabilization	11.6	9.6–14.7	Approx. 55% of all types of cans[d]
A & P	Increasing market share	"General promotive" (low-margin policy)	13.0	9.7–18.8	n.a.
du Pont	Target return on investment—no specific figure given	(a) Charging what traffic will bear over long run (b) Maximum return for new products—"life cycle" pricing	25.9	19.6–34.1	n.a.
Esso (Standard Oil of N.J.)	"Fair-return" target—no specific figure given	(a) Maintaining market share (b) Price stabilization	16.0	12.0–18.9	n.a.
General Electric	20% on investment (after taxes); 7% on sales (after taxes)	(a) Promotive policy on new products (b) Price stabilization on nationally advertised products	21.4	18.4–26.6	—[e]

General Foods	33 1/3% gross margin: ("1/3 to make, 1/3 to sell, and 1/3 for profit"); expectation of realizing target only on new products	(a) Full line of food products and novelties (b) Maintaining market share	12.2	8.9–15.7	n.a.
General Motors	20% on investment (after taxes)	Maintaining market share	26.0	19.9–37.0	50% of passenger automobiles[f]
Goodyear	"Meeting competitors"	(a) Maintain "position" (b) Price stabilization	13.3	9.2–16.1	n.a.
Gulf	Follow price of most important marketer in each area	(a) Maintain market share (b) Price stabilization	12.6	10.7–16.7	n.a.
International Harvester	10% on investment (after taxes)	Market share: ceiling of "less than a dominant share of any market"	8.9	4.9–11.9	Farm tractors, 28–30%; combines, cornpickers, tractor plows, cultivators, mowers, 20–30%; cotton pickers, 65%; light & light-heavy trucks, 5–18%; medium-heavy to heavy-heavy, 12–30%
Johns-Manville	Return on investment greater than last 15-year average (about 15% after taxes); higher target for new products	(a) Market share not greater than 20% (b) Stabilization of prices	14.9	10.7–19.6	n.a.
Kennecott	Stabilization of prices		16.0	9.3–20.9	n.a.
Kroger	Maintaining market share	Target return of 20% on investment before taxes[g]	12.1	9.7–16.1	n.a.
National Steel	Matching the market–price follower	Increase market share	12.1	7.0–17.4	5%

TABLE 1. (Continued)

Company	*Principal Pricing Goal*	*Collateral Pricing Goal*	*Rate of Return on Investment (After Taxes) 1947–1955*[a]		*Average Market Share*[b]
			Avg.	Range	
Sears Roebuck	Increasing market share (8–10% regarded as satisfactory share)	(a) Realization of traditional return on investment of 10–15% (after taxes) (b) General promotive (low margin) policy	5.4	1.6–10.7	5–10% average (twice as large a share in hard goods v. soft goods)
Standard Oil (Indiana)	Maintain market share	(a) Stabilize prices (b) Target-return on investment (none specified)	10.4	7.9–14.4	n.a.
Swift	Maintenance of market share in livestock buying and meat packing		6.9	3.9–11.1	Approximately 10% nationally[h]
Union Carbide	Target return on investment[i]	Promotive policy on new products; "life cycle" pricing on chemicals generally	19.2	13.5–24.3	—[j]
U.S. Steel	8% on investment (after taxes)	(a) Target market share of 30% (b) Stable price (c) Stable margin	10.3	7.6–14.8	Ingots and steel, 30%; blast furnaces, 34%; finished hot-rolled products, 35%; other steel mill products, 37%[k]

[a]Federal Trade Commission, *Rates of Return (After Taxes) for Identical Companies in Selected Manufacturing Industries, 1940, 1947–55*, Washington [1957], pp. 28–30, except for the following companies whose rates were computed by the author using the methods outlined in the Commission Report: A & P, General Foods, Gulf, International Harvester, Kroger, National Steel, Sears Roebuck, and Swift.

[b]As of 1955, unless otherwise indicated. Source of data is company mentioned unless noted otherwise.

[c]*U.S. v. Alcoa et al.*, "Stipulation Concerning Extension of Tables III–X," dated May 31, 1956, U.S. District Court for the Southern District of New York.

[d]As of 1939. U.S. Department of Justice, *Western Steel Plants and the Tin Plate Industry*, 79th Cong., 1st Sess., Doc. No. 95, p. L 1.

[e]The company states that on the average it aims at not more than 22 to 25 per cent of any given market. Percentages for individual markets or products were not made available, but it is estimated that in some markets, e.g., electrical turbines, General Electric has 60 per cent of the total market. *Cf.* Standard and Poor's, *Industry Surveys*, "Electrical-Electronic-Basic Analysis," Aug. 9, 1956, p. E 21.

[f]Federal Trade Commission, *Industrial Concentration and Product Diversification in the 1000 Largest Manufacturing Companies: 1950*, Washington, Jan. 1957, p. 113.

[g]Target return on investment evidently characterizes company policy as much as target market share. In making investment decisions the company is quoted as follows: "The Kroger Co. normally expected a return on investment of at least 20% before taxes." See McNair, Burnham, and Hersum, *Cases in Retail Management*, New York 1957, pp. 205 ff.

[h]This represents the average share of total industry shipments of the four largest firms in 1954. *Cf. Concentration in American Industry*, Report of Subcommittee on the Judiciary, U.S. Senate, 85th Cong., 1st Sess., Washington 1957, p. 315.

[i]In discussions with management officials various profit-return figures were mentioned, with considerable variation among divisions of the company. No official profit target percentage was given, but the author estimates the *average* profit objective for the corporation to be approximately 35% before taxes, or an effective rate after taxes of about 18%.

[j]Chemicals account for 30% of Carbide's sales, most of which are petro-chemicals, a field that the company opened thirty years ago and still dominates; plastics account for 18%—the company sells 40% of the two most important plastics (vinyl and polyethylene); alloys and metals account for 26% of sales—top U.S. supplier of ferroalloys (e.g., chrome, silicon, manganese), and the biggest U.S. titanium producer; gases account for 14% of sales—estimated to sell 50% of oxygen in the U.S.; carbon, electrodes, and batteries account for 12% of sales—leading U.S. producer of electrodes, refractory carbon, and flashlights and batteries; and miscellaneous—leading operator of atomic energy plants, a leading producer of uranium, the largest U.S. producer of tungsten, and a major supplier of vanadium. *Cf.* "Union Carbide Enriches the Formula," *Fortune*, Feb. 1957, pp. 123 ff.; Standard and Poor's, *Industry Surveys*, "Chemicals-Basic Analysis," Dec. 20, 1956, p. C44; and "Annual Report for 1955 of the Union Carbide and Carbon Corporation."

[k]The range of the corporation's capacity as a percentage of total industry capacity varies from 15% to 54%, as of January 1957. For more detail see *Administered Prices, Hearings Before the Subcommittee on Antitrust and Monopoly of the Senate Committee on the Judiciary*, 85th Cong., 1st Sess., Pt. 2, *Steel*, Washington 1958, pp. 335–36.

given year, over the long haul, or both; but in most cases the target was regarded as a long-run objective. The average of the targets mentioned was 14 per cent (after taxes); only one was below 10 per cent; and the highest was 20 per cent.

Under this pricing system both costs and profit goals are based not upon the volume level which is necessarily expected over a short period, but rather on standard volume; and the margins added to standard costs are designed to produce the target profit rate on investment, assuming standard volume to be the long-run average rate of plant utilization. In effect, the procedure is designed to prevent cyclical or shorter-run changes in volume or product-mix from unduly affecting price, with the expectation that the averaging of fluctuations in cost and demand over the business cycle will produce a particular rate of return on investment.

Firms that were conscious of shooting for a particular target return on investment in their price policies were those that sold products in a market or markets more or less protected and in which the companies were leaders in their respective industries. In Alcoa, du Pont, Esso, General Electric, General Motors, International Harvester, Johns-Manville, Union Carbide, and U.S. Steel, the pricing of many products was hinged to this particular objective, and with the expectation of being able to reach the target return. Target-return pricing was usually tied in with a long-run view of prices, especially on new products where an "orderly" stepping down ("cascading") of prices was followed by du Pont, Union Carbide, and Alcoa.

A distinction should be made, however, between those companies that use target return on investment as a rigid and primary guide to pricing and those to whom it is more useful as a benchmark in an area where prices otherwise might be subject to wide and dangerous variations.[6]

[6]To illustrate, the use of rate-of-return pricing by U.S. Steel (likened by its officials to a public utility's "fair return"), apparently has not always been consistently followed. Under market pressure, U.S. Steel has at times had to accept much less than this return; when desperate for business, as in 1938, its competitors offered substantial concessions below published prices on almost every type of business. A very different situation shows up in the discussions of the target return by officials of General Motors. Instead of vainly attempting to realize its target in good years and bad, General Motors takes a long-run view and has sufficient assurance of its retention of a minimum market share to accept a diminished profit note in years when diminished output bears a heavy unallocated overhead. Du Pont seems to assume its ability to realize a target return, especially in connection with new products. The same could be said for Union Carbide, the other chemical producer in the sample. International Harvester, although as vulnerable as U.S. Steel to wide swings in volume of business, appeared to be less worried by competitors' ability to jeopardize its prices based

Columns 4 and 5 of Table 1 show the average and range of the profit rates realized by the twenty companies over the 1947–1955 period. It will be noted that the target figures are *less* than the actual returns: for the nine-year period, the target-return companies earned on the average slightly more to substantially more than their indicated profit objective (International Harvester being the only exception). Also, there is a rather wide range in the profit rates for each company.[7]

The actual profit rates may be higher than the targets for several possible reasons: (a) the targets may only be nominal or minimal goals (which is suggested by footnote 7); (b) the generally prosperous nature of the period in question in which company operations exceeded "normal" or average percentage of capacity upon which costs and prices were determined; and (c) some of the companies have found that pricing on an historical-cost basis using the company's traditional objective does not provide adequate capital for replacement and expansion at current costs, and accordingly have made allowance for this factor in their pricing formulas.[8] Thus, if actual profit rates were "adjusted" for changes in the price level, the actual profits would more closely approximate the stated targets.

Whichever of the foregoing may be the most plausible explanation of the differences between actual and target profit rates, the findings indicate that a distinction must be made between year-to-year and secular profits objectives. The evidence on actual profit rates, taken in conjunction with the targets mentioned, raises serious questions whether these companies are attempting to "maximize" profits on a year-to-year basis. Moreover, to construe the actual profit rates (as against target rates) as evidence of a long-run maximization policy would

---

on long-run normal cost and return. Harvester was not able to maintain its prices during the great depression, and there is no evidence that such reductions as it made correspond merely to changes in direct cost. But in spite of frank admission by Harvester's management that the company was faced by tough competition, company officials appeared to be much more independent in their pricing policy than U.S. Steel.

[7]If the lowest figure for each firm is omitted, however, the low side of the range of returns approximates the target figure. This is especially true of Alcoa, du Pont, Johns-Manville, Union Carbide, and U.S. Steel.

[8]When U.S. Steel, for example, announces an increase in its base prices, it usually justifies its action in terms of increased direct costs, especially labor costs. But that rising capital costs have also influenced the prices set in recent years is suggested by President Hood's announcement in connection with the $8.50 increase in 1956:

"The new prices do not provide a solution to the problem that United States Steel faces with respect to inadequate depreciation allowances for the replacement of obsolete and outworn facilities, nor do they attempt to provide a solution to the many problems attending the expansion program upon which United States Steel is currently engaged." *New York Times*, August 7, 1956, p. 10.

require the demonstration that the prices charged were based not upon the targets but on what the firms believed they could get as a maximum. In any event, for this sample of firms and for this time period, there are limitations upon profit maximization as an adequate explanation of the relationships between profit targets and actual profit rates.

It is perhaps significant that there has been an increasing tendency in recent years for the companies in the sample to adopt some form of target-return pricing, either across-the-board or at least for particular products. In a few cases it was found that managements had developed a target-return policy between the time of the first interviews with the company and subsequent interviews several years later. The reasons for this movement toward greater use of a target-return approach are varied, but the major influences seem to have been: (a) an increasing awareness of and concern by managements for profit-capital-investment planning and capital budgeting, especially in the conglomerate company within which there is keen competition for capital funds by many units; (b) the desire for a good common denominator for evaluating the performance of divisions and product groups; (c) the wartime experiences of most of the companies with "cost-plus," "cost plus fixed fee," and other contractual arrangements with the government which focused attention on the return of investment; and (d) the emulation, by competitors and others, of successful large companies which have followed a target-return policy for many years (several companies in the sample mentioned that they had patterned their general target-return policy after that of du Pont or General Motors).

It is not surprising that new products above all are singled out for target-return pricing. Since they have no close rivals, new products are usually expected to produce a predetermined level of profit return on the investment represented.[9] No rigid length of time after the intro-

[9]A good example of the kinds of data utilized in determining which new products will be added or which existing facilities will be expanded is one company's procedure for capital investment decisions. The request by a division for new funds shows (a) estimated new commitment (new fixed investment, working capital, and noncapital expenditures); (b) estimated total utilized investment (the new investment plus transfer of existing investment); (c) estimated annual operating income (i.e., income before depreciation, amortization, depletion, other income and income taxes); and (d) estimated return on investment income, which is shown both as a ratio to the new commitment and the total utilized investment. No figure was mentioned as a minimum return; normally new products were expected to return better than the corporate average, but expansions of existing facilities have been made on a projected return of no greater than 20 to 25 per cent before taxes.

An elaborate check-off list is designed to insure attention to various aspects of

duction of the product was mentioned in which the target is supposed to be achieved. However, the time horizon is more short range vis-á-vis established products in the sense that the target payout is delineated from the start.[10] Accordingly, pricing may take the form of "skimming" the market by exploiting the inelasticity of demand in different markets (maintaining a selected price as long as actual or potential competition permits), or a "penetration" price policy designed to develop mass markets via relatively low prices, provided a rapid expansion of the market and higher returns may be obtained later. This approach is most typical of du Pont, Union Carbide, Alcoa, International Harvester, and General Foods. The prescribed target for new products is usually higher than on established products, at least initially. But the target approach is not limited to unique products; it is also typical of low-unit-profit high-volume commodities (e.g., steel, aluminum, and chemicals).

Minimum target profit figures also are used by most of the companies as a basis for sloughing off products and in arriving at "make-or-buy" decisions. An exact minimum target figure was rarely mentioned, but good justifications were required of operating divisions or product departments when returns consistently fell below the corporate average. Not infrequently, officers made statements along the following lines: "If the average corporate return were, say, 20 per cent and the return on investment for a particular item kept falling below 10 per cent, it would be dropped unless (a) a good customer needs it in order to keep a full line, or (b) it is a by-product anyhow, and anything it brings in is really gravy."

---

projected demand, supply, costs, and competition. Of particular interest are such items as: capacities, captive requirements and future expansion plans of competitors; company's estimated market share before and after expansion; degree of diversity of customers; extent to which success of venture depends upon short- or long-term contracts; the effects of changes in tariff rates on competition from abroad; selling prices used for sales to other units of the company; shape of short-run unit cost curve; comparative cost position of competitors; the degree to which an alternative exists of either making or buying important intermediates; flexibility of proposed facilities for production of other products; the probabilities of obsolescence of the process or products; and the relative position of the company with respect to research and development, technical knowledge, labor supply, patents, and raw materials.

[10]The problem here is not simply one of the target return and target payout period, but rather one of balancing the desire to recoup development and other investment costs as rapidly as possible against the desire to prolong the period from distinctiveness to obsolescence by discouraging potential competitors with a relatively low-price or low-profits policy. The most rapid recovery of investment mentioned was one year, with two years not infrequently mentioned, especially where the innovative monopoly was not expected to last long or process secrecy was not secure. Also, there did not appear to be any consistent relationship between the presence of patent protection and the payout period.

A variety of explanations was given by the companies to justify the particular size of the profit target used as a guide in pricing decisions. The most frequently mentioned rationalizations included: (a) fair or reasonable return, (b) the traditional industry concept of fair return in relation to risk factors, (c) desire to equal or better the corporation average return over a recent period, (d) what the company felt it could get as a long-run matter, and (e) use of a specific profit target as a means of stabilizing industry prices. At least one of the foregoing, and most frequently the first, was mentioned by the companies interviewed, and in a few cases the entire list was offered as justification for the company profit goal.

This reinforces the observation made earlier that no one single objective or policy rules all price-making in any given company. In fact, in many companies a close interrelationship exists among target-return pricing, desire to stabilize prices, and target market-share (either a minimum or maximum objective); this is especially true of U.S. Steel, Union Carbide, and Johns-Manville. It would seem, however, that a target-return approach is ordinarily incompatible with a market-share policy; that is, if a company desires to expand its share of the market, it will be inclined to place less emphasis on rigid adherence to a predetermined target.

IV. STABILIZATION OF PRICE AND MARGIN

The drive for stabilized prices by companies like U.S. Steel, Alcoa, International Harvester, Johns-Manville, du Pont, and Union Carbide involves both expectation of proper reward for duty done, i.e., "proper" prices, and a sense of *noblesse oblige*. Having earned what is necessary during poor times to provide an adequate return, they will refrain from upping the price as high as the traffic will bear in prosperity. Likewise, in pricing different items in the product line, there will be an effort (sustained in individual cases by the pricing executive's conscience) to refrain from exploiting any item beyond the limit set by cost-plus.

The distinction between target return on investment as a pricing philosophy and cost-plus pricing in the companies surveyed is difficult to define. Some of the companies that clearly employ the target-return-on-investment procedure in pricing new products—the area of most frequent use of target-return pricing—use cost-plus pricing for other products. The difference between the two rationalizations lies in the extent to which the company is willing to push beyond the limits of a pricing method to some average-return philosophy. According to a General Motors executive, the target plays a prominent role in the formulation of the cost-plus method.[11] But in the case of International Harvester, U.S. Steel, A & P, Johns-Manville, Alcoa, or Union Carbide, it seems fair to say that the pricing executive set the prices of many products on a cost-plus basis (except where competition precludes such action) without questioning the appropriateness of the traditional mark-up.

Cost-plus, therefore, may be viewed as one step on the road to return-on-investment as a guide, or precept for price policy. But some firms never go any farther. The standard can be accepted as self-sufficient; just as the target-return perhaps needs no modification to make it accord with profit maximization (with all the necessary qualifications). Pricing executives seldom look beyond the particular formula with which they are accustomed to justify their decisions. They differentiate between price policies according to the degree of control they exercise; but not by the gap between the price policy and an ideal of profit maximization. They appear as ready to accept cost-plus at a reasonable volume as an ultimate standard for pricing as any other principle.

V. TARGET MARKET-SHARE

A maximum or minimum share of the market as a determinant of pricing policy was listed almost as frequently, and seemed to govern policy almost to the same extent as target-return on investment. Share of the market was ordinarily thought of in terms of a maximum, bearing witness to the power of the corporations interviewed. Being giants, they were careful to limit themselves; they apparently did not wish to gobble up any market they entered, unless it was one which they had created, like nylon, asbestos pipe, aluminum screen wire, cable products, or some synthetic chemical.

Hence, the target share of the market as a guide to pricing tended to be used for those products in which the firm did not, at the outset, enjoy a patent or innovative monopoly. Du Pont made no mention of shooting for a given share of the cellophane or nylon market, nor did Union Carbide in the Prestone market; Johns-Manville set no limit to

[11] [illegible] Donaldson Brown, "Pricing in Relation to Financial Control," *Manag. and Admin.*, Feb. 1924, 7: 195–98, 283–86, 417–22. This may seem to be a rather old reference, but General Motors officials cited it so frequently as an accurate representation of their present-day pricing that it warrants emphasis.

its market share in specialized insulation materials; American Can was not thinking in terms of winning against stiff competition a moderate share of the market for vacuum packed can; nor was Alcoa in the wire and cable market. But a General Electric official spoke at length of the company's policy of not exceeding 50 per cent of any given market because it then would become too vulnerable to competition.[12] Johns-Manville officials likewise indicated that product and sales development are geared to attaining a given percentage of the market for a product line. The company endeavors, executives indicated, to maintain the offensive, rather than to be subject to attack because of their large product share. The company felt strongly that 20 per cent of competitive markets was the maximum share in which it was interested. This policy ruled in those areas where Johns-Manville was *not* the price leader. It stresses sales, service, and superior quality of its product in order to maintain its prices somewhat above those of its competitors. Apparently the program of reaching no more than a given market-share and of moving ahead against competition does not find expression in price reductions.

It is not possible to reach any general conclusions from comparisons of target market-shares and actual share of business realized by the companies mentioning this as a policy for pricing purposes. This is due on the one hand to the unwillingness of the companies to specify in detail particular target-share percentages, and on the other to the lack of sufficiently detailed information for the companies in question, especially for the highly diversified firms. Patently, most of these companies have very significant proportions of national markets.[13]

[12]He stated, "The company would rather be pushing to expand a 25 per cent share than defending a 50 per cent share." As a matter of fact, he indicated, there were few instances where G.E. had more than 22 to 25 per cent of a market. In substance, this means that when G.E. enters an appliance field with a new product, it will price to match its competitors. The company believes that it has been a downward price leader on appliances generally, however, and that both its postwar attempt to lead in price reductions and its long-term reduction in margins (its over-all margins were said to be only 58 per cent as high as in 1940) demonstrates that it has not been content merely to follow the ruling price after moving into a field.

[13]One interesting example of the connection between pricing (livestock bidding), market share, and investment policy is found in Swift. An analysis of livestock buying raises the question whether there is something of an understanding by the major packers of what constitutes their "normal share" of the animals sold in given public stockyards, which was the essence of the Department of Justice's complaint (1948) against Armour, Swift, Cudahy, and Wilson (since dismissed). It would seem that the relative constancy of the proportions of livestock purchased by the principal meat packers is traceable in large part to the short-run fixity of plant capacity, the desire to keep that plant operating at least up to a specific minimum level of utilization (governed partly by labor commit-

VI. "MEETING OR MATCHING COMPETITION"

To some of the officials interviewed, the requirement that the product price "meet competition" appeared, at first glance, to preclude the existence of any pricing policy at all. Meeting competition according to their view cannot be regarded as a rationalization of action; it is the action itself.

The rationalization of this policy of meeting competition is far from elaborate; at first blush it is perhaps unnecessary. How can "meeting competition" be dignified as one out of several alternative guides to action? In chemicals, du Pont seems to apply a rule of thumb of adopting the going price in the markets for many standardized products where it never had or else had lost the leadership—e.g., carbon tetrachloride, hydrogen peroxide, disodium phosphate, nitric acid, hydrochloric acid, and various rubber chemicals. Moreover, in the case of many products selling on a freight-equalization basis, prices were not set at a high executive level; the pricing in many cases had not been reviewed for years, having been established beyond the ken of anyone now in the organization. Yet, even here there is perhaps more discretion than the officials are willing or accustomed to admit. In the pricing of neozone, du Pont was forced—though it had introduced the chemical—to change its price policy because of the tactics of competitors, who shifted the basing point. But need the matter have stopped there? Was there not a decision by du Pont to go no further than matching the Akron-based price? In many other cases du Pont undoubtedly could, if it chose, have altered the basing points or other features of the marketing of chemicals of which it produced more than an inconsequential market share.

In many cases the policy of meeting competition appears to be materially influenced by market-share psychology. Esso Standard, while going to great lengths to devise a cost-plus theory, has modified it when and where it seemed necessary or desirable. Standard of Indiana was even more specific in basing its policies on "meeting"—or forestalling—competition. Esso and, to a much lesser extent, Standard

ments), and the ever present threat that another packer may secure a larger share of the animals and the market for dressed meats. In view of these considerations, the percentages of animals purchased by the major packers would logically evidence substantial constancy over periods of weeks or months in given markets. But, unless this same approach is carried over into the planning of plant sizes in new locations (or enlargement of established plants), as well as the rate of utilization of these facilities, this would seem to be an insufficient explanation for the long-run stability of shares.

of Indiana refrained from publishing or trying to reduce to definiteness the details of the policy. A number of questions related to the companies' rationalizations are basic to understanding the functioning of the policy, for clearly neither company changed prices instantaneously when facing "competition": Did they meet the exact price charged, at the refinery or to the retail dealer? How long did a substandard price have to prevail before it could undermine a cost-plus price? Whose competitive price brought action? How were competitors rated in effectiveness? Answers to these questions are basic to an understanding of the policy. But the oil companies have not divulged the facts that would permit full and consistent treatment of the theory of "meeting competition" as seen by their managements.

It seems also that in some cases the companies are not simply meeting competition—they are preventing it. This appears to have been the purpose of A & P in localizing price cuts to make matters difficult for a competitive store on its opening day, or General Foods in reducing the price of Certo and Sur-Jell in the Northwest where rival pectins were strong.[14] Standard of Indiana, a dominant seller not overfond of price wars, may easily justify meeting competition locally on the basis that the policy offers a permanent threat to potential price-cutters.

In other cases, the companies are aware of specific competitive products whose prices must be matched by their own if volume is to be expanded. Union Carbide knew that its synthetic organic chemicals, like the various alcohols, had to meet or undersell the price of the natural products if the investment was ever to be returned. In other cases, where a standardized commodity—e.g., bakery flour, livestock feeds, and frozen fish sold by General Foods, flour by General Mills, or wholesale meat by Swift—is simply marketed at a price over which no firm, or even small group of firms, can have control, then pricing policy ceases to have meaning. The phrase "meeting competition" is either inapplicable or inaccurate, since there is no specific competition to meet—only the market price.

[14]This information was not provided by the companies when interviewed, but is based on statements in the A & P antitrust case and the General Foods F.T.C. case made by officials of the respective companies. An A & P official of the Atlantic Division, for example, said, "It might be necessary for us to operate unprofitably for several weeks . . . reducing our line of [sic] 10% several weeks prior to the time the competitor plans to open so that people in the community will be impressed with our low prices. . . ." *U.S. v. New York Great Atlantic and Pacific Tea Co., Inc.*, 67 F. Supp. 626 (1946), p. 668; see also *ibid.*, pp. 667, 669, and Government Brief, pp. 909, 931; and General Foods, F.T.C. Docket No. 5675, Complaint, July 7, 1949.

VII. OTHER RATIONALIZATIONS

There are other pegs on which managements hang pricing decisions. In view of American Can's undisputed (at least until 1954) leadership in the metal container industry, and its bargaining power vis-à-vis both its suppliers and customers, it is somewhat surprising that the company should not have set out an explicit pricing goal in terms of return on investment. The management seems to be more concerned with the assurance of funds for innovating research than any particular target return on investment, although the maintenance of its market share through its closing-machine leasing policy indirectly accomplishes the same objective. The company's pricing policy could be construed as "marginal" in the sense that it automatically (via its contracts) transmits to its customers increases or decreases in costs of materials (tin plate) or labor in the can factories. In turn, this adjustability in price seems to have had the effect of stabilizing American Can's margin, the price of its services as the owner of can-closing equipment and engineering services, and, at the same time, the price of cans throughout the canning season.

The companies cited many instances involving the need for resolution of conflicts of interest between integrated and non-integrated firms and between established giants and newcomers, which displaced the usual bases for their pricing decisions. The Robinson-Patman and Sherman Acts, even when they have not been the basis for actions against the companies, were used as fundamental rationalizations of policy.

VIII. A COMPOSITE VIEW OF PRICING OBJECTIVES

Because it is big the large firm envisages itself as a part of a socially integrated group, with responsibilities for the whole pipeline and production (including full-line offerings) and associated distribution. They see themselves in a continuing relationship not only with their own distributors, but even with dealers and ultimate customers, and with their suppliers—even when the latter lacked, or especially when they lacked, the bargaining power of a larger firm. The market, in effect, is regarded as a creature of the firm, and the firm has the responsibility for preserving these relationships and perpetuating its own position.

The size of these firms also makes them an obvious target for antitrust suits, legislation, Congressional investigation, and similar restraining forces. To a certain extent, size thus entails a vulnerability and generates a sense of *noblesse oblige*. This is reinforced by the disposition of the government and the community generally to look on and appeal to these firms as "pattern-setters" for industry generally; and in pricing they are expected to avoid taking full advantage of immediate profit opportunities. This attitude is perhaps most clearly expressed in the *Economic Report of the President* of January 1957, which stated:

> Specifically, business and labor leadership have the responsibility to reach agreements on wages and other labor benefits that are fair to the rest of the community as well as to those persons immediately involved. . . . *And business must recognize the broad public interest in price set on their products and services.* (p. 3, italics added.)

From this point, it is an easy step to the position taken by the typical large firm that it is entitled to a "just price" and "fair return" on investment. In the case of some companies, like U.S. Steel, the resolution of conflicts of interest between integrated and nonintegrated firms, between established giants and newcomers, and between the pattern-setter and the community generally, has modified company price policy to a point where even the managements have come to refer to it as akin to that of a public utility. This may be a logical development in cases where unpleasant experiences of cutthroat competition—especially in fairly standardized products like steel, copper, gasoline, and aluminum—have generated a disposition by management to avoid price changes except through periodic, thoroughly considered, and well-publicized alterations in recognized base prices. By relating price revisions to changes in direct costs (especially increases in wage costs), the firm avoids the annoyance to itself and its customers (who they claim vastly prefer stable prices) of frequent changes in price structure.

This desire for stabilized pricing, oftentimes described with a blanket adjective as "administered," usually implies that the company or companies set some kind of target to which their price policies conform. The price, according to this view, is under the control of one firm acting as the price leader or a group of firms that make policy for the industry. The contention of the business executives themselves is that an administered price, like the tank-wagon price of gasoline, far from being an independent creation of the price leader, is merely a device for approximating a market equilibrium. According to this view, there are so many possibilities of substitution of one product for another, or an off-brand for a name brand, that the limits of discretion are much narrower than is generally supposed. Administration of prices, officials contend, thus merely avoids the decision to use cutthroat competition—which itself would be another form of administered pricing; it also avoids temporary exploitation of shortages. Refraining from raising prices when a higher price is necessary to equate supply with demand, is also justified by management on the grounds that over the long run higher prices would disturb equilibrium by bringing unneeded capacity into the industry. But it is impossible to accept the conventional justification for leadership. It can masquerade as resulting in a genuine "equilibrium" only if the word is made equivalent to whatever is the decision of the leading firms.

The foregoing data, above all, make it clear that management's approach to pricing is based upon *planned* profits. The company proceeds on the assumption of the need for a certain amount of capital to undertake the investment in plant expansion and new facilities which are envisaged for the long haul in order to maintain and/or improve market position. In some cases, quite in contrast to the thinking of management before the second world war, this desire to hold position and to penetrate wider markets requires that capital investment should be planned with built-in excess capacity (this is best illustrated by the fact that prices are premised on the assumption of operating at a rate of 75 or 80 per cent of capacity, which is assumed to be the long-run normal). In deciding upon which products and productive facilities will be added or expanded, the top-level corporation appropriations committee relies upon estimates of return on utilized investment. The only way in which price policy can be viewed in such companies as these, with their wide variety of products and selling in a large number of different markets, is in terms of profits-investment ratios. This criterion serves as an effective guide for pricing decisions at divisional and departmental levels. If we are to speak of "administered" decisions in the large firm, it is perhaps more accurate to speak of administered *profits* rather than administered *prices*.

IX. CONCLUSIONS

The principal purpose of this paper has been to contribute to our knowledge of the actual process by which prices are formed in industry, with the expectation that the data will help in constructing a more realistic theory of the firm capable of yielding useful predictions of industrial price behavior. The general hypothesis which emerges is that (a) the large company has a fairly well-defined pricing goal that is related to a long-range profit horizon; (b) its management seeks—especially in multiproduct multimarket operations—a simultaneous decision with respect to price, cost, and product characteristics; and (c) its pricing formulas are handy devices for checking the internal consistency of the separate decisions as against the general company objective. Under this hypothesis no single theory of the firm—and certainly no single motivational hypothesis such as profit-maximization—is likely to impose an unambiguous course of action for the firm for any given situation; nor will it provide a satisfactory basis for valid and useful predictions of price behavior.

In pursuit of price policies that will yield the maximum satisfaction of the company's community of interests, the findings show that one company will prefer stability, another will seek to expand its market share, or to engage in continuous discovery and pre-emption of new fields, while others will be content to meet competition, to satisfy a set target, or to aim at combinations and variations of these goals. It seems reasonable to conclude that the pricing policies are in almost every case equivalent to a company policy that represents an order of priorities and choice from among competing objectives rather than policies tested by any simple concept of profits maximization. Managerial specialists down the line are given a framework of requirements that must be met, while managers at the top, of course, are free to and do change these requirements to meet particular situations.[15]

Another relevant aspect of the data for theoretical analysis is the conception of the market held by managements of large corporations. Individual products, markets, and pricing are not considered in isolation; the unit of decision-making is the enterprise, and pricing and marketing strategies are viewed in this global context. Because of the tremendously complex joint-cost problems and the lack of knowledge of actual relationships between costs and output or sales, on the one hand, and the joint-revenue aspects of multiproduct companies, on the other, pricing is frequently done for product groups with an eye to the over-all profit position of the company. This means that costing of products ends up as a result of price policy rather than the reverse. In view of the various external pressures on the company and the nature of the strategy of the enterprise, however, it is doubtful if prices would

[15] "The managerial philosophy not only calls into question the assumption of profit maximization as a workable description of entrepreneurial behavior but denies the institutional basis of the classical profit motivation." E. S. Mason, "The Apologetics of 'Managerialism'," *Journal of Business,* Volume 31 (January 1958), p. 6.

bear any closer relationship to actual costs were detailed cost data available to management. The incentive to realize target rates of profits for the long haul better suits the objectives of management-controlled companies than any desire to profiteer or to seek windfall profits.

It might appear that there are conflicts between the objectives of price leaders and price followers, e.g., between such companies as U.S. Steel and National Steel. Actually, however, it is a matter of leaders having fairly well-defined target objectives, whereas price followers evidently do not have independent targets. Their objective, especially where undifferentiated products make up the bulk of the product line, will be determined by the target set by the price leader. If the target is acceptable, the follower is content to hold a market share and will adjust price policy accordingly.

In more general cases, including differentiated product markets as well as undifferentiated, the extent to which companies—with the dimensions and diversification of those under discussion—serve as leaders or followers on individual products or product groups depends upon the profit-importance of a particular product in a given company's line, the nature of the product—whether a producer or a consumer good—and the size and degree of diversification of companies with which there are product overlaps. Moreover, the manner in which interfirm policies will be coordinated will depend upon the above factors as they bear upon particular products, plus the over-all objectives of the enterprise as a unit and its general market strategy.

A further implication of the findings for the theory of the firm is the relationship found between price and investment decisions. The information on this aspect is limited, but nevertheless the setting of and attempt to follow specific target returns on investment are manifest at two separate levels of operations: short-run pricing and investment decisions. The investment decision presupposes a price (and usually a market-share) assumption, which, in turn, determines short-run price decisions thereafter. Thus, investment decisions in effect are themselves a form of pricing decision, and over time become an inherent part of price policy.

Finally, the general approach of these large corporations to price policy, and the attendant price behavior, raise some important issues for public policy. Their very size—both absolutely and relatively—permits the managements to select from among various alternative courses of action. This is a fairly clear manifestation of economic or market power. In partial reflection of this power, plus a variety of other reasons related to their size, vulnerability to public criticism, and potential antitrust action, these corporations tend to behave more and more like public utilities, especially the target-return-minded companies. To complicate the issue further, target-return pricing implies a policy of stable or rigid pricing, even though exceptions are found within particular product lines.

A crucial question raised by these facets of policy is: What is the net impact on economic growth and stability? More specifically, do target-return pricing, profits planning, and the attendant price behavior, tend to promote or inhibit stability and growth? Much more adequate empirical data on corporation objectives and detailed study of individual company pricing, profits, and investment planning over the course of economic fluctuations are needed before answers can be given to this question.

20. RETAIL STRATEGY AND THE CLASSIFICATION OF CONSUMER GOODS*

Louis P. Bucklin

When Melvin T. Copeland published his famous discussion of the classification of consumer goods, shopping, convenience, and specialty goods, his intent was clearly to create a guide for the development of marketing strategies by manufacturers.[1] Although his discussion involved retailers and retailing, his purpose was to show how consumer buying habits affected the type of channel of distribution and promotional strategy that a manufacturer should adopt. Despite the controversy which still surrounds his classification, his success in creating such a guide may be judged by the fact that through the years few marketing texts have failed to make use of his ideas.

The purpose of this article is to attempt to clarify some of the issues that exist with respect to the classification, and to extend the concept to include the retailer and the study of retail strategy.

CONTROVERSY OVER THE CLASSIFICATION SYSTEM

The starting point for the discussion lies with the definitions adopted by the American Marketing Association's Committee on Definitions for the classification system in 1948.[2] These are:

Convenience Goods: Those consumers' goods which the cus-

*Reprinted from the *Journal of Marketing*, national quarterly publication of the American Marketing Association (January, 1963), pp. 51–56.

[1]Melvin T. Copeland, "Relation of Consumers' Buying Habits to Marketing Methods," *Harvard Business Review*, Vol. 1 (April, 1923), pp. 282–289.

[2]Definitions Committee, American Marketing Association, "Report of the Definitions Committee," *Journal of Marketing*, Vol. 13 (October, 1948), pp. 202–217, at p. 206, p. 215.

tomer purchases frequently, immediately, and with the minimum of effort.

Shopping Goods: Those consumers' goods which the customer in the process of selection and purchase characteristically compares on such bases as suitability, quality, price and style.

Specialty Goods: Those consumers' goods on which a significant group of buyers are habitually willing to make a special purchasing effort.

This set of definitions was retained in virtually the same form by the Committee on Definitions in its latest publication.[3]

Opposing these accepted definitions stands a critique by Richard H. Holton.[4] Finding the Committee's definitions too imprecise to be able to measure consumer buying behavior, he suggested that the following definitions not only would represent the essence of Copeland's original idea, but be operationally more useful as well.

Convenience Goods: Those goods for which the consumer regards the probable gain from making price and quality comparisons as small compared to the cost of making such comparisons.

Shopping Goods: Those goods for which the consumer regards the probable gain from making price and quality comparisons as large relative to the cost of making such comparisons.

Specialty Goods: Those convenience or shopping goods which have such a limited market as to require the consumer to make a special effort to purchase them.

Holton's definitions have particular merit because they make explicit the underlying conditions that control the extent of a consumer's shopping activities. They show that a consumer's buying behavior will be determined not only by the strength of his desire to secure some good, but by his perception of the cost of shopping to obtain it. In other words, the consumer continues to shop *for all goods* so long as he feels that the additional satisfactions from further comparisons are at least equal to the cost of making the additional effort. The distinction between shopping and convenience goods lies principally in the degree of satisfaction to be secured from further comparisons.

[3]Definitions Committee, American Marketing Association, *Marketing Definitions*, (Chicago: American Marketing Association, 1960), pp. 11, 21, 22.

[4]Richard H. Holton, "The Distinction Between Convenience Goods, Shopping Goods, and Specialty Goods," *Journal of Marketing*, Vol. 23 (July, 1958), pp. 53–56.

The Specialty Good Issue

While Holton's conceptualization makes an important contribution, he has sacrificed some of the richness of Copeland's original ideas. This is essentially David J. Luck's complaint in a criticism of Holton's proposal.[5] Luck objected to the abandonment of the *willingness* of consumers to make a special effort to buy as the rationale for the concept of specialty goods. He regarded this type of consumer behavior as based upon unique consumer attitudes toward certain goods and not the density of distribution of those goods. Holton, in a reply, rejected Luck's point; he remained convinced that the real meaning of specialty goods could be derived from his convenience goods, shopping goods continuum, and market conditions.[6]

The root of the matter appears to be that insufficient attention has been paid to the fact that the consumer, once embarked upon some buying expedition, may have only one of two possible objectives in mind. A discussion of this aspect of consumer behavior will make possible a closer synthesis of Holton's contributions with the more traditional point of view.

A Forgotten Idea

The basis for this discussion is afforded by certain statements, which the marketing profession has largely ignored over the years, in Copeland's original presentation of his ideas. These have regard to the extent of the consumer's awareness of the precise nature of the item he wishes to buy, *before* he starts his shopping trip. Copeland stated that the consumer, in both the case of convenience goods and specialty goods, has full knowledge of the particular good, or its acceptable substitutes, that he will buy before he commences his buying trip. The consumer, however, lacks this knowledge in the case of a shopping good.[7] This means that the buying trip must not only serve the objective of purchasing the good, but must enable the consumer to discover which item he wants to buy.

The behavior of the consumer during any shopping expedition may, as a result, be regarded as heavily dependent upon the state of his

[5]David J. Luck, "On the Nature of Specialty Goods," *Journal of Marketing*, Vol. 24 (July, 1959), pp. 61–64.

[6]Richard H. Holton, "What is Really Meant by 'Specialty' Goods?" *Journal of Marketing*, Vol. 24 (July, 1959), pp. 64–67.

[7]Melvin T. Copeland, same reference as footnote 1, pp. 283–284.

decision as to what he wants to buy. If the consumer knows precisely what he wants, he needs only to undertake communication activities sufficient to take title to the desired product. He may also undertake ancillary physical activities involving the handling of the product and delivery. If the consumer is uncertain as to what he wants to buy, then an additional activity will have to be performed. This involves the work of making comparisons between possible alternative purchases, or simply search.

There would be little point, with respect to the problem of classifying consumer goods, in distinguishing between the activity of search and that of making a commitment to buy, if a consumer always performed both before purchasing a good. The crucial point is that he does not. While most of the items that a consumer buys have probably been subjected to comparison at some point in his life, he does not make a search before each purchase. Instead, a past solution to the need is frequently remembered and, if satisfactory, is implemented.[8] Use of these past decisions for many products quickly moves the consumer past any perceived necessity of undertaking new comparisons and leaves only the task of exchange to be discharged.

REDEFINITION OF THE SYSTEM

Use of this concept of problem solving permits one to classify consumer buying efforts into two broad categories which may be called shopping and nonshopping goods.

Shopping Goods

Shopping goods are those for which the consumer *regularly* formulates a new solution to his need each time it is aroused. They are goods whose suitability is determined through search before the consumer commits himself to each purchase.

The motivation behind this behavior stems from circumstances which tend to perpetuate a lack of complete consumer knowledge about the nature of the product that he would like to buy.[9] Frequent changes in price, style, or product technology cause consumer information to become obsolete. The greater the time lapse between purchases, the more obsolete will his information be. The consumer's

[8]George Katona, *Psychological Analysis of Economic Behavior* (New York: McGraw-Hill Book Co., Inc., 1951), p. 47.
[9]Same reference, pp. 67–68.

needs are also subject to change, or he may seek variety in his purchases as an actual goal. These forces will tend to make past information inappropriate. New search, due to forces internal and external to the consumer, is continuously required for products with purchase determinants which the consumer regards as both important and subject to change.[10]

The number of comparisons that the consumer will make in purchasing a shopping good may be determined by use of Holton's hypothesis on effort. The consumer, in other words, will undertake search for a product until the perceived value to be secured through additional comparisons is less than the estimated cost of making those comparisons. Thus, shopping effort will vary according to the intensity of the desire of the consumer to find the right product, the type of product and the availability of retail facilities. Whether the consumer searches diligently, superficially, or even buys at the first opportunity, however, does not alter the shopping nature of the product.

Nonshopping Goods

Turning now to nonshopping goods, one may define these as products for which the consumer is both willing and able to use stored solutions to the problem of finding a product to answer a need. From the remarks on shopping goods it may be generalized that nonshopping goods have purchase determinants which do not change, or which are perceived as changing inconsequentially, between purchases.[11] The consumer, for example, may assume that price for some product never changes or that price is unimportant. It may be unimportant because either the price is low, or the consumer is very wealthy.

Nonshopping goods may be divided into convenience and specialty goods by means of the concept of a preference map. Bayton introduces this concept as the means to show how the consumer stores information about products.[12] It is a rough ranking of the relative desirability of the different kinds of products that the consumer sees as possible satisfiers for his needs. For present purposes, two basic types of preference maps may be envisaged. One type ranks all known product alternatives equally in terms of desirability. The other ranks one

[10]George Katona and Eva Mueller, "A Study of Purchase Decisions in Consumer Behavior," Lincoln Clark, editor, *Consumer Behavior* (New York: University Press, 1954), pp. 30–87.

[11]Katona, same reference as footnote 8, p. 68.

[12]James A. Bayton, "Motivation, Cognition, Learning—Basic Factors in Consumer Behavior," *Journal of Marketing*, Vol. 22 (January, 1958), pp. 282–289, at p. 287. [See pp. 107–118 of this anthology — eds.].

particular product as so superior to all others that the consumer, in effect, believes this product is the only answer to his need.

Distinguishing the Specialty Good

This distinction in preference maps creates the basis for discriminating between a convenience good and a specialty good. Clearly, where the consumer is indifferent to the precise item among a number of substitutes which he could buy, he will purchase the most accessible one and look no further. This is a convenience good. On the other hand, where the consumer recognizes only one brand of a product as capable of satisfying his needs, he will be willing to bypass more readily accessible substitutes in order to secure the wanted item. This is a specialty good.

However, most nonshopping goods will probably fall in between these two polar extremes. Preference maps will exist where the differences between the relative desirability of substitutes may range from the slim to the well marked. In order to distinguish between convenience goods and specialty goods in these cases, Holton's hypothesis regarding consumer effort may be employed again. A convenience good, in these terms, becomes one for which the consumer has such little preference among his perceived choices that he buys the item which is most readily available. A specialty good is one for which consumer preference is so strong that he bypasses, or would be willing to bypass, the purchase of more accessible substitutes in order to secure his most wanted item.

It should be noted that this decision on the part of the consumer as to how much effort he should expend takes place under somewhat different conditions than the one for shopping goods. In the nonshopping good instance the consumer has a reasonably good estimate of the additional value to be achieved by purchasing his preferred item. The estimate of the additional cost required to make this purchase may also be made fairly accurately. Consequently, the consumer will be in a much better position to justify the expenditure of additional effort here than in the case of shopping goods where much uncertainty must exist with regard to both of these factors.

The New Classification

The classification of consumer goods that results from the analysis is as follows:

Convenience Goods: Those goods for which the consumer, before his need arises, possesses a preference map that indicates a willingness to purchase any of a number of known substitutes rather than to make the additional effort required to buy a particular item.

Shopping Goods: Those goods for which the consumer has not developed a complete preference map before the need arises, requiring him to undertake search to construct such a map before purchase.

Specialty Goods: Those goods for which the consumer, before his need arises, possesses a preference map that indicates a willingness to expend the additional effort required to purchase the most preferred item rather than to buy a more readily accessible substitute.

EXTENSION TO RETAILING

The classification of the goods concept developed above may now be extended to retailing. As the concept now stands, it is derived from consumer attitudes or motives toward a *product*. These attitudes, or product motives, are based upon the consumer's interpretation of a product's styling, special features, quality, and social status of its brand name, if any. Occasionally the price may also be closely associated with the product by the consumer.

Classification of Patronage Motives

The extension of the concept to retailing may be made through the notion of patronage motives, a term long used in marketing. Patronage motives are derived from consumer attitudes concerning the retail establishment. They are related to factors which the consumer is likely to regard as controlled by the retailer. These will include assortment, credit, service, guarantee, shopping ease and enjoyment, and usually price. Patronage motives, however, have never been systematically categorized. It is proposed that the procedure developed above to discriminate among product motives be used to classify consumer buying motives with respect to retail stores as well.

This will provide the basis for the consideration of retail marketing strategy and will aid in clearing up certain ambiguities that would otherwise exist if consumer buying motives were solely classified by product factors. These ambiguities appear, for example, when the consumer has a strong affinity for some particular brand of a product, but little interest in where he buys it. The manufacturer of the product, as a result, would be correct in defining the product as a specialty item if the consumer's preferences were so strong as to cause him to eschew more readily available substitutes. The retailer may regard it as a convenience good, however, since the consumer will make no special effort to purchase the good from any particular store. This problem is clearly avoided by separately classifying product and patronage motives.

The categorization of patronage motives by the above procedure results in the following three definitions. These are:

Convenience Stores: Those stores for which the consumer, before his need for some product arises, possesses a preference map that indicates a willingness to buy from the most accessible store.

Shopping Stores: Those stores for which the consumer has not developed a complete preference map relative to the product he wishes to buy, requiring him to undertake a search to construct such a map before purchase.

Specialty Stores: Those stores for which the consumer, before his need for some product arises, possesses a preference map that indicates a willingness to buy the item from a particular establishment even though it may not be the most accessible.

The Product-patronage Matrix

Although this basis will now afford the retailer a means to consider alternative strategies, a finer classification system may be obtained by relating consumer product motives to consumer patronage motives. By cross-classifying each product motive with each patronage motive, one creates a three-by-three matrix, representing nine possible types of consumer buying behavior. Each of the nine cells in the matrix may be described as follows:

1. *Convenience Store–Convenience Good*: The consumer, represented by this category, prefers to buy the most readily available brand of product at the most accessible store.
2. *Convenience Store–Shopping Good*: The consumer selects his purchase from among the assortment carried by the most accessible store.
3. *Convenience Store–Specialty Good*: The consumer purchases his favored brand from the most accessible store which has the item in stock.
4. *Shopping Store–Convenience Good*: The consumer is indiffer-

ent to the brand of product he buys, but shops among different stores in order to secure better retail service and/or lower retail price.

5. *Shopping Store–Shopping Good*: The consumer makes comparisons among both retail controlled factors and factors associated with the product (brand).
6. *Shopping Store–Specialty Good*: The consumer has a strong preference with respect to the brand of the product, but shops among a number of stores in order to secure the best retail and/or price for this brand.
7. *Specialty Store–Convenience Good*: The consumer prefers to trade at a specific store, but is indifferent to the brand of product purchased.
8. *Specialty Store–Shopping Good*: The consumer prefers to trade at a certain store, but is uncertain as to which product he wishes to buy and examines the store's assortment for the best purchase.
9. *Specialty Store–Specialty Good*: The consumer has both a preference for a particular store and a specific brand.

Conceivably, each of these nine types of behavior might characterize the buying patterns of some consumers for a given product. It seems more likely, however, that the behavior of consumers toward a product could be represented by only three or four of the categories. The remaining cells would be empty, indicating that no consumers bought the product by these methods. Different cells, of course, would be empty for different products.

THE FORMATION OF RETAIL STRATEGY

The extended classification system developed above clearly provides additional information important to the manufacturer in the planning of his marketing strategy. Of principal interest here, however, is the means by which the retailer might use the classification system in planning his marketing strategy.

Three Basic Steps

The procedure involves three steps. The first is the classification of the retailer's potential customers for some product by market segment, using the nine categories in the consumer buying habit matrix to define the principal segments. The second requires the retailer to determine the nature of the marketing strategies necessary to appeal to each market segment. The final step is the retailer's selection of the market segment, and the strategy associated with it, to which he will sell. A simplified, hypothetical example may help to clarify this process.

A former buyer of dresses for a department store decided to open her own dress shop. She rented a small store in the downtown area of a city of 50,000, ten miles distant from a metropolitan center of several hundred thousand population. In contemplating her marketing strategy, she was certain that the different incomes, educational backgrounds, and tastes of the potential customers in her city meant that various groups of these women were using sharply different buying methods for dresses. Her initial problem was to determine, by use of the consumer buying habit matrix, what proportion of her potential market bought dresses in what manner.

By drawing on her own experience, discussions with other retailers in the area, census and other market data, the former buyer estimated that her potential market was divided, according to the matrix, in the following proportions.

TABLE 1

PROPORTION OF POTENTIAL DRESS MARKET IN EACH MATRIX CELL

Buying habit	*% of market*
Convenience store–convenience good	0
Convenience store–shopping good	3
Convenience store–specialty good	20
Shopping store–convenience good	0
Shopping store–shopping good	35
Shopping store–specialty good	2
Specialty store–convenience good	0
Specialty store–shopping good	25
Specialty store–specialty good	15
	100

This analysis revealed four market segments that she believed were worth further consideration. (In an actual situation, each of these four should be further divided into submarket segments according to other possible factors such as age, income, dress size required, location of residence, etc.) Her next task was to determine the type of marketing mix which would most effectively appeal to each of these segments. The information for these decisions was derived from the characteristics of consumer behavior associated with each of the defined segments. The following is a brief description of her assessment of how elements of the marketing mix ought to be weighted in order to formulate a strategy for each segment.

A Strategy for Each Segment

To appeal to the convenience store-specialty good segment she felt that the two most important elements in the mix should be a highly accessible location and selection of widely-accepted brand merchandise. Of somewhat lesser importance, she found, were depth of assortment, personal selling, and price. Minimal emphasis should be given to store promotion and facilities.

She reasoned that the shopping store-shopping good requires a good central location, emphasis on price, and a broad assortment. She ranked store promotion, accepted brand names and personal selling as secondary. Store facilities would, once again, receive minor emphasis.

The specialty store-shopping good market would, she believed, have to be catered to with an exceptionally strong assortment, a high level of personal selling and more elaborate store facilities. Less emphasis would be needed upon prominent brand names, store promotions, and price. Location was of minor importance.

The specialty store-specialty good category, she thought, would require a marketing mix heavily emphasizing personal selling and highly elaborate store facilities and service. She also felt that prominent brand names would be required, but that these would probably have to include the top names in fashion, including labels from Paris. Depth of assortment would be secondary, while least emphasis would be placed upon store promotion, price, and location.

Evaluation of Alternatives

The final step in the analysis required the former dress buyer to assess her abilities to implement any one of these strategies, given the degree of competition existing in each segment. Her considerations were as follows. With regard to the specialty store-specialty good market, she was unprepared to make the investment in store facilities and services that she felt would be necessary. She also thought, since a considerable period of time would probably be required for her to build up the necessary reputation, that this strategy involved substantial risk. Lastly, she believed that her experience in buying high fashion was somewhat limited and that trips to European fashion centers would prove burdensome.

She also doubted her ability to cater to the specialty store-shopping good market, principally because she knew that her store would not be large enough to carry the necessary assortment depth. She felt that this same factor would limit her in attempting to sell to the shopping store-shopping good market as well. Despite the presence of the large market in this segment, she believed that she would not be able to create sufficient volume in her proposed quarters to enable her to compete effectively with the local department store and several large department stores in the neighboring city.

The former buyer believed her best opportunity was in selling to the convenience store-specialty good segment. While there were already two other stores in her city which were serving this segment, she believed that a number of important brands were still not represented. Her past contacts with resources led her to believe that she would stand an excellent chance of securing a number of these lines. By stocking these brands, she thought that she could capture a considerable number of local customers who currently were purchasing them in the large city. In this way, she believed, she would avoid the full force of local competition.

Decision

The conclusion of the former buyer to use her store to appeal to the convenience store-specialty good segment represents the culmination to the process of analysis suggested here. It shows how the use of the three-by-three matrix of consumer buying habits may aid the retailer in developing his marketing strategy. It is a device which can isolate the important market segments. It provides further help in enabling the retailer to associate the various types of consumer behavior with those elements of the marketing mix to which they are sensitive. Finally, the analysis forces the retailer to assess the probability of his success in attempting to use the necessary strategy in order to sell each possible market.

21. PARALLEL SYSTEMS OF PROMOTION AND DISTRIBUTION*

Leo V. Aspinwall

The sponsor of a product must decide how it is to be promoted and what channels to use for its physical distribution. He is confronted with a variety of possibilities both for stimulating demand and for moving his product to the consumer. It turns out that there is a parallel relationship between these two aspects of the marketing problem with a distribution system and its appropriate counterpart in promotion usually occurring together. This pairing of systems occurs because the promotion and distribution requirements of a product are both

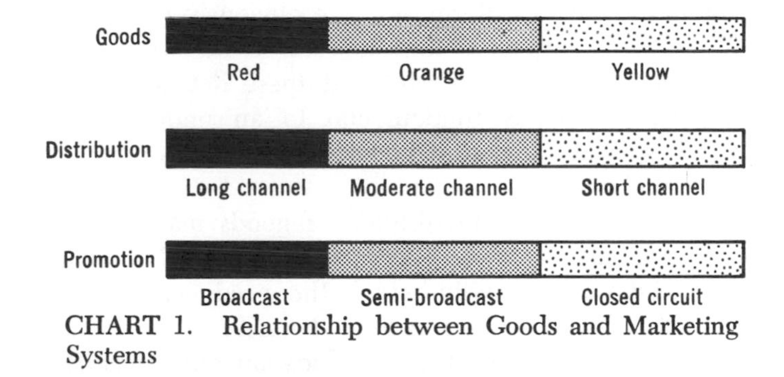

CHART 1. Relationship between Goods and Marketing Systems

dependent on the marketing characteristics of the goods. It was further shown that this array could be translated into a numerical scale and presented in simple graphic form. The purpose of the present article is to indicate how the position of a product on this scale can be used to

*Reprinted from *Cost and Profit Outlook* (October, 1956), by permission of the author.

identify the parallel systems of promotion and distribution which should be used in marketing the product.

THE PARALLEL SYSTEMS THEORY

This set of ideas has come to be designated as the parallel systems theory. It is the kind of theory which is intended to be helpful in resolving fundamental practical issues in marketing. Theory alone cannot settle all the details of a marketing plan. It may save much time and effort by indicating the starting point for planning and the appropriate matching of systems of promotion and distribution. The gross margin earned on a product provides the fund which must cover the costs of marketing distribution and marketing promotion. The management of this fund involves many of the most critical decisions with which marketing executives have to deal. Even slight errors of judgment in this regard may spell the difference between profit and loss.

The parallel systems theory begins with a simple thesis which may be stated as follows: The characteristics of goods indicate the manner of their physical distribution and the manner of promotion must parallel that physical distribution. Thus, we have parallel systems, one for physical distribution and one for promotion. The movement of goods and the movement of information are obviously quite different processes. It was to be expected that specialized facilities would be developed for each function. The fact that these developments take place along parallel lines is fundamental to an understanding of marketing. A few special terms must be introduced at this point for use in discussing parallel systems.

A channel for the physical distribution of goods may be either a short channel or a long channel. The shortest channel, of course, is represented by the transaction in which the producer delivers the product directly to its ultimate user. A long channel is one in which the product moves through several stages of location and ownership as from the factory to a regional warehouse, to the wholesaler's warehouse, to a retail store, and finally to the consumer. The parallel concepts in promotion may be compared to contrasting situations in electronic communication. On the one hand there is the closed circuit through which two people can carry on a direct and exclusive conversation with each other. On the other hand there is broadcast communication such as radio and television whereby the same message can be communicated to many people simultaneously.

In general, long channels and broadcast promotion are found together in marketing while short channels and closed circuit or direct promotion are found together. The parallel systems theory attempts to show how these relationships arise naturally out of the marketing characteristics of the goods.

CHARACTERISTICS OF GOODS AND MARKETING SYSTEMS

Goods may be arrayed according to their marketing characteristics as red, orange, and yellow. Marketing systems can be arrayed in similar and parallel fashion. Red goods call for long channels and broadcast promotion. Yellow goods call for short channels and closed circuit promotion. Orange goods are intermediate as to their marketing characteristics and, hence, are intermediate as to the kind of distribution and promotion systems which they require. There is a continuous gradation from red to yellow and from broadcast to direct methods of marketing.

One of the fundamental marketing characteristics of goods is replacement rate. That is the frequency with which the average consumer in the market buys the product or replenishes the supply of it carried in his household inventory. Red goods are goods with a high replacement rate. A market transaction which occurs with high frequency lends itself to standardization and specialization of function. The movement of goods and the movement of information each becomes clearly marked and separate. Opportunity arises for a number of specialized marketing agencies to participate in distribution, and the result is what has been called the "long channel." Messages to the ultimate user become as standardized as the product itself. This type of information and persuasion does not need to follow the long distribution channel from step to step in its transmission from producer to consumer. Such messages are broadcast to consumers through both electronic and printed advertising media which provide a more appropriate channel.

Yellow goods are low in replacement rate and high in other marketing characteristics such as adjustment. Requirements for this class of goods tend to vary from one user to another. Adjustment embraces a variety of means by which goods are fitted to individual requirements. The marketing process remains relatively costly and a large percentage of gross margin necessarily goes along with high adjustment. The opportunity for standardization and specialization is slight compared to that of red goods. Physical movement and promotion remain more closely associated, with a two-way communication concerning what is available and what is needed finally resulting in the delivery of the custom-made product. A transaction between a man and his tailor would illustrate this type of marketing. Many kinds of industrial equipment are specially designed for the given user and would also be at the extreme yellow end of the scale. The short channel is prevalent in such situations and all promotion or related communication moves through a closed circuit.

Many products lie in the middle range which has been designated as orange goods. They have been produced to standard specifications but with the knowledge that they will have to be adapted in greater or less degree in each individual installation. The replacement rate is high enough to offer moderate opportunity for standardization and specialization. At least one intermediary is likely to enter the picture, such as an automobile dealer buying from the manufacturer and selling to the consumer or an industrial distributor serving as a channel between two manufacturers. The car sold to customers may be of the same model and yet be substantially differentiated to meet individual preferences as to color and accessories. Broadcast media are used in promotion but not on the same scale relatively as for soaps or cigarettes. The industrial distributor is often supported in his efforts by specialty salesmen or sales engineers employed by the manufacturer. Advertising of a semi-broadcast character is likely to be used. That is to say that messages are specially prepared for various segments of the market for which the appeal of the product is expected to be somewhat different. This approach lies between the standardized message to all users on the one hand and the individualized closed circuit negotiation on the other.

One qualification which may properly be suggested at this point is that marketing systems are not quite so flexible as this discussion suggests, but must conform to one type or another. Thus a channel for physical distribution could have two steps or three steps but not two and a half. Nevertheless the picture of continuous variation along a scale is generally valid because of the combinations which are possible. A producer may sell part of his output through wholesalers who service retailers and sell the remainder direct to retailers. The proportions may vary over time so that one channel presently becomes dominant rather than the other. Similarly broadcast promotion may gradually assume greater importance in the marketing mix even though a large but declining amount of adjustment is involved in some individual sales.

MOVEMENT OF GOODS AND MOVEMENT OF INFORMATION

It is a readily observable fact that the number of separate and distinct items in any stock of goods increases as replacement rate decreases. A drug store, for example, has to sell more separate items to achieve the same volume of sales as a grocery store. An exclusive dress shop will need more variation in styles and models than a store operating in the popular price range. Paint brushes, files, or grinding wheels will be made up in a great multiplicity of specifications to serve the industrial market as compared to the few numbers which suffice for the household user. Red goods by their very nature are those in which a single item is bought frequently because it meets the requirements of many occasions for use while in the yellow goods more numerous items with less frequent sales are required for a more accurate matching of diverse and differentiated use situations.

APPLICATION TO A MANAGEMENT PROBLEM

A short time ago a project was undertaken for a well-known manufacturer whose operation is such that the range of products his company manufactures covers the scale from red goods to yellow goods. In following the reasoning of the characteristics of goods theory and the parallel systems theory he was able to locate a certain product in its position on the base line. He drew the ordinate representing this product and found from the diagram that the distribution indicated was a modified direct distribution and that accordingly a considerable amount of direct promotion should be used. In reviewing what actually was being done with this product he knew that promotion was mostly broadcast while the distribution was a modified direct. Thus, promotion and distribution were not running parallel and such a finding for this product provided a substantial explanation of the poor performance this product was making. Research had confirmed that it was an excellent product and that it was priced correctly so that a reasonable volume of sales should have been expected. The planned sales for the product were not realized and to correct this situation a more extensive broadcast promotion program was launched, but from this program little or no increase in sales was realized. At this point the manufacturer decided that it would be worth a try to follow out the indicated promotional and distributional plan shown in the parallel systems theory analysis. A program of direct promotion was initiated and results were immediately forthcoming. The full sales expectations were realized and the manufacturer decided to establish a special division to handle the product which since that time has produced even more sales at costs considerably below the estimated costs.

A somewhat closer look at this case revealed that broadcast promotion was reaching thousands of people who were in no way qualified users of the product and that the type of advertising message was such that qualified users were unable to specify the product even if they wished to do so. A careful study of the problem showed that the direct promotion had produced all of the sales results. Thus the cost of the broadcast promotion had to be borne by qualified users and the result was a higher price than would have been needed if direct promotional means had been employed. The final result of this operation was that prices were lowered and the profit position for the manufacturer and all institutions in the distribution channel was improved.

By making analyses of products and their distribution and promotional programs, it will be found that many products are not in conformity with the parallel systems theory, and yet seem to be successful products. This would not of itself disprove the theory. Such results might indicate that better results might be had if the programs were modified in the direction indicated by the theory. This can often be done at a comparatively small cost by using test sales areas in which the adjustment can be made without affecting the national system in which the product may be operating. The results from such experimentation should confirm the analysis made under the parallel systems theory. A large amount of case material has been collected on the parallel systems theory but there seems to be an almost endless variety of cases and there is a need for constantly studying the problem in the light of the improvements in communications and distribution.

CONCLUSION

A further definition for broadcast promotion seems to be needed as well as for direct promotion. Whenever promotional means are used, without knowledge in advance of the identity of prospective users, the promotional means is considered to be broadcast. The firm employing broadcast promotional means relies upon the chance contact with potential customers for the product or service. The broadcast distributional means for such a product are so arranged that the customer for the product who has been reached by this type of promotion can exercise his choice conveniently and quickly. Retail stores are available within a short radius of the consumer who may wish to purchase the product. Thus, the sales gap is shortened both as to time and distance and the effectiveness of the broadcast means of promotion is enhanced. The key fact that makes this type of marketing economical is that while the prospective users are unidentified, they represent a large proportion of the general public which will be exposed to the broadcast message. The opposite of broadcast promotion is direct promotion. The definition of direct promotion turns on the fact that the recipient of the direct communication is known in advance, so that the message reaches the intended purchaser by name and address or by advance qualification of the prospect as to his need and ability to purchase the product. The most direct means would be a salesman who calls upon a selected prospect whose address and name is known in advance, and where judgment has been passed upon his need for the product, and whose ability to pay for the product has been ascertained. The next in order might be a direct first-class letter or telegram sent to a prospect. Then perhaps door-to-door selling or mailing to persons found on selected mailing lists. These selected means of direct promotion used show a widening sales gap between the customer and the product. It is readily seen that broadcast promotion creates the widest sales gap. At the same time it can readily be seen that the marketing radius over which the customer may have to search for the

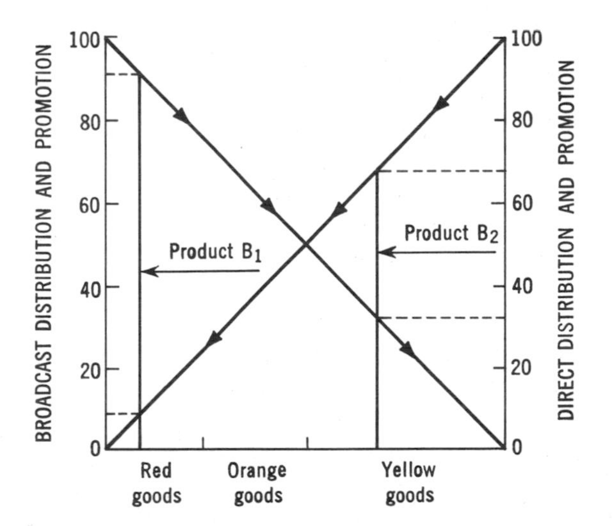

CHART 2. Parallel Systems Theory

product is increased. Compensating for this increased radius are the more intensive means of promotion that result from direct promotion, which will induce the customer willingly to undertake greater inconveniences of time and distance in order to procure the product.

These definitions relate directly back to the characteristics of goods theory. Whenever a high replacement is involved it becomes physically impossible to effect distribution by direct means. Such a situation calls for mass selling and mass movement of goods wherein all economies of volume selling and goods handling are brought into play. The low gross margin on the individual transaction requires that the aggregate gross margin resulting from mass selling be ample to get the job done. It seems ludicrous to think of fashioning cigarettes to the customers' needs at the point of sale, putting on filters and adjusting lengths to king size. The gross margin required to do such a job would put cigarettes in the price class of silverware and the number of people who could purchase on that basis would be very small. But mounting a diamond in a special setting is not at all ludicrous, because the gross margin available is large enough to undertake such adjustment. It would be redundant to go through the whole list of characteristics since it is perfectly clear what the relationships would be.

These two theories are excellent marketing tools and aid materially in understanding the marketing processes and their interactions. At the same time they may become dangerous tools in the hands of those who are not skilled in marketing. Even the experienced practitioners need to be fully cognizant of the technological advances as they occur and how these advances affect marketing processes. Skill in use of these tools should increase with experience in applying them to actual marketing situations.

22. AN EXPERIMENTAL METHOD FOR ESTIMATING DEMAND*

Edgar A. Pessemier

A generous increase in the available empirical data concerning demand for individual branded products would be of considerable value to economists and businessmen. For the economist these data would provide an important foundation of fact upon which the structure of microeconomic price theory could rest. For the businessman they would yield helpful indications about how buyers evaluated his brand, as well as the brands of competitors, thereby removing some of the guesswork from decisions concerning price, product design, and promotional activities. Consequently, it is interesting to find that relatively little has been done to obtain demand schedules for individual branded goods.[1] Why has this been the case? The answer can be found principally in the problem of measurement. When an attempt is made to estimate demand under market conditions, an extended period of observation is required, and the cost of gathering data is often high. Furthermore, the use of a protracted period of observation introduces a variety of uncontrolled variables whose effect cannot be accurately isolated and assessed. It appears that, so long as the market is used as the source of data, there is little hope of overcoming these difficulties.

THE EXPERIMENTAL APPROACH

Hope is held, however, for obtaining simple approximations of the demand for branded goods by gathering information about the be-

*Reprinted from *Journal of Business* (October 1960), pp. 373–383, by permission of the University of Chicago Press, © The University of Chicago Press, 1960.

[1]For a summary of much of the work done in this area, see Edward R. Hawkins, "Methods of Estimating Demand," *Journal of Marketing*, April, 1957, pp. 428–38.

havior of buyers in a controlled environment.[2] If the length of time between buying decisions is greatly reduced, buyers' actions can be observed without having to evaluate such disturbing factors as changes in the branded product, its promotion, its method of distribution, and its competition, or changes in the economic or psychological characteristics of the industry's buyers. By this procedure *all important influences on the buyer, except price, can be held constant* so that the independent effect of changes in price can be observed. The crucial problem that must be dealt with when research is conducted in this manner is the preservation of a sufficiently realistic situation to insure that subjects will respond in the experimental setting in approximately the same way they would in the marketplace: the state of *ceteris paribus* must include as a necessary condition an experimental environment that is not unworkably artificial.

Since this discussion is limited to an analysis of the demand for consumer goods of relatively modest unit price, the personal experience of the buyer of such goods is easy to describe. He seeks to satisfy his wants by purchasing goods from existing institutions and assortments, and he has limited time, information, and funds to use in gaining these ends. By the acts of gathering satisfactions in the market, he is expressing personal judgments about the relative value of what the market has to offer. When taken over a given period of time, the sum of the preference-motivated actions of all buyers represents demand. In other words, within the limits of the consumer's capacity to act, demand for a product depends on how consumers evaluate the product's relative worth. Since in the market it is often difficult to determine the demands or preferences for branded products over a moderate range of price variation, the question naturally arises: Can it be done in a controlled environment? An affirmative answer can be given *provided* the buyer can be placed in a position where the consequences of his actions in the experimental environment will have an impact on his well-being and conduct similar to what they would have in the market: the experimental conditions should be *psychologically equivalent* to the market, not necessarily physically identical. If the experimental situation is made "real" by duplicating those aspects

[2]During 1957 three reports appeared concerning important groups of game experiments: Cycil C. Herrmann and John B. Stewart, "The Experimental Game," *Journal of Marketing*, July, 1957, pp. 12–30; *Basic Research Report on Consumer Behavior* (Philadelphia: Alderson & Sessions, April, 1957), pp. 1-01–6-05; and Donald Davidson and Patrick Suppes, with Sidney Siegal, *Decision Making* (Stanford, Calif.: Stanford University Press, 1957); see also Edgar A. Pessemier, "A New Way To Determine Buying Decisions," *Journal of Marketing*, October, 1959, pp. 41–46.

of the market which influence buyer action, then the experimental results will closely parallel the decisions made by consumers confronted by similar conditions in everyday life.

The experiments reported here were designed to accomplish this end by having subjects go on simulated shopping trips. As it would have been on a real shopping trip, the subject's goal was to maximize the satisfaction he could obtain from prevailing market conditions and limited funds. Each participant in the experiment was told how much money he had to spend, the assortment of brands available in each class of goods from which he was to make a purchase, and the price of each item. In every case the subject made purchase decisions from assortments that contained goods which he purchased frequently for his own personal use. The participant in the experiment could maximize the satisfaction he might obtain on any one of the simulated shopping trips by selecting the brands he preferred in light of the price at which they could be purchased. Since he had a stated sum available, the act of making the selections also determined the amount of change he would receive. The experiment was administered to groups ranging in size from twenty to fifty subjects, and at the conclusion of the experiment one member of each group, selected at random, actually received the merchandise and change called for by his decisions during one of his simulated shopping trips. It seems fair to state that a reasonably close parallel to real shopping conditions was maintained during the experiment and that useful information was obtained about consumer behavior.

Although maintaining psychological equivalence was one of the principal objectives of the experiment, it should be noted that it is not essential that subjects respond precisely as they would in a real market environment. It is necessary only that any deviation which may exist be predictable. Had the study reported here been designed to do more than explore the potential value of the experimental method in deriving schedules of demand, deviations in behavior could have been examined under a number of experimental procedures. As additional experiments are undertaken, the method employed should be varied to gain sharper insights into the impact on experimental subjects of such factors as the form of presentation, the procedure followed in modifying price, the types of incentives offered, the number and complexity of the purchase decisions, and the time allowed to complete a simulated shopping trip. If a larger sample representative of the population of buyers of each class of goods is used in a future study, an examination of the behavior of various classes of buyers would also be a promising area for exploration. For example, it could be instructive to examine demand schedules for groups of subjects possessing distinct personal, social, and economic characteristics.

DESIGN AND ADMINISTRATION OF THE EXPERIMENT

The experiment was administered to 228 students at Washington State University during the spring of 1959. Although convenience in handling groups was an important consideration in selecting the experimental subjects, it was possible to obtain subjects representing all social class levels and a wide range of fields of major interest. However, a higher proportion of males, upperclassmen, and business administration majors were present than would be expected in a random sample drawn from the population of approximately six thousand resident students. An extensive statistical analysis of the effect of characteristics of buyers was beyond the scope of this study, but a limited check was made which failed to uncover significant bias introduced by the particular composition of the experimental subjects.

Before the experiment began, the subjects were polled to determine whether they purchased items for their own use from four classes of goods—toothpaste, cigarettes, toilet soap, and headache remedies—and, if they did, what brands they customarily purchased. In addition to the form used to gather these facts, two sets of assortment sheets, or lists of brands, were compiled and duplicated in advance. These sheets listed seven brands of toothpaste, ten brands of cigarettes, eleven brands of toilet soap, and six brands of headache remedies and included all the brands available at the student bookstore in these classifications.[3] Because of the convenient location of the student bookstore, the particular lines of merchandise that it stocks, and the absence of effective competition, student patronage was very high. Since each assortment that was used paralleled one found in a retail store in which the subjects frequently shopped, presumably subjects were familiar with the brands and their usual prices.

On the basis of the brand preferences indicated by the subjects, it was possible to modify the prices of each subject's preferred brands on sets of assortment sheets.[4] By raising the price of the subject's preferred brands on each of a number of assortment sheets, subjects were

[3]Each classification also carried one or two additional items labeled "a new brand", this was included in the assortment to measure the tendency of consumers to buy a new brand when switching brands.

[4]To eliminate positional bias, the positions of brands in a column and the positions of sheets in a series were randomized.

offered their preferred brands at various increases in price while the other brands remained available at the regular price. By entering the regular price of a subject's preferred brands on a series of assortment sheets on which the prices of all brands had been reduced, it was possible to offer *all* but the subject's preferred brands at various reductions in price. Other than these changes in price, the conditions under which the subjects made their buying decisions were unaltered. As a result, subjects were given assortments from which to make selections on simulated shopping trips that *required the subject to decide whether he would buy the brand he preferred or whether he would change his usual purchasing behavior because of the difference in price.*

When the two series, containing a total of twenty simulated shopping trips, had been prepared for each individual, the experiment was administered to groups of subjects. The subjects were shown samples of the merchandise contained in the assortment sheets, and told that they had $1.75 available on each shopping trip. This sum was large enough to permit a subject to purchase the highest-priced item in each of the four classifications, if he chose to do so, and still receive change. Although the subjects were requested to assume that they had a current need for the merchandise included in the assortments, they were permitted to postpone making a purchase if they would walk a block to investigate the offerings in another store. As a result, subjects were expected to purchase a fixed number of items, but they were given an opportunity to shop.[5] In addition, the subjects were told that at the conclusion of the experiment one member of the group, chosen at random, would receive the actual merchandise and change called for by his decisions on one of his shopping trips. Finally, the subjects were asked to make the twenty simulated shopping trips, selecting those items on each trip which would give them the greatest satisfaction from a mix of merchandise and change.

Several additional precautions were taken to reduce any tendency subjects might have to try to win approval by acting "rationally." First, subjects were given no indication of what "rational" conduct might be. Second, they were asked to shop at the same speed and react in the same manner as they would on a real shopping trip. And, finally, subjects were allowed to handle the assortment sheets on which they recorded their buying decisions in a manner which would prevent the identification of a set of responses with a particular individual.

[5]Because of the type of goods purchased, it was not surprising to find that only three subjects elected to investigate a second set of assortments.

On the average, the experiment was explained and administered to a group in less than thirty minutes. If it had been practical to assemble all subjects in a single location, the nearly fifteen thousand buying decisions which were recorded could have been recorded in little more than a half hour.[6] The important point is that a large amount of data about the behavior of consumers was accumulated rapidly at low cost. Even if subjects had been handled singly, at least one hundred buying decisions could have been recorded in an experimental environment in less than one-half hour.

In the course of the experiment it developed that five individuals were members of more than one group. As a check on consistency, they were permitted to take part in two sets of simulated shopping trips, several hours to several days apart. About 85 per cent of the decisions recorded on the second series were in direct agreement with the decisions made during the original series. And, in almost all cases where disagreement existed, the magnitudes of the differences were small.

SPECIAL USE OF "DEMAND"

As a consequence of the methods employed in the experiments, the terms "demand curves" and "demand schedules," although similar to those used in economics, are used here in a special sense. For example, with reference to Brand A toothpaste, Figure 1 shows that 81 individuals bought Brand A at its regular price of 31 cents. When the price of Brand A increased to 32 cents and all other brands remained at their regular price, 31 cents, 67 subjects continued to buy Brand A, and 14 switched to other brands of toothpaste. A like interpretation may be given to the remaining points on the upper portion of Brand A's "demand curve" as well as to the upper halves (above solid dots) of all the "demand curves" in this article.

The bottom half of the "demand curve" for Brand A was not obtained by simply lowering the price of Brand A. To do so would have required a four- to fivefold increase in the number of buying decisions made by every subject, since it would have been necessary to reduce individually the price of six brands of toothpaste, ten brands of toilet soap, and so on, through a full range of price reductions. Cutting

[6]All 288 subjects made twenty simulated shopping trips and could have bought one item from each of four classifications on each trip. Some subjects, however, did not buy goods from all four classifications, since they did not normally either buy or use the goods included in the classifications, i.e., cigarettes for the non-smoker.

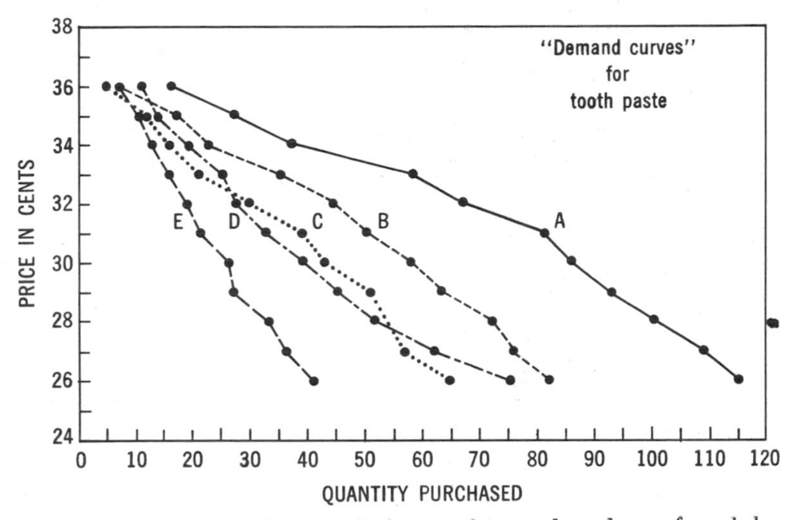

FIGURE 1. "Demand curves" for toothpaste brands preferred by twenty or more subjects.

the number of classifications included in an exploratory study or risking excessive fatigue on the part of subjects was undesirable. Therefore, the alternative of simultaneously reducing the price of all but the subject's preferred brand was adopted. The effect of this procedure was to eliminate the advantage a brand would have by being the only one available at a reduced price. In the case of Brand A, Figure 1 shows that, among those subjects who normally purchased brands other than Brand A, there were five individuals who would switch to Brand A if it and all other non-preferred brands were reduced to 30 cents. If Brand A had been the only brand offered at this one-cent reduction in price, additional switching to Brand A might have occurred. Under these circumstances switching would not have been the result of a secondary preference for Brand A so much as the result of the more direct price appeal possessed by Brand A when compared to other brands. In other words, the bottom halves of the "demand curves" understate the effect of price reductions, and the understatement should be more pronounced as the magnitude of the reduction increases.

For some purposes of comparison, "demand schedules" of the type used here may be superior to those that comply with the usual definition of demand. For example, if a seller is interested in patterns of secondary brand preference, exclusive of switching occurring principally on the basis of subjects selecting the lowest-priced item, then the procedure followed in this study would be superior. On the other hand, there will be many instances when a measure of demand in accordance with the traditional definition will be required, and a way around the difficulties associated with increasing the number of buying decisions will have to be found. If data were being gathered to aid in the solution of a specific problem, it would be practical to work with a single classification and obtain the required data without running the risk of excessive fatigue on the part of subjects.

RESULTS

The "demand curves" for the more popular brands included in the study are shown in Figures 1–4. The original price and number of buyers who preferred the brand at that price are indicated by a solid dot adjacent to the letter designating the brand. Prices and quantities are shown through the range of a 5-cent increase and a 5-cent decrease.[7] The price elasticities for the total change to that point have been computed for increases and decreases in price of 1 cent, 2 cents, etc., through 5 cents (Table 1). The elasticities displayed for price reductions are subject to the qualifications outlined in the preceding section and are used exclusively for purposes of comparing one brand to another. Average price elasticities for a classification have also been computed for toothpaste and cigarettes. Since these represent a weighted arithmetic average of the elasticities of all individual brands in the classification, they should not be interpreted as applying to total industry demand.

[7]An estimate of the reliability for points above the original price on a "demand curve" for the student population used in the experiment may be illustrated as follows: Let p be the probability that a person who has been chosen at random from the subpopulation of buyers of Brand A toothpaste will *not* switch to another brand if the price of Brand A is increased by three cents. A point estimate of p, call it p, is given by the fraction 37/81, the proportion of experimental subjects preferring Brand A who continued to buy it after the price of Brand A had been increased from 31 cents to 34 cents. A 90 per cent confidence interval on p is given by the formula:

$$p - 1.645\sqrt{\frac{pq}{n}} \leq p \leq p + 1.645\sqrt{\frac{pq}{n}}$$

For a price increase of 3 cents on Brand A tooth paste, the 90 per cent confidence interval is: $.37 < p < .55$

A similar procedure could be used for the points below the original price on a "demand curve" by letting p be the probability of choosing a person at random from the subpopulation of buyers of all brands of toothpaste other than Brand A who will switch to Brand A if all brands but the one originally preferred by the person are reduced in price by a given amount.

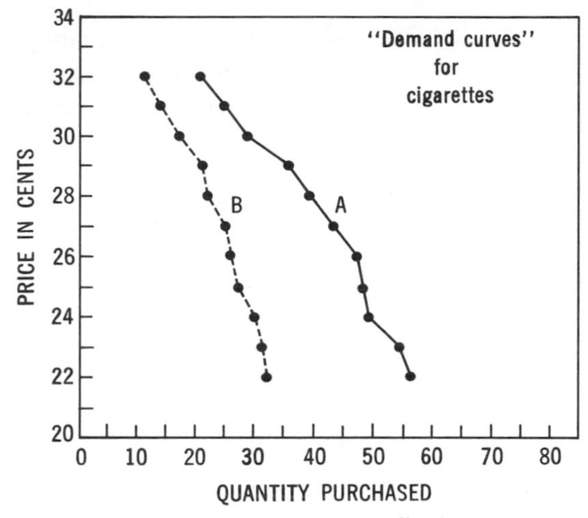

FIGURE 2. "Demand curves" for cigarette brands preferred by twenty or more subjects.

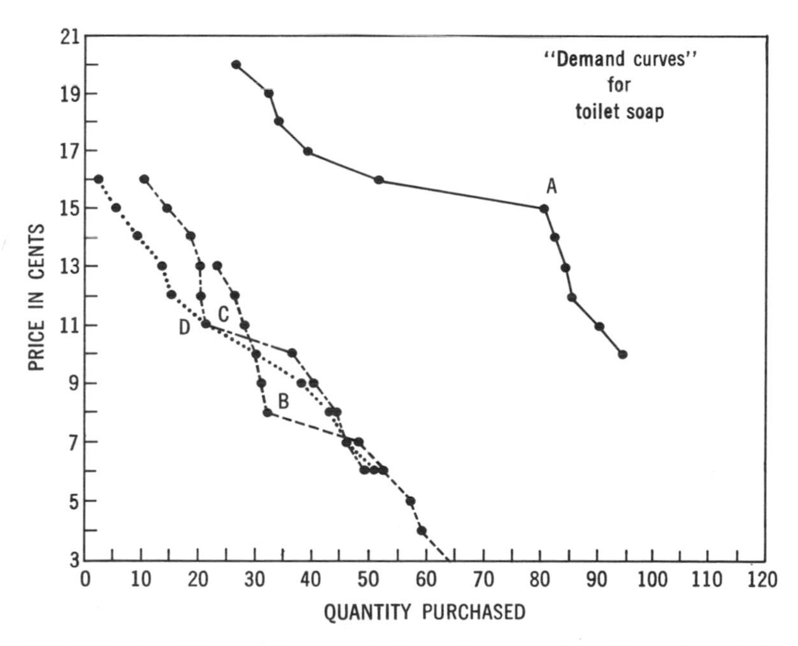

FIGURE 3. "Demand curves" for toilet-soap brands preferred by twenty or more subjects.

Although it is impossible to generalize about the behavior of all buyers, it is interesting to review some of the characteristics of demand displayed by those who took part in the simulated shopping trips. For simplicity, each classification will be discussed separately. To facilitate identification, the brands in each classification are lettered in alphabetical order beginning with the most popular brand and, in the text, the subscript "$_t$" is used for toothpaste, "$_c$" for cigarettes, "$_s$" for toilet soap, and "$_h$" for headache remedies; thus, for example, Brand B_t designates the second most popular brand of toothpaste.

Toothpaste The "demand curves" in Figure 1 and the elasticities shown in Table 1 reveal that the subjects varied a good deal in the strength of their brand preferences for toothpaste. For example, Brand A_t, with its large share of the market, gains far less relatively by reducing its price than does Brand E_t, which holds a small share of the market. In addition, Brand E_t loses less relatively by increasing its price than does Brand A_t. The strategic position of a leading brand like Brand A_t will be discussed in the following section but it is worth note here that the relatively lower price elasticity of Brand E_t under price increases may be attributable in part to the specific medicinal properties of the product, not shared by the other brands in the assortment. Further, when all brands are taken together, a relatively

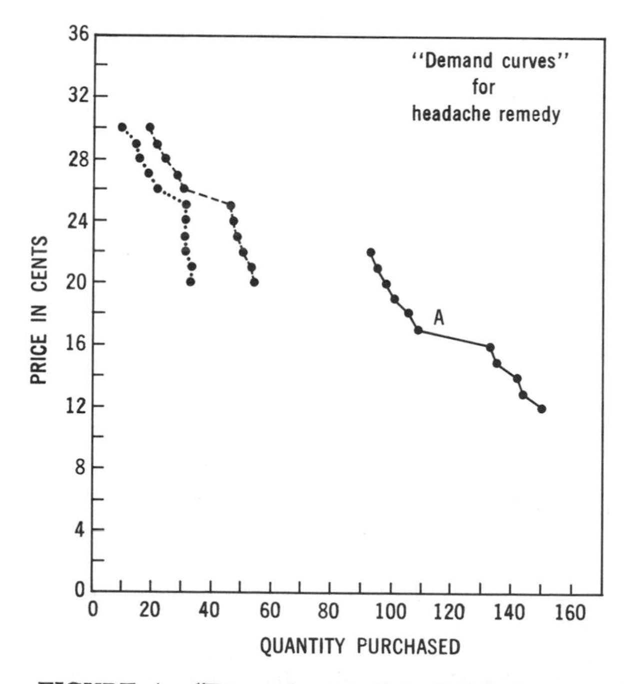

FIGURE 4. "Demand curves" for headache-remedy brands preferred by twenty or more subjects.

high degree of price elasticity may be observed that remains rather stable over the range in which price was varied.

Cigarettes The data displayed in Figure 2 and Table 1 show that, for the classification as a whole, brands of cigarettes are less price-elastic than are brands of toothpaste. On the other hand, the elasticities for cigarettes, like those for toothpaste, remain fairly uniform over the range that price varied. Both leading brands of cigarettes, Brand A_c and Brand B_c, gain a good deal less relatively from a reduction in price than do the brands that hold the remaining share of the market. The tendency of leading brands to gain less relatively from a price reduction than do minor brands shows up in both the cigarette and toothpaste classifications. As in the case of the toothpaste, the original prices of all brands of cigarettes were identical. Therefore, to gain an important share of student patronage, a brand had to utilize effectively differential non-price appeals that would prove attractive to a sizable proportion of the buyers. To the degree that a brand was successful in doing so, it reduced the number of buyers who could be easily switched to the brand on the basis of the particular product and promotion appeals it employed. In other words, fewer buyers remain that such a brand could attract because of its past success and the particular form of differentiation it adopted. In other instances, minor brands attracted buyers by somewhat narrower appeals that particularly fill the needs of a smaller group. By concentrating on these special needs, minor brands may make it difficult for the general appeals of the more popular brands to be effective.

Toilet Soap In contrast to the two preceding classifications, where the original prices of the brands were identical, a distinctly different condition existed in the toilet-soap classification. Here, the leading brand sold regularly at 15 cents, the second most popular brand at 8 cents, and the next two brands in order of popularity sold originally at 11 cents. The kinked demand curve for brand A_s may be attributed in large measure to the producer's early promotion of a distinct appeal to the consumer's desire for social acceptability. Besides gaining a sizable share of the market through its product and promotion policies, the producer appears to have priced the product to take advantage of the brand's marketing characteristics. If the price of Brand A_s is increased, buyers will be lost in large numbers, but relatively few buyers will be gained if price is reduced by small amounts. On the other hand, Brand B_s holds a very strong price position but a smaller market share. This brand will lose few buyers as a result of small

TABLE 1

"PRICE ELASTICITY OF DEMAND" FOR SELECTED BRANDS*

PRODUCT	ORIGINAL PRICE (Cents)	CHANGE IN PRICE FROM ORIGINAL PRICE (Cents)									
		+5	+4	+3	+2	+1	−1†	−2†	−3†	−4†	−5†
Toothpaste:											
Brand A....	31	5.0	5.2	5.6	4.4	5.4	1.9	2.3	2.4	2.7	2.6
Brand B....	31	5.5	5.1	5.8	6.2	3.7	5.0	4.0	4.5	4.0	4.0
Brand C....	31	5.4	5.6	6.1	7.2	7.2	3.2	4.8	3.7	3.6	4.1
Brand D....	31	5.3	5.9	4.7	3.8	4.7	5.6	5.6	5.9	5.5	5.9
Brand E....	31	4.4	3.7	5.5	3.7	3.0	7.4	4.4	5.9	5.5	5.9
All Brands‡	31	4.9	4.9	5.3	5.1	4.1	4.1	4.1	4.2	4.3	4.5
Cigarettes:											
Brand A....	27	3.4	3.6	2.9	2.2	2.5	2.5	1.6	1.3	1.7	1.6
Brand B....	27	3.0	3.0	2.9	2.2	3.2	1.1	1.1	1.8	1.6	1.5
All Brands‡	27	3.4	3.2	3.8	2.3	3.4	3.7	2.5	3.2	3.7	3.5
Toilet soap:											
Brand A....	15	2.0	2.3	2.9	3.8	5.4	0.4	0.4	0.3	0.5	0.5
Brand B....	8	0.7	0.4	0.3	0.3	0.3	4.0	2.5	2.1	1.7	1.7
Brand C....	11	2.0	2.1	2.2	2.3	3.5	4.0	4.0	3.5	3.0	2.9
Brand D....	11	1.2	0.9	0.5	0.3	0.5	7.9	5.0	4.0	3.3	2.9
Headache remedy:											
Brand A....	15	0.4	0.5	0.5	0.6	0.4	3.3	1.8	1.5	1.2	1.1
Brand B....	25	2.9	3.4	4.0	4.9	8.7	0.5	0.5	0.7	1.0	0.9
Brand C....	25	3.6	3.4	4.3	5.2	8.9	0.0	0.0	0.0	0.4	0.3

*Coefficient of elasticity = $[p/(p - p')]\ [q' - q)/q]$, where p = original price, p' = altered price, q = quantity demanded at original price, and q' = quantity demanded at altered price.

Basic data from which elasticities of individual brands were computed may be read directly from Figures 1–4. Brands preferred by less than twenty subjects have been excluded.

†See discussion in text of the interpretation of demand that is appropriate for price reductions.

‡A weighted arithmetic average of the elasticities of all brands in the classification.

increases in price and, if able to lower its modest price, it can attract substantial numbers of new buyers. Had the toilet-soap assortment found in a typical supermarket been used in the experiment, doubtless Brand B_s would have faced active price competition. Because such competition was absent, economy-minded subjects were not given an acceptable alternative until the price of Brand B_s increased to a marked degree. In the case of Brand C_s and D_s, both display a high degree of price elasticity when their prices are reduced, but there is a marked difference in the elasticities when their prices are increased. When Brand D_s is compared to Brand C_s, the buyers of Brand D_s show very strong brand loyalty. If the differences in original price are considered, Brand D_s also displays this characteristic when compared to Brands A_s and B_s. A partial explanation of the loyalty evidenced by the buyers of Brand D_s is found in the fact that this soap is used by a number of buyers both as a toilet soap and as a shaving soap.

Headache Remedies This classification, like the toilet-soap classification, contains items with different original prices. In this instance, however, the lowest-priced item, Brand A_h, has by far the largest share of the market. Like Brand B_s, the lowest-priced toilet soap, it is highly price-inelastic when its price is increased and moderately price-elastic when its price is reduced. Brands B_h and C_h, both higher-priced items, have kinked demand curves characteristic of the differentiated premium product, but in this classification these brands have been unable to attain an important market share. For the group of subjects studied here, the results of product differentiation appear to be less successful for a headache remedy than for a toilet soap. For both headache remedies and toilet soaps the atypical nature of the assortment and of the subjects limits what may be said about the over-all pricing policies of the various brands. In particular, the presence of only one brand in the lower price range creates an unusual assortment for both toilct soap and headache remedies.

CONCLUSIONS

Since the experiment reported here was exploratory, the findings cited are necessarily little more than illustrative of some kinds of facts about consumer behavior that can be obtained under simulated market conditions. Despite this limitation, it is fair to conclude that controlled experiments offer large promise as a means of attacking a variety of important problems in business and economics that have remained unsolved in the absence of basic facts concerning consumer behavior. For example, it should be practical to employ experimental methods to test the hypothesis that for a given classification there exists a well-defined optimum market share for a single brand. It may also be possible to gain insights into thc rclative effectiveness of marketing several brands with strong differential appeals, in contrast to expanding the market for a single brand. Further, a better understanding might be developed concerning the degree to which a brand in a given market can expand or protect its market share by price and non-price appeals. The list of similar problems is long, too long to be included here, and the potential applications of research results range from shaping antitrust policy to developing short-range marketing programs for brand-promoters. The essential point is that the tools of experimental research appear to offer a potentially fruitful means of attacking these problems. By imaginative design and application of experimental methods of research, it is reasonable to expect that the base of facts can be greatly broadened and important progress made toward finding solutions to a number of stubborn problems.

23. ARE CHANNELS OF DISTRIBUTION WHAT THE TEXTBOOKS SAY?*

Phillip McVey

Perhaps Wroe Alderson said as much as is safe to say when he described a marketing channel as a group of firms which "constitute a loose coalition engaged in exploiting joint opportunity in the market."[1]

THEORY AND ACTUALITY

Certainly too much is said about channel relationships in many published textbooks for businessmen and students, if one is to look for proof in current marketing practice. The picture usually given is one of long lists of various types of middlemen and facilitating agencies, which differ minutely but precisely in functions performed. Alignments of particular types are presented as "right" or "customary" for a given commodity or type of producer. Furthermore, it is often implied that it is the producer who selects all the links in the channel and establishes the working arrangements with them, down to and including the outlet which sells his goods to the final user.

Several popular college textbooks in marketing illustrate this manufacturer-oriented approach to channel planning.[2] One reason for fairly

*Reprinted from the *Journal of Marketing*, national quarterly publication of the American Marketing Association (January, 1960), pp. 61–64.

[1]Wroe Alderson, "The Development of Marketing Channels," in Richard M. Clewett (editor), *Marketing Channels for Manufactured Products* (Homewood, Illinois; Richard D. Irwin, Inc., 1954), p. 30.

[2]Examples are found in: T. N. Beckman, H. H. Maynard, and W. R. Davidson, *Principles of Marketing*, sixth edition (New York, The Ronald Press Company, 1957), pp. 44–45. C. F. Phillips and D. J. Duncan, *Marketing Principles and Methods*, third edition (Homewood, Illinois; Richard D. Irwin, Inc., 1956), p. 562. M. P. McNair, M. P. Brown, D. S. R. Leighton, and W. B. England, *Problems in Marketing*, second edition (New York, McGraw-Hill Book Company, Inc., 1957), p. 66.

standard treatment of channel-building is that the growth of marketing knowledge has proceeded from a description of the activities of existing business firms, leaning heavily on data provided by the U.S. Censuses of Wholesale and Retail Trade. The framework appears orderly and well planned. But little recognition is given to the probability that some channel sequences "just grew" like Topsy, without direction or intent of known parents.

The Census method of counting, whereby each separate establishment is assigned to a single traditional category on the basis of a *major-portion-of-dollar-volume* rule, tends to produce more orderliness in the picture than probably exists. It tends to obscure a great deal of "promiscuous distribution" and channel-jumping. The Census rule, like the Procrustean bed of Greek mythology, effectively reduces the number of categories into which firms are sorted, and avoids hybrid, nondescript classifications.

Yet hybridity is too common among marketing firms to be ignored. For example, almost any wholesaler will do some business at retail; similarly, it is not uncommon for a broker to find himself holding title to a given lot of goods, thus becoming temporarily a merchant middleman. A realistic classification may require the use of relative terms to identify types of operation, according to a range of variables—for example, the *degree* to which a firm caters to a given customer group, or the *frequency* with which a function is performed.

Further study of marketing textbooks may lead a reader to conclude that: (a) middlemen of many types are available to any manufacturer in any market to which he wishes to sell, and within each type there is an ample selection of individual firms; (b) the manufacturer habitually controls the selection and operation of individual firms in his channel; and (c) middlemen respond willingly as *selling agents* for the manufacturer rather than as *purchasing agents* for a coveted group of customers to whom the middlemen sell.

Yet none of these conclusions is entirely valid.

In a product line such as fashion apparel, a garment maker may have an extremely limited choice of types of middlemen: the selling agent, the broker, the direct-buying retailer, or the chain store buying office. The general absence of service wholesalers from this line of trade is not correctible by manufacturers' *fiat*.

In a particular market area, the choice may be even more limited. Of individual firms of a given type, there may be no choice at all. These limitations arise, of course, because of the free choices made by the middlemen as to locations, customer groups, and product assortments they elect to sell.

IS THE "CHANNEL" AN ACADEMIC CONCEPT?

Integrated action up and down a channel is a rare luxury in marketing. Why? It may be that the "channel of distribution" is a concept that is principally academic in usage and unfamiliar to many firms selling to and through these channels.

Instead of a channel, a businessman is likely to concern himself merely with suppliers and customers. His dealings are not with all of the links in the channel but only with those immediately adjacent to him, from which he buys and to which he sells. He may little know nor care what becomes of his products after they leave the hands of some merchant middleman who has paid him for them and released him to return to problems involving his special functions. A manufacturer may not even consider himself as standing at the head of a channel, but only as occupying a link in a channel that begins with his suppliers.

Policies

Choice of a channel is not open to any firm unless it has considerable freedom of action in matters of marketing policy. Other areas of policy seem to be treated with more respect. For example, it is well recognized that a *price* policy is an authoritarian privilege open only to those sellers who possess power to withhold goods from the market in considerable quantities, or who have the choice of alternative markets and the means to solicit them. Usually a differentiated product is necessary. Therefore, a wheat farmer can seldom have anything resembling a price policy.

Likewise, a *design* policy is meaningful only when variations in product characteristics have been understood and accepted by customers to be of significance. Manufacturers of semi-finished or component parts, or of textile "gray goods" cannot enjoy this luxury in most cases.

Similarly, the selection of a multi-stage channel is not the prerogative of a manufacturer unless his franchise is coveted by the middlemen he seeks, as being more valuable to them than their franchise would be to him.

Names such as Sears Roebuck & Company, Macy's, or Kroger mean a great deal more to the customers of these retailers than do the brand names of most of the items sold in their stores. These firms control the channels for many products, even to the point of bringing into existence some manufacturing firms needed to fill gaps in their assortments. In the same manner some national wholesalers, holding the reins of a huge distributive system, are more powerful than either their suppliers or their customers. In such extreme cases the power position is obvious. The big company, regardless of its position in the channel, tries to make its plans and policies effective by taking the initiative for co-ordinated action.

UNCERTAINTY AMONG SMALLER FIRMS

As to the many thousands of middlesize and small companies that truly characterize American marketing, the power position is speculative, vacillating, and ephemeral. Strength in certain market areas, the temporary success of a product, ability to perform a certain needed type of financing or promotional effort—these and similar factors enable companies to assume power.

On the other hand, financial reverses, an unfortunate sales campaign, or even the lack of accurate market news—these factors can shift power elsewhere, possibly to another link in the channel or to another firm in the same link. In any case, the opportunity of any firm is contingent upon the willingness of others to use it as a link in the channel.

Comparison with Advertising Media

Selection of middlemen has been likened to the selection of advertising media. In both instances the task is to find a vehicle which has an existing coverage (or circulation) which coincides with the market desired. A region blanketed with a neat mosaic of distributors' territories will appear on a map much like the same region covered by television stations.

However, there is an important difference. Seldom does an advertising medium restrict its availability. The advertiser's product need not be sold first to the medium on the grounds of self-interest. Only occasionally will a middleman accept any product he is offered. The requirement that he invest his own money and effort forces him to be selective in terms of probable outcome or profit. No seller can afford to neglect the task of selling *to* the middlemen he seeks, as well as *through* them. Nearly every comprehensive campaign of consumer advertising allots substantial effort to dealer promotion and distributor promotion. Indeed, much consumer advertising is undertaken primarily for the stimulating effect it will have upon middlemen.

Middlemen's Reactions

Middlemen's reactions to new-product offerings probably deserve more attention from manufacturers than usual. Wholesalers and retailers, as well as agent middlemen, enjoy an excellent position from which to make keen judgments of a product's probable successes within local markets. Free from the manufacturer's proclivity to "fall in love with the product," but not primarily concerned with its ultimate usage characteristics, middlemen who are alert merchandisers can look at the product with an eye to salability alone.

Yet it is common practice for manufacturers to force acceptance with a heavy barrage of consumer advertising, introductory high-markup offers, free merchandise, combination deals, co-operative advertising schemes, and the like. These may have the effect of "mesmerizing" middlemen, and clouding the issue of the product's own rate of initial acceptance.

Lack of effective vertical communication in most channels is a serious deterrent. Possibly no other proof of the weakness of manufacturers' control over channels is so convincing as their inability to obtain facts from their own ultimate and intermediate markets. Information that could be used in product development, pricing, packaging, or promotion-planning is buried in non-standard records of middlemen, and sometimes purposely secreted from suppliers.

Channels research is one of the most frustrating areas of marketing investigation, since it requires access to data collected by firms which are independent, remotely situated, and suspicious. Unless given incentive to do so, middlemen will not maintain separate sales records by brands sold. Extracting the needed figures by preferred units of measure is often a hopeless task. To get such data, one producer of pipe tools adopted a device commonly used with electric appliances: a "warranty registration" questionnaire attached to the tools. Ostensibly designed to validate users' damage claims, its true purpose was to discover where, when, how, and by whom the tools had been sold.

Communication downward from the manufacturer is also faulty, placing in doubt the claim that all links in the channel are bound together by common objectives. For example, it is seldom practical to disclose a forthcoming promotional plan in all its details and to ask the middlemen whether the plan will be timely, acceptable, and supportable by their efforts. To do so would jeopardize the advantage of surprise, usually a significant competitive stratagem. Yet the value of synchronized, co-ordinated action on any new plan by all firms in the channel is obvious.

MIDDLEMEN'S VIEWS

Channel Building

To the extent that any middleman can do so, he should think of himself primarily as a purchasing agent for his customers, and only secondarily as a selling agent for his suppliers. The planning of his product line will proceed from an analysis of a finite customer group in which he is interested . . . to the selection of goods capable of satisfying those needs . . . and then to the choice of available suppliers who can provide those goods. Of course, he may actually begin his assortment with one or more basic products, chosen by him as a way of defining the area of customer needs in which he elects to deal.

From that point on, however, his chief stock in trade becomes not the franchises of important suppliers, but rather his customer group. He is interested in selling any product which these customers desire to buy from him. The attractiveness of any new offering by a supplier is not to be judged by the size of the markup or commission, nor the unusual nature of the product, nor details of its manufacture, nor the promises of manufacturer's advertising support.

The key question is: Does it fit the line? That is, does it complement the other products that he sells, in terms of salability to precisely the same group of buyers? His list of customers is probably less subject to intentional revision than are many other aspects of his business. Is it not at this point, then, that channel building starts?

Some unusual product combinations may result from this approach. A manufacturers' agent selling baby garments in the Southwest took on a line of printed business forms, which the small retailers on whom he called were seeking. An Omaha wholesaler successfully added grocery products to his liquor business. A Cleveland distributor of welding equipment rejected a portable farm welder offered by his principal supplier, since he had no contact with farmers, but was interested in carrying a line of warehouse tractors and lift trucks.

Approach to New Prospects

In some cases a middleman may deem it worth-while to shift from his current customer group to a new list of prospects, in order to find a market for a particularly promising new product. In the main, however, he will not do so. His approach to new prospects is based on their close similarity to those now on his customer list. To all these persons he attempts to become known as a helpful specialist in a well-defined set of recurring needs. The scope of his line, and the interrelation of products in it, must be known to the bulk of his customers. Scrambled merchandising, or stocking of unrelated items, will tend to split his market into many small groups.

Assortment Sales

Furthermore, the middleman attempts to weld all of his offerings into a family of items which he can sell in combination, as a packaged assortment, to individual customers. His selling efforts are directed primarily at obtaining orders for the assortment, rather than for individual items. Naturally the greatest *numbers* of his transactions will seldom be made in this way; but often his greatest volume and more profitable sales to "blue-chip" accounts will be assortment sales.

Catering to assortment sales has considerable significance to channel operation, because the kind of sales service which a middleman can offer a single-product supplier is affected thereby. Since he is relatively disinterested in pushing individual items, the middleman is criticized for failure to stress a given brand, or for the poor quality of his salesmen's product knowledge, his disuse of suppliers' advertising materials, his neglect of certain customers (who may be good prospects for individual items but not for the assortment), and even for his unrefined systems of record keeping, in which brand designations may be lost.

THE MIDDLEMAN AS AN INDEPENDENT MARKET

The middleman is not a hired link in a chain forged by a manufacturer, but rather an independent market, the focus of a large group of customers for whom he buys. Subsequent to some market analysis of his own, he selects products and suppliers, thereby setting at least one link in the channel.

After some experimentation, he settles upon a method of operation, performing those functions he deems inescapable in the light of his own objectives, forming policies for himself wherever he has freedom to do so. Perhaps these methods and policies conform closely to those of a Census category of middleman, but perhaps they do not.

It is true that his choices are in many instances tentative proposals.

He is subject to much influence from competitors, from aggressive suppliers, from inadequate finances and faulty information, as well as from habit. Nonetheless, many of his choices are independent.

As he grows and builds a following, he may find that his prestige in his market is greater than that of the suppliers whose goods he sells. In some instances his local strength is so great that a manufacturer is virtually unable to tap that market, except through him. In such a case the manufacturer can have no channel policy with respect to that market.

24.

A MODEL FOR PREDICTIVE MEASUREMENTS OF ADVERTISING EFFECTIVENESS*

Robert J. Lavidge and Gary A. Steiner

What are the functions of advertising? Obviously the ultimate function is to help produce sales. But all advertising is not, should not, and cannot be designed to produce immediate purchases on the part of all who are exposed to it. Immediate sales results (even if measurable) are, at best, an incomplete criterion of advertising effectiveness.

In other words, the effects of much advertising are "long-term." This is sometimes taken to imply that all one can really do is wait and see—ultimately the campaign will or will not produce.

However, if something is to happen in the long run, something must be happening in the short run, something that will ultimately lead to eventual sales results. And this process must be measured in order to provide anything approaching a comprehensive evaluation of the effectiveness of the advertising.

Ultimate consumers normally do not switch from disinterested individuals to convinced purchasers in one instantaneous step. Rather, they approach the ultimate purchase through a process or series of steps in which the actual purchase is but the final threshold.

SEVEN STEPS

Advertising may be thought of as a force, which must move people up a series of steps:

1. Near the bottom of the steps stand potential purchasers who are completely *unaware of the existence* of the product or service in question.

*Reprinted from the *Journal of Marketing*, national quarterly publication of the American Marketing Association (October, 1961), pp. 59–62.

2. Closer to purchasing, but still a long way from the cash register, are those who are merely *aware of its existence.*
3. Up a step are prospects who *know what the product has to offer.*
4. Still closer to purchasing are those who have favorable attitudes toward the product—those who *like the product.*
5. Those whose favorable attitudes have developed to the point of *preference* over all other possibilities are up still another step.
6. Even closer to purchasing are consumers who couple preference with a desire to buy and the *conviction* that the purchase would be wise.
7. Finally, of course, is the step which translates this attitude into actual *purchase.*

Research to evaluate the effectiveness of advertisements can be designed to provide measures of movement on such a flight of steps.

The various steps are not necessarily equidistant. In some instances the "distance" from awareness to preference may be very slight, while the distance from preference to purchase is extremely large. In other cases, the reverse may be true. Furthermore, a potential purchaser sometimes may move up several steps simultaneously.

Consider the following hypotheses. The greater the psychological and/or economic commitment involved in the purchase of a particular product, the longer it will take to bring consumers up these steps, and the more important the individual steps will be. Contrariwise, the less serious the commitment, the more likely it is that some consumers will go almost "immediately" to the top of the steps.

An impulse purchase might be consummated with no previous awareness, knowledge, liking, or conviction with respect to the product. On the other hand, an industrial good or an important consumer product ordinarily will not be purchased in such a manner.

DIFFERENT OBJECTIVES

Products differ markedly in terms of the role of advertising as related to the various positions on the steps. A great deal of advertising is designed to move people up the final steps toward purchase. At an extreme is the "Buy Now" ad, designed to stimulate immediate overt action. Contrast this with industrial advertising, much of which is not intended to stimulate immediate purchase in and of itself. Instead, it is designed to help pave the way for the salesman by making the prospects aware of his company and products, thus giving them knowledge and favorable attitudes about the ways in which those products or services might be of value. This, of course, involves movement up the lower and intermediate steps.

Even within a particular product category, or with a specific product, different advertisements or campaigns may be aimed primarily at different steps in the purchase process—and rightly so. For example, advertising for new automobiles is likely to place considerable emphasis on the lower steps when new models are first brought out. The advertiser recognizes that his first job is to make the potential customer aware of the new product, and to give him knowledge and favorable attitudes about the product. As the year progresses, advertising emphasis tends to move up the steps. Finally, at the end of the "model year" much emphasis is placed on the final step—the attempt to stimulate immediate purchase among prospects who are assumed, by then, to have information about the car.

The simple model assumes that potential purchasers all "start from scratch." However, some may have developed negative attitudes about the product, which place them even further from purchasing the product than those completely unaware of it. The first job, then, is to get them off the negative steps—before they can move up the additional steps which lead to purchase.

THREE FUNCTIONS OF ADVERTISING

The six steps outlined, beginning with "aware," indicate three major functions of advertising. The first two, awareness and knowledge, relate to *information or ideas*. The second two steps, liking and preference, have to do with favorable *attitudes or feelings* toward the product. The final two steps, conviction and purchase, are to produce *action*—the acquisition of the product.

These three advertising functions are directly related to a classic psychological model which divides behavior into three components or dimensions:

1. The *cognitive* component—the intellectual, mental, or "rational" states.
2. The *affective* component—the "emotional" or "feeling" states.
3. The *conative or motivational* component—the "striving" states, relating to the tendency to treat objects as positive or negative goals.

This is more than a semantic issue, because the actions that need to be taken to stimulate or channel motivation may be quite different from those that produce knowledge. And these, in turn, may differ from actions designed to produce favorable attitudes toward something.

FUNCTIONS OF ADVERTISING RESEARCH

Among the first problems in any advertising evaluation program are to:

1. Determine what steps are most critical in a particular case, that is, what the steps leading to purchase are for most consumers.
2. Determine how many people are, at the moment, on which steps.
3. Determine which people on which steps it is most important to reach.

Advertising research can then be designed to evaluate the extent to which the advertising succeeds in moving the specified "target" audience(s) up the critical purchase steps.

Table 1 summarizes the stair-step model, and illustrates how several common advertising and research approaches may be organized according to their various "functions."

Over-all and Component Measurements

With regard to most any product there are an infinite number of additional "sub-flights" which can be helpful in moving a prospect up the main steps. For example, awareness, knowledge, and development of favorable attitudes toward a specific product feature may be helpful in building a preference for the line of products. This leads to the concept of other steps, subdividing or "feeding" into the purchase steps, but concerned solely with more specific product features or attitudes.

Advertising effectiveness measurements may, then, be categorized into:

1. Over-all or "global" measurements, concerned with measuring the results—the consumers' positions and movement on the purchase steps.
2. Segment or component measurements, concerned with meas-

TABLE 1

ADVERTISING AND ADVERTISING RESEARCH RELATED TO THE MODEL

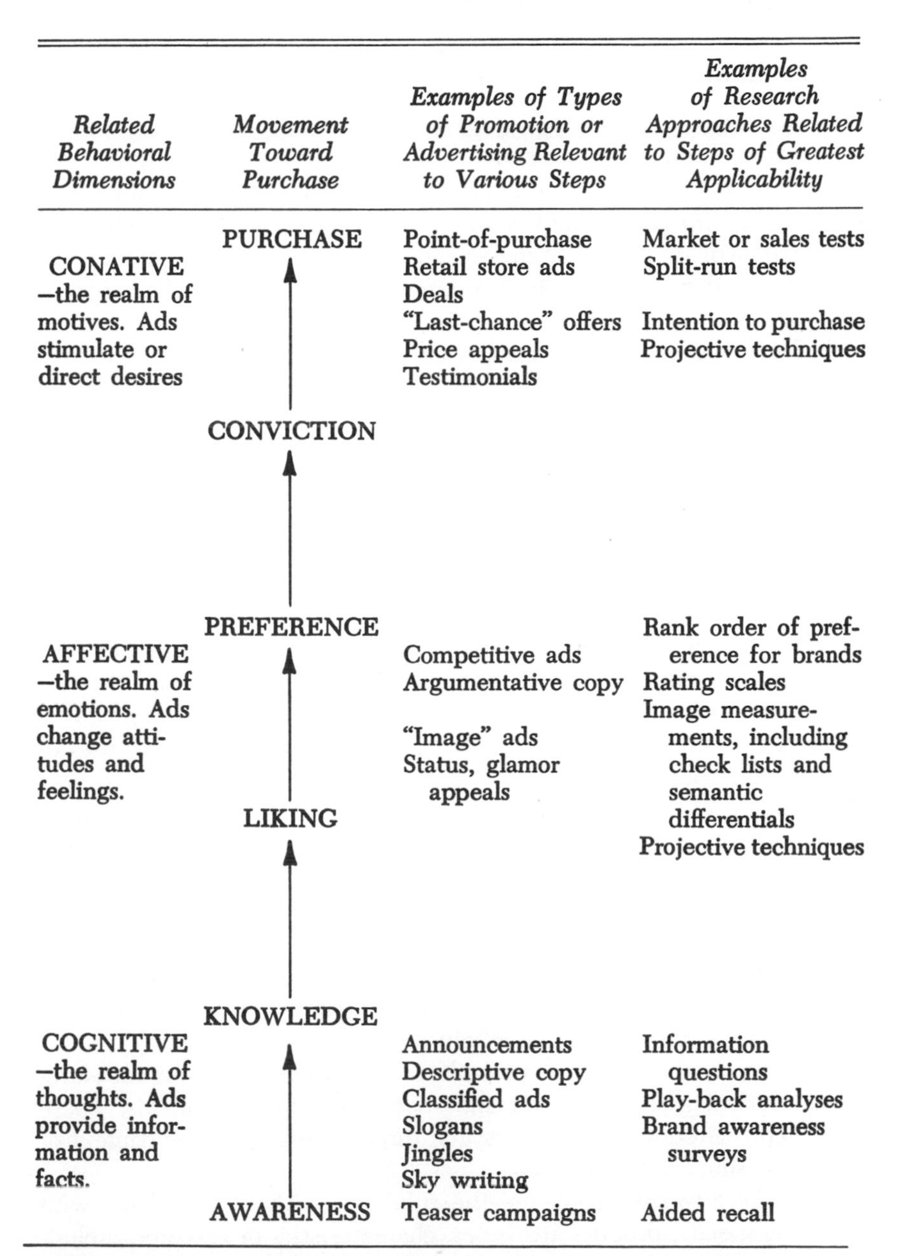

Related Behavioral Dimensions	*Movement Toward Purchase*	*Examples of Types of Promotion or Advertising Relevant to Various Steps*	*Examples of Research Approaches Related to Steps of Greatest Applicability*
	PURCHASE	Point-of-purchase	Market or sales tests
CONATIVE —the realm of motives. Ads stimulate or direct desires	↑	Retail store ads Deals "Last-chance" offers Price appeals Testimonials	Split-run tests Intention to purchase Projective techniques
	CONVICTION ↑		
	PREFERENCE		Rank order of preference for brands
AFFECTIVE —the realm of emotions. Ads change attitudes and feelings.	↑	Competitive ads Argumentative copy "Image" ads Status, glamor appeals	Rating scales Image measurements, including check lists and semantic differentials
	LIKING ↑		Projective techniques
	KNOWLEDGE		
COGNITIVE —the realm of thoughts. Ads provide information and facts.	↑	Announcements Descriptive copy Classified ads Slogans Jingles Sky writing	Information questions Play-back analyses Brand awareness surveys
	AWARENESS	Teaser campaigns	Aided recall

uring the relative effectiveness of various means of moving people up the purchase steps—the consumers' positions on ancillary flights of steps, and the relative importance of these flights.

Measuring Movement on the Steps

Many common measurements of advertising effectiveness have been concerned with movement up either the first steps or the final step on the primary purchase flight. Examples include surveys to determine the extent of brand awareness and information and measures of purchase and repeat purchase among "exposed" versus "unexposed" groups.

Self-administered instruments, such as adaptations of the "semantic differential" and adjective check lists, are particularly helpful in providing the desired measurements of movement up or down the middle steps. The semantic differential provides a means of scaling attitudes with regard to a number of different issues in a manner which facilitates gathering the information on an efficient quantitative basis. Adjective lists, used in various ways, serve the same general purpose.

Such devices can provide relatively spontaneous, rather than "considered," responses. They are also quickly administered and can contain enough elements to make recall of specific responses by the test participant difficult, especially if the order of items is changed. This helps in minimizing "consistency" biases in various comparative uses of such measurement tools.

Efficiency of these self-administered devices make it practical to obtain responses to large numbers of items. This facilitates measurement of elements or components differing only slightly, though importantly, from each other.

Carefully constructed adjective check lists, for example, have shown remarkable discrimination between terms differing only in subtle shades of meaning. One product may be seen as "rich," "plush," and "expensive," while another one is "plush," "gaudy," and "cheap."

Such instruments make it possible to secure simultaneous measurements of both *global* attitudes and *specific* image components. These can be correlated with each other and directly related to the content of the advertising messages tested.

Does the advertising change the thinking of the respondents with regard to specific product attributes, characteristics or features, including not only physical characteristics but also various image elements such as "status"? Are these changes commercially significant?

The measuring instruments mentioned are helpful in answering these questions. They provide a means for correlating changes in specific attitudes concerning image components with changes in global attitudes or position on the primary purchase steps.

Testing the Model

When groups of consumers are studied over time, do those who show more movement on the measured steps eventually purchase the product in greater proportions or quantities? Accumulation of data utilizing the stair-step model provides an opportunity to test the assumptions underlying the model by measuring this question.

THREE CONCEPTS

This approach to the measurement of advertising has evolved from three concepts:

1. Realistic measurements of advertising effectiveness must be related to an understanding of the functions of advertising. It is helpful to think in terms of a model where advertising is likened to a force which, if successful, moves people up a series of steps toward purchase.
2. Measurements of the effectiveness of the advertising should provide measurements of changes at all levels on these steps —not just at the levels of the development of product or feature awareness and the stimulation of actual purchase.
3. Changes in attitudes as to specific image components can be evaluated together with changes in over-all images, to determine the extent to which changes in the image components are related to movement on the primary purchase steps.

25. ADVERTISING: A PROBLEM IN INDUSTRIAL DYNAMICS*

Jay W. Forrester

How well is the impact of advertising on other company operations taken into account in advertising policies?

How adequate—in aim and content as well as in amount—is advertising research?

How can a sudden change in advertising expenditures designed to get prospects to buy quicker create havoc in other distribution operations and in the factory?

What are the time effects of a periodic sales promotion on the costs of manufacture and of distribution?

How does the mission and social justification of advertising vary from stage to stage in a product's life cycle?

The thoughtful top executive looks at advertising differently from most advertising managers, copywriters, and researchers. He sees advertising as but *one* of many tools available to management for influencing the forces that determine company success. Having no personal involvement in advertising, he readily agrees that it is a powerful and important influence in our present-day economy, but he does not think of it as an end in itself. He would properly feel that its goal is not merely to generate impact or consumer awareness, that its primary purpose is not even merely to sell. Instead, advertising should operate as part of a team for creating long-range profitable company success—with a special emphasis on those words "long-range" and "profitable."

This viewpoint makes quite a difference. If we look at advertising the way so many specialists do, much of the current thinking and

*Reprinted from *Harvard Business Review*, Vol. 37 (March-April, 1959), pp. 100-110.

research about the subject might make sense. But if we look at advertising from a top-management viewpoint, a great deal of the work that has been going on does not add up at all.

I think it is time that we ask some different kinds of questions about advertising—questions that I would like to see more executives pressing upon their advertising managers and research agencies, and that more scholars and educators should be looking into. In this article I shall suggest the kinds of inquiries which I have in mind, and outline briefly a new way of thinking that should help provide answers to them.

LEADING PROBLEMS

The worries which the top executive has—or might well have—about advertising do not concern matters such as readable copy, exciting graphics, program ratings, and choice of media. To him, such topics should be of only secondary importance. The real problems are far more basic. They include such matters as the time and scope relationships of advertising to other company functions, the aims and nature of advertising research, and the relationship of the agency to the company client.

Purposes and Functions

For example, how adequately do advertising policies and measurements recognize some of the very long-delayed responses and aftereffects that exist? Advertising campaigns that look successful from the short-term view of a few weeks may have delayed reactions that are detrimental over a period of several years. Advertising schedules improperly related to market and production conditions can produce disastrous shifts in the *timing* of sales without increasing long-run total sales; or can produce peaks and valleys in the sales pattern which do nothing but increase factory and distribution costs. As for measurements made on this season's advertising effectiveness, they may be seriously misinterpreted because they include a long series of past market, product, and advertising conditions.

Again, consider the narrowness of scope of many advertising operations. How well are they integrated with product design and production? All too often product improvement exists only in the advertising office and not in the engineering and manufacturing departments. Too often advertising creates a product image which is not supported by the product itself; or it builds a picture of a company personality which is not reflected by company salesmen and service men. Advertising is often used as a fire department to cope with crises which might better have been handled as a coordinated program of fire prevention.

What is the purpose of advertising? Advertising is part of the flow of communications which ties our economic system together. But does advertising always communicate? It often tries to sell qualities that are not present in the product. At the other extreme, it often fails to mention features that set the product apart from and above its competitors. If there is any serious effort to communicate, it seems to get lost in an advertising-industry fascination with the psychological behavior of the consumer. The emphasis seems to be on how to force the consumer in a certain direction or on how to get the buyer to purchase in spite of himself.

Direction of Research

At a different level there is the question of what advertisers are asking of their advertising research agencies and organizations. It seems to me that most of advertising research is superficial and deals with symptoms, not causes.

Let us begin by setting a standard. What is true research? It should be the seeking for fundamental principles. It should be the search for laws governing physical or social behavior. The successful results of such an effort have enduring value in explaining and predicting what happens.

Research is not the mere measurement of performance. In fact, performance measurement lies at the opposite end of the product sequence from research. Over-all performance measurement may tell us something of the *quality* of the prior research, but the measurement itself does *not* constitute the research. Take, for example, the relationship of physical research to a specific product:

> In producing jet engines we start by studying the characteristics of new metals and the chemistry of fuels, and by extending our knowledge of the laws of thermodynamics. That is research. The results have some permanence. Not only will they be useful in future jet engines, but also they will contribute to the entire fields of metallurgy and power generation. On the research foundation, we carry out development, product design, production, sale, installation, and use. Then and only then, do we finally

verify the effectiveness of our efforts by measuring the performance of the equipment produced. And note that this measurement of performance is not the research but the ultimate *evaluation* of the quality of the original research, as well as of the succeeding design and production.

By contrast, advertising seems to start at the design step. The advertising is turned out, and then a performance measurement is attempted. The research step has been skipped, and the final measurement is misleadingly called research.

What would the research step include if it were not skipped? The company should, I believe, strive for lasting answers to such basic questions as:

What is the real relationship of a secondhand market to new-product sales?

What fraction of sales represents the actual rate of product usage and what fraction represents a one-time building up of the necessary product inventory in the customer's hands?

What are the typical phases in the development of a style fad as a guide to future design plans?[1]

Is advertising being used as a tool to help to stabilize factory production and employment, or is it causing cyclical fluctuation in orders and profits?

When are sales being primarily influenced by advertising, when by underlying demand and need, when by general economic conditions?

Are we measuring how many television sets are tuned to programs, or how many magazine advertisements are being noticed, when we should be determining how well the public is satisfied with our product?

Do current sales correlated against the latest advertising campaign tell us whether or not we are, for example, merely selling in March what we would otherwise have sold in June?

Are we attributing to advertising results which really arise from price changes?

Is advertising trying to overcome a product deficiency which might better be corrected in the laboratory?

In short, it seems to me that most advertising research measures the composite results of campaigns and does not establish enduring principles to guide future work. Much stands to be gained by changing the

[1]See Dwight E. Robinson, "Fashion Theory and Product Design," HBR (November–December, 1958), p. 126.

emphasis of research, by asking different questions and seeking different answers. We have—or are rapidly acquiring—the know-how. Will we get the right direction and support from top management?

In time, the answer is certain to be yes. Already some companies are beginning research programs into the true nature and purpose of advertising.[2] Also, some consulting organizations and academic institutions are beginning to delve into the basic market forces and their interactions rather than being content with gross over-all measurements of sales changes.[3]

Effort and Organization

Businessmen might well be uneasy about advertising research for still other reasons. For one thing, is the *amount* of it anywhere near adequate? I doubt that there is any other function in industry where management bases so much expenditure on such scanty knowledge. The advertising industry spends 2% or 3% of its gross dollar volume on what it calls "research," and even if this were really true research, the small amount would be surprising. However, I estimate that less than a tenth of this amount would be considered research *plus* development as these terms are defined in the engineering and product-research departments of companies. In other words, probably no more than 1/5 of 1% of total advertising expenditure is used to achieve an enduring understanding of how to spend the other 99.8%.

Apparently, therefore, the advertising industry as a whole is characterized by a different attitude toward research and progress than, say, the electronic, chemical, or aircraft industries in their product research. Why? I do not feel that the explanation has much to do with the ethics, ideals, or innate competence of advertising men; in these respects they seem to measure up as well as other people (best-selling books to the contrary). But I do suspect that superficial, defeatist attitudes toward research reflect the way the industry is organized and the way responsibilities are subdivided. For example:

> Advertising *should* be an integral part of corporate operation. The amount, timing, character, and objectives of outlays *should* be geared to the status of product research, manufacturing, inventories, and price, and to the moral and ethical standards by

[2] See "A Profit Yardstick for Advertising," *Business Week* (November 22, 1958), p. 49.

[3] See Wroe Alderson, "Measuring the Sales Effectiveness of Advertising—A Progress Report," *Proceedings of the Fourth Annual Conference of the Advertising Research Foundation,* October 2, 1958.

which the corporation wishes to be known. Instead, in actual practice, advertising is separated by barriers even stronger than those that impede the integration of other corporate functions! Not only is advertising in a separate corporate department where there is little access to information about marketing and distribution operations, let alone operations in manufacturing or research, but most of the work is carried out in a separate company—the advertising agency.

To compound the difficulties which agencies would have under the best of circumstances (and those difficulties would be considerable in view of the present state of the art), it has become the practice for companies to judge the performance of an agency on immediate results. This short-range view is accentuated by our practices of rapid executive rotation and by our short-term executive evaluation methods such as the return-on-investment measure. I have even noticed that one television survey service plans to have viewers' sets permanently wired to a central electronic computer. The advertiser can then learn his audience rating every 90 seconds. In such an environment can management expect dedication to the long-run welfare of the corporation when this conflicts with the immediate present?

For example, over a period of 20 or 30 years, a number of our large corporations have developed a reputation for honesty and the delivery of the best value that the existing technology could provide. Such a reputation will persist for 10 years or more whether or not currently justified. It is to be expected that under extreme pressure for immediate results, marketing and pricing methods could take advantage of this carefully built reputation to the detriment of future customer confidence.

TIME RELATIONSHIPS

So much for the problems of advertising. To deal constructively with these problems I want to suggest an approach that I call "industrial dynamics," and which is described in my previous HBR article ("Industrial Dynamics: A Major Breakthrough for Decision Makers," July-August, 1958). In general terms, this means recognizing the company not as a collection of separate functions but as a system in which the *flows* of information, materials, manpower, capital equipment, and money set up forces that determine the basic tendencies toward growth, fluctuation, and decline.

Such an approach has a great deal to offer advertising because it takes *time relationships* into account. Proper recognition of the effects of time in advertising and market actions should go far in clarifying the existing controversies in the advertising field. For instance, answering the argument over the social value of advertising in our economic system depends on the relationship of advertising to the life cycle of the particular product. Advertising can be the mainspring of our capitalist system when it is used to communicate information about new products, but when used to sustain continued sales growth beyond the saturation level of an older product, it can actually increase costs, produce an economic loss, and eventually lead to the downfall of the very product whose success it was intended to enhance.

Effects of Sudden Increase

Of the many possible illustrations of time effects in advertising I shall take only a few. A good example to start with is the campaign designed to get customers to buy more quickly. Such campaigns are, of course, fairly common, and a typical situation can be simplified without doing too much injustice to reality.

To begin, what are some of the effects on an industry as a whole of consumers' decisions to defer purchases for a while? A hypothetical product market (or, more precisely, a subgroup of consumers) is shown in Exhibit 1. Here is a pool of "prospective customers" who are

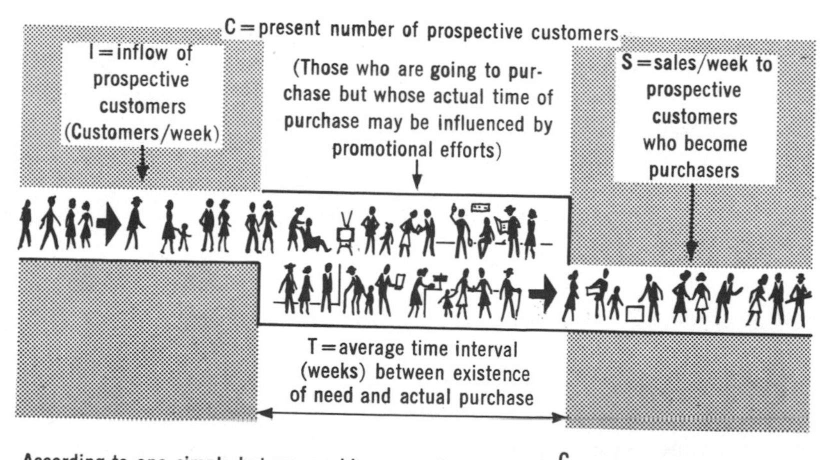

According to one simple but reasonable assumption: $S = \frac{C}{T}$ at all times.

In the "steady state" (uniform, stable operation): $S = I$ and $C = I \times T = S \times T$.

During changes from one level of sales to another: S does not equal I; C does not equal $I \times T$ or $S \times T$.

EXHIBIT 1. Constant Inflow of Customers

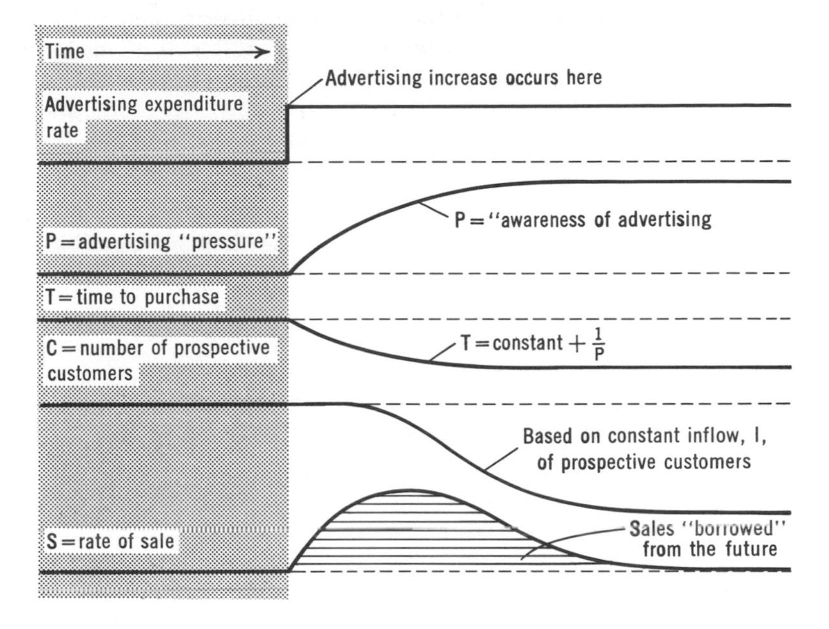

EXHIBIT 2. Effects of Sudden Advertising Increase

aware of their impending need to buy a product but who have not yet purchased it. To see what can happen, assume that the inflow of prospective customers is constant. This represents a demand which is created by natural circumstances and not by advertising. For example, it might represent the demand for refrigerators on the part of house builders where the builder knows as soon as he starts a house that he will need to purchase a refrigerator.

On the average, the prospective customer will exist as such for a certain period of time before actually buying. This period may be very different for different products—for refrigerators it may be 20 weeks, for raincoats 20 days. If advertising has *any* effect on these prospective customers, it must take the form of influencing the average length of time before they make a purchase. (Note that we are talking about only one possible effect of advertising. In this part of the market, advertising can affect the time of purchase but not total long-term sales. Long-term sales are controlled entirely by the inflow of prospective customers, here assumed constant but, in reality, affected by still other dynamic aspects of advertising.)

Looking at Exhibit 2, we see some effects of a sudden change in advertising expenditure rate. Taking the curves in order, from the top of the chart to the bottom:

The curve at the top shows the increase in advertising.

The second curve shows a buildup in what I call advertising "pressure." By this I simply mean the persuasiveness of the advertising to the prospective customer. It builds up more gradually than the actual increase in advertising because of the time that is required for the advertising campaign to achieve full effect.

The third curve shows the decrease in the average waiting time, a change which results from increased advertising pressure.

Reducing the average waiting time before purchase causes the total number of prospective customers in the pool to decrease. This is known in the fourth curve.

In the last curve, at the bottom of Exhibit 2, we see the actual sales rate. It rises as the waiting time is reduced and the pool of prospective customers is partially depleted. Sales then fall again to the initial rate. It is impossible for sales to stay at a higher level because in the circumstances, as set forth in Exhibit 1, the inflow of new prospective customers is constant.

Note that as soon as steady-state conditions have been reestablished, the outflow or sales rate must necessarily equal the inflow of prospective customers. The shaded area under the last curve of Exhibit 2 therefore represents sales "borrowed" from the future.

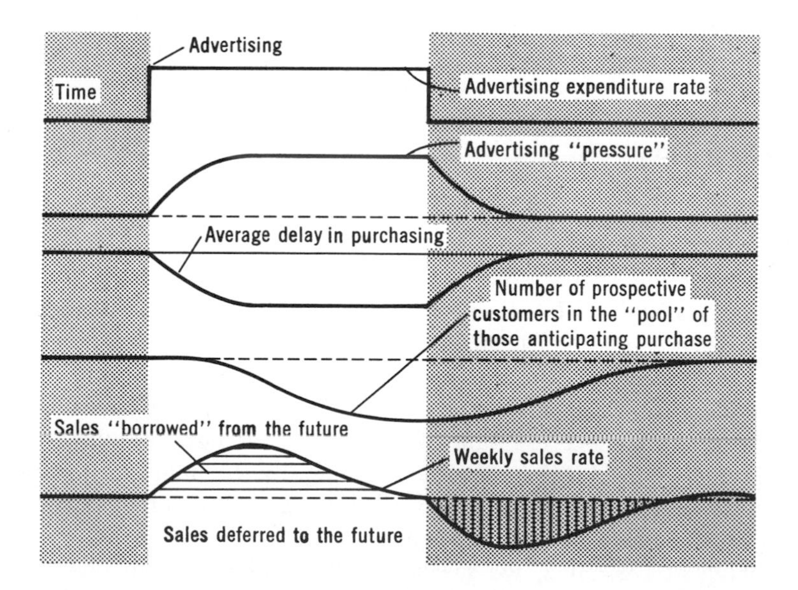

EXHIBIT 3. Effects of Terminating Campaign

If the time from the beginning of the advertising campaign to the peak of the sales curve should be several weeks or several months long, it would be very easy and natural for management to mistake the rising sales level for a permanent improvement attributable to the advertising campaign itself.

Campaign Aftermath

See now what happens when the advertising campaign is terminated. Exhibit 3 is like Exhibit 2 except that the advertising campaign increases, runs at a higher level for a period of time, and then returns to its original level. Advertising pressure rises gradually, reaches a saturation, and, after the end of the advertising campaign, falls off. Likewise, the average delay before the prospective customer buys is reduced, reaches a new lower value, and, after the end of the advertising campaign, rises gradually to its original length of time. The initial increase in sales causes the number of prospective customers in the pool to drop to a lower level. After the end of the advertising campaign, as the lowest curve shows, the system relaxes back to its initial longer waiting period during which time sales fall below their average value.

The net result of the campaign: sales have simply been moved from the second shaded section of the curve to the first shaded section without affecting the total sales for the entire period. I believe that we would expect the behavior shown here to be an important part of the market pattern in consumer durable goods. It may even be very significant in clothing and expendables.

Fluctuations Exaggerated

Earlier I referred to the troublesome tendency to think of advertising as a subject by itself, without relating its behavior to the behavior of other company operations and vice versa. Let us now, therefore, trace the effects of an advertising change more deeply into the company, adding retail and factory sales to our distribution picture. In Exhibit 4 we see another series of response curves (all hypothetical, yet reflecting a considerable amount of composite company experience):

> In the first curve we assume that the inflow of prospective customers has suddenly increased because the need for or popularity of the product has increased.

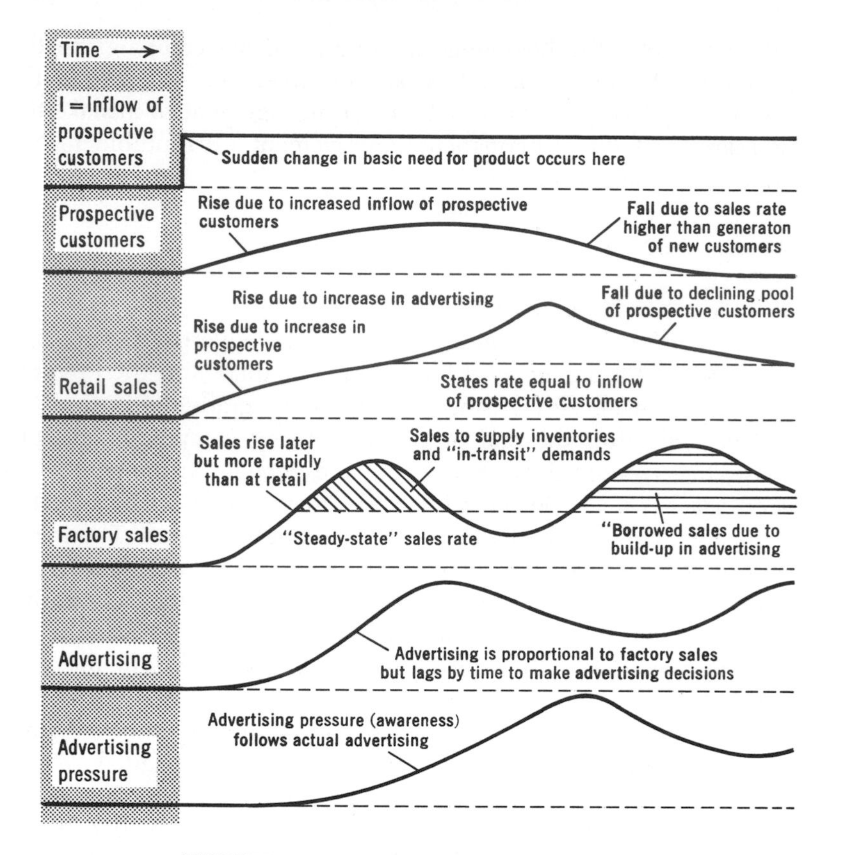

EXHIBIT 4. Permanent Increase in Demand

As the market grows, we find in the second curve that the number of buyer prospects in the pool will gradually rise.

Actual sales will correspondingly begin to increase, as shown by the third curve.

When retail sales increase, it is customary, as we all know, for higher inventory levels to be carried at the different levels of distribution. Also, for a higher level of business there must be more orders and goods in transit in the supply pipelines of the system. Consequently, as we see in the fourth curve, the factory sales start rising. They are later than retail sales because of the time delays in the placing of orders. However, once they start to rise, they rise more rapidly and to a higher peak than the actual retail sales because of the inventory and pipeline influences.

In many companies the advertising level is, in fact, determined as a fraction of the sales and production forecast. In the fifth curve is shown the rise in advertising expenditure which might follow the factory sales in such a company. This advertising expenditure is delayed by the length of time necessary to make advertising decisions and to act on them.

The curve at the bottom shows the advertising pressure or awareness on the part of the prospective consumers.

Note that as advertising pressure begins to rise, it further boosts the rising retail sales curve (third curve). This new retail rise occurs at a time when the factory sales have already satisfied the initial inventory demands of the system and have fallen to their new steady-state level corresponding to the new rate of inflow of prospective customers. The peak in the middle of the retail sales curve then produces another peak at the factory (fourth curve).

This kind of graphical analysis is totally unsatisfactory except to convey an impression of *some* of the time relationships that management should analyze. In a system of this kind, with retail sales affecting factory sales, which in turn affect advertising, which in turn affect retail sales, it is necessary to treat the entire system as a closed-loop, information-feedback system to learn its behavior. The over-all behavior is not divulged by any analysis of one piece at a time.

The need is for the more comprehensive type of analysis outlined in my previous HBR article. Turning back to that article (particularly Exhibit D), the interested reader can see in some detail how changes in the level of advertising expenditures proportional to planned sales might, in a typical distribution system, produce devastating peaks and

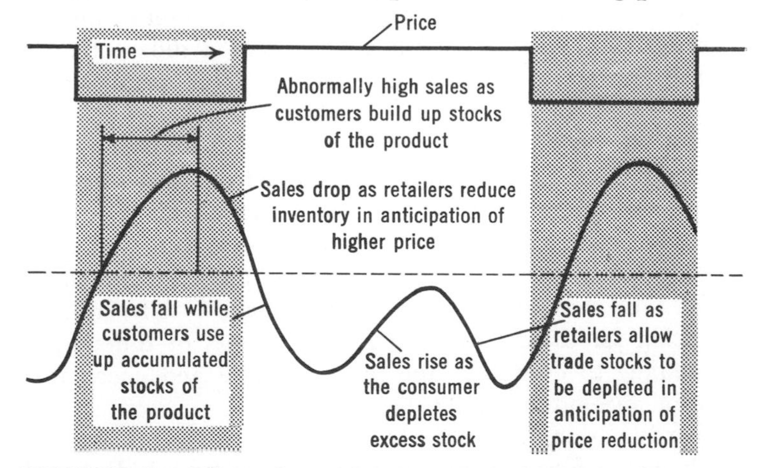

EXHIBIT 5. Effect of Periodic Price-Reduction Sales Promotions on Factory Sales

valleys in the factory production and inventory curves. Can management afford not to know more about these effects?

Periodic Sales Promotion

Let us turn now to some other time effects of advertising, as shown in Exhibit 5.

Numerous products are promoted both by advertising and by price discounts on a periodic basis. As a result, a sales pattern of the sort illustrated in Exhibit 5 can develop. Sales rise during the promotion but fall sharply thereafter as customers use their accumulated stocks of the product. Sales then begin to rise back toward normal as customers deplete their excess stocks and re-enter the market. Sales from the factory then take another sharp drop as *retailers* allow their stocks to be depleted in anticipation of restocking at lower prices during the forthcoming sales promotion.

Again we have a price and advertising pattern that probably has little effect on total long-run sales but can have serious repercussions on the cost of manufacture and distribution.

Product Life Cycle

Exhibit 6 shows the typical life cycle of a product from its introduction as an innovation through the phases of market growth, market maturity, and finally sales decline as it is replaced by some successor. The typical profitability peak rises to its maximum value ahead of the sales peak and then declines, sometimes to the point of unprofitability. This kind of growth pattern has, of course, a different duration for different products. For automobiles it may be 90 years long; for hula hoops it is probably 90 days.

It might be worthwhile to ponder the mission and extent of advertising during this life cycle. During product introduction, advertising tells customers of the existence of the new product. This is communication in its most useful form and is essential to the growth and development of our economy. In the market growth phase, competing product designs will show true product technological differentiation. Here advertising serves to stress the relative merits of differing products, thus helping to crystallize the most effective and acceptable design and to enhance product utility.

Advertising as a percentage of sales probably falls during the market growth period because total sales are rising so rapidly. In fact, we might expect a minimum fraction of sales going into advertising near

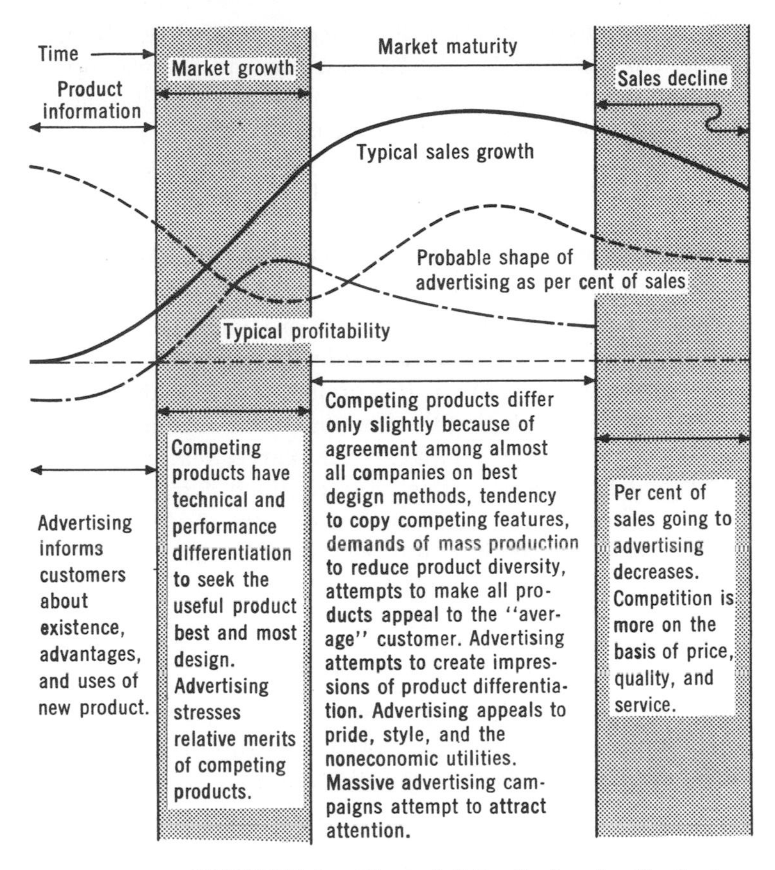

EXHIBIT 6. Typical Life Cycle of a Product

the end of this phase because it is often characterized by demand exceeding production capacity with very little incentive to attempt to expand the market more rapidly.

As market maturity sets in, sales begin to hit the saturation level. Here the serious problems develop. Poor products fall by the wayside. Those that remain tend to be similar to one another, for the reasons given in Exhibit 6. Advertising may attempt to create product differentiation which does not, in fact, exist in the actual design. It sometimes becomes a shouting contest to attract customers by sheer volume.

It is in this phase that advertising becomes vulnerable to social criticism. I believe that we can trace much of the popular writing against advertising today to the fact that an unusually large number of our products are now in the market maturity phase. This simultaneous appearance of many products at the same stage of their life cycle has its origins in World War II. The big wartime and postwar upsurge in technological development which took place has now brought many new products to the market maturity phase together. This can be seen in such industrial lines as automobiles, synthetic textile fibers, household appliances, frozen foods, packaged food mixes, television sets, soaps and detergents.

After the reshuffle which takes place during the market maturity phase, price, quality, and service will probably take precedence over sheer advertising volume in the selling of products. This last phase of the product life cycle may still be highly successful for many companies. We will see those firms in the profit struggle that have made a sufficiently early start in laying the foundation for customer satisfaction and confidence. For other companies the market maturity phase simply marks the last desperate attempt to continue living as they did in the highly profitable market growth period. But at this point a company which persists in living in the past sooner or later awakes to find itself bankrupt.

Relation to Investment

Advertising also affects capital investment, as shown in Exhibit 7. It was noted earlier that management often steps up the percentage and also the total volume of advertising in the maturity phase of the product life cycle. If this promotional effort has any effect, it will probably be

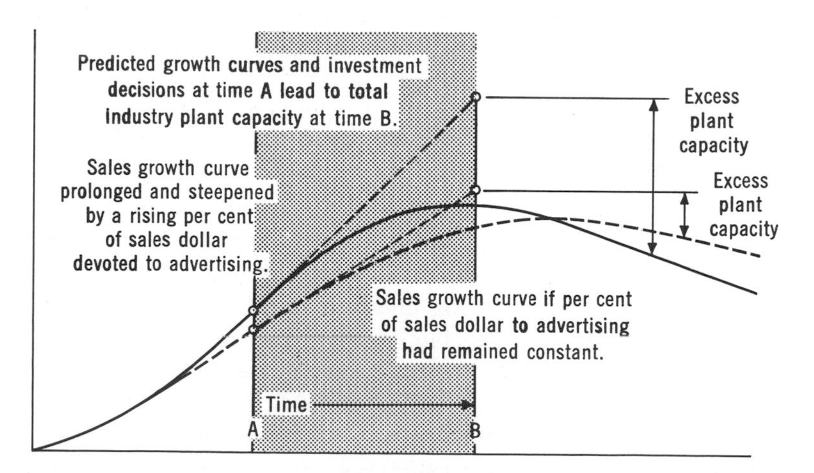

EXHIBIT 7. Possible Interaction of Promotional Efforts and Capital Investment

to sustain market growth at the expense of a more rapid fall in later sales.

Now, one finds in many industrial situations that extrapolating the current market trend is a highly favored technique in planning future production plant capacity. Note in comparing the two curves in Exhibit 7 how advertising can contribute to overestimating production capacity and thus lead to excess and unused production facilities at a later time.

CONCLUSION

I have described only some fragments of the dynamic marketing picture in which advertising plays a role. Numerous other critical time relationships also exist.

In trying to assess the combined implications of these many factors, intuition is totally unreliable (though it may provide dependable judgments on individual questions). We must turn instead to methods developed in the study of engineering and military-weapons systems. The most effective procedure follows five steps:

1. The available intuition, judgment, and experience about the firm's operations are drawn together.
2. These estimates and guesses are formulated mathematically into a single coherent system—or model. Such a formulation can be sufficiently comprehensive to include all the practical considerations that seem important.
3. The behavior of this system is then studied through digital computer simulation methods. The consequences of errors in the initial guesses can be determined and corrections made. At this point analysts are in a position to determine which factors and relationships are critical in company operations and which are unimportant. For example, the choice of advertising media might not have so much impact on the *company* as the timing of promotion campaigns.
4. After the critical factors have been identified, field measurements can be devised to secure needed data. This sequential approach conserves effort in the expensive field phase of the program.
5. The series of steps is repeated on a continuing basis to refine one's understanding and to introduce newly discovered factors.

Research into the fundamental nature of the industrial system and the consumer market is already getting under way in a number of places. Some industrial companies are beginning it, and so are a few consulting firms and a number of universities.

At the present time, perhaps only one tenth of 1% of the nation's advertising budget goes toward what can properly be called "research and development" for improving advertising effectiveness. I venture to predict that, within a few years, 5% of total advertising expenditures will be devoted to true research and development, not including field measurement of advertising campaign results. Percentage wise, this is a tremendous increase—but is not every bit of it needed? The advertising industry seems to be built on a foundation of sand. Until management takes as much interest in understanding advertising in a conceptual way as it does in understanding physics and new products, the situation will not improve.

The challenge and new frontier in our capitalist society during the next three decades is not space flight but the science of management and economics. It is in management and economics, not on the moon or Mars, that the current international competition will be won. The American corporation is the heart of the American economic system. How well we fare will depend on how well American corporate management understands its job.

26. THE WHEEL OF RETAILING*

Stanley C. Hollander

"The wheel of retailing" is the name Professor Malcolm P. McNair has suggested for a major hypothesis concerning patterns of retail development. This hypothesis holds that new types of retailers usually enter the market as low-status, low-margin, low-price operators. Gradually they acquire more elaborate establishments and facilities, with both increased investments and higher operating costs. Finally they mature as high-cost, high-price merchants, vulnerable to newer types who, in turn, go through the same pattern. Department-store merchants, who originally appeared as vigorous competitors to the smaller retailers and who have now become vulnerable to discount house and supermarket competition, are often cited as prime examples of the wheel pattern.[1]

Many examples of conformity to this pattern can be found. Nevertheless, we may ask: (1) Is this hypothesis valid for all retailing under all conditions? (2) How accurately does it describe total American retail development? (3) What factors cause wheel-pattern changes in retail institutions?

The following discussion assembles some of the slender empirical evidence available that might shed some light on these three questions. In attempting to answer the third question, a number of hypotheses should be considered that marketing students have advanced concerning the forces that have shaped retail development.

*Reprinted from the *Journal of Marketing*, national quarterly publication of the American Marketing Association (July, 1960), pp. 37–42.

[1]M. P. McNair, "Significant Trends and Developments in the Postwar Period," in A. B. Smith (editor), *Competitive Distribution in a Free, High-Level Economy and Its Implications for the University* (Pittsburgh: University of Pittsburgh Press, 1958), pp. 1–25 at pp. 17–18.

TENTATIVE EXPLANATIONS OF THE WHEEL

(A) Retail Personalities New types of retail institutions are often established by highly aggressive, cost-conscious entrepreneurs who make every penny count and who have no interest in unprofitable frills. But, as P. D. Converse has suggested, these men may relax their vigilance and control over costs as they acquire age and wealth. Their successors may be less competent. Either the innovators or their successors may be unwilling, or unable, to adjust to changing conditions. Consequently, according to this view, deterioration in management causes movement along the wheel.[2]

(B) Misguidance Hermann Levy has advanced the ingenious, if implausible, explanation that retail trade journals, seduced by profitable advertising from the store equipment and supply industry, coax merchants into superfluous "modernization" and into the installation of overly elaborate facilities.[3]

(C) Imperfect Competition Although retail trade is often cited as the one type of business that approaches the Adam Smith concept of perfect competition, some economists have argued that retailing actually is a good example of imperfect competition. These economists believe that most retailers avoid direct price competition because of several forces, including resale price maintenance, trade association rules in some countries, and, most important, the fear of immediate retaliation. Contrariwise, the same retailers feel that service improvements, including improvements in location, are not susceptible to direct retaliation by competitors. Hence, through a ratchet process, merchants in any established branch of trade tend to provide increasingly elaborate services at increasingly higher margins.[4]

(D) Excess Capacity McNair attributes much of the wheel effect to the development of excess capacity, as more and more dealers enter any branch of retail trade.[5] This hypothesis rests upon an imperfect competition assumption, since, under perfect competition excess ca-

[2]P. D. Converse, "Mediocrity in Retailing," *Journal of Marketing*, Vol. 23 (April, 1959), pp. 419–420.

[3]Hermann Levy, *The Shops of Britain* (London: Kegan Paul, Trench, Trubner & Co., 1947), pp. 210–211.

[4]D. L. Shawver, *The Development of Theories of Retail Price Determination* (Urbana: University of Illinois Press, 1956), p. 92.

[5]Same reference as footnote 1.

pacity would simply reduce margins until the excess vendors were eliminated.

(C) Secular Trend J. B. Jeffreys has pointed out that a general, but uneven, long-run increase in the British standard of living provided established merchants with profitable opportunities for trading up. Jefferys thus credits adjustments to changing and wealthier market segments as causing some movement along the wheel. At the same time, pockets of opportunity have remained for new, low-margin operations because of the uneven distribution of living-standard increases.[6]

(F) Illusion Professor B. Holdren has suggested in a recent letter that present tendencies toward scrambled merchandising may create totally illusory impressions of the wheel phenomenon. Store-wide average margins may increase as new, high-markup lines are added to the product mix, cvcn though the margins charged on the original components of that mix remain unchanged.

DIFFICULTIES OF ANALYSIS

An examination of the actual development of retail institutions here and abroad does shed some light on both the wheel hypothesis and its various explanations. However, a number of significant difficulties hinder the process.

(1) Statements concerning changes in retail margins and expenses are the central core of the wheel hypothesis. Yet valid information on historical retail expense rates is very scarce. Long-run changes in percentage margins probably do furnish fairly reliable clues to expense changes, but this is not true over short or intermediate periods. For example, 1957 furniture-store expense rates were about 5 percentage points higher than their 1949–1951 average, yet gross margins actually declined slightly over the same period.[7]

(2) Historical margin data are somewhat more plentiful, but these also have to be dredged up from fragmentary sources.[8]

[6] J. B. Jefferys, *Retail Trading in Great Britain*, 1850–1950 (Cambridge: Cambridge University Press, 1954), various pages, especially p. 96.

[7] Cited in Fabian Linden, "Department Store Operations," *Conference Board Business Record*, Vol. 14 (October, 1958), pp. 410–414, at p. 411.

[8] See Harold Barger, *Distribution's Place in the American Economy Since 1869* (Princeton: Princeton University Press, 1955).

(3) Available series on both expenses and margins merely note changes in retailers' outlays and receipts. They do not indicate what caused those changes and they do not report changes in the costs borne by suppliers, consumers, or the community at large.

(4) Margin data are usually published as averages that may, and frequently do, mask highly divergent tendencies.

(5) A conceptual difficulty presents an even more serious problem than the paucity of statistics. When we talk about "types" of retailers, we think of classifications based upon ways of doing business and upon differences in price policy. Yet census categories and other systems for reporting retail statistics are usually based upon major differences in commodity lines. For example, the "pineboard" druggists who appeared in the 1930s are a "type" of retailing for our purposes. Those dealers had cruder fixtures, charged lower prices, carried smaller assortments, gave more attention to turnover, and had less interest in prescriptions than did conventional druggists. Yet census reports for drugstores necessarily included all of the pineboards that maintained any sort of prescription department.

Discount houses provide another example of an important, but amorphous, category not reflected in census classifications. The label "discount house" covers a variety of retailers. Some carry stocks, others do not. Some have conventional store facilities, whereas others operate in office buildings, lofts, and warehouses. Some feature electrical appliances and hard goods, while others emphasize soft goods. Some pose as wholesalers, and others are practically indistinguishable from all other popular priced retailers in their fields. Consequently discount dealers' operating figures are likely to be merged into the statistics reported for other appliance, hardware, or apparel merchants.

EXAMPLES OF CONFORMITY

British

British retailing provides several examples of conformity to the wheel pattern. The grocery trade has gone through several wheel-like evolutions, according to a detailed analysis made by F. G. Pennance and B. S. Yamey.[9] Established firms did initiate some changes and

[9] F. G. Pennance and B. S. Yamey, "Competition in the Retail Grocery Trade, 1850–1939," *Economica*, Vol. 22 (March, 1955), pp. 303–317.

some margin reductions, so that the pattern is obscured by many cross currents. But the major changes seem to have been due to the appearance and then the maturation, first, of department-store food counters; then, of chain stores; and finally, of cut-price cash-and-carry stores. Now supermarkets seem to be carrying the pattern through another evolution.[10]

Jefferys also has noted a general long-run upgrading in both British department stores and chains.[11] Vague complaints in the co-operative press and a decline in consumer dividend rates suggest that wheel-like changes may have occurred in the British co-operative movement.[12]

American

Very little is known about retail margins in this country before the Civil War. Our early retail history seems to have involved the appearance, first, of hawkers, walkers, and peddlers; then, of general stores; next, of specialty stores; and finally, of department stores. Each of these types apparently came in as a lower-margin, lower-price competitor to the established outlets, and thus was consistent with the wheel pattern. We do not know, however, whether there was simply a long-run decline in retail margins through successive improvements in retail efficiency from one type to another (contrary to the wheel pattern), or whether each of the early types was started on a low-margin basis, gradually "up-graded," and so provided room for the next entrant (in accordance with the pattern).

The trends toward increasing margins can be more easily discerned in many branches of retailing after the Civil War. Barger has described increases over the years 1869–1947 among important retail segments, including department stores, mail-order firms, variety stores, and jewelry dealers. He attributes much of the pre-World War I rise in department-store margins to the absorption of wholesaling functions. Changes in merchandise mix, such as the addition of soda fountains and cafeterias to variety stores and the upgrading of mail-order merchandise, seem to have caused some of the other increases. Finally, he believes changes in customer services have been a major force in

[10] "La Methode Americaine," *Time*, Vol. 74 (November 16, 1959), pp. 105–106.
[11] Same reference as footnote 6.
[12] "Battle of the Dividend," *Co-operative Review*, Vol. 36 (August, 1956), p. 183; "Independent Commission's Report," *Co-operative Review*, Vol. 38 (April, 1958), pp. 84–89; "£52 Million Dividend in 1957," *Co-operative Review*, Vol. 38 (August, 1958), pp. 171–172.

raising margins.[13] Fabian Linden has extended Barger's observations to note similar 1949–1957 margin increases for department stores, variety chains, and appliance dealers.[14]

Some other examples of at least partial conformity to the wheel pattern may be cited. Many observers feel that both discount-house services and margins have increased substantially in recent years.[15] One major discount-house operator has stated that he has been able to keep his average markup below 12%, in spite of considerable expansion in his facilities and commodity mix.[16] However, the concensus seems to be that this probably is an exception to the general rule.

A study of gasoline pricing has pointed out how many of the so-called "off-brand" outlets have changed from the "trackside" stations of pre-war days. The trackside dealers typically maintained unattractive and poorly equipped installations, at out-of-the-way locations where unbranded gasoline was sold on a price basis. Today many of them sell well-promoted regional and local brands, maintain attractive, efficient stations, and provide prompt and courteous service. Some still offer cut prices, but may have raised their prices and margins up to or above national brand levels.[17] Over time, many of the pineboard druggists also seem to have become converted to fairly conventional operations.[18]

NON-CONFORMING EXAMPLES

Foreign

In underdeveloped countries, the relatively small middle- and upper-income groups have formed the major markets for "modern" types of retailing. Supermarkets and other modern stores have been introduced in those countries largely at the top of the social and price

[13]Same reference as footnote 8, p. 82.

[14]See footnote 7.

[15]D. A. Loehwing, "Resourceful Merchants," *Barron's*, Vol. 38 (November 17, 1958), p. 3.

[16]S. Masters, quoted in "Three Concepts of Retail Service," *Stores*, Vol. 41 (July–August, 1959), pp. 18–21.

[17]S. M. Livingston and T. Levitt, "Competition and Retail Gasoline Prices," *The Review of Economics and Statistics*, Vol. 41 (May, 1959), pp. 119–132 at p. 132.

[18]Paul C. Olsen, *The Marketing of Drug Products* (New Brunswick: Rutgers University Press, 1948), pp. 130–132.

scales, contrary to the wheel pattern.[19] Some non-conforming examples may also be found in somewhat more industrialized environments. The vigorous price competition that developed among Japanese department stores during the first three decades of this century seems directly contrary to the wheel hypothesis.[20] B. S. Yamey's history of resale price maintenance also reports some price-cutting by traditional, well-established British merchants who departed from the wheel pattern in the 1880s and 1890s.[21] Unfortunately, our ignorance of foreign retail history hinders any judgment of the representatives of these examples.

American

Automatic merchandising, perhaps the most "modern" of all American retail institutions, departed from the wheel pattern by starting as a high-cost, high-margin, high-convenience type of retailing.[22] The department-store branch movement and the concomitant rise of planned shopping centers also has progressed directly contrary to the wheel pattern. The early department-store branches consisted of a few stores in exclusive suburbs and some equally high-fashion college and resort shops.

Only in relatively recent years have the branches been adjusted to the changing and more democratic characteristics of the contemporary dormitory suburbs. Suburban shopping centers, too, seem to have appeared first as "Manhasset Miracle Miles" and "Ardmores" before reaching out to the popular price customers. In fact, complaints are still heard that the regional shopping centers have displayed excessive resistance to the entry of really aggressive, low-margin outlets.[23] E. R.

[19] H. S. Hettinger, "Marketing in Persia," *Journal of Marketing*, Vol. 15 (January, 1951), pp. 289–297; H. W. Boyd, Jr., R. M. Clewett, & R. L. Westfall, "The Marketing Structure of Venezuela," *Journal of Marketing*, Vol. 22 (April, 1958), pp. 391–397; D. A. Taylor, "Retailing in Brazil," *Journal of Marketing*, Vol. 24 (July, 1959), pp. 54–58; J. K. Galbraith and R. Holton, *Marketing Efficiency in Puerto Rico* (Cambridge: Harvard University Press, 1955), p. 35.

[20] G. Fukami, "Japanese Department Stores," *Journal of Marketing*, Vol. 18 (July, 1953), pp. 41–49 at p. 42.

[21] "The Origins of Resale Price Maintenance," *The Economic Journal*, Vol. 62 (September, 1952), pp. 522–545.

[22] W. S. Fishman, "Sense Makes Dollars," *1959 Directory of Automatic Merchandising* (Chicago: National Automatic Merchandising Association, 1959), p. 52; M. V. Marshall, *Automatic Merchandising* (Boston: Graduate School of Business Administration, Harvard University, 1954), pp. 108–109, 122.

[23] P. E. Smith, *Shopping Centers* (New York: National Retail Merchants' Association, 1956), pp. 11–12; M. L. Sweet, "Tenant-Selection Policies of Regional Shopping Centers," *Journal of Marketing*, Vol. 23 (April, 1959), pp. 399–404.

A. Seligman and R. A. Love's study of retail pricing in the 1930s suggests that pressures on prices and margins were generated by all types of retailers. The mass retailing institutions, such as the department and chain stores, that had existed as types for many decades were responsible for a goodly portion of the price cutting.[24] As McNair has pointed out, the wheel operated very slowly in the case of department stores.

Finally, Harold Barger has described the remarkable stability of overall distributive margins during the years 1919–1947.[25] Some shifting of distributive work from wholesalers to retailers apparently affected their relative shares of the total margins during this period, but this is not the type of change contemplated by the wheel pattern. Of course, the stability Barger notes conceivably could have been the result of a perfectly smooth functioning of the pattern, with the entrance of low-margin innovators providing exactly the right balance for the upcreep of margins in the longer established types. But economic changes do not come in smooth and synchronized fashion, and Barger's data probably should indicate considerably wider oscillations if the wheel really set the mold for all retailing in the post-war period.

CONCLUSIONS

The number of non-conforming examples suggests that the wheel hypothesis is not valid for all retailing. The hypothesis, however, does seem to describe a fairly common pattern in industrialized, expanding economies. Moreover, the wheel is not simply an illusion created by scrambled merchandising, as Holdren suggests. Undoubtedly some of the recent "upcreep" in supermarket average margins is due to the addition of nonfood and other high margin lines. But in recent years the wheel pattern has also been characteristic of department-store retailing a field that has been relatively unreceptive to new commodity groups.[26]

In some ways, Jefferys' secular trend explanation appears most reasonable. The tendency of many established retailers to reduce prices and margins during depressions suggests also that increases may

[24]E. R. A. Seligman and R. A. Love, *Price Cutting and Price Maintenance* (New York: Harper & Brothers, 1932).

[25]Same reference as footnote 8, pp. ix, x.

[26]R. D. Entenberg, *The Changing Competitive Position of Department Stores in the United States by Merchandise Lines* (Pittsburgh: University of Pittsburgh Press, 1957), p. 52.

be a result of generally prospering environments. This explanation helps to resolve an apparent paradox inherent in the wheel concept. Why should reasonably skilled businessmen make decisions that consistently lead their firms along seemingly profitable routes to positions of vulnerability? Jefferys sees movement along the wheel as the result of sensible, business-like decisions to change with prospering market segments and to leave the poorer customers to low-margin innovators. His explanation is supported by the fact that the vulnerability contemplated by the wheel hypothesis usually means only a loss of market share, not a loss of absolute volume. At least in the United States, though, this explanation is partially contradicted by studies showing that prosperous consumers are especially prone to patronize discount houses. Also they are equally as likely to shop in supermarkets as are poorer consumers.[27]

The imperfect competition and excess capacity hypotheses also appear highly plausible. Considerably more investigation is needed before their validity can be appraised properly. The wheel pattern developed very slowly, and very recently in the department-store field. Yet market imperfections in that field probably were greater before the automobile gave the consumer shopping mobility. Major portions of the supermarket growth in food retailing and discount-house growth in appliance distribution occurred during periods of vastly expanding consumption, when excess capacity probably was at relatively low levels. At the moment there is little evidence to suggest any clear-cut correlation between the degree of market imperfection and the appearance of the wheel pattern. However, this lack may well be the result of the scarcity of empirical studies of retail competition.

Managerial deterioration certainly must explain some manifestations of the wheel, but not all. Empires rise and fall with changes in the quality of their leadership, and the same thing seems true in business. But the wheel hypothesis is a hypothesis concerning types of retailing and not merely individual firms. Consequently, the managerial-deterioration explanation holds true only if it is assumed that new people entering any established type of retailing as the heads of both old and new companies are consistently less competent than the first generation. Again, the fact that the wheel has operated very slowly in some fields suggests that several successive managerial generations can avoid wheel-like maturation and decay.

[27]R. Holton, *The Supply and Demand Structure of Food Retailing Services, A Case Study* (Cambridge: Harvard University Press, 1954).

IV

Marketing Strategy

Once the marketing manager has made his analysis of consumers and of market forces, he can design a marketing strategy to take advantage of the opportunities disclosed by these analyses. His design is guided by his marketing philosophy. The selections on marketing strategy begin with Levitt's action-oriented restatement of the rationale of the marketing concept. Levitt's article is perhaps the literature's most vivid description of the role of the marketing concept in managerial thinking.

Bordon's paper reviews the concept of the marketing mix and stresses the interdependence of mix elements in designing a marketing strategy. The following four articles explore certain of these decision areas in greater depth. Smith contrasts the consequences of alternative approaches to product decisions; Oxenfeldt examines the pricing problem as a sequential process; Magee advocates approaching the distribution problem from a systems viewpoint; and Dean's article explores the effect of the manner of classifying advertising expenses on decision-making in the promotional area.

The remaining two articles represent pioneering applications of decision theory to marketing management. Buzzell and Slater review the concept of decision theory and illustrate the application of these ideas to a hypothetical bakery market. Green's article illustrates the use of Bayesian statistics in marketing decision-making.

27. MARKETING MYOPIA*

Theodore Levitt

Every major industry was once a growth industry. But some that are now riding a wave of growth enthusiasm are very much in the shadow of decline. Others which are thought of as seasoned growth industries have actually stopped growing. In every case the reason growth is threatened, slowed, or stopped is *not* because the market is saturated. It is because there has been a failure of management.

FATEFUL PURPOSES

The failure is at the top. The executives responsible for it, in the last analysis, are those who deal with broad aims and policies. Thus:

> The railroads did not stop growing because the need for passenger and freight transportation declined. That grew. The railroads are in trouble today not because the need was filled by others (cars, trucks, airplanes, even telephones), but because it was *not* filled by the railroads themselves. They let others take customers away from them because they assumed themselves to be in the railroad business rather than in the transportation business. The reason they defined their industry wrong was because they were railroad-oriented instead of transportation-oriented; they were product-oriented instead of customer-oriented.
>
> Hollywood barely escaped being totally ravished by television. Actually, all the established film companies went through drastic reorganizations. Some simply disappeared. All of them got into trouble not because of TV's inroads but because of their own

*Reprinted from Edward C. Bursk and John F. Chapman (eds.), *Modern Marketing Strategy* (Cambridge, Mass.: Harvard University Press), © 1964 by the President and Fellows of Harvard College, originally published in the *Harvard Business Review,* Vol. 38 (July-August, 1960), pp. 45–46.

> myopia. As with the railroads, Hollywood defined its business incorrectly. It thought it was in the movie business when it was actually in the entertainment business. "Movies" implied a specific, limited product. This produced a fatuous contentment which from the beginning led producers to view TV as a threat. Hollywood scorned and rejected TV when it should have welcomed it as an opportunity—an opportunity to expand the entertainment business.
>
> Today TV is a bigger business than the old narrowly defined movie business ever was. Had Hollywood been customer-oriented (providing entertainment), rather than product-oriented (making movies), would it have gone through the fiscal purgatory that it did? I doubt it. What ultimately saved Hollywood and accounted for its recent resurgence was the wave of new young writers, producers, and directors whose previous successes in television had decimated the old movie companies and toppled the big movie moguls.

There are other less obvious examples of industries that have been and are now endangering their futures by improperly defining their purposes. I shall discuss some in detail later and analyze the kind of policies that lead to trouble. Right now it may help to show what a thoroughly customer-oriented management *can* do to keep a growth industry growing, even after the obvious opportunities have been exhausted; and here there are two examples that have been around for a long time. They are nylon and glass—specifically, E. I. duPont de Nemours & Company and Corning Glass Works:

> Both companies have great technical competence. Their product orientation is unquestioned. But this alone does not explain their success. After all, who was more pridefully product-oriented and product-conscious than the erstwhile New England textile companies that have been so thoroughly massacred? The DuPonts and the Cornings have succeeded not primarily because of their product or research orientation but because they have been thoroughly customer-oriented also. It is constant watchfulness for opportunities to apply their technical know-how to the creation of customer-satisfying uses which accounts for their prodigious output of successful new products. Without a very sophisticated eye on the customer, most of their new products might have been wrong, their sales methods useless.

Aluminum has also continued to be a growth industry, thanks to the efforts of two wartime-created companies which deliberately set about creating new customer-satisfying uses. Without Kaiser Aluminum & Chemical Corporation and Reynolds Metals Company, the total demand for aluminum today would be vastly less than it is.

Error of Analysis

Some may argue that it is foolish to set the railroads off against aluminum or the movies off against glass. Are not aluminum and glass naturally so versatile that the industries are bound to have more growth opportunities than the railroads and movies? This view commits precisely the error I have been talking about. It defines an industry, or a product, or a cluster of know-how so narrowly as to guarantee its premature senescence. When we mention "railroads," we should make sure we mean "transportation." As transporters, the railroads still have a good chance for every considerable growth. They are not limited to the railroad business as such (though in my opinion rail transportation is potentially a much stronger transportation medium than is generally believed).

What the railroads lack is not opportunity, but some of the same managerial imaginativeness and audacity that made them great. Even an amateur like Jacques Barzun can see what is lacking when he says:

> "I grieve to see the most advanced physical and social organization of the last century go down in shabby disgrace for lack of the same comprehensive imagination that built it up. [What is lacking is] the will of the companies to survive and to satisfy the public by inventiveness and skill."[1]

SHADOW OF OBSOLESCENCE

It is impossible to mention a single major industry that did not at one time qualify for the magic appellation of "growth industry." In each case its assumed strength lay in the apparently unchallenged superiority of its product. There appeared to be no effective substitute for it. It was itself a runaway substitute for the product it so triumphantly replaced. Yet one after another of these celebrated industries has come under a shadow. Let us look briefly at a few more of them, this time taking examples that have so far received a little less attention:

[1]Jacques Barzun, "Trains and the Mind of Man," *Holiday*, February 1960, p. 21.

Dry cleaning This was once a growth industry with lavish prospects. In an age of wool garments, imagine being finally able to get them safely and easily clean. The boom was on.

Yet here we are 30 years after the boom started and the industry is in trouble. Where has the competition come from? From a better way of cleaning? No. It has come from synthetic fibers and chemical additives that have cut the need for dry cleaning. But this is only the beginning. Lurking in the wings and ready to make chemical dry cleaning totally obsolescent is that powerful magician, ultrasonics.

Electric utilities This is another one of those supposedly "no-substitute" products that has been enthroned on a pedestal of invincible growth. When the incandescent lamp came along, kerosene lights were finished. Later the water wheel and the steam engine were cut to ribbons by the flexibility, reliability, simplicity, and just plain easy availability of electric motors. The prosperity of electric utilities continues to wax extravagant as the home is converted into a museum of electric gadgetry. How can anybody miss by investing in utilities, with no competition, nothing but growth ahead?

But a second look is not quite so comforting. A score of nonutility companies are well advanced toward developing a powerful chemical fuel cell which could sit in some hidden closet of every home silently ticking off electric power. The electric lines that vulgarize so many neighborhoods will be eliminated. So will the endless demolition of streets and service interruptions during storms. Also on the horizon is solar energy, again pioneered by nonutility companies.

Who says that the utilities have no competition? They may be natural monopolies now, but tomorrow they may be natural deaths. To avoid this prospect, they too will have to develop fuel cells, solar energy, and other power sources. To survive, they themselves will have to plot the obsolescence of what now produces their livelihood.

Grocery stores Many people find it hard to realize that there ever was a thriving establishment known as the "corner grocery store." The supermarket has taken over with a powerful effectiveness. Yet the big food chains of the 1930's narrowly escaped being completely wiped out by the aggressive expansion of independent supermarkets. The first genuine supermarket was opened in 1930, in Jamaica, Long Island. By 1933 supermarkets were thriving in California, Ohio, Pennsylvania, and elsewhere. Yet the established chains pompously ignored them. When they chose to notice them, it was with such derisive descriptions as "cheapy," "horse-and-buggy," "cracker-barrel store-keeping," and "unethical opportunities."

The executive of one big chain announced at the time that he found it "hard to believe that people will drive for miles to shop for foods and sacrifice the personal service chains have perfected and to which Mrs. Consumer is accustomed."[2] As late as 1936, the National Wholesale Grocers convention and the New Jersey Retail Grocers Association said there was nothing to fear. They said that the supers' narrow appeal to the price buyer limited the size of their market. They had to draw from miles around. When imitators came, there would be wholesale liquidations as volume fell. The current high sales of the supers was said to be partly due to their novelty. Basically people wanted convenient neighborhood grocers. If the neighborhood stores "cooperate with their suppliers, pay attention to their costs, and improve their services," they would be able to weather the competition until it blew over.[3]

It never blew over. The chains discovered that survival required going into the supermarket business. This meant the wholesale destruction of their huge investments in corner store sites and in established distribution and merchandising methods. The companies with "the courage of their convictions" resolutely stuck to the corner store philosophy. They kept their pride but lost their shirts.

Self-Deceiving Cycle

But memories are short. For example, it is hard for people who today confidently hail the twin messiahs of electronics and chemicals to see how things could possibly go wrong with these galloping industries. They probably also cannot see how a reasonably sensible businessman could have been as myopic as the famous Boston millionaire who 50 years ago unintentionally sentenced his heirs to poverty by stipulating that his entire estate be forever invested exclusively in electric streetcar securities. His posthumous declaration, "There will always be a big demand for efficient urban transportation," is no consolation to his heirs who sustain life by pumping gasoline at automobile filling stations.

Yet, in a casual survey I recently took among a group of intelligent business executives, nearly half agreed that it would be hard to hurt

[2]For more details see M. M. Zimmerman, *The Super Market: A Revolution in Distribution* (New York, McCraw-Hill Book Company, Inc., 1955), p. 48.
[3]Ibid., pp. 45–47.

their heirs by tying their estates forever to the electronics industry. When I then confronted them with the Boston street car example, they chorused unanimously, "That's different!" But is it? Is not the basic situation identical?

In truth, *there is no such thing* as a growth industry, I believe. There are only companies organized and operated to create and capitalize on growth opportunities. Industries that assume themselves to be riding some automatic growth escalator invariably descend into stagnation. The history of every dead and dying "growth" industry shows a self-deceiving cycle of bountiful expansion and undetected decay. There are four conditions which usually guarantee this cycle:

1. The belief that growth is assured by an expanding and more affluent population.
2. The belief that there is no competitive substitute for the industry's major product.
3. Too much faith in mass production and in the advantages of rapidly declining unit costs as output rises.
4. Preoccupation with a product that lends itself to carefully controlled scientific experimentation, improvement, and manufacturing cost reduction.

I should like now to begin examining each of these conditions in some detail. To build my case as boldly as possible, I shall illustrate the points with reference to three industries—petroleum, automobiles, and electronics—particularly petroleum, because it spans more years and more vicissitudes. Not only do these three have excellent reputations with the general public and also enjoy the confidence of sophisticated investors, but their managements have become known for progressive thinking in areas like financial control, product research, and management training. If obsolescence can cripple even these industries, it can happen anywhere.

POPULATION MYTH

The belief that profits are assured by an expanding and more affluent population is dear to the heart of every industry. It takes the edge off the apprehensions everybody understandably feels about the future. If consumers are multiplying and also buying more of your product or service, you can face the future with considerably more comfort than if the market is shrinking. An expanding market keeps the manufacturer from having to think very hard or imaginatively. If thinking is an intellectual response to a problem, then the absence of a problem leads to the absence of thinking. If your product has an automatically expanding market, then you will not give much thought to how to expand it.

One of the most interesting examples of this is provided by the petroleum industry. Probably our oldest growth industry, it has an enviable record. While there are some current apprehensions about its growth rate, the industry itself tends to be optimistic. But I believe it can be demonstrated that it is undergoing a fundamental yet typical change. It is not only ceasing to be a growth industry, but may actually be a declining one, relative to other business. Although there is widespread unawareness of it, I believe that within 25 years the oil industry may find itself in much the same position of retrospective glory that the railroads are now in. Despite its pioneering work in developing and applying the present-value method of investment evaluation, in employee relations, and in working with backward countries, the petroleum business is a distressing example of how complacency and wrongheadedness can stubbornly convert opportunity into near disaster.

One of the characteristics of this and other industries that have believed very strongly in the beneficial consequences of an expanding population, while at the same time being industries with a generic product for which there has appeared to be no competitive substitute, is that the individual companies have sought to outdo their competitors by improving on what they are already doing. This makes sense, of course, if one assumes that sales are tied to the country's population strings, because the customer can compare products only on a feature-by-feature basis. I believe it is significant, for example, that not since John D. Rockefeller sent free kerosene lamps to China has the oil industry done anything really outstanding to create a demand for its product. Not even in product improvement has it showered itself with eminence. The greatest single improvement, namely, the development of tetraethyl lead, came from outside the industry, specifically from General Motors and DuPont. The big contributions made by the industry itself are confined to the technology of oil exploration, production, and refining.

Asking for Trouble

In other words, the industry's efforts have focused on improving the *efficiency* of getting and making its product, not really on improving the generic product or its marketing. Moreover, its chief product has continuously been defined in the narrowest possible terms, namely, gasoline, not energy, fuel, or transportation. This attitude has helped assure that:

> Major improvements in gasoline quality tend not to originate in the oil industry. Also, the development of superior alternative fuels comes from outside the oil industry, as will be shown later.
>
> Major innovations in automobile fuel marketing are originated by small new oil companies that are not primarily preoccupied with production or refining. These are the companies that have been responsible for the rapidly expanding multipump gasoline stations, with their successful emphasis on large and clean layouts, rapid and efficient driveway service, and quality gasoline at low prices.

Thus, the oil industry is asking for trouble from outsiders. Sooner or later, in this land of hungry inventors and entrepreneurs, a threat is sure to come. The possibilities of this will become more apparent when we turn to the next dangerous belief of many managements. For the sake of continuity, because this second belief is tied closely to the first, I shall continue with the same example.

Idea of Indispensability

The petroleum industry is pretty much persuaded that there is no competitive substitute for its major product, gasoline—or if there is, that it will continue to be a derivative of crude oil, such as diesel fuel or kerosene jet fuel.

There is a lot of automatic wishful thinking in this assumption. The trouble is that most refining companies own huge amounts of crude oil reserves. These have value only if there is a market for products into which oil can be converted—hence the tenacious belief in the continuing competitive superiority of automobile fuels made from crude oil.

This idea persists despite all historic evidence against it. The evidence not only shows that oil has never been a superior product for any purpose for very long, but it also shows that the oil industry has never really been a growth industry. It has been a succession of different businesses that have gone through the usual historic cycles of growth, maturity, and decay. Its over-all survival is owed to a series of miraculous escapes from total obsolescence, of last minute and unexpected reprieves from total disaster reminiscent of the Perils of Pauline.

Perils of Petroleum

I shall sketch in only the main episodes:

First, crude oil was largely a patent medicine. But even before that fad ran out, demand was greatly expanded by the use of oil in kerosene lamps. The prospect of lighting the world's lamps gave rise to an extravagant promise of growth. The prospects were similar to those the industry now holds for gasoline in other parts of the world. It can hardly wait for the underdeveloped nations to get a car in every garage.

In the days of the kerosene lamp, the oil companies competed with each other and against gaslight by trying to improve the illuminating characteristics of kerosene. Then suddenly the impossible happened. Edison invented a light which was totally nondependent on crude oil. Had it not been for the growing use of kerosene in space heaters, the incandescent lamp would have completely finished oil as a growth industry at that time. Oil would have been good for little else than axle grease.

Then disaster and reprieve struck again. Two great innovations occurred, neither originating in the oil industry. The successful development of coal-burning domestic central-heating systems made the space heater obsolescent. While the industry reeled, along came its most magnificent boost yet—the internal combustion engine, also invented by outsiders. Then when the prodigious expansion for gasoline finally began to level off in the 1920's, along came the miraculous escape of a central oil heater. Once again, the escape was provided by an outsider's invention and development. And when that market weakened, wartime demand for aviation fuel came to the rescue. After the war the expansion of civilian aviation, the dieselization of railroads, and the explosive demand for cars and trucks kept the industry's growth in high gear.

Meanwhile centralized oil heating—whose boom potential had only recently been proclaimed—ran into severe competition from natural gas. While the oil companies themselves owned the gas that now competed with their oil, the industry did not originate the natural gas revolution, nor has it to this day greatly profited from its gas ownership. The gas revolution was made by newly formed transmission companies that marketed the product with an aggressive ardor. They started a magnificent new industry, first against the advice and then against the resistance of the oil companies.

By all the logic of the situation, the oil companies themselves should have made the gas revolution. They not only owned the gas; they also were the only people experienced in handling, scrubbing, and using it, the only people experienced in pipeline technology and transmission, and they understood heating problems. But, partly because they knew that natural gas would compete with their own sale of heating oil, the oil companies poohpoohed the potentials of gas.

The revolution was finally started by oil pipeline executives who, unable to persuade their own companies to go into gas, quit and organized the spectacularly successful gas transmission companies. Even after their success became painfully evident to the oil companies, the latter did not go into gas transmission. The multibillion dollar business which should have been theirs went to others. As in the past, the industry was blinded by its narrow preoccupation with a specific product and the value of its reserves. It paid little or no attention to its customers' basic needs and preferences.

The postwar years have not witnessed any change. Immediately after World War II the oil industry was greatly encouraged about its future by the rapid expansion of demand for its traditional line of products. In 1950 most companies projected annual rates of domestic expansion of around 6% through at least 1975. Though the ratio of crude oil reserves to demand in the Free World was about 20 to 1, with 10 to 1 being usually considered a reasonable working ratio in the United States, booming demand sent oil men searching for more without sufficient regard to what the future really promised. In 1952 they "hit" in the Middle East; the ratio skyrocketed to 42 to 1. If gross additions to reserves continue at the average rate of the past five years (37 billion barrels annually), then by 1970 the reserve ratio will be up to 45 to 1. This abundance of oil has weakened crude and product prices all over the world.

Uncertain Future

Management cannot find much consolation today in the rapidly expanding petrochemical industry, another oil-using idea that did not originate in the leading firms. The total United States production of petrochemicals is equivalent to about 2% (by volume) of the demand for all petroleum products. Although the petrochemical industry is now expected to grow by about 10% per year, this will not offset other drains on the growth of crude oil consumption. Furthermore, while petrochemical products are many and growing, it is well to remember that there are nonpetroleum sources of the basic raw material, such as coal. Besides, a lot of plastics can be produced with relatively little oil. A 50,000-barrel-per-day oil refinery is now considered the absolute minimum size for efficiency. But a 5,000-barrel-per-day chemical plant is a giant operation.

Oil has never been a continuously strong growth industry. It has grown by fits and starts, always miraculously saved by innovations and developments not of its own making. The reason it has not grown in a smooth progression is that each time it thought it had a superior product safe from the possibility of competitive substitutes, the product turned out to be inferior and notoriously subject to obsolescence. Until now, gasoline (for motor fuel, anyhow) has escaped this fate. But, as we shall see later, it too may be on its last legs.

The point of all this is that there is no guarantee against product obsolescence. If a company's own research does not make it obsolete, another's will. Unless an industry is especially lucky, as oil has been until now, it can easily go down in a sea of red figures—just as the railroads have, as the buggy whip manufacturers have, as the corner grocery chains have, as most of the big movie companies have, and indeed as many other industries have.

The best way for a firm to be lucky is to make its own luck. That requires knowing what makes a business successful. One of the greatest enemies of this knowledge is mass production.

PRODUCTION PRESSURES

Mass-production industries are impelled by a great drive to produce all they can. The prospect of steeply declining unit costs as output rises is more than most companies can usually resist. The profit possibilities look spectacular. All effort focuses on production. The result is that marketing gets neglected.

John Kenneth Galbraith contends that just the opposite occurs.[4] Output is so prodigious that all effort concentrates on trying to get rid of it. He says this accounts for singing commercials, desecration of the countryside with advertising signs, and other wasteful and vulgar practices. Galbraith has a finger on something real, but he misses the strategic point. Mass production does indeed generate great pressure to "move" the product. But what usually gets emphasized is selling, not marketing. Marketing, being a more sophisticated and complex process, gets ignored.

[4] *The Affluent Society* (Boston, Houghton Mifflin Company, 1958), pp. 152–160.

The difference between marketing and selling is more than semantic. Selling focuses on the needs of the seller, marketing on the needs of the buyer. Selling is preoccupied with the seller's need to convert his product into cash; marketing with the idea of satisfying the needs of the customer by means of the product and the whole cluster of things associated with creating, delivering, and finally consuming it.

In some industries the enticements of full mass production have been so powerful that for many years top management in effect has told the sales departments, "You get rid of it; we'll worry about profits." By contrast, a truly marketing-minded firm tries to create value-satisfying goods and services that consumers will want to buy. What it offers for sale includes not only the generic product or service, but also how it is made available to the customer, in what form, when, under what conditions, and at what terms of trade. Most important, what it offers for sale is determined not by the seller but by the buyer. The seller takes his cues from the buyer in such a way that the product becomes a consequence of the marketing effort, not vice versa.

Lag in Detroit

This may sound like an elementary rule of business, but that does not keep it from being violated wholesale. It is certainly more violated than honored. Take the automobile industry:

> Here mass production is most famous, most honored, and has the greatest impact on the entire society. The industry has hitched its fortune to the relentless requirements of the annual model change, a policy that makes customer orientation an especially urgent necessity. Consequently the auto companies annually spend millions of dollars on consumer research. But the fact that the new compact cars are selling so well in their first year indicates that Detroit's vast researches have for a long time failed to reveal what the customer really wanted. Detroit was not persuaded that he wanted anything different from what he had been getting until it lost millions of customers to other small car manufacturers.
>
> How could this unbelievable lag behind consumer wants have been perpetuated so long? Why did not research reveal consumer preferences before consumers' buying decisions themselves revealed the facts? Is that not what consumer research is for—to find out before the fact what is going to happen? The answer is that Detroit never really researched the customer's wants. It only researched his preferences between the kinds of things

which it had already decided to offer him. For Detroit is mainly product-oriented, not customer-oriented. To the extent that the customer is recognized as having needs that the manufacturer should try to satisfy, Detroit usually acts as if the job can be done entirely by product changes. Occasionally attention gets paid to financing, too, but that is done more in order to sell than to enable the customer to buy.

As for taking care of other customer needs, there is not enough being done to write about. The areas of the greatest unsatisfied needs are ignored, or at best get stepchild attention. These are at the point of sale and on the matter of automotive repair and maintenance. Detroit views these problem areas as being of secondary importance. That is underscored by the fact that the retailing and servicing ends of this industry are neither owned and operated nor controlled by the manufacturers. Once the car is produced, things are pretty much in the dealer's inadequate hands. Illustrative of Detroit's arm's-length attitude is the fact that, while servicing holds enormous sales-stimulating, profit-building opportunities, only 57 of Chevrolet's 7,000 dealers provide night maintenance service.

Motorists repeatedly express their dissatisfaction with servicing and their apprehensions about buying cars under the present selling setup. The anxieties and problems they encounter during the auto buying and maintenance processes are probably more intense and widespread today than 30 years ago. Yet the automobile companies do not *seem* to listen to or take their cues from the anguished consumer. If they do listen, it must be through the filter of their own preoccupation with production. The marketing effort is still viewed as a necessary consequence of the product, not vice versa, as it should be. That is the legacy of mass production, with its parochial view that profit resides essentially in low-cost full production.

What Ford Put First

The profit lure of mass production obviously has a place in the plans and strategy of business management, but it must always *follow* hard thinking about the customer. This is one of the most important lessons that we can learn from the contradictory behavior of Henry Ford. In a sense Ford was both the most brilliant and the most senseless marketer in American history. He was senseless because he refused to give the customer anything but a black car. He was brilliant because he fashioned a production system designed to fit market needs. We habitually celebrate him for the wrong reason, his production genius.

His real genius was marketing. We think he was able to cut his selling price and therefore sell millions of $500 cars because his invention of the assembly line had reduced the costs. Actually he invented the assembly line because he had concluded that at $500 he could sell millions of cars. Mass production was the *result* not the cause of his low prices.

Ford repeatedly emphasized this point, but a nation of production-oriented business managers refuses to hear the great lesson he taught. Here is his operating philosophy as he expressed it succinctly:

> "Our policy is to reduce the price, extend the operations, and improve the article. You will notice that the reduction of price comes first. We have never considered any costs as fixed. Therefore we first reduce the price to the point where we believe more sales will result. Then we go ahead and try to make the prices. We do not bother about the costs. The new price forces the costs down. The more usual way is to take the costs and then determine the price, and although that method may be scientific in the narrow sense; it is not scientific in the broad sense, because what earthly use is it to know the cost if it tells you that you cannot manufacture at a price at which the article can be sold? But more to the point is the fact that, although one may calculate what a cost is, and of course all of our costs are carefully calculated, no one knows what a cost ought to be. One of the ways of discovering . . . is to name a price so low as to force everybody in the place to the highest point of efficiency. The low price makes everybody dig for profits. We make more discoveries concerning manufacturing and selling under this forced method than by any method of leisurely investigation."[5]

Product Provincialism

The tantalizing profit possibilities of low unit production costs may be the most seriously self-deceiving attitude that can afflict a company, particularly a "growth" company where an apparently assured expansion of demand already tends to undermine a proper concern for the importance of marketing and the customer.

The usual result of this narrow preoccupation with so-called concrete matters is that instead of growing, the industry declines. It usually means that the product fails to adapt to the constantly chang-

[5]Henry Ford, *My Life and Work* (New York, Doubleday, Page & Company, 1923), pp. 146–147.

ing patterns of consumer needs and tastes, to new and modified marketing institutions and practices, or to product developments in competing or complementary industries. The industry has its eyes so firmly on its own specific product that it does not see how it is being made obsolete.

The classical example of this is the buggy whip industry. No amount of product improvement could stave off its death sentence. But had the industry defined itself as being in the transportation business rather than the buggy whip business, it might have survived. It would have done what survival always entails, that is, changing. Even if it had only defined its business as providing a stimulant or catalyst to an energy source, it might have survived by becoming a manufacturer of, say, fanbelts or air cleaners.

What may some day be a still more classical example is again, the oil industry. Having let others steal marvelous opportunities from it (e.g., natural gas, as already mentioned, missile fuels, and jet engine lubricants), one would expect it to have taken steps never to let that happen again. But this is not the case. We are now getting extraordinary new developments in fuel systems specifically designed to power automobiles. Not only are these developments concentrated in firms outside the petroleum industry, but petroleum is almost systematically ignoring them, securely content in its wedded bliss to oil. It is the story of the kerosene lamp versus the incandescent lamp all over again. Oil is trying to improve hydrocarbon fuels rather than to develop *any* fuels best suited to the needs of their users, whether or not made in different ways and with different raw materials from oil.

Here are some of the things which nonpetroleum companies are working on:

> Over a dozen such firms now have advanced working models of energy systems which, when perfected, will replace the internal combustion engine and eliminate the demand for gasoline. The superior merit of each of these systems is their elimination of frequent, time-consuming, and irritating refueling stops. Most of these systems are fuel cells designed to create electrical energy directly from chemicals without combustion. Most of them use chemicals that are not derived from oil, generally hydrogen and oxygen.
>
> Several other companies have advanced models of electric storage batteries designed to power automobiles. One of these is an aircraft producer that is working jointly with several elec-

tric utility companies. The latter hope to use off-peak generating capacity to supply overnight plug-in battery regeneration. Another company, also using the battery approach, is a medium-size electronics firm with extensive small-battery experience that it developed in connection with its work on hearing aids. It is collaborating with an automobile manufacturer. Recent improvements arising from the need for high-powered miniature power storage plants in rockets have put us within reach of a relatively small battery capable of withstanding great overloads or surges of power. Germanium diode applications and batteries using sintered-plate and nickel-cadmium techniques promise to make a revolution in our energy sources.

Solar energy conversion systems are also getting increasing attention. One usually cautious Detroit auto executive recently ventured that solar-powered cars might be common by 1980.

As for the oil companies, they are more or less "watching developments," as one research director put it to me. A few are doing a bit of research on fuel cells, but almost always confined to developing cells powered by hydrocarbon chemicals. None of them are enthusiastically researching fuel cells, batteries, or solar power plants. None of them are spending a fraction as much on research in these profoundly important areas as they are on the usual run-of-the-mill things like reducing combustion chamber deposit in gasoline engines. One major integrated petroleum company recently took a tentative look at the fuel cell and concluded that although "the companies actively working on it indicate a belief in ultimate success . . . the timing and magnitude of its impact are too remote to warrant recognition in our forecasts."

One might, of course, ask: Why should the oil companies do anything different? Would not chemical fuel cells, batteries, or solar energy kill the present product lines? The answer is that they would indeed, and that is precisely the reason for the oil firms having to develop these power units before their competitors, so they will not be companies without an industry.

Management might be more likely to do what is needed for its own preservation if it thought of itself as being in the energy business. But even that would not be enough if it persists in imprisoning itself in the narrow grip of its tight product orientation. It has to think of itself as taking care of customer needs, not finding, refining, or even selling oil. Once it genuinely thinks of its business as taking care of people's transportation needs, nothing can stop it from creating its own extravagantly profitable growth.

"Creative Destruction"

Since words are cheap and deeds are dear, it may be appropriate to indicate what this kind of thinking involves and leads to. Let us start at the beginning—the customer. It can be shown that motorists strongly dislike the bother, delay, and experience of buying gasoline. People actually do not buy gasoline. They cannot see it, taste it, feel it, appreciate it, or really test it. What they buy is the right to continue driving their cars. The gas station is like a tax collector to whom people are compelled to pay a periodic toll as the price of using their cars. This makes the gas station a basically unpopular institution. It can never be made popular or pleasant, only less unpopular, less unpleasant.

To reduce its unpopularity completely means eliminating it. Nobody likes a tax collector, not even a pleasantly cheerful one. Nobody likes to interrupt a trip to buy a phantom product, not even from a handsome Adonis or a seductive Venus. Hence, companies that are working on exotic fuel substitutes which will eliminate the need for frequent refueling are heading directly into the outstretched arms of the irritated motorists. They are riding a wave of inevitability, not because they are creating something which is technologically superior or more sophisticated, but because they are satisfying a powerful customer need. They are also eliminating noxious odors and air pollution.

Once the petroleum companies recognize the customer-satisfying logic of what another power system can do, they will see that they have no more choice about working on an efficient, long-lasting fuel (or some way of delivering present fuels without bothering the motorist) than the big food chains had a choice about going into the supermarket business, or the vacuum tube companies had a choice about making semiconductors. For their own good the oil firms will have to destroy their own highly profitable assets. No amount of wishful thinking can save them from the necessity of engaging in this form of "creative destruction."

I phrase the need as strongly as this because I think management must make quite an effort to break itself loose from conventional ways. It is all too easy in this day and age for a company or industry to let its sense of purpose become dominated by the economies of full production and to develop a dangerously lopsided product orientation. In short, if management lets itself drift, it invariably drifts in the direction of thinking of itself as producing goods and services, not customer satisfactions. While it probably will not descend to the depths of telling its salesmen, "You get rid of it; we'll worry about profits," it can, without knowing it, be practicing precisely that formula for withering decay. The historic fate of one growth industry after another has been its suicidal product provincialism.

DANGERS OF R & D

Another big danger to a firm's continued growth arises when top management is wholly transfixed by the profit possibilities of technical research and development. To illustrate I shall turn first to a new industry—electronics—and then return once more to the oil companies. By comparing a fresh example with a familiar one, I hope to emphasize the prevalence and insidiousness of a hazardous way of thinking.

Marketing Shortchanged

In the case of electronics, the greatest danger which faces the glamorous new companies in this field is not that they do not pay enough attention to research and development, but that they pay *too much* attention to it. And the fact that the fastest growing electronics firms owe their eminence to their heavy emphasis on technical research is completely beside the point. They have vaulted to affluence on a sudden crest of unusually strong general receptiveness to new technical ideas. Also, their success has been shaped in the virtually guaranteed market of military subsidies and by military orders that in many cases actually preceded the existence of facilities to make the products. Their expansion has, in other words, been almost totally devoid of marketing effort.

Thus, they are growing up under conditions that come dangerously close to creating the illusion that a superior product will sell itself. Having created a successful company by making a superior product, it is not surprising that management continues to be oriented toward the product rather than the people who consume it. It develops the philosophy that continued growth is a matter of continued product innovation and improvement.

A number of other factors tend to strengthen and sustain this belief:

(1) Because electronic products are highly complex and sophisticated, managements become top-heavy with engineers and

scientists. This creates a selective bias in favor of research and production at the expense of marketing. The organization tends to view itself as making things rather than satisfying customer needs. Marketing gets treated as a residual activity, "something else" that must be done once the vital job of product creation and production is completed.

(2) To this bias in favor of product research, development, and production is added the bias in favor of dealing with controllable variables. Engineers and scientists are at home in the world of concrete things like machines, test tubes, production lines, and even balance sheets. The abstractions to which they feel kindly are those which are testable or manipulatable in the laboratory, or, if not testable, then functional, such as Euclid's axioms. In short, the managements of the new glamour-growth companies tend to favor those business activities which lend themselves to careful study, experimentation, and control—the hard, practical, realities of the lab, the shop, the books.

What gets shortchanged are the realities of the *market*. Consumers are unpredictable, varied, fickle, stupid, shortsighted, stubborn, and generally bothersome. This is not what the engineer-managers say, but deep down in their consciousness it is what they believe. And this accounts for their concentrating on what they know and what they can control, namely, product research, engineering, and production. The emphasis on production becomes particularly attractive when the product can be made at declining unit costs. There is no more inviting way of making money than by running the plant full blast.

Today the top-heavy science-engineering-production orientation of so many electronics companies works reasonably well because they are pushing into new frontiers in which the armed services have pioneered virtually assured markets. The companies are in the felicitous position of having to fill, not find markets; of not having to discover what the customer needs and wants, but of having the customer voluntarily come forward with specific new product demands. If a team of consultants had been assigned specifically to design a business situation calculated to prevent the emergence and development of a customer-oriented marketing viewpoint, it could not have produced anything better than the conditions just described.

Stepchild Treatment

The oil industry is a stunning example of how science, technology, and mass production can divert an entire group of companies from their main task. To the extent the consumer is studied at all (which is not much), the focus is forever on getting information which is designed to help the oil companies improve what they are now doing. They try to discover more convincing advertising themes, more effective sales promotional drives, what the market shares of the various companies are, what people like or dislike about service station dealers and oil companies, and so forth. Nobody seems as interested in probing deeply into the basic human needs that the industry might be trying to satisfy as in probing into the basic properties of the raw material that the companies work with in trying to deliver customer satisfactions.

Basic questions about customers and markets seldom get asked. The latter occupy a stepchild status. They are recognized as existing, as having to be taken care of, but not worth very much real thought or dedicated attention. Nobody gets as excited about the customers in his own backyard as about the oil in the Sahara Desert. Nothing illustrates better the neglect of marketing than its treatment in the industry press:

> The centennial issue of the *American Petroleum Institute Quarterly*, published in 1959 to celebrate the discovery of oil in Titusville, Pennsylvania, contained 21 feature articles proclaiming the industry's greatness. Only one of these talked about its achievements in marketing, and that was only a pictorial record of how service station architecture has changed. The issue also contained a special section on "New Horizons," which was devoted to showing the magnificent role oil would play in America's future. Every reference was ebulliently optimistic, never implying once that oil might have some hard competition. Even the reference to atomic energy was a cheerful catalogue of how oil would help make atomic energy a success. There was not a single apprehension that the oil industry's affluence might be threatened or a suggestion that one "new horizon" might include new and better ways of serving oil's present customers.
>
> But the most revealing example of the stepchild treatment that marketing gets was still another special series of short articles on "The Revolutionary Potential of Electronics." Under that heading this list of articles appeared in the table of contents:
>
> "In the Search for Oil"
> "In Production Operations"
> "In Refinery Processes"
> "In Pipeline Operations"

Significantly, every one of the industry's major functional areas is listed, *except* marketing. Why? Either it is believed that electronics holds no revolutionary potential for petroleum marketing (which is palpably wrong), or the editors forgot to discuss marketing (which is more likely, and illustrates its stepchild status).

The order in which the four functional areas are listed also betrays the alienation of the oil industry from the consumer. The industry is implicitly defined as beginning with the search for oil and ending with its distribution from the refinery. But the truth is, it seems to me, that the industry begins with the needs of the customer for its products. From that primal position its definition moves steadily backstream to areas of progressively lesser importance, until it finally comes to rest at the "search for oil."

Beginning & End

The view that an industry is a customer-satisfying process, not a goods-producing process, is vital for all businessmen to understand. An industry begins with the customer and his needs, not with a patent, a raw material, or a selling skill. Given the customer's needs, the industry develops backwards, first concerning itself with the physical *delivery* of customer satisfactions. Then it moves back further to *creating* the things by which these satisfactions are in part achieved. How these materials are created is a matter of indifference to the customer, hence the particular form of manufacturing, processing, or what-have-you cannot be considered as a vital aspect of the industry. Finally, the industry moves back still further to *finding* the raw materials necessary for making its products.

The irony of some industries oriented toward technical research and development is that the scientists who occupy the high executive positions are totally unscientific when it comes to defining their companies' over-all needs and purposes. They violate the first two rules of the scientific method—being aware of and defining their companies' problems, and then developing testable hypotheses about solving them. They are scientific only about the convenient things, such as laboratory and product experiments. The reason that the customer (and the satisfaction of his deepest needs) is not considered as being "the problem" is not because there is any certain belief that no such problem exists, but because an organizational lifetime has conditioned management to look in the opposite direction. Marketing is a stepchild.

I do not mean that selling is ignored. Far from it. But selling, again, is not marketing. As already pointed out, selling concerns itself with the tricks and techniques of getting people to exchange their cash for your product. It is not concerned with the values that the exchange is all about. And it does not, as marketing invariably does, view the entire business process as consisting of a tightly integrated effort to discover, create, arouse, and satisfy customer needs. The customer is somebody "out there" who, with proper cunning, can be separated from his loose change.

Actually, not even selling gets much attention in some technologically minded firms. Because there is a virtually guaranteed market for the abundant flow of their new products, they do not actually know what a real market is. It is as if they lived in a planned economy, moving their products routinely from factory to retail outlet. Their successful concentration on products tends to convince them of the soundness of what they have been doing, and they fail to see the gathering clouds over the market.

CONCLUSION

Less than 75 years ago American railroads enjoyed a fierce loyalty among astute Wall Streeters. European monarchs invested in them heavily. Eternal wealth was thought to be the benediction for anybody who could scrape a few thousand dollars together to put into rail stocks. No other form of transportation could compete with the railroads in speed, flexibility, durability, economy, and growth potentials. As Jacques Barzun put it, "By the turn of the century it was an institution, an image of man, a tradition, a code of honor, a source of poetry, a nursery of boyhood desires, a sublimest of toys, and the most solemn machine—next to the funeral hearse—that marks the epochs in man's life."[6]

Even after the advent of automobiles, trucks, and airplanes, the railroad tycoons remained imperturbably self-confident. If you had told them 60 years ago that in 30 years they would be flat on their backs, broke, and pleading for government subsidies, they would have thought you totally demented. Such a future was simply not considered possible. It was not even a discussable subject, or an askable question, or a matter which any sane person would consider worth speculating about. The very thought was insane. Yet a lot of insane notions now have matter-of-fact acceptance—for example, the idea of 100-ton tubes

[6]Op. cit., p. 20.

of metal moving smoothly through the air 20,000 feet above the earth, loaded with 100 sane and solid citizens casually drinking martinis—and they have dealt cruel blows to the railroads.

What specifically must other companies do to avoid this fate? What does customer orientation involve? These questions have in part been answered by the preceding examples and analysis. It would take another article to show in detail what is required for specific industries. In any case, it should be obvious that building an effective customer-oriented company involves far more than good intentions or promotional tricks; it involves profound matters of human organization and leadership. For the present, let me merely suggest what appear to be some general requirements.

Visceral Feel of Greatness

Obviously the company has to do what survival demands. It has to adapt to the requirements of the market, and it has to do it sooner rather than later. But mere survival is a so-so aspiration. Anybody can survive in some way or other, even the skid-row bum. The trick is to survive gallantly, to feel the surging impulse of commercial mastery; not just to experience the sweet smell of success, but to have the visceral feel of enterpreneurial greatness.

No organization can achieve greatness without a vigorous leader who is driven onward by his own pulsating *will to succeed.* He has to have a vision of grandeur, a vision that can produce eager followers in vast numbers. In business, the followers are the customers. To produce these customers, the entire corporation must be viewed as a customer-creating and customer-satisfying organism. Management must think of itself not as producing products but as providing customer-creating value satisfactions. It must push this idea (and everything it means and requires) into every nook and cranny of the organization. It has to do this continuously and with the kind of flair that excites and stimulates the people in it. Otherwise, the company will be merely a series of pigeonholed parts, with no consolidating sense of purpose or direction.

In short, the organization must learn to think of itself not as producing goods or services but as *buying customers,* as doing the things that will make people *want* to do business with it. And the chief executive himself has the inescapable responsibility for creating this environment, this viewpoint, this attitude, this aspiration. He himself must set the company's style, its direction, and its goals. This means he has to know precisely where he himself wants to go, and to make sure the whole organization is enthusiastically aware of where that is. This is a first requisite of leadership, for *unless he knows where he is going, any road will take him there.*

If any road is okay, the chief executive might as well pack his attaché case and go fishing. If an organization does not know or care where it is going, it does not need to advertise that fact with a ceremonial figurehead. Everybody will notice it soon enough.

28.

THE CONCEPT OF THE MARKETING MIX*

Neil H. Borden

I have always found it interesting to observe how an apt or colorful term may catch on, gain wide usage, and help to further understanding of a concept that has already been expressed in less appealing and communicative terms. Such has been true of the phrase "marketing mix," which I began to use in my teaching and writing some 15 years ago. In a relatively short time it has come to have wide usage. This note tells of the evolution of the marketing mix concept.

The phrase was suggested to me by a paragraph in a research bulletin on the management of marketing costs, written by my associate, Professor James Culliton.[1] In this study of manufacturers' marketing costs he described the business executive as a

> "decider," an "artist"—a "mixer of ingredients," who sometimes follows a recipe as he goes along, sometimes adapts a recipe to the ingredients immediately available, and sometimes experiments with or invents ingredients no one else has tried.

I liked his idea of calling a marketing executive a "mixer of ingredients," one who is constantly engaged in fashioning creatively a mix of marketing procedures and policies in his efforts to produce a profitable enterprise.

For many years previous to Culliton's cost study the wide variations in the procedures and policies employed by managements of manufacturing firms in their marketing programs and the correspondingly wide variation in the costs of these marketing functions, which Culliton

*Reprinted from *Journal of Advertising Research*, © Advertising Research Foundation, Inc. (June, 1964), pp. 2–7.

[1]James W. Culliton, *The Management of Marketing Costs* (Boston: Division of Research, Graduate School of Business Administration, Harvard University, 1948).

aptly ascribed to the varied "mixing of ingredients," had become increasingly evident as we had gathered marketing cases at the Harvard Business School. The marked differences in the patterns or formulae of the marketing programs not only were evident through facts disclosed in case histories, but also were reflected clearly in the figures of a cost study of food manufacturers made by the Harvard Bureau of Business Research in 1929. The primary objective of this study was to determine common figures of expenses for various marketing functions among food manufacturing companies, similar to the common cost figures which had been determined in previous years for various kinds of retail and wholesale businesses. In this manufacturer's study we were unable, however, with the data gathered to determine common expense figures that had much significance as standards by which to guide management, such as had been possible in the studies of retail and wholesale trades, where the methods of operation tended toward uniformity. Instead, among food manufacturers the ratios of sales devoted to the various functions of marketing such as advertising, personal selling, packaging, and so on, were found to be widely divergent, no matter how we grouped our respondents. Each respondent gave data that tended to uniqueness.

Culliton's study of marketing costs in 1947–48 was a second effort to find out, among other objectives, whether a bigger sample and a more careful classification of companies would produce evidence of operating uniformities that would give helpful common expense figures. But the result was the same as in our early study: there was wide diversity in cost ratios among any classifications of firms which were set up, and no common figures were found that had much value. This was true whether companies were grouped according to similarity in product lines, amount of sales, territorial extent of operations, or other bases of classification.

Relatively early in my study of advertising, it had become evident that understanding of advertising usage by manufacturers in any case had to come from an analysis of advertising's place as one element in the total marketing program of the firm. I came to realize that it is essential always to ask: what overall marketing strategy has been or might be employed to bring about a profitable operation in light of the circumstances faced by the management? What combination of marketing procedures and policies has been or might be adopted to bring about desired behavior of trade and consumers at costs that will permit a profit? Specifically, how can advertising, personal selling, pricing, packaging, channels, warehousing, and the other elements of a marketing program be manipulated and fitted together in a way that will give a profitable operation? In short, I saw that every advertising management case called for a consideration of the strategy to be adopted for the total marketing program, with advertising recognized as only one element whose form and extent depended on its careful adjustment to the other parts of the program.

The soundness of this viewpoint was supported by case histories throughout my volume, *The Economic Effects of Advertising*.[2] In the chapters devoted to the utilization of advertising by business, I had pointed out the innumerable combinations of marketing methods and policies that might be adopted by a manager in arriving at a marketing plan. For instance, in the area of branding, he might elect to adopt an individualized brand or a family brand. Or he might decide to sell his product unbranded or under private label. Any decision in the area of brand policy in turn has immediate implications that bear on his selection of channels of distribution, sales force methods, packaging, promotional procedure, and advertising. Throughout the volume the case materials cited show that the way in which any marketing function is designed and the burden placed upon the function are determined largely by the overall marketing strategy adopted by managements to meet the market conditions under which they operate. The forces met by different firms vary widely. Accordingly, the programs fashioned differ widely.

Regarding advertising, which was the function under focus in the economic effects volume, I said at one point:

> In all the above illustrative situations it should be recognized that advertising is not an operating method to be considered as something apart, as something whose profit value is to be judged alone. An able management does not ask, "Shall we use or not use advertising," without consideration of the product and of other management procedures to be employed. Rather the question is always one of finding a management formula giving advertising its due place in the combination of manufacturing methods, product form, pricing, promotion and selling methods, and distribution methods. As previously pointed out different formulae, i.e., different combinations of methods, may be profitably employed by competing manufacturers.

From the above it can be seen why Culliton's description of a marketing manager as a "mixer of ingredients" immediately appealed to me as an apt and easily understandable phrase, far better than my

[2]Neil H. Borden, *The Economic Effects of Advertising* (Homewood, Illinois: Richard D. Erwin, 1942).

previous references to the marketing man as an empiricist seeking in any situation to devise a profitable "pattern" or "formula" of marketing operations from among the many procedures and policies that were open to him. If he was a "mixer of ingredients," what he designed was a "marketing mix."

It was logical to proceed from a realization of the existence of a variety of "marketing mixes" to the development of a concept that would comprehend not only this variety, but also the market forces that cause managements to produce a variety of mixes. It is the problems raised by these forces that lead marketing managers to exercise their wits in devising mixes or programs which they hope will give a profitable business operation.

To portray this broadened concept in a visual presentation requires merely:

1. A list of the important elements or ingredients that make up marketing programs.
2. A list of the forces that bear on the marketing operation of a firm and to which the marketing manager must adjust in his search for a mix or program that can be successful.

The list of elements of the marketing mix in such a visual presentation can be long or short, depending on how far one wishes to go in his classification and sub-classification of the marketing procedures and policies with which marketing managements deal when devising marketing programs. The list of elements which I have employed in my teaching and consulting work covers the principal areas of marketing activities which call for management decisions as revealed by case histories. I realize others might build a different list. Mine is as follows:

Elements of the Marketing Mix of Manufacturers

1. *Product Planning*—policies and procedures relating to:
   a. Product lines to be offered—qualities, design, etc.
   b. Markets to sell—whom, where, when, and in what quantity.
   c. New product policy—research and development program.
2. *Pricing*—policies and procedures relating to:
   a. Price level to adopt.
   b. Specific prices to adopt—odd-even, etc.
   c. Price policy—one-price or varying price, price maintenance, use of list prices, etc.
   d. Margins to adopt—for company, for the trade.

3. *Branding*—policies and procedures relating to:
   a. Selection of trade marks.
   b. Brand policy—individualized or family brand.
   c. Sale under private label or unbranded.
4. *Channels of Distribution*—policies and procedures relating to:
   a. Channels to use between plant and consumer.
   b. Degree of selectivity among wholesalers and retailers.
   c. Efforts to gain cooperation of the trade.
5. *Personal Selling*—policies and procedures relating to:
   a. Burden to be placed on personal selling and the methods to be employed in:
      1. Manufacturer's organization.
      2. Wholesale segment of the trade.
      3. Retail segment of the trade.
6. *Advertising*—policies and procedures relating to:
   a. Amount to spend—i.e., the burden to be placed on advertising.
   b. Copy platform to adopt:
      1. Product image desired.
      2. Corporate image desired.
   c. Mix of advertising—to the trade, through the trade, to consumers.
7. *Promotions*—policies and procedures relating to:
   a. Burden to place on special selling plans or devices directed at or through the trade.
   b. Form of these devices for consumer promotions, for trade promotions.
8. *Packaging*—policies and procedures relating to:
   a. Formulation of package and label.
9. *Display*—policies and procedures relating to:
   a. Burden to be put on display to help effect sale.
   b. Methods to adopt to secure display.
10. *Servicing*—policies and procedures relating to:
    a. Providing service needed.
11. *Physical Handling*—policies and procedures relating to:
    a. Warehousing.
    b. Transportation.
    c. Inventories.
12. *Fact Finding and Analysis*—policies and procedures relating to:
    a. Securing, analysis, and use of facts in marketing operations.

Also, if one were to make a list of all the forces which managements weigh at one time or another when formulating their marketing mixes, it would be very long indeed, for the behavior of individuals and groups in all spheres of life has a bearing, first, on what goods and services are produced and consumed, and, second, on the procedures that may be employed in bringing about exchange of these goods and services. However, the important forces which bear on marketers, all arising from the behavior of individuals or groups, may readily be listed under four heads, namely, the behavior of consumers, the trade, competitors, and government.

The next outline contains these four behavioral forces with notations of some of the important behavioral determinants within each force. These must be studied and understood by the marketer, if his marketing mix is to be successful. The great quest of marketing management is to understand the behavior of humans in response to the stimuli to which they are subjected. The skillful marketer is one who is a perceptive and practical psychologist and sociologist, who has keen insight into individual and group behavior, who can foresee changes in behavior that develop in a dynamic world, who has creative ability for building well-knit programs because he has the capacity to visualize the probable response of consumers, trade, and competitors to his moves. His skill in forecasting response to his marketing moves should well be supplemented by a further skill in devising and using tests and measurements to check consumer or trade response to his program or parts thereof, for no marketer has so much prescience that he can proceed without empirical check.

Here, then, is the suggested outline of forces which govern the mixing of marketing elements. This list and that of the elements taken together provide a visual presentation of the concept of the marketing mix.

Market Forces Bearing on the Marketing Mix

1. *Consumers' Buying Behavior*—as determined by their:
   a. Motivation in purchasing.
   b. Buying habits.
   c. Living habits.
   d. Environment (present and future, as revealed by trends, for environment influences consumers' attitudes toward products and their use of them).
   e. Buying power.
   f. Number (i.e., how many).
2. *The Trade's Behavior*—wholesalers' and retailers' behavior, as influenced by:

a. Their motivations.
b. Their structure, practices, and attitudes.
c. Trends in structure and procedures that portend change.

3. *Competitors' Position and Behavior*—as influenced by:
   a. Industry structure and the firm's relation thereto.
      1. Size and strength of competitors.
      2. Number of competitors and degree of industry concentration.
      3. Indirect competition—i.e., from other products.
   b. Relation of supply to demand—oversupply or undersupply.
   c. Product choices offered consumers by the industry—i.e., quality, price, service.
   d. Degree to which competitors compete on price vs. non-price bases.
   e. Competitors' motivations and attitudes—their likely reponse to the actions of other firms.
   f. Trends technological and social, portending change in supply and demand.
4. *Government Behavior*—controls over marketing:
   a. Regulations over products.
   b. Regulations over pricing.
   c. Regulations over competitive practices.
   d. Regulations over advertising and promotion.

When building a marketing program to fit the needs of his firm, the marketing manager has to weigh the behavioral forces and then juggle marketing elements in his mix with a keen eye on the resources with which he has to work. His firm is but one small organism in a large universe of complex forces. His firm is only a part of an industry that is competing with many other industries. What does the firm have in terms of money, product line, organization, and reputation with which to work? The manager must devise a mix of procedures that fit these resources. If his firm is small, he must judge the response of consumers, trade, and competition in light of his position and resources and the influence that he can exert in the market. He must look for special opportunities in product or method of operation. The small firm cannot employ the procedures of the big firm. Though he may sell the same kind of product as the big firm, his marketing strategy is likely to be widely different in many respects. Innumerable instances of this fact might be cited. For example, in the industrial goods field, small firms often seek to build sales on a limited and highly specialized line, whereas industry leaders seek patronage for full lines. Small firms often elect to go in for regional sales rather than attempt the national distribution practiced by larger companies. Again, the company of limited resources often elects to limit its production and sales to products whose potential is too small to attract the big fellows. Still again, companies with small resources in the cosmetic field not infrequently have set up introductory marketing programs employing aggressive personal selling and a "push" strategy with distribution limited to leading department stores. Their initially small advertising funds have been directed through these selected retail outlets, with the offering of the products and their story told over the signatures of the stores. The strategy has been to borrow kudos for their products from the leading stores' reputations and to gain a gradual radiation of distribution to smaller stores in all types of channels, such as often comes from the trade's follow-the-leader behavior. Only after resources have grown from mounting sales has a dense retail distribution been aggressively sought and a shift made to place the selling burden more and more on company-signed advertising.

The above strategy was employed for Toni products and Stoppette deodorant in their early marketing stages when the resources of their producers were limited (cf. case of Jules Montenier, Inc. in Borden and Marshall).[3] In contrast, cosmetic manufacturers with large resources have generally followed a "pull" strategy for the introduction of new products, relying on heavy campaigns of advertising in a rapid succession of area introductions to induce a hoped-for, complete retail coverage from the start (cf. case of Bristol-Meyers Company in Borden and Marshall).[4] These introductory campaigns have been undertaken only after careful programs of product development and test marketing have given assurance that product and selling plans had high promise of success.

Many additional instances of the varying strategy employed by small versus large enterprises might be cited. But those given serve to illustrate the point that managements must fashion their mixes to fit their resources. Their objectives must be realistic.

LONG VS. SHORT TERM ASPECTS OF MARKETING MIX

The marketing mix of a firm in a large part is the product of the evolution that comes from day-to-day marketing. At any time the mix represents the program that a management has evolved to meet the

[3]Neil H. Borden and M. V. Marshall, *Advertising Management: Text and Cases* (Homewood, Illinois: Richard D. Irwin, 1959), pp. 498–518.
[4]*Ibid.*, pp. 518–33.

problems with which it is constantly faced in an ever-changing, ever-challenging market. There are continuous tactical maneuvers: a new product, aggressive promotion, or price change initiated by a competitor must be considered and met; the failure of the trade to provide adequate market coverage or display must be remedied; a faltering sales force must be reorganized and stimulated; a decline in sales share must be diagnosed and remedied; an advertising approach that has lost effectiveness must be replaced; a general business decline must be countered. All such problems call for a management's maintaining effective channels of information relative to its own operations and to the day-to-day behavior of consumers, competitors, and the trade. Thus, we may observe that short-range forces play a large part in the fashioning of the mix to be used at any time and in determining the allocation of expenditures among the various functional accounts of the operating statement.

But the overall strategy employed in a marketing mix is the product of longer-range plans and procedures dictated in part by past empiricism and in part, if the management is a good one, by management foresight as to what needs to be done to keep the firm successful in a changing world. As the world has become more and more dynamic, blessed is that corporation which has managers who have foresight, who can study trends of all kinds—natural, economic, social, and technological—and, guided by these, devise long-range plans that give promise of keeping their corporations afloat and successful in the turbulent sea of market change. Accordingly, when we think of the marketing mix, we need to give particular heed today to devising a mix based on long-range planning that promises to fit the world of five or ten or more years hence. Provision for effective long-range planning in corporate organization and procedure has become more and more recognized as the earmark of good management in a world that has become increasingly subject to rapid change.

To cite an instance among American marketing organizations which have shown foresight in adjusting the marketing mix to meet social and economic change, I look upon Sears Roebuck and Company as an outstanding example. After building an unusually successfully mail order business to meet the needs of a rural America, Sears management foresaw the need to depart from its marketing pattern as a mail order company catering primarily to farmers. The trend from a rural to an urban United States was going on apace. The automobile and good roads promised to make town and city stores increasingly available to those who continued to be farmers. Relatively early, Sears launched a chain of stores across the land, each easily accessible by highway to both farmer and city resident, and with adequate parking space for customers. In time there followed the remarkable telephone and mail order plan directed at urban residents to make buying easy for Americans when congested city streets and highways made shopping increasingly distasteful. Similarly, in the areas of planning products which would meet the desires of consumers in a fast-changing world, of shaping its servicing to meet the needs of a wide variety of mechanical products, of pricing procedures to meet the challenging competition that came with the advent of discount retailers, the Sears organization has shown a foresight, adaptability, and creative ability worthy of emulation. The amazing growth and profitability of the company attest to the foresight and skill of its management. Its history shows the wisdom of careful attention to market forces and their impending change in devising marketing mixes that may assure growth.

USE OF THE MARKETING MIX CONCEPT

Like many concepts, the marketing mix concept seems relatively simple, once it has been expressed. I know that before they were ever tagged with the nomenclature of "concept," the ideas involved were widely understood among marketers as a result of the growing knowledge about marketing and marketing procedures that came during the preceding half century. But I have found for myself that once the ideas were reduced to a formal statement with an accompanying visual presentation, the concept of the mix has proved a helpful device in teaching, in business problem solving, and, generally, as an aid to thinking about marketing. First of all, it is helpful in giving an answer to the question often raised as to "what is marketing?" A chart which shows the elements of the mix and the forces that bear on the mix helps to bring understanding of what marketing is. It helps to explain why in our dynamic world the thinking of management in all its functional areas must be oriented to the market.

In recent years I have kept an abbreviated chart showing the elements and the forces of the marketing mix in front of my classes at all times. In case discussion it has proved a handy device by which to raise queries as to whether the student has recognized the implications of any recommendation he might have made in the areas of the several elements of the mix. Or, referring to the forces, we can question whether all the pertinent market forces have been given due consideration. Continual reference to the mix chart leads me to feel that the students' understanding of "what marketing is" is strengthened. The constant presence and use of the chart leaves a deeper understanding that marketing is the devising of programs that successfully meet the forces of the market.

In problem solving the marketing mix chart is a constant reminder of:

1. The fact that a problem seemingly lying in one segment of the mix must be deliberated with constant thought regarding the effect of any change in that sector on the other areas of marketing operations. The necessity of integration in marketing thinking is ever present.
2. The need of careful study of the market forces as they might bear on problems in hand.

In short, the mix chart provides an ever-ready checklist as to areas into which to guide thinking when considering marketing questions or dealing with marketing problems.

MARKETING: SCIENCE OR ART?

The quest for a "science of marketing" is hard upon us. If science is in part a systematic formulation and arrangement of facts in a way to help understanding, then the concept of the marketing mix may possibly be considered a small contribution in the search for a science of marketing. If we think of a marketing science as involving the observation and classification of facts and the establishment of verifiable laws that can be used by the marketer as a guide to action with assurance that predicted results will ensue, then we cannot be said to have gotten far toward establishing a science. The concept of the mix lays out the areas in which facts should be assembled, these to serve as a guide to management judgment in building marketing mixes. In the last few decades American marketers have made substantial progress in adopting the scientific method in assembling facts. They have sharpened the tools of fact finding—both those arising within the business and those external to it. Aided by these facts and by the skills developed through careful observation and experience, marketers are better fitted to practice the art of designing marketing mixes than would be the case had not the techniques of gathering facts been advanced as they have been in recent decades. Moreover, marketers have made progress in the use of the scientific method in designing tests whereby the results from mixes or parts of mixes can be measured.

Thereby marketers have been learning how to subject the hypotheses of their mix artists to empirical check.

With continued improvement in the search for and the recording of facts pertinent to marketing, with further application of the controlled experiment, and with an extension and careful recording of case histories, we may hope for a gradual formulation of clearly defined and helpful marketing laws. Until then, and even then, marketing and the building of marketing mixes will largely lie in the realm of art.

29.

PRODUCT DIFFERENTIATION AND MARKET SEGMENTATION AS ALTERNATIVE MARKETING STRATEGIES*

Wendell R. Smith

During the decade of the 1930's, the work of Robinson and Chamberlin resulted in a revitalization of economic theory. While classical and neoclassical theory provided a useful framework for economic analysis, the theories of perfect competition and pure monopoly had become inadequate as explanations of the contemporary business scene. The theory of perfect competition assumes homogeneity among the components of both the demand and supply sides of the market, but diversity or heterogeneity had come to be the rule rather than the exception. This analysis reviews major marketing strategy alternatives that are available to planners and merchandisers of products in an environment characterized by imperfect competition.

DIVERSITY IN SUPPLY

That there is a lack of homogeneity or close similarity among the items offered to the market by individual manufacturers of various products is obvious in any variety store, department store, or shopping center. In many cases the impact of this diversity is amplified by advertising and promotional activities. Today's advertising and promotion tends to emphasize appeals to *selective* rather than *primary* buying motives and to point out the distinctive or differentiating features of the advertiser's product or service offer.

The presence of differences in the sales offers made by competing

*Reprinted from the *Journal of Marketing*, national quarterly publication of the American Marketing Association (July, 1956), pp. 3–8.

suppliers produces a diversity in supply that is inconsistent with the assumptions of earlier theory. The reasons for the presence of diversity in specific markets are many and include the following:

1. Variations in the production equipment and methods or processes used by different manufacturers of products designed for the same or similar uses.
2. Specialized or superior resources enjoyed by favorably situated manufacturers.
3. Unequal progress among competitors in design, development, and improvement of products.
4. The inability of manufacturers in some industries to eliminate product variations even through the application of quality control techniques.
5. Variations in producers' estimates of the nature of market demand with reference to such matters as price sensitivity, color, material, or package size.

Because of these and other factors, both planned and uncontrollable differences exist in the products of an industry. As a result, sellers make different appeals in support of their marketing efforts.

DIVERSITY OR VARIATIONS IN CONSUMER DEMAND

Under present-day conditions of imperfect competition, marketing managers are generally responsible for selecting the over-all marketing strategy or combination of strategies best suited to a firm's requirements at any particular point in time. The strategy selected may consist of a program designed to bring about the *convergence* of individual market demands for a variety of products upon a single or limited offering to the market. This is often accomplished by the achievement of product differentiation through advertising and promotion. In this way, variations in the demands of individual consumers are minimized or brought into line by means of effective use of appealing product claims designed to make a satisfactory volume of demand *converge* upon the product or product line being promoted. This strategy was once believed to be essential as the marketing counterpart to standardization and mass production in manufacturing because of the rigidities imposed by production cost considerations.

In some cases, however, the marketer may determine that it is better to accept *divergent* demand as a market characteristic and to adjust product lines and marketing strategy accordingly. This implies ability to merchandise to a heterogeneous market by emphasizing the precision with which a firm's products can satisfy the requirements of one or more distinguishable market segments. The strategy of product differentiation here gives way to marketing programs based upon measurement and definition of market differences.

Lack of homogeneity on the demand side may be based upon different customs, desire for variety, or desire for exclusiveness or may arise from basic differences in user needs. Some divergence in demand is the result of shopping errors in the market. Not all consumers have the desire or the ability to shop in a sufficiently efficient or rational manner as to bring about selection of the most needed or most wanted goods or services.

Diversity on the demand side of the market is nothing new to sales management. It has always been accepted as a fact to be dealt with in industrial markets where production to order rather than for the market is common. Here, however, the loss of precision in the satisfying of customer requirements that would be necessitated by attempts to bring about convergence of demand is often impractical and, in some cases, impossible. However, even in industrial marketing, the strategy of product differentiation should be considered in cases where products are applicable to several industries and may have horizontal markets of substantial size.

LONG-TERM IMPLICATIONS

While contemporary economic theory deals with the nature of product differentiation and its effects upon the operation of the total economy, the alternative strategies of product differentiation and market segmentation have received less attention. Empirical analysis of contemporary marketing activity supports the hypothesis that, while product differentiation and market segmentation are closely related (perhaps even inseparable) concepts, attempts to distinguish between these approaches may be productive of clarity in theory as well as greater precision in the planning of marketing operations. Not only do strategies of differentiation and segmentation call for differing systems of action at any point in time, but the dynamics of markets and marketing underscore the importance of varying degrees of diversity *through time* and suggest that the rational selection of marketing strategies is a requirement for the achievement of maximum functional effectiveness in the economy as a whole.

If a rational selection of strategies is to be made, an integrated approach to the minimizing of total costs must take precedence over separate approaches to minimization of production costs on the one hand and marketing costs on the other. Strategy determination must be regarded as an over-all management decision which will influence and require facilitating policies affecting both production and marketing activities.

DIFFERENCES BETWEEN STRATEGIES OF DIFFERENTIATION AND SEGMENTATION

Product differentiation and market segmentation are both consistent with the framework of imperfect competition.[1] In its simplest terms, *product differentiation* is concerned with the bending of demand to the will of supply. It is an attempt to shift or to change the slope of the demand curve for the market offering of an individual supplier. This strategy may also be employed by a group of suppliers such as a farm cooperative, the members of which have agreed to act together. It results from the desire to establish a kind of equilibrium in the market by bringing about adjustment of market demand to supply conditions favorable to the seller.

Segmentation is based upon developments on the demand side of the market and represents a rational and more precise adjustment of product and marketing effort to consumer or user requirements. In the language of the economist, segmentation is *disaggregative* in its effects and tends to bring about recognition of several demand schedules where only one was recognized before.

Attention has been drawn to this area of analysis by the increasing number of cases in which business problems have become soluble by doing something about marketing programs and product policies that overgeneralize both markets and marketing effort. These are situations where intensive promotion designed to differentiate the company's products was not accomplishing its objective—cases where failure to recognize the reality of market segments was resulting in loss of market position.

While successful product differentiation will result in giving the marketer a horizontal share of a broad and generalized market, equally successful application of the strategy of market segmentation tends to produce depth of market position in the segments that are effectively

[1]Imperfect competition assumes lack of uniformity in the size and influence of the firms or individuals that comprise the demand or supply sides of a market.

defined and penetrated. The differentiator seeks to secure a layer of the market cake, whereas one who employs market segmentation strives to secure one or more wedge-shaped pieces.

Many examples of market segmentation can be cited; the cigarette and automobile industries are well-known illustrations. Similar developments exist in greater or lesser degree in almost all product areas. Recent introduction of a refrigerator with no storage compartment for frozen foods was in response to the distinguishable preferences of the segment of the refrigerator market made up of home freezer owners whose frozen food storage needs had already been met.

Strategies of segmentation and differentiation may be employed simultaneously, but more commonly they are applied in sequence in response to changing market conditions. In one sense, segmentation is a momentary or short-term phenomenon in that effective use of this strategy may lead to more formal recognition of the reality of market segments through redefinition of the segments as individual markets. Redefinition may result in a swing back to differentiation.

The literature of both economics and marketing abounds in formal definitions of product differentiation. *From a strategy viewpoint*, product differentiation is securing a measure of control over the demand for a product by advertising or promoting differences between a product and the products of competing sellers. It is basically the result of sellers' desires to establish firm market positions and/or to insulate their business against price competition. Differentiation tends to be characterized by heavy use of advertising and promotion and to result in prices that are somewhat above the equilibrium levels associated with perfectly competitive market conditions. It may be classified as a *promotional* strategy or approach to marketing.

Market segmentation, on the other hand, consists of viewing a heterogeneous market (one characterized by divergent demand) as a number of smaller homogeneous markets in response to differing product preferences among important market segments. It is attributable to the desires of consumers or users for more precise satisfaction of their varying wants. Like differentiation, segmentation often involves substantial use of advertising and promotion. This is to inform market segments of the availability of goods or services produced for or presented as meeting their needs with precision. Under these circumstances, prices tend to be somewhat closer to perfectly competitive equilibrium. Market segmentation is essentially a *merchandising* strategy, merchandising being used here in its technical sense as representing the adjustment of market offerings to consumer or user requirements.

THE EMERGENCE OF THE SEGMENTATION STRATEGY

To a certain extent, market segmentation may be regarded as a force in the market that will not be denied. It may result from trial and error in the sense that generalized programs of product differentiation may turn out to be effective in some segments of the market and ineffective in others. Recognition of, and intelligent response to, such a situation necessarily involves a shift in emphasis. On the other hand, it may develop that products involved in marketing programs designed for particular market segments may achieve a broader acceptance than originally planned, thus revealing a basis for convergence of demand and a more generalized marketing approach. The challenge to planning arises from the importance of determining, preferably in advance, the level or degree of segmentation that can be exploited with profit.

There appear to be many reasons why formal recognition of market segmentation as a strategy is beginning to emerge. One of the most important of these is decrease in the size of the minimum efficient producing or manufacturing unit required in some product areas. American industry has also established the technical base for product diversity by gaining release from some of the rigidities imposed by earlier approaches to mass production. Hence, there is less need today for generalization of markets in response to the necessity for long production runs of identical items.

Present emphasis upon the minimizing of marketing costs through self-service and similar developments tends to impose a requirement for better adjustment of products to consumer demand. The retailing structure, in its efforts to achieve improved efficiency, is providing less and less sales push at point of sale. This increases the premium placed by retailers upon products that are presold by their producers and are readily recognized by consumers as meeting their requirements as measured by satisfactory rates of stock turnover.

It has been suggested that the present level of discretionary buying power is productive of sharper shopping comparisons, particularly for items that are above the need level. General prosperity also creates increased willingness "to pay a little more" to get "just what I wanted."

Attention to market segmentation has also been enhanced by the recent ascendancy of product competition to a position of great economic importance. An expanded array of goods and services is competing for the consumer's dollar. More specifically, advancing technology is creating competition between new and traditional materials with reference to metals, construction materials, textile products, and in many other areas. While such competition is confusing and difficult to analyze in its early stages, it tends to achieve a kind of balance as various competing materials find their markets of maximum potential as a result of recognition of differences in the requirements of market segments.

Many companies are reaching the stage in their development where attention to market segmentation may be regarded as a condition or cost of growth. Their *core* markets have already been developed on a generalized basis to the point where additional advertising and selling expenditures are yielding diminishing returns. Attention to smaller or *fringe* market segments, which may have small potentials individually but are of crucial importance in the aggregate, may be indicated.

Finally, some business firms are beginning to regard an increasing share of their total costs of operation as being fixed in character. The higher costs of maintaining market position in the channels of distribution illustrate this change. Total reliance upon a strategy of product differentiation under such circumstances is undesirable, since market share available as a result of such a promotion-oriented approach tends to be variable over time. Much may hinge, for example, upon week-to-week audience ratings of the television shows of competitors who seek to outdifferentiate each other. Exploitation of market segments, which provides for greater maximization of consumer or user satisfactions, tends to build a more secure market position and to lead to greater over-all stability. While traditionally, high fixed costs (regarded primarily from the production viewpoint) have created pressures for expanded sale of standardized items through differentiation, the possible shifting of certain marketing costs into the fixed area of the total cost structure tends to minimize this pressure.

CONCLUSION

Success in planning marketing activities requires precise utilization of both product differentiation and market segmentation as components of marketing strategy. It is fortunate that available techniques of marketing research make unplanned market exploration largely unnecessary. It is the obligation of those responsible for sales and marketing administration to keep the strategy mix in adjustment with market structure at any given point in time and to produce in marketing strategy at least as much dynamism as is present in the market. The ability of business to plan in this way is dependent upon the maintenance of a flow of market information that can be provided by marketing research as well as the full utilization of available techniques of cost accounting and cost analysis.

Cost information is critical because the upper limit to which market segmentation can be carried is largely defined by production cost considerations. There is a limit to which diversity in market offerings can be carried without driving production costs beyond practical limits. Similarly, the employment of product differentiation as a strategy tends to be restricted by the achievement of levels of marketing costs that are untenable. These cost factors tend to define the limits of the zone within which the employment of marketing strategies or a strategy mix dictated by the nature of the market is permissive.

It should be emphasized that while we have here been concerned with the differences between product differentiation and market segmentation as marketing strategies, they are closely related concepts in the setting of an imperfectly competitive market. The differences have been highlighted in the interest of enhancing clarity in theory and precision in practice. The emergence of market segmentation as a strategy once again provides evidence of the consumer's preeminence in the contemporary American economy and the richness of the rewards that can result from the application of science to marketing problems.

30. MULTI-STAGE APPROACH TO PRICING*

Alfred R. Oxenfeldt

Of all the areas of executive decision, pricing is perhaps the most fuzzy. Whenever a price problem is discussed by a committee, divergent figures are likely to be recommended without a semblance of consensus. Although unanimity in marketing decisions is a custom more remarkable in its occurrence than in its absence, agreement in pricing decisions is even more rare.

This article accordingly presents a long-run, policy-oriented approach to pricing which should reduce the range of prices considered in specific situations and consequently improve the decisions which result. This approach, which to the best of my knowledge is new, calls for the price decision to be made in six successive steps, each one narrowing the alternatives to be considered at the next step.

Is this method just another mechanical pricing formula? Hardly, for it is my conviction that the quest for mechanical pricing methods is unduly optimistic, if not downright naive. Nevertheless, many businessmen consistently employ almost mechanical formulas for pricing. They do this even though they scoff at the claim that there are reliable fixed formulas for handling personnel problems or making advertising or capital outlay decisions. Certainly, experience has not produced recipes that guarantee correct decisions in any sphere of business. The best of them only apply under normal conditions, and it is most rare indeed that conditions resembling normalcy prevail.

On the other hand, many discussions of pricing present a long list of factors to be "taken into account," carefully weighed and balanced, and then subjected to a process called "judgment." While a specific

*Reprinted from Edward C. Bursk and John F. Chapman (eds.), *Modern Marketing Strategy* (Cambridge, Mass.: Harvard University Press), © 1964 by the President and Fellows of Harvard College, originally published in the *Harvard Business Review,* Vol. 38 (July-August, 1960), pp. 125–33.

price is thus arrived at, this does not alter the fact that intelligent and experienced business executives using the method will arrive at widely different price decisions—all based on the same information.

Yet, even if mechanical pricing formulas are the hope of the optimistic, it would be excessively pessimistic to resign ourselves to a *formless* consideration of all the relevant factors and to a random exercise of judgment. Many things are known about the subject that would be extremely helpful to those responsible for making such decisions.

SEQUENTIAL STAGES

In order to organize the various pieces of information and considerations that bear on price decisions, a multi-stage approach to pricing can be a very helpful tool. This method sorts the major elements in a pricing decision into six successive stages:

1. Selecting market targets.
2. Choosing a brand "image."
3. Composing a marketing mix.
4. Selecting a pricing policy.
5. Determining a pricing strategy.
6. Arriving at a specific price.

The sequence of the stages is an essential part of the method, for each step is calculated to simplify the succeeding stage and to reduce the likelihood of error. One might say that this method divides the price decision into manageable parts, each one logically antecedent to the next. In this way, the decision at each stage facilitates all subsequent decisions. This approach might also be regarded as a process of selective search, where the number of alternatives deserving close consideration is reduced drastically by making the decision in successive stages. Of course, one could arrive at the same result by simultaneously considering all the factors mentioned—but it might require a computer to do so.

While it appears that this approach is applicable over a broad range of industry and trade, the great diversity of business situations precludes the possibility of its being a universally applicable method. No rigid approach, and certainly not the one presented here, offers a guarantee of reaching the best—or even a satisfactory—price decision. It must be adapted to prevailing circumstances; consequently, information, experience, and the application of rigorous logic are required for its optimum utilization.

I. MARKET TARGETS

A going concern is "committed," confined, and tied down by several important circumstances which can be altered only over a considerable period of time. It must live with many conditions, even while it may attempt to alter them. Also, an operating business possesses specified resources on which it will strive to capitalize in achieving its objectives. For example, a firm will have:

A fixed production location, given physical facilities, and a particular production and sales labor force.

A set of distribution arrangements through which the firm generally sells, including particular distributors with whom it has established relationships.

Contracts with suppliers, customers, laborers, and lenders of funds.

A portfolio of customers who have a definite opinion of the firm's reliability, and the quality of its offerings and service.

These commitments and resources of a firm contain pricing implications. Mainly, they determine the type of product that it can make, the type of service it can render, and its probable costs of operation. What is more, these circumstances form the basis for the most fundamental pricing decision that management should make—namely, the types of customers, or market segments, it will attempt to cultivate.

By virtue of its fixed commitments, then, a firm is limited to the several market segments it can reasonably hope to capture. It has customer connections on which it can capitalize, and it has a variety of strengths and weaknesses that limit its choice among potential submarkets for intensive cultivation.

Two examples drawn from the TV set industry will help to clarify this crucial first stage. Certainly, no two firms could possibly exemplify all situations, nor is it possible for an outsider to explain satisfactorily why specific decisions were made in specific cases. However, these illustrations are intended to indicate what factors management must consider if it is to apply the multi-stage approach. They do *not* describe how management reasoned or what would have been the best decision under the circumstances.

ZENITH RADIO

First, consider the pricing problem of the Zenith Radio Corporation at the time it started to produce TV sets in 1948:

This company, which is one of the two largest TV set producers now, dropped out of the automobile radio business in order to manufacture television sets. (At that time, it was the largest single producer of automobile radios, but this business was not very profitable.) Zenith possessed these resources and was subject to these commitments and limitations that could have influenced its selection of market targets in the TV business—

It had production facilities in Chicago that had been designed for and used in radio production for many years; its labor force and supervisory personnel were familiar with the electronics business. The firm had substantial manufacturing skills in electronics because of its work for the military during and after World War II. Zenith could assess its manufacturing capabilities as very substantial, but not outstanding.

Financially, Zenith was also in a very strong and liquid position and could readily have undertaken heavy expenditures at this time.

But Zenith's outstanding resource was a distributor and dealer organization that was as good as that possessed by any other firm in the nation. Its dealers commanded strong loyalty among their clientele not only in small communities but also in large cities—a most vital fact in view of the technical character of TV and the great power that retailers wield over consumer choices of such products. Here Zenith was helped by the fact that it had acquired an excellent reputation for quality products in radios; for many years, it was the Cadillac of the radio industry. Zenith management, like all other radio manufacturers who entered the television business, decided to sell its sets through the distributor organization it had already created; its distributors, in turn, would sell them mainly to dealers already buying Zenith radios.

There were also several other peripheral advantages. Zenith was closely identified, in the minds of many consumers, with hearing aids which were widely advertised as much on grounds of moderate price as in terms of high quality. Further, Zenith started to telecast, experimentally, in the Chicago market even before World War II and had some local identification as a telecaster, as well as a manufacturer. Its products were strongly favored in the Chicago market.

In summary, Zenith Radio could count on its strong distributor and retail organizations as its outstanding resource, while recognizing that it did not possess any particular advantage in costs of manufacture or quality of product and, in fact, that its behavior in the television business was necessarily circumscribed by its radio and hearing aid business. Zenith's management would have required very strong reasons to choose as its market targets customers who were very different from those who bought its radios and hearing aids.

Under these circumstances, Zenith management might have decided to attempt to reach customers at almost all levels of income. Partly, it could do this by including "low-end" and promotional models in its line; partly because television sets were sold on installment credit involving modest monthly charges and partly because, at least in the early years, television purchases were spread rather evenly over all income groups.

On the other hand, Zenith management, as its first step, might well expect to cultivate particularly those consumers who were conservative and quality-conscious, who felt a strong loyalty to particular appliance retailers, who were located mainly in small cities and towns. On this basis the Zenith customer targets would not include "snobs" who, at that time, favored the Dumont brand and, to a lesser degree, the RCA set. Also they would not include bargain hunters. Rather Zenith's customers would be the kind of people who feel that "you get what you pay for." (Zenith would presumably capitalize on its strong position in the Chicago area by special measures aimed at that market.)

Columbia Broadcasting

Now contrast Zenith's position with that of Columbia Broadcasting System, Inc. when it started to produce and sell TV sets under its own brand name in 1953:

> CBS resources and commitments were altogether different from those possessed by Zenith, with the result that the two companies could have been expected to cultivate different market targets. Specifically, in the case of Columbia Broadcasting—
>
> CBS executives were primarily familiar with the management of entertainment talent and the creation and servicing of a network of stations. Although its phonograph record and Hi-Fi phonograph business did involve a type of production and distribution experience, CBS was completely new to major appliance manufacturing and possessed no suitable distribution facilities whatsoever for appliances.
>
> In addition, CBS acquired production facilities when it entered the TV business that were of relatively poor quality. The size, location, equipment, plant layout, and employee facilities of the Air King firm, which CBS acquired, were widely recognized as mediocre or below. Many people familiar with that company and with the TV industry strongly doubted that Air

> King's management was capable of establishing a prestige national brand and producing the high quality product needed to support a quality reputation.
>
> On the other hand, CBS had some genuine pluses in its favor. Its radio and television networks were the largest, and enjoyed great prestige at the time CBS entered the TV set business. Also, by virtue of its telecasting facilities, it could advertise its sets during unsponsored programs at virtually no out-of-pocket cost. It could, moreover, get the advertising support—mainly through testimonials from outstanding personalities like Arthur Godfrey, Edward R. Murrow, Jack Benny, and others—for little or no cost.

To what kinds of customers could a firm with these resources and limitations appeal?

One way that CBS might have adjusted to its particular combination of resources and weaknesses would have been to select as its chief consumer market target the metropolitan customer who is anxious to be associated with prestigeful figures, vulnerable to advertising over radio and TV, prepared to pay a premium price, and relatively unfamiliar with or insensitive to technical performance features. But this market target would hardly have been very large in the first instance; moreover, CBS management must have recognized that many other firms were cultivating this type of customer.

It would appear, then, that CBS was compelled to select its market targets mainly in terms of distributors and retailers, rather than ultimate consumers. Whereas Zenith already possessed a strong distributor and dealer organization, CBS had to construct one. Only after it secured representation on the market could it hope to sell to consumers.

CBS management must have realized that whatever it did in an effort to win distributors and dealers would also influence the kind of customers it could hope to attract. For example, if it had to extend big markups to distributors and retailers to get them to handle its sets (combined with the fact that its production facilities were mediocre), CBS would be compelled to charge a relatively high retail price for its sets. In turn, it would have to rely on intensive advertising to persuade consumers to pay these higher prices and find methods of making its sets appear luxurious and worth the high price.

In addition to having to accept the fact of a relatively high-price product, CBS would feel the pressure to concentrate on customers in the large metropolitan centers, because of the need to build large sales volume rapidly in order to get its production costs in line with those of its competitors. Even as early as 1953, the large metropolitan markets were pervaded by severe price competition among set manufacturers and relatively little emphasis on quality and brand loyalty on the part of retailers. Independent distributors were leaving the business because of great manufacturer pressure to gain heavy sales volume. Hence CBS could not have much hope of obtaining strong independent distributors for its line in most metropolitan markets, but would have to look ahead to a considerable period during which it "supported" both distributors and key retailers to obtain an organization that would distribute its sets.

OTHER CASES

Zenith and CBS have been cited as companies that would have been justified in placing relatively little weight on price in their selection of target submarkets. These companies mainly had to avoid alienating customers by charging prices that were far out of line with other companies' prices. Not all TV set manufacturers could have taken this approach, however. Thus:

> Companies like Admiral, Emerson, and producers of private brands were under pressure to cultivate customers who place heavy emphasis on price. Why? Because in some cases they lacked the personnel and financial resources to sustain a claim of quality and style superiority; or, because their experience in the major appliance business before adding a line of TV receivers could have indicated that they had won acceptance mainly among customers who want moderate quality at prices below the average; or, finally, because their chief asset was a very efficient manufacturing organization that could imitate the products of their more progressive rivals at low cost.

Other industries offer clear examples of firms that selected as market targets persons who were not particularly interested in high intrinsic quality or style. Specifically:

> A fairly obvious example is the Scripto pencil, which offers satisfactory performance at minimum cost. Apparently the customers Scripto selected for intensive cultivation were those who would want a pencil to write with and not for display, a pencil they could afford to lose or misplace.
>
> Some producers of private brands of aspirin likewise have selected as market targets those persons who know of the fundamental similarity of aspirin quality and who actively desire to minimize their outlays for this product.

These examples illustrate a point that may not have been particularly clear in the discussion of the Zenith and CBS examples: *one important criterion in the selection of market targets is customer awareness of and sensitivity to price.*

II. BRAND "IMAGE"

Once management has defined the submarkets it wishes to cultivate most actively, it must select the methods it will use to achieve its goal.

Success in the market place for more and more products seems to depend on creating a favorable general image (often vague and formless) of the product or company among prospective customers. The selection and development of this image become of prime importance and have a direct bearing on price, as will be explained subsequently. A favorable image is especially important when one sells consumers' goods, but only rarely is it completely unimportant even in the sales of producers' goods. Buyers' very perceptions are affected by their prior attitudes, the actions and opinions of others, first impressions and early associations. It is a rare firm that can ignore the total impression its potential customers have of it and of what it is selling.

The firm's selection of its company and brand image should be dictated by the types of customers it is trying to attract. Submarkets may be likened to targets at which the seller is firing, and "images" are powerful weapons that can be used to hit the targets.

Almost every going concern has invested—often very heavily— in the creation of a favorable image. Most businesses know what image they wish to achieve and are concerned lest they or their products fail to have a favorable "meaning" to potential customers. At the very minimum, almost every management knows there are certain images that customers might have of it and its product that would prove disastrous.

The type of image a firm can create of itself and its wares depends to a considerable degree, again, on its fixed commitments and resources. With its physical and personnel resources, there is a limit to what it can do to alter the prevailing opinions—for they reflect all that the company was and did in the past. In that sense, the basic commitments limit the type of image a firm can establish, how much time it will require to establish it, and the cost. Even as brand image is frequently an effective weapon in cultivating particular submarkets, price helps to create the brand image. It is for this reason that the selection of a brand image which is consistent with the firm's market targets implies particular forms of price behavior.

Let us carry our original examples a little further. Given the market targets that they might have selected, as explained earlier, what brand image could Zenith and CBS try to create?

Alternative Qualities

As in the selecting of market targets, every firm has only a few *reasonable* alternatives from which to choose its desired image. For example:

> Zenith already possessed a brand image that contributed strongly to its success in the radio and hearing aid business. Even if another image might have been advantageous for its television business, Zenith's management could hardly afford to injure the bird already in hand. Consequently, Zenith would be obliged to perpetuate for its TV line the brand image it had already established in its other activities. As it happened, that image was altogether suitable for its TV set business.
>
> To implement this line of thinking, Zenith would be obliged to establish the image of a "premium" product and of a company that was old-time, conservative, and mainly concerned with quality and craftsmanship. Above all, it would seek to avoid high-pressure selling, emphasis on price, and shoddiness of product. In styling, it could pursue a safe policy of including a wide variety of styles, while being especially careful not to alienate its conservative small-town customers with models too far in the vanguard of modern design.
>
> CBS faced a very different choice with regard to brand image. It, too, could not afford to jeopardize its eminent position in the radio and TV network field, for those activities were very profitable and would always remain its major sources of income. Except for this limitation, CBS had a relatively free choice of brand images.
>
> CBS could well undertake to be the style leader in the industry. This image would be consistent with relatively inefficient manufacturing facilities, concentration on selling in the metropolitan market, and the necessity of charging a high retail price. It would appear that few brand images other than for advanced styling and for gimmicks would have been consistent with the resources and limitations on CBS at this time.
>
> In contrast to Zenith and CBS, other TV sets producers sought a brand image that did have an important price ingredient.

Again, most producers of private brands, Admiral, Emerson, and others, often featured price in their advertising and apparently sought to sensitize prospective customers to price. They could purposely become identified as firms that were not afraid to discuss price and that seemed confident they offered better values than their competitors.

Many firms outside the TV set industry attempt to establish a brand image that has a heavy price ingredient. Among producers, one finds Caron boasting that its Joy perfume is the most expensive, and Chock-Full-of-Nuts implying much the same thing about its coffee. Without being explicit, some retailers seem to claim that no stores charge more than they—and, strangely, this image is a source of strength. The retail world is full of stores that claim that they are never knowingly undersold; on the other hand, it is difficult to name manufacturers who claim that their product is the cheapest on the market—probably because of the implication that theirs is also the brand of lowest quality. (Automobile manufacturers occasionally claim to be the "cheapest of the low-price three," but none has occupied that position long.)

III. MARKETING MIX

The third stage in multi-stage pricing calls for the selection of a combination of sales promotion devices that will create and re-enforce the desired company and product brand image and achieve maximum sales for the planned level of dollar outlays. In this stage, a role must be assigned to price. The role in which price is cast should be selected only after assessment is made as to the relative effectiveness and appropriateness of each sales promotion device that might be employed. The short-term gains of certain sales promotion devices may entail injury to the image objectives of the firm. Conflicts of such a nature must be resolved at this stage.

Then, too, a firm might achieve precisely the *desired* image and still find customers very hard to get. It is not enough to establish the desired image; it must be an *effective* image. Furthermore, even though a firm may establish highly favorable impressions of itself and its wares, the company and its products must live up to the image they foster. Not only must its product be "within reach" in price, but it must be accessible by being offered through convenient channels of distribution, and must be sold in outlets where customers like to buy.

The third stage builds directly upon the second. The need to conform to the prior decision about company and brand image greatly limits the number of price alternatives that a price setter can reasonably consider.

The marketing mix decision at this stage need not be translated into specific dollars and cents amounts to be devoted to each sales promotion device; however, it does at least call for crude answers to the following questions:

How heavily to advertise?
How much for salesmen?
How much for product improvement?
How much of an assortment to carry?
How large an inventory to hold?
How best to provide speedy delivery?
How much emphasis on price appeal?

The composition of a marketing mix (arrived at by answering the type of questions just listed) is admittedly very difficult and highly subjective. But the job is facilitated greatly when answers are subjected to the test of conforming to the desired company and brand image and to the firm's fixed commitments.

Few firms can afford to switch "images," usually because they have invested heavily in them in prior years and should, therefore, not abandon them lightly. Moreover, past images persist and blur any future attempts at image building. Although it cannot easily scrap its brand image, a firm can vary its marketing mix within moderate limits and remain consistent with the image it seeks to create. Thus, the selection of an image sets limits and gives direction to the decision about the elements to be included in marketing mix. In that way, it facilitates the decision and also increases the likelihood that it will be correct. However, it does not isolate a single marketing mix as the only correct one.

Marketing the Image

How might have Zenith, CBS, and other TV set manufacturers composed a marketing mix, if they had reasoned about market targets and brand image along the lines of the foregoing discussion? Let us see:

> In Zenith's case, price clearly would have had to be subordinated as a sales appeal. The company could have placed major emphasis on quality of product, subdued advertising, and reliable service, while placing its product with retailers who would en-

hance the reputation of the brand. By these measures, Zenith could have re-enforced the image of a high quality and reliable producer.

In the case of CBS, the role of price in the marketing mix would not have been subject to much control. As explained, it might have been forced to charge a high price; if so, most of its other actions would have been dictated by that fact. It could have relied very heavily on radio and TV advertising to generate consumer preference, and justified its high price by adding externals to the set—particularly attractive styling, an expensive furniture appearance, or special features of some sort. It could not have reasonably hoped to get very much support from retailers who commanded strong loyalty among their patrons.

Other TV set producers adopted quite different market mixes from those that Zenith and CBS would have selected if they had reasoned along these lines. Some, however, apparently had no conscious marketing mix philosophy and, therefore, seemed to improvise and stumble from one crisis to another. Nevertheless, in their bids for patronage, some TV set producers apparently placed relatively heavy reliance on advertising including mainly RCA, General Electric, Westinghouse, and Sylvania). Others made strong quality claims (like Dumont and Andrea). Still others placed chief emphasis on styling (Magnavox).

IV. DETERMINING POLICY

The fourth stage in multi-stage pricing calls for the selection of a pricing policy. But before a pricing policy can be determined, answers to the following questions must be obtained:

How should our price compare with "average" prices in the industry? Specifically, should we be 2% above or 4% below the average? And, when we speak of the average, which firms' prices are we going to include in the computation?

How fast will we meet price reductions or increases by rivals?

How frequently will it be advisable to vary price? To what extent is stability of price advantageous?

Should the firm make use of "fair trade" price maintenance?

How frequently should the firm run price promotions?

These are simply illustrative of the aspects of a pricing policy which management can and should spell out in proper sequence. By virtue of having made the evaluations and decisions called for in the first three stages, management will find itself limited in the number of choices on these points.

In addition, each company must take account of the valuations placed on its product-service "package" as well as the valuations of rival products by the market segments it is most anxious to cultivate. On the basis of such considerations, plus its target market segments and marketing mix, it will decide whether it can afford to charge much more or less than its rivals.

"Bracketing" the Price

Before proceeding further, let us summarize. Surely, a price setter would be some distance from a specific price decision even after completing the fourth step. We must ask ourselves whether he would not also have covered considerable distance toward a price decision. By taking account of the firm's basic commitments and resources, the images it desires to establish, its decision about marketing mix, and the selection of a detailed pricing policy, has not the price setter reached the point where he is very strongly circumscribed in the price decision he will ultimately make? To illustrate Step Four, let us carry our two main examples—Zenith and CBS—about as far as they can be taken and see what pricing policy these companies might have adopted:

> If the Zenith management had selected the market targets set forth here and made the same decisions regarding brand image and marketing mix, it would have had little trouble in selecting a pricing policy. It would have felt obliged to charge a price somewhat above the average in the market and to minimize emphasis on price in its advertising. Moreover, it could have varied price relatively infrequently to the consumer—except possibly in some of the large metropolitan markets where neither consumers nor retailers are loyal to anything or anyone, except their own pecuniary interests.
>
> In Zenith's pricing policy, the preservation of distributor and retailer loyalty would have figured very prominently in its thinking. It would be compelled to sacrifice long-term price advantages in order to protect its distributors and retailers from financial loss due to price change.
>
> CBS, on the other hand, need not have concerned itself much with dealer and retailer loyalty. It had none and must have realized that it would not have been able to create a loyal distribution structure unless it were willing to make very large financial outlays. If it had reconciled itself to a not-too-loyal distrib-

utor and dealer organization, CBS could have conducted sales promotions and varied price frequently and by large amounts. It could have emphasized price in these promotions, but presumably only when combined with strong emphasis on alleged high quality and superior styling. CBS need not have felt obliged to match the prices charged by its competitors, but it could not have afforded to have its retailers' margins be out of line on the low side.

Since it commanded no loyalty from its retailers, CBS was, in fact, compelled to buy their sales support. This it could do, primarily by offering a higher than average margin. (CBS could also have attempted to solve its distribution problem by granting exclusive privileges to a small number of retail outlets. In the case of the TV industry, such a policy has been used successfully by Magnavox. However, this company had already sewed up the strong quality retailers who were capable of producing large volume. As a result, CBS was shut out of this pattern of distribution.)

Although Zenith and CBS apparently would have been obliged to charge more than the average by the foregoing line of thinking, other TV producers were wise to take a very different tack, mainly because of their different resources and commitments. For example, Admiral and Emerson have tended to charge somewhat less than average, while General Electric has not adopted a very consistent price position.

V. PRICING STRATEGY

It is difficult to draw a sharp line between policy and strategy, but it is possible and useful to make some sort of distinction between them. Policy is formulated to deal with anticipated and foreseeable situations of a recurrent type. However, markets frequently are beset and dominated by *special* situations that basic policy was not designed to meet. For example:

A Congressional committee might threaten to investigate the company's or the industry's pricing arrangements.

A sizable firm may have fallen into a desperate financial situation so that it was forced to raise cash through a liquidation of its inventories.

A large new firm may have entered the market.

Business may have fallen off precipitately for the entire industry or economy.

The company may have introduced a model that is either a "dud" or a "sure winner."

Special situations like these ordinarily require an adjustment in price—and the formulation of a strategy to guide management in setting price *during the time that the special* situation endures.

There generally are several strategies which would be compatible with the firm's basic commitments and resources, its market targets, its image objectives, its convictions about the relative emphasis to attach to various elements in the marketing mix, and its specific pricing policies. Others would be incompatible with earlier decisions and therefore might endanger precious values. A threat to one's very survival might justify a scrapping of these, but impetuousness, short-sightedness or avarice would not. Explicit recognition of these earlier stages of the pricing decision should prevent hasty short-run actions that are painful, but quite common.

No effort will be made to discuss the Zenith and CBS examples in connection with the formulation of a pricing strategy. They have already been stretched far enough to illustrate the application of the multi-stage approach to pricing—especially in the most difficult stages. The reader, might, however, speculate about how, within the framework of the approach outlined here, both Zenith and CBS management could have responded to a great pricing crisis in the TV set industry. This occurred in the fall of 1953 when Westinghouse suddenly reduced its TV sets by approximately 20% during the very heart of the selling season. We may speculate that adherence to decisions regarding market targets, brand image, marketing mix, and price policy would have prevented both Zenith and CBS from reducing their prices to the levels set by Westinghouse Electric Corporation.

VI. SPECIFIC PRICE

Here is the final step—the selection of a specific price. At this point, the price setter will usually find himself sharply circumscribed in the specific sums he can charge. Nevertheless, he usually will have some range of price possibilities that are consistent with the decisions made in the preceding five stages of the price decision. How may he best select among the alternatives?

To the extent that he is able, he should be guided by the arithmetic of pricing—that is, by a comparison of the costs and revenues of the alternative prices within the zone delimited by the prior stages of his pricing decision. Once he has taken into account his market targets, brand image, marketing mix, pricing policy, and strategy, he can afford to ignore everything but the calculations of costs and revenues. *The first five stages of decision are designed to take account of the business considerations which may be ignored if one selects price solely on the basis of prevailing cost and revenue conditions.*

It often is impossible to obtain reliable information about sales at different prices; this difficulty is present whatever method of pricing one employs. But the multi-stage policy approach facilitates research and experimentation into demand conditions by limiting the number of alternatives to be considered.

The price that would be established under this multi-stage policy approach would rarely be the same as that set by balancing marginal cost and marginal revenue. The former probably would exclude, as incompatible with the firm's basic commitments and resources, desired brand image, and so on, the prices that would be most profitable in the very short term.

THE ADVANTAGES

First, this approach breaks up the pricing decision into six relatively manageable pieces. In that way, it introduces order into the weighing of the many considerations bearing on price. This approach, therefore, should increase the likelihood that all major factors will be taken into account and that their large number will not overwhelm the price setter.

Second, this method of pricing reduces the risk that the price setter will destroy the firm's valuable investments in corporate and brand images. Also, it requires the price setter to determine and take into account the limitation on the firm's freedom of decision. In that way, it would discourage the pricing executive from undertaking what he is powerless to accomplish. Similarly, the multi-stage policy approach should militate against a short-run policy of opportunism that would sacrifice long-term values.

Third, the multi-stage policy approach to pricing should be valuable to those executives who are compelled to delegate pricing responsibilities. In the first place, high-level executives are virtually required by the method to make the decisions for several stages, which thus limits their dependence on their subordinates. In the second place, as explained, it simplifies the making of a price decision so that greater success can be expected. Then, too, its use should make it easier for subordinates to raise questions and obtain advice from their superiors, should they be unable to reach a decision.

Fourth, this approach to pricing puts considerable emphasis on the intangibles that are involved in pricing—particularly on the total impression that customers have of the vendor and of the things he sells. Price is far more than a rationing device that determines which potential customers will be able to afford to make a purchase. Generally it is one of the most important actions in creating an impression of the firm among potential customers. Especially as tangible differences among rival products shrink, these intangibles will grow in significance for marketing success.

THE LIMITATIONS

This approach does not indicate all the considerations that should be taken into account at each stage in the pricing decision. In other words, the price setter is compelled to isolate the significant factors operating at each stage and weigh them for himself.

Second, this approach does not indicate what price to charge in any specific situation. The most that can be claimed for it is that it narrows down the zone of possible prices to the point where it may not matter a great deal which particular price is selected. As stated at the outset, one must beware of any pricing method that does lead to a single price, for such a method could not possibly take into account all of the special circumstances which are relevant to a price decision and which vary so greatly from market to market and from time to time.

Third, this method does not guide price setters in recognizing the factors that dominate the market at any time and in knowing when to switch basic strategies. Also, there may well be more than one dominant condition which must be considered in selecting a basic strategy.

On balance, then, the multi-stage approach to pricing at best only takes an executive fairly close to this ultimate destination. Although the multi-stage policy approach does not do the whole job of pricing, the part of the job that is left is relatively easy to finish in many cases. Where this is not so, one can only assume that the task would be almost hopeless without the assistance of a method that reduces the pricing decision to a series of relatively manageable steps in a prescribed sequence.

CONCLUSION

The multi-stage policy approach outlined here differs from usual approaches to pricing in two major respects. First, it demands a long-range view of price by emphasizing the enduring effects of most price actions on company and brand image. One might say this approach constructs a policy framework for the price decision. And, second, it allows the price decision to be made in stages, rather than requiring a simultaneous solution of the entire price problem.

31. THE LOGISTICS OF DISTRIBUTION*

John F. Magee

American business is awakening to a new, exciting opportunity to improve service and reduce costs—better management of the flow of goods from plant to user. Capitalizing on this opportunity means:

> Thinking of the physical distribution process as a *system* in which, just as in a good hi-fi system, all the components and functions must be properly balanced.
>
> Taking a fresh look at the responsibilities, capabilities, and organizational positions of executives in traffic, warehouse management, inventory control, and other functions which make up the over-all system.
>
> Re-examining the company's physical plant and distribution procedures in the light of technical advances in such areas as transportation, data processing, and materials handling.

In this article I shall first examine the pressing need for improved management of companies' distribution systems. Then I shall outline some of the most promising ways by which progress in "industrial logistics" can be achieved, with special attention to the implications of technological advances for policy, the problems of getting started with a new look at a company's system, and the steps that should be taken in making a good distribution study.

STUBBORN PRESSURES

The need for progress in distribution is a product of not one but several trends—trends in costs, in product-line policy, and in the

*Reprinted from *Harvard Business Review*, Vol. 38 (July-August, 1960), pp. 89–101,

market place. More often than not, the challenge posed is to the system as a whole, not just to the particular part or function where trouble is most obvious.

Rising Costs

For years, businessmen and economists have looked with mixed feelings on the increase in distribution costs in our economy. Over the past half century, tremendous strides have been made in reducing the costs of production, but these feats have not been duplicated in other areas. If the over-all efficiency of companies is to continue to improve, management must turn its attention increasingly to holding distribution costs in line. Physical distribution costs in particular, estimated by some to represent the third largest component in the total cost of business operation, are a logical center for management attention.

The problems of cutting these costs pose certain new and interesting questions for business. Whereas in many production operations it has been possible in the past to substitute a machine for human labor and to cut the cost of one operation without seriously disturbing the rest of the production system, this is hardly the case in efforts to cut physical distribution costs. Indiscriminate cost reduction in any one of the individual cost elements, such as inventory maintenance, warehousing, transportation, or clerical activities, can have a disastrous effect on the efficiency of the system as a whole. To illustrate this point:

> Suppose we cut inventories. Certainly a reduction in inventories will save capital investment and the costs of supplying capital, and it may save some expenses in storage, taxes, and insurance. On the other hand, an indiscriminate reduction in inventory levels may seriously impair the reliability of delivery service to customers and the availability of products in the field. An inventory reduction which saves money but destroys competitive position is hardly a contribution to a more effective distribution system.
>
> We can cut transportation costs, perhaps, by changing to methods showing lower cost per ton-mile, or by shipping in larger quantities and taking advantage of volume carload or truckload rates. But if lower transportation costs are achieved at the expense of slower or less frequent movement of goods, we face the risk of: (a) cutting the flexibility and responsiveness of the distribution system to changes in customer requirements; (b) requiring greater field inventories to maintain service; (c) creating greater investment requirements and obsolescence risks.

Similarly, blanket refusal to allow cost increases in any one part can wipe out opportunities to make the system as a whole more efficient. For instance:

> New methods of high-speed data communications and processing may in fact increase the clerical costs of operating the distribution system. On the other hand, they may cut down delays in feeding information back to govern production operations and to control lags in getting material moving into the distribution system in response to customer demand. Thus, they may actually cut *total* distribution system costs because of their impact on improved production and inventory control.

It takes a careful analysis of the total physical distribution system to know whether net costs will be increased or decreased by efforts to cut the cost of any one component.

Proliferating Product Lines

Physical distribution systems in recent years have been put under tremendous pressure induced by changes in product-line characteristics. Until recently, for example, products like typewriters, light bulbs, appliances, and plumbing fixtures were largely utilitarian, with differences in product characteristics rather closely related to function. A typewriter manufacturer did not have to worry about matching typewriter color to office décor or type style to company "image." Light bulbs used to be white and sometimes clear, and they varied by wattage. Now, however, typewriters come in pastels and two-tones. Light bulbs are sold not only to provide light but atmosphere, with a corresponding increase in the number of products that have to be shipped, stocked, and controlled. Appliances and plumbing fixtures are available to customers not only in the classical antiseptic white, but in a wide range of color and style combinations. In short, style and individuality have become strong competitive weapons.

In an almost unending list of products in the consumer field, variations in color, packaging, and other features have imposed heavy burdens on the distribution system. In the marketing of industrial goods, variations in grade, color, and size have had a similar impact. In paper manufacture, for example, the wide variety of package sizes required for consumer products has led carton manufacturers to demand correspondingly wide ranges of kraft board roll widths from paper manufacturers, and these demands have created difficult problems of scheduling, inventory control, and distribution.

The growth and change in product-line characteristics in both consumer and industrial products have meant that manufacturing plants have had more items to make, and the distribution system has had more items to handle and stock. More items mean lower volume per item and correspondingly higher unit handling inventory and storage costs. Take, for example, just the impact on inventory requirements of substituting three items for one:

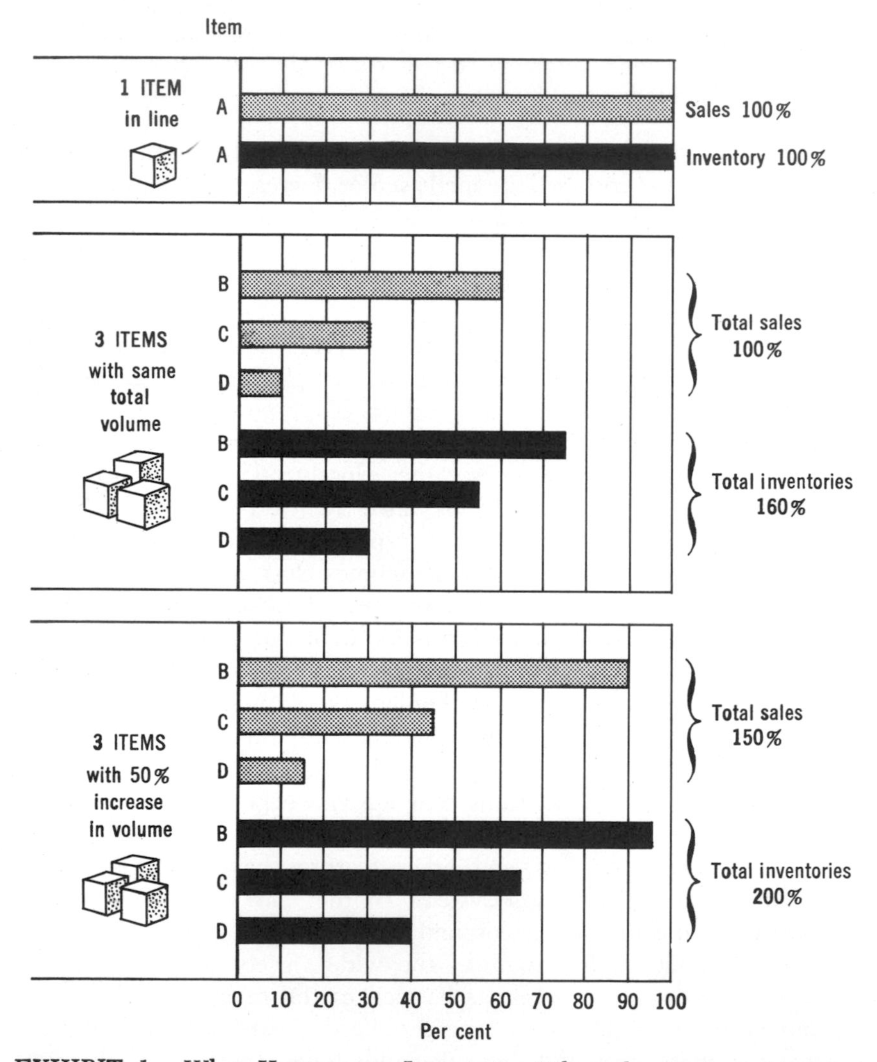

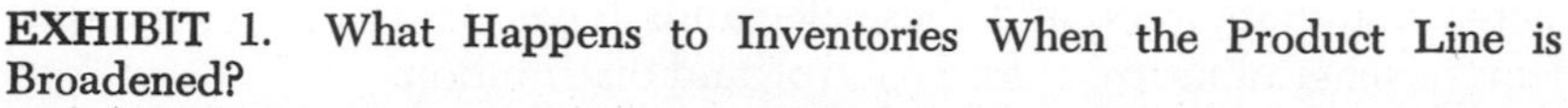
EXHIBIT 1. What Happens to Inventories When the Product Line is Broadened?

Suppose we have substituted items B, C, and D for an old item A. If sales among these items are broken down 60% to B, 30% to C, and 10% to D, with no over-all increase in sales compared to the volume on the old item A, then Exhibit I shows what is likely to happen to field inventory requirements—an increase of more than 60%. (This figure is based on characteristic relationships between inventory and sales in companies with which I am familiar. In general, the larger the sales, the lower inventory can be relative to sales. Thus, product D with 10% of sales needs a much higher proportion of inventory than product B, with 60% of the sales.)

At a carrying cost of 20% a year, this increase represents a handsome expense for maintaining competitive position.

Let us be optimistic, however, and assume that items B, C, and D do more than yield the same total volume; let us assume that total volume increases by 50%. Even so, the inventory requirements would double, and inventory cost per unit sold would increase over 30%—a substantial source of pressure on the distribution system.

These figures illustrate the impact of small-volume items on the cost of operating the distribution system. Yet diversity of product sales is characteristic in American businesses, whether selling in consumer or industrial markets. Exhibit II shows the typical relationship between the number of items sold and the proportion of sales they account for. The figures are based on the records of a large number of firms in the consumer and industrial products fields. The exhibit reveals that while 10–20% of total items sold characteristically yield 80% of the sales, half of the items, in the line account for less than 4% of the sales. It is the bottom half of the product line that imposes a great deal of the difficulty, expense, and investment on the distribution system.

Alternative Courses

Increased cost, selling, and product-line pressures suggest that management should take a hard look at alternative distribution patterns, as a means of cutting logistics costs without a major sacrifice in service. Here are a few of the possibilities:

The company can carry central stocks of low-selling items only. To get the right balance of transportation costs, handling costs, and service, it may be necessary to stock these items at one central point and ship them against individual customer orders as the latter arise, perhaps by expedited service or air freight.

For many items in the line, a good compromise may be to carry some low- or middle-volume items in only a few large regional warehouses, as a compromise between the excessive storage costs incurred from broad-scale stocking and the transportation and service penalties incurred by attempting to meet demand from manufacturing points alone.

Warehouse points can be consolidated. With improvements in transportation and in mechanical material- and data-handling methods, large opportunities exist in many businesses for cutting down on the number of field warehouse points. With increased volume through the individual warehouses, carrying a broader product line at the local points begins to make greater economic sense.

Sales-Generating Capacity

The first and most basic job of the distribution system is to get customers, to turn interest and orders into sales. As business has grown more competitive and the public has become harder to please, management has focused increasing attention on the *quality* of its logistical operations. What can be done to make products more readily available for purchase in local markets? What improvements can be made in

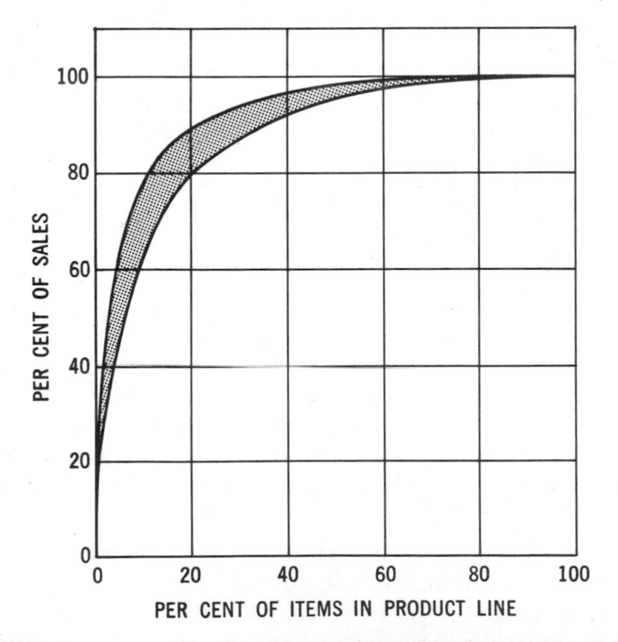

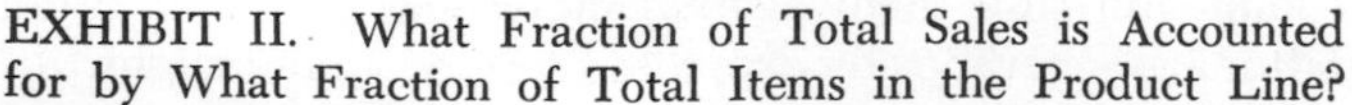
EXHIBIT II. What Fraction of Total Sales is Accounted for by What Fraction of Total Items in the Product Line?

backing up product merchandising and advertising programs with adequate deliveries and service? Obviously, questions like these are affected by cost considerations, but as marketing objectives they deserve individual attention.

In analyzing the capacity of a distribution system to produce sales, executives will do well to examine three key characteristics:

1. *Location*—It has been estimated, for example, that from 5 distribution points a company can reach 33% of the U.S. consumer market within a day; while from 25 warehouse locations, 80% can be reached in one day.
2. *Inventories*—Judging from my own and associates' experience, approximately 80% more inventory is needed in a typical business to fill 95% of the customers' orders out of stock than to fill only 80%.
3. *Responsiveness*—The ability of a system to transmit needs back to the supplying plant and get material needed into the field determines how quickly the business can shift with changes in customer preferences to meet demand with minimum investment and cost.

REVOLUTION IN TECHNOLOGY

The pressures on distribution methods have led to exciting new technological advances for getting goods to the user at lower cost to the company—with less labor and materials expended and less capital tied up in inventories and facilities. When these advances are introduced in proper balance, the distribution process can better meet the needs of the consumer. Major technological changes are now taking place in transportation, information handling, and material handling. Let us examine each of them in turn.

Costs vs. Transport Time

Transportation thinking has been dominated too long by preoccupation with the direct traffic bill. Too much attention has been paid to transport cost per ton-mile and not enough to the contribution transportation makes to the effectiveness of the distribution system as a whole.

Railroad rate structures are to an outsider an eye-opening illustration of what can happen when a transportation system is put under the cost-per-ton-mile pressure for too long. Rail rate structures, despite frequent attempts to introduce some rationale, have degenerated into an unbelievable hodgepodge of unrealistic and uneconomic rate compromises as the roads have succumbed to the pressure of giving each shipper the lowest cost per ton-mile, often at the expense of service. While improvements in equipment, such as the introduction of the diesel locomotive, have led to greater efficiency on the track, in some cases at least the longer trains and increased classification problems that have resulted have meant little or no net increase in over-all distribution efficiency. The gap between traffic and marketing thinking is painfully evident in many companies' distribution methods; little has been done to relate transportation methods and service to the objectives of the distribution system in support of marketing efforts.

Transportation costs are important indeed, but they are only part of the story. For example, think of the value of materials in transit:

> Data collected on sample shipments in various parts of the country indicate that material may spend one to two weeks in transit and that the capital value of assets tied up in the transportation system may, depending on the pressure for capital, add as much as 1% to the economic cost of the goods.
>
> Service, or reliability of the transport system, is also important. Goods must get to the user promptly and reliably, to permit him to operate systematically with low inventories.
>
> The direct and indirect costs of damage in transport are another large item in the traffic bill that at times gets overlooked in the pressure for low cost per ton-mile.

Clearly, transport time is one of the key determinants of the efficiency of the distribution system. Its impact is not vivid or dramatic, and executives do not always appreciate what a difference it makes, but in a great many companies it is a significant factor in financing. To take a simple illustration:

> Suppose that in a company doing an annual business of $100 million, time in transit is reduced from 14 days to 2. Time between reorders is 14 days, communication and processing time is 4 days, and field stocks average $12.5 million. In such a situation the reduction in transit time might well lead to a reduction in distribution inventory investment of $6 million, made up of: (1) a reduction of $3.3 million in transit, i.e., 12 days' sales; (2) a reduction of $2.7 million in inventories required to protect customer service resulting from a faster, more flexible distribution system response.

Speeding up Service

Changes in transportation leading to improved opportunities in distribution have been truly revolutionary since World War II. Major superhighway systems have been built, truck speeds have increased substantially and so have trailer capacities. The growth in the use of trucking for industrial distribution is now well known. The stimulus from subsidies is only part of the story; trucks have been able to compete at characteristically higher ton-mile costs because they have offered speed, reliability, and flexibility to shippers.

Without a doubt railroads are responding to this challenge. A recent survey showed that almost all Class I railroads are offering some form of piggyback or expedited motor-carrier service. At least some railroads are showing new merchandising awareness in concentrating on customer service. Whether the industry will be able, in the face of inherent limitations, to reverse the decline in its share of manufacturers' freight business is still an open question.

Air freight represents a challenge to both rail and over-the-road haulers. Today most industry executives still tend to view air freight as a luxury, as a service available for "orchids and emergencies." However the trend in air freight rates has been sharply downward in recent years. With new planes coming into service, even further reductions can be projected—down to 8 cents to 12 cents a ton-mile from present day rates of approximately 22 cents. Much depends on the success of efforts to develop aircraft equipped for freight handling and for flexible operation under a wide range of conditions (for example, modest runway lengths), and to build up the ground service needed to match air-handling speeds so as to avoid the danger faced by the railroads—the collapse of service as a result of concentration on mass, low-cost, terminal-to-terminal movement.

Impact of New Methods

What is the significance of the ferment in transportation methods? For one thing, improvement in local truck service opens up opportunities to serve wide-flung markets through fewer and larger distribution points. With larger distribution centers, the chance that mechanized material handling and storage systems will pay off is enhanced, and inventory requirements are reduced through consolidation.

To suggest the size of the opportunity, one analysis with which I am familiar showed that cutting the number of field distribution points for a national product line from 50 to 25 would increase total transport costs 7% but cut inventories 20% and cut *total* physical distribution costs 8% (the latter representing roughly a 1% cut in the total cost of delivered product). This was accomplished at the cost of serving a few small markets—about 5% of the total—with second-day instead of first-day delivery.

Rapid truck or air service increases the feasibility of relying on shipments from a few central points to back up service. Here are two ways in which this can be employed:

(1) The many low-volume items in the typical product line, the items on which local storage and handling costs outweigh the penalty costs of expedited shipment, can be held centrally and moved to the market where they are needed, as needed. For example, the bottom 50% of the product line, which as Exhibit II shows often accounts for only 4% of sales, may require 25% or more of the warehousing costs and inventory capital charges. Turnover of the stocks of these items is often only one eighth that of the high-volume half of the line. In a *relatively* high number of cases, special shipments could be made at a cost well below that of storing the items at local distribution centers.

(2) If there are substantial reserve stocks designed to protect customer service located in the field, it is possible to pare them down in the knowledge that additional supplies can be moved in promptly to meet sudden customer demands.

In a typical distribution system a large share of the inventory—as much as 90%—is carried to protect delivery service to customers in the face of fluctuating demand and system delays. This safety stock is most likely to be used at the end of the reorder cycle, when stocks hit their low point before new receipts. Exhibit III illustrates a common situation, with safety stocks being partly depleted at intervals just before a new shipment arrives. During the period of the first reorder, demand has been heavy. In many reorder cycles, however, stocks will not be touched at all; this is the case before the second reorder in the illustration (middle of the chart) comes in. Note that inventory in transit represents a fairly significant proportion of the whole.

How much of safety stocks is actually used depends on the reorder system and level of service maintained. Typically, the last 10% may be needed only once or twice a year—a turnover rate roughly one sixth the average; and the last 30% may be needed only two to four times a year. Warehouses and inventory carrying charges on this portion of

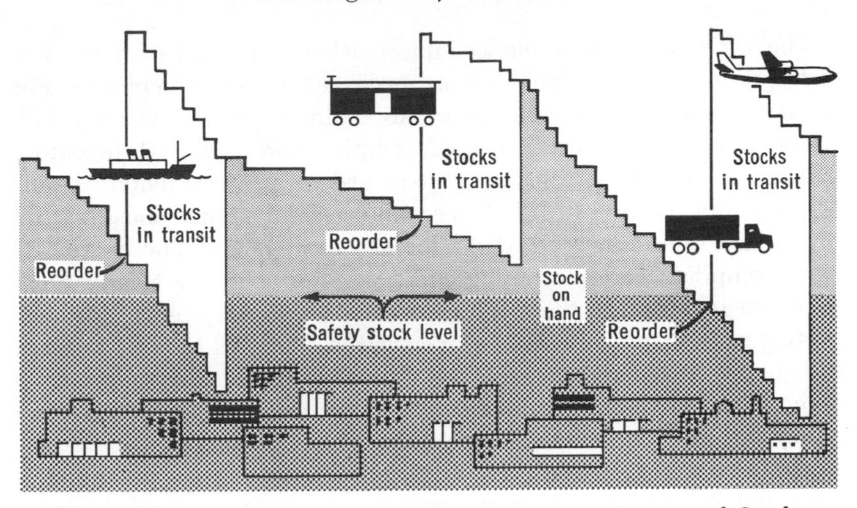

EXHIBIT III. What is the Characteristic Inventory Pattern of Stocks on Hand in the Typical Company?

inventory, then, may easily run to 10%–20% of the sales they make possible.

There is an opportunity in many companies for management to cut material held in the field and back up customer service through regularized high-speed delivery service. This possibility will deserve increasing attention from management as the costs of high-speed transport, communication, and data processing drop.

Information Processing

Revolutionary data-processing methods were noisily battering at established business methods some six or seven years ago, but the impact was more in noise generated than in accomplishment. Now that a lot of the superficial excitement has died away, however, a broad and solid structure of accomplishment in modern data-processing techniques is quietly being built.

For one thing, computers seem to have become much more broadly accepted than anticipated. When the earliest internally programmed machines were announced, computer manufacturers' optimistic estimates were in the dozens. Today the number of machines installed or in the process of installation is in the thousands. In support of computing or processing facilities, great improvements are taking place in communications systems, especially systems designed to feed into or out of computers. In distribution management, fast, reliable communication is equally as important as fast, reliable processing.

The *use* being made of modern information-processing equipment in distribution is just as significant as its broad market acceptance. For instance, machines are being used to maintain local inventory balances, forecast near-term demand, employ forecasts and inventory balances as inputs in calculating item orders, prepare tentative purchase orders, allocate item balances among stock points, and draw up production schedules and work force requirements. These are not mere compiling and accounting functions, nor it is fair to call them "decision making." In these functions, the machine systems are interpreting rules or procedures to work out the decisions implicit in them in light of the facts of the situation. In other words, the equipment is doing what we would like intelligent clerks to do: diligently following policy and weighing costs to arrive at day-to-day actions.

The forecasting function in particular deserves special attention. I refer not to the longer term economic forecasts, annual business forecasts, or even shorter term (e.g., quarterly) business predictions, but to short-term forecasts of sales, item by item, over the replenishment lead time. These forecasts are made implicitly or explicitly in every inventory control system. In most companies they are left up to the individual stock clerk or inventory controller to make as best he can, usually with little or no training or guides. Management will spend hundreds of hours of industrial engineering time simplifying or improving a job method here and there to take a few pennies out of labor cost. Yet the stock clerk making inventory control forecasts may, through his control over product distribution and assets tied up in inventories, be costing his company many pennies indeed.

Many people still argue that one cannot forecast routinely because intuition and background knowledge count too heavily. They fail to recognize that objective procedures for short-term prediction of item sales have the same merits as, say, routing and tooling lists in a shop. Experience leaves little doubt that great gains can be made by substituting powerful systematic methods for casual or unrecognized ones.[1]

Changes in Material Handling

Mechanization is slowly spreading from the making of things to their handling in distribution. For instance:

One company in the clothing industry has installed a new data-processing system first to handle sales orders and then inventory

[1]See Robert G. Brown, "Less Risk in Inventory Estimates," HBR July–August 1959, p. 104.

control and production-scheduling systems. At the same time, it has been developing a bin-and-conveyer system which will permit economical mechanization of order-filling activities. The goal toward which both of these efforts are directed is a unified system in which the customer order not only serves as an input in automatic order handling but will also, after suitable internal mechanical processing, activate the warehouse system to select and consolidate the customer's order. This customer order data will also be processed internally for inventory management and production planning purposes.

How will such changes in warehousing and materials handling influence the planning of distribution systems? The effects will take least three forms:

1. *Integration of systems for (a) material storage and transport and (b) information handling*—This development should create opportunities for significant "automation" of the distribution function and for reduction of manual drudgery. Ultimate full-scale mechanization of materials handling will not only require redesign of warehouse and transport facilities, but will have an impact on design of products and packages as well.
2. *Pressure to reduce the number of distribution points or warehouses*—Mechanized warehouses cost money. One way to improve the efficiency of capital utilization is of course to increase throughput.
3. *Pressure to concentrate ownership of warehousing facilities*—Mechanization takes capital. This factor will be another force behind the tendency for manufacture, distribution, and maintenance service to become integrated under one ownership roof.

GETTING STARTED

Some managers view the opportunities presented by changes in distribution technology with about the same air with which a bear views a porcupine: the possibilities look interesting, but where can you start to get your teeth in?

Improvements in distribution efficiency cost money. Higher speed, more flexible transport generally costs more per ton-mile. Mechanized warehousing systems or material-handling systems are not cheap. The cost of working out, installing, and testing new information-processing systems may make direct clerical cost savings look like a rather thin return on investment. In fact, direct payoffs from distribution changes (e.g., modified transport methods leading to a direct cut in transport costs) may often be small or nonexistent. The payoffs, often handsome ones, are likely to be indirect, coming about from "tradeoffs" such as paying a higher transport bill to save material investment, putting in warehouse investment to cut over-all shipping costs, and so on.

Because tradeoffs so often are involved, it is not always easy for management to get an aggressive, functionally operated group of people to think *through* the problems. It is not easy for men in production, sales, warehousing, traffic, merchandising, and accounting to grasp other functions' needs or express their own needs in terms which make the advantages of tradeoff and balance clear. Many times the distribution *system* has been run too long as a collection of more or less independent *functions*. Any changes, any tradeoffs to get the system into better, more economical balance, any modifications to take advantage in the whole system of new technical developments—these are bound to be disruptive and to some extent resisted.

The difficulties in facing up to a searching look at the distribution system are not confined to the individual functions concerned. Some of the toughest questions arise at the general management level. For example:

What degree of sales service is the system to provide? How far will the firm go to meet customers' service desires?

What standards are to be used to judge investment in facilities and inventory so that it can be weighed against any cost savings that are made possible?

What policy will the company take toward ownership and operation of the distribution, transport, warehousing, and information-processing facilities? Will the company operate its own facilities, lease them, contract for services, or rely on independent businesses to perform some or all of the necessary distribution system functions?

What is the company's policy toward employment stabilization? To what extent is the company prepared to pay higher distribution costs to absorb demand variations and to level employment?

Approach to the Issues

Grappling with all of these problems is like untangling a tangled skein of yarn. Each decision has an impact on other choices and for this reason is hard to pin down. The distribution problem is a system problem, and it must be looked at as such. If it is examined in total and if the experience and methods available for studying it are used, the issues just mentioned can be resolved in an orderly, mutually compatible way.

In my experience, three key conditions have, when present, made for a sound distribution system study and an effective implementation program.

(1) Recognition by company management that improving distribution means examining the full physical distribution system.
(2) Use of quantitative systems analysis or operations research methods to show clearly the nature of tradeoffs and the relation between system operation and company policies.
(3) Cooperative work by men knowledgeable in sales and marketing, transportation, materials handling, materials control, and information handling.

In the following sections we shall see the need for these conditions asserting itself again and again as we go through the steps of making a good distribution study.

MAKING THE STUDY

How should a distribution system study be made? What principal steps should be taken? As far as I know, there is no formula for the approach. The relative emphasis put on different phases of the study can vary, as can also the degree of detail; the order of analysis can be changed; and so on. But there are important steps to take at some point in any study, and I shall discuss them in logical order.

1. Data on the company's markets should be organized in a helpful way The distribution system study starts with a study of customers. This does not need to be a field interview program; to a large extent what is required is the organization of market facts which are available. Occasionally, a moderate amount of skilled field interview work may be desirable to obtain customers' estimates of service requirements and their comparison of the company with its competition.

A great deal of useful information can be obtained by analysis of sales data. Here are some of the key questions of interest:

> Are we servicing several fundamentally different markets through different distribution channels? Are these markets located differently? Do they buy in different patterns, in different

quantities, and with different service and stock availability requirements?

How are our sales distributed among customers? We have found that the top 10% of a company's customers characteristically account for from 60% to 80% or even more of its business.

Do the same customers tend to buy our high-volume items as well as slow-moving items? The answer to this question has an important bearing on how the slow-moving items, for which distribution and sales service costs are often relatively high, should be handled. Few companies seem to have really examined this problem, though strong opinions on it exist in most.

2. *Statistical analyses of product characteristics should be made, with special attention to the nature of sales fluctuations* Sometimes the facts about products can be established fairly readily. An example is the susceptibility of items in the line to spoilage or damage. The degree to which sales volume is concentrated among a few fast moving items (as illustrated in EXHIBIT II) can often be ascertained rather quickly, too. But data of this kind do not tell us nearly enough.

Statistical analysis is needed to establish certain key sales characteristics of the product line, all related to the *variability* of item sales. The significance of variability must be emphasized. Business managers are used to thinking in terms of averages or average rates, but the answers to many important questions affecting distribution system design depend on the characteristics of short-term sales variations about the average.

Most items exhibit unexpected day-to-day variations in sales about the average or expected level. In some cases the fluctuations are extremely wide and short-term in character; in other cases they are quite steady and predictable. The statistical characteristics of these variations determine in a very significant way how a distribution system will work and how it should be designed to operate economically.

3. *In analyzing sales variations, special attention should be paid to size, time, area, and volatility* Executives interested in the practical implications of short-term sales variations might focus on the following questions:

How big are the ups and downs? The magnitude of sales variations *over the replenishment lead time* will determine how large the inventory of an item must be to maintain a desired level of delivery service. The amount of an item on hand at a field point or on order must always equal the maximum reasonable demand over the lead time. Thus, the bigger the sales fluctuations, the more inventory of an item must be carried in the distribution system—at local warehouses, at the factory—to provide a given level of delivery service.

Are the variations correlated from one time period to the next? If one day's sales are above or below average, are the chances considerably better than 50–50 that the next day's sales will be above or below average, too? If sales are highly correlated from one week to the next, or from one month to the next, this means that the range of accumulated variation over the replenishment lead time increases nearly in proportion to the lead time itself. Doubling the warehouse lead time would nearly double the range of sales variations and the inventory requirements, while cutting the lead time in half would cut inventory requirements nearly in proportion. If sales are *not* correlated from one period to the next, chance variations tend to offset to some degree; doubling the lead time would increase inventory requirements only 40%–50%, while cutting it in half would cut inventories 30% or so.

High correlation in sales puts a premium on cutting lead times to make the distribution system react faster, perhaps through more expensive but higher speed transport, communications, and sales-information processing. By contrast, lower correlation means it may be more economical to let lead times lengthen and save expense in information handling and transport at the cost of somewhat higher inventories. EXHIBIT IV illustrates all this graphically for a hypothetical firm:

The dotted line represents transport, handling, and data-processing costs, tending to fall as a longer lead time permits less frequent reordering and slower, less expensive methods of shipment. The solid lines represent unit inventory costs, increasing nearly in proportion to lead time in the case of high sales correlation (dashed line) and at a slower rate in the case of low correlation (broken line). The higher the correlation, the further the point of minimum total cost is shifted toward the left—that is toward a shorter lead time—even in the face of higher transport, handling, and processing costs.

Are sales variations correlated between areas or markets? Is an unexpected increase in an item's sales in, say, the Pittsburgh area likely to coincide with an increase in Cleveland, or are variations unrelated from one market to another? Some causes of expected sales variations may affect a wide geographic re-

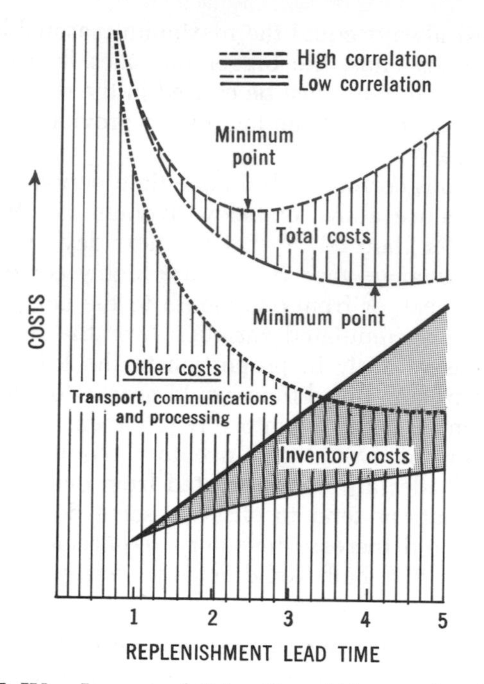

EXHIBIT IV. Impact of Sales Correlation on Lead Time Cost

gion (e.g. weather, rumors); others may be related entirely to local conditions (e.g., individual customers' plans).

The degree of cross-correlation in chance sales variations occurring in different markets has a significant influence on warehouse location decisions. For example, if the cross-correlation is low, so that chance variations in sales in one market tend to offset those in another, there is a potentially substantial economy in consolidating warehouses, in having fewer distribution points to serve the same total market. But if the cross-correlation is high, little would be saved to offset possibly greater transportation costs.

How do sales variations compare among items? Are sales of high-volume items relatively more stable than sales of low-volume items? Generally (but not always), one finds evidence that the higher the sales volume of an item, the more stable will be sales, relatively speaking. Differences in the sales volatility of products influence distribution system choices. The more changeable the sales of an item, other things being equal, the better the chances that centralized stocking in regional distribution centers or plants will be advantageous.

4. Inventory functions should be examined and related to other company needs Characteristically inventories are made up of: (a) stock in transit; (b) supplies arising from periodic shipments; (c) reserves carried to protect service in the face of unusual demand (safety stock). In some businesses, inventories are also carried to accommodate seasonal sales patterns and to permit a smoothed load to be put on manufacturing. These inventory functions and methods for analyzing have already been discussed in HBR[2] and there is no need to outline them again here. Suffice it to say that one important job in a distribution study is to identify the functions actually served by inventories and to characterize the factors—e.g., transport times, reordering principles used, and service requirements—that are responsible for existing inventory levels and costs.

5. The costs of warehouse storage and handling, traffic or freight, and clerical procedures should be determined Many of these costs are difficult to obtain from normal company accounting records or engineering studies; direct unit costs often just are not maintained in these records. However, statistical analyses of operating cost records can often serve quite adequately.

Warehouse costs are as good an illustration as any of the approach I have in mind. Included here are:

a. The costs of holding inventory These are generally related to the average or maximum inventory level in a distribution center and include space rent (including maintenance and janitor services, heat, and so on) and inventory costs (taxes, obsolescence and spoilage, and especially the cost of capital tied up in inventory). In our experience, careful study of the storage bill typically yield costs of 20%-35% per year on the capital value of the inventory, depending on the financial resources and policies of the company.

b. The costs of handling These include the costs of physically moving material into and out of storage or through terminal marshaling areas.

[2]See John F. Magee, "Guides to Inventory Policy: Part I. Functions and Lot Size," January–February 1956, p. 49; "Part II. Problems of Uncertainty," March–April 1956, p. 103; "Part III. Anticipating Future Needs," May–June 1956, p. 57; and Robert G. Brown, op. cit. See also John F. Magee, *Production Planning and Inventory* (New York, McGraw-Hill Book Company, Inc., 1958) and Robert G. Brown, *Statistical Forecasting for Inventory Control* (New York, McGraw-Hill Book Company, Inc., 1959).

What is wanted here are cost factors which can be used to calculate the warehousing and handling costs under different system plans. These factors usually take the form of:

A fixed charge per warehouse per year × number of warehouses (the fixed charge is generally $5,000–$10,000 per warehouse per year, depending on the character of space).

Warehousing cost per year per unit in inventory × average inventory in the system.

Handling cost per year per unit through the warehouse.

These cost factors can be built up from an engineering study or derived from statistical analysis of existing cost data. They will, of course, differ for different types of facilities and operating methods. For example, a mechanized warehouse operation will of course have a quite different order of costs from a nonmechanized operation.

Clerical cost factors for alternate operating systems can be derived in similar fashion. Transport costs must also be collected, usually in the form of specimen rates collated with shipment volumes for alternate transport methods. Such possibilities as in-transit privileges, "marriage" of shipments, and forwarding schemes should be reviewed.

6. *Management should analyze alternative distribution plans on paper* The effect of alternative numbers of warehouses, changed locations, different transport methods, and different response times should be tested, using the methods of inventory analysis and programing techniques. Existing manufacturing capacities and locations may be used as a starting point. Alternatively—or as a second step in the analysis—the effect of changes in manufacturing facilities, in capacities, or in the product assigned to individual plants can be tested.

The first broad system studies are used to see where the biggest payoffs or traps may be. On paper, it is possible to make some arbitrary changes in lead times, warehouse locations, plant capacities, flexibility and so on to see what the gross impact on distribution costs will be and thus whether detailed implementation studies are justified. It is important that the system study be based on current demand conditions, such as gross volume, product mix, and regional balance, as well as demand conditions projected roughly five to ten years ahead.

The facilities analysis is a step-by-step process. As the studies proceed, they will indicate potentially useful modifications in the distribution system. For example, a high concentration of sales among a few customers may indicate the need for special distribution plans, or the degree of concentration among products and the statistical characteristics of demand will suggest the need for regional stocking, changed warehouse numbers or locations, or similar alternatives. Again, an inventory study may indicate payoff possibilities in reducing lead times, in modifying service standards or in introducing new, more flexible transport and handling methods.

Generally, as a result of broad analyses of facilities and operations, special studies will be indicated. Such studies as these may be in order:

> Detailed analysis of the information-processing methods and costs to (a) take advantage of advancing technology to improve forecasting and control and (b) cut replenishment lead times.
>
> Investigation of the costs of employment variations and manufacturing changes. Additional inventory—or changes in production technology—may be justified to minimize these costs. If so, however, the additions or changes should be clearly recognized; "manufacturing cost" is too often a lame excuse for careless, inefficient management of materials in distribution.
>
> Study of product redesign or regrouping, especially where the product line may have evolved without much thought having been given to logistics concepts.
>
> Analysis of special ordering procedures, stock locations, and transport methods for handling low-volume items.

ORGANIZATION PLANS

Distribution system management poses some puzzling organization problems to the typical, functionally organized firm. Distribution is not a sales function; it is not traffic management; it is not a manufacturing responsibility. It is an aspect of *all* of these functions. At the same time, the effectiveness of its managers will determine the conditions under which men in the individual functions must work.

Most companies prefer not to put all aspects of distribution management—sales order processing and analysis, field stock control, warehouses, traffic, production control—under one organizational unit, but to divide responsibility among several interested units. Such a division leads, however, to difficulty principally because of failure to (a) recognize the need for specific coordinated distribution systems planning, (b) specify planning and control responsibilities, and (c) set up performance measures consistent with over-all system efficiency and with assigned responsibilities.

In revising an organization to meet current needs and in keeping it up to date, executives should try to have five questions uppermost in their minds:

1. What are the necessary planning steps, policy decisions, and operating decisions to be made?
2. Who is the right person to make each of the decisions?
3. What information does he need, and how can he get it most expeditiously?
4. Does each person know how to recognize an emergency calling for nonroutine action? Does he know how to resolve it?
5. What performance measures reflect what is expected of each person in terms of the operation of the whole system?

CONCLUSION

To sum up, a number of pressures have piled up on today's distribution systems. As manufacturing efficiency has increased and product cost has come down, costs have grown. Physical distribution costs are a significant share of these.

Business in many fields is becoming increasingly competitive, with competition taking new forms, including availability of goods and reliability of delivery. Product changes are forcing new pressures on the distribution system—more items to carry, faster obsolescence, lower unit sales and inventory turnover. In particular, changes in merchandising practices, such as the introduction of style as a merchandising weapon, have significantly complicated the distribution problem. Pressures for improvement in logistics also include internal forces—for example, the need to stabilize production and insulate production levels from short-term fluctuations in sales.

In the face of these trends, a number of revolutionary changes have taken place. Substantial improvements have come about in essentially all forms of transportation methods. Tremendous strides forward have been made in information-handling methods, including schemes for assimilating and processing data dealing with product demand and with the need for replenishment. Materials-handling methods, ranging from mechanized stock keeping to extensions of the pallet concept to eliminate item-by-item handling, have been gaining acceptance. Finally, and perhaps as important as improvement in physical facilities and concepts, there has been progress in ways of looking at the logistics problem and at methods for analyzing distribution systems.

Long-Run Implications

So far, we have seen farsighted companies taking advantage of the changes I have described by redesigning their distribution systems to cut costs and increase the support given to sales programs. The next step is now beginning to be felt—the insinuation of distribution concepts into certain aspects of long-term planning and capital budgeting, especially the analysis of facility requirements, the location of distribution points, and the determination of financial requirements to support distribution.

Of course, we must avoid the trap of thinking that all management problems will be resolved in terms of efficient distribution. Nevertheless, the long-range impact of distribution-system thinking on production, on product design, and on manufacturing location may be substantial. Perhaps one of the most significant changes will be in concepts of organization, in the assignment of functions and responsibilities. Efficient physical distribution poses a challenge to business in integrating what is essentially a system approach with the functional approaches that hitherto have tended to govern business organization planning.

In the long run, at least two possible directions are open for making a wide variety of products available in local markets. On the one hand, manufacturers can move toward centralized manufacture, with the specialty or small-volume items being made in enough volume to permit reasonable manufacturing economy and then being moved rapidly, perhaps by air freight, to the local markets as needed. On the other hand, management can try to achieve diversity through superficial differences built into a few basic product lines. Low-cost mass transport methods, perhaps rail freight, can be used to move parts and components from centralized manufacturing points with heavy equipment into widespread local assembly or modification plants. At the local points, the final touches can be put on the product to meet customer demand.

One thing seems sure: the choice of distribution system each company makes will have a significant impact on product design, plant investment, and organization. Industrial logistics and trends in logistics technology will receive increasing attention from business, along with markets, capital resources, and product development, in the formulation of corporate plans for the decade ahead.

32. DOES ADVERTISING BELONG IN THE CAPITAL BUDGET?*

Joel Dean

Should advertising be budgeted as an expense or as an investment?

Advertising is now book-kept and budgeted as though its benefits were used up immediately, like purchased electricity. Management thinks about advertising as it is book-kept, as a current expense. The decision as to how much a corporation should spend on persuasion is made by the same criteria as for materials used up in the factory—impact upon the current P&L. The advertising budget is part of the *operating* budget.

So far as is known, no corporation puts advertising in its capital budget. But maybe it belongs there. Several disinterested parties say so:

> The stock market says it belongs there. It says the benefits derived from promotional outlays are just as capitalizable as the tangible assets that the bookkeeper does capitalize. It says this when Bristol Myers sells at ten times its book value.
>
> Corporation presidents occasionally say it belongs there, especially when they evoke *investment* in advertising to justify poor current profits.
>
> New entrants into an industry say advertising belongs in the capital budget. They say it by including the promotional outlays required to build brand-acceptance as an integral part of the total investment required to break into the business.
>
> Antitrust economists say advertising belongs in the capital budget. They say it by viewing brand-acceptance, which is built up by promotion, as just as substantial a barrier to entry as the investment required in buildings and machinery.

*Reprinted from the *Journal of Marketing*, national quarterly publication of the American Marketing Association (October, 1966), pp. 15–21.

It is just possible that the bookkeeper's guide to top-management thinking about advertising is wrong.

THE APPROACH

The plan of this article is, first, to find whether promotion is an investment; second, to consider how to optimize it if it is an investment; and third, to speculate on the probabilities that this novel approach, even if theoretically valid, will do any good.

The approach here to the problem of how much to invest in advertising is formal and objective, rather than intuitive. The premise is that the overriding goal of the corporation is to maximize profits. The viewpoint is that of an economist concerned with managerial finance.

This article is confined to the conceptual framework for deciding how much to invest in promotion. Measurement problems are not examined, nor the mechanics of application. The analysis is presented in terms of advertising, but is equally applicable to all forms of persuasion. Advertising is used as an example simply because it is the purest and most indisputable form of selling cost, and for many firms also the largest.

My thesis is as follows. Most advertising is, in economic essence, an investment. How much to spend on advertising is, therefore, a problem of investment economics. A new approach is required—economic and financial analysis of futurities. This approach focuses on future after-tax cash flows and centers on the profit-productivity of capital.

IS PROMOTION AN INVESTMENT?

To determine whether, as a matter of economics, outlays for advertising and other forms of promotion constitute an investment, rather than a current expense, is our first task.

So we must bravely face three basic questions concerning the economics of investment in corporate persuasion:

A. Precisely what is a business investment; how is it distinguished from a current expense?
B. Just what are promotional costs; how should they be distinguished from production costs?
C. What are the distinctive characteristics of promotional outlays; do they disqualify promotion for investment treatment?

A. Concept of Investment

What distinguishes a business investment from a current expense? An investment is an outlay made today to achieve benefits in the future. A current expense is an outlay whose benefits are immediate. The question is not how the outlay is treated in conventional accounting, how it is taxed, or whether the asset is tangible or intangible. The hallmark of an investment is futurity.

B. Concept of Promotional Costs

Precisely what are promotional costs? How do they differ from production costs?

Promotional costs are outlays to augment the demand for the product—that is, to shift its price-quantity demand schedule upward, so that more will be sold at a given price. In contrast, production costs are all outlays required to meet this demand.

This different dividing line means that some costs which are conventionally classified as marketing costs, for example, physical distribution, are here viewed as part of production costs. It means also that some costs usually viewed as production costs, for example, inspection, are here viewed as promotional costs, even though they are incurred in the factory.

This is the cost-dichotomy needed for clear thinking about promotional investments. A clear idea of the purpose of an outlay is indispensable for a useful estimate of its effectiveness. Moreover, the criterion for optimization is quite different for production costs than for promotional costs. For production, it is sheer cost-minimization; for promotion, it is not cost-minimization but something much more intricate, as we shall see.

C. Distinctive Traits of Promotional Outlays

Do promotional investments differ from unimpeachable corporate investments in ways that make it impractical to manage them like true investments?

Promotional investments *are* different from traditional corporate investments—for example, capital tied up in machinery. The question is whether these differences call for a different intellectual apparatus for measuring productivity and rationing the firm's capital.

Promotional investments *are book-kept differently*. They are not capitalized and not depreciated. But this does not keep them from being investments. They tie up capital with equal inflexibility and do so with similar expectation of future benefits.

Promotional investments *are taxed differently*. Unlike acknowledged investments, they are deductible against income fully at the time of outlay, regardless of the delay of benefits. The fact that the tax collector is oblivious to promotional investments increases their productivity. Immediate tax writeoff of the entire outlay halves the investment after tax and steps up its true rate of return.

Promotional investments *are generally spread out over time* and usually can be adjusted in amount in relatively small steps. However, this is irrelevant in determining whether or not they are true investments.

Most promotional investments *have an indeterminate economic life*. Brand-acceptance "planted in the head" of a teenager by television may influence his purchases for 50 minutes or 50 years. But uncertainty of duration of the benefits does not make the promotional outlay any less an investment. The obsolescence-life of a computer is also quite uncertain.

Promotional investments *have multiple benefits* which can be reaped in optional ways. The profitability of augmented demand may be taken out either in higher prices or in larger volume. But this is not unique to promotional investments. Usually factory modernization not only saves labor, but also increases capacity and improves product-quality and employee morale.

Promotional investments *usually have irregular and diverse time-shapes in their benefits streams*. But this is a common characteristic of many tangible investments. Some oil wells, for example, come in as gushers, have an unexpected midlife rejuvenation from repressuring, and live out a tranquil old age as pumpers.

Promotional investments *have a benefit-stream which is difficult to measure and to predict*. But they share this characteristic with many forms of outlay conventionally classified as capital expenditures. Obsolescence of chemical-processing equipment, for example, is hard to predict, yet vitally affects its rate of return.

Promotional investments *are provocative*; they may induce rivals to retaliate. This adds to the difficulty of measuring and predicting benefits. Tangible investments, however, can also provoke competitors' reactions in ways that erode their profitability (for example, retail store modernization).

All this adds up to the fact that promotional investments do have unusual characteristics, different from many other investments that now fight for funds in the capital budget. However, these traits either are not distinctive, or if they are, do not destroy the essential investment-character of the promotional outlays.

All promotional outlays are now conventionally viewed exclusively as current expenses. Some are, if the time lag of benefits is sufficiently short; but others are instead true investments, because the delay in their benefits is substantial. Most promotion is a *mixture*, and the richness of the investment-mix varies over a wide range.

HOW TO OPTIMIZE INVESTMENT IN PROMOTION

Granted that much advertising is largely an investment in economic reality, how should a corporation determine how much it should invest in promotion? To solve this problem, we need answers to the following questions:

a. Does a satisfactory solution for the problem already exist?
b. Why has such an important problem remained unsolved?
c. To what corporate goal should the solution be geared?
d. How does promotion tie into other ways of getting business?
e. What are the determinants of the productivity of capital invested in promotion?
f. What concepts of measurement are needed to calibrate productivity of capital?
g. What is the most appropriate yardstick of capital productivity for promotional investments?
h. How would rate-of-return rationing work for investments in corporate persuasion?

A. Problem Unsolved

Has the problem of how much a corporation should spend on advertising and other forms of persuasion been already satisfactorily solved?

The problem is important. The answer is crucial to the competitive success of many firms, and may involve vast expenditures.

In the future, it is likely to be even more vital. Depersonalized distribution, increased urbanization, rising consumer affluence, revolutionary advances in technology, and bigger economies of scale in some promotional media are dynamic forces which will make the decision as to how much to invest in promotion a jugular issue for many corporations in the next decade.

Surprisingly, this crucial problem is not yet solved. Despite yards of computer print-outs and millions of dollars spent on advertising research, most corporations do not really know whether their promotional outlays should be half or twice as large as they now are.

B. Reasons for Failure

Why has such an important problem remained unsolved? There are three main causes.

The first cause is *failure to acknowledge the importance of futurity.* The full impact of most promotional outlays upon demand is delayed with associated uncertainty. Hence, the conceptual framework of analysis that management needs for solving this problem is the kind that is used in modern, sophisticated management of conventional corporate capital appropriations.

A second cause *is lack of a conceptual apparatus whose orientation is economic.* The problem of optimizing promotional investment is basically a matter of managerial economics, that is, balancing incremental promotional investment against predicted benefits, so as to augment sales most profitably.

The third cause of failure is *the difficulty of measuring the effectiveness of promotional outlays.* Their impacts on demand are diffused, delayed, and intricately interwoven with other forces. To make the kind of investment approach needed to produce practical benefits will require an open mind, fresh concepts, substantial research spending, and great patience.

C. Overriding Corporate Goal

What is the corporate goal to which the solution of optimum investment in promotion should be geared?

Promotional outlays, like other expenditures, should be judged in terms of their contribution to attainment of the corporation's objectives. Most companies have several goals, some of which conflict; but the solution for the problem of how much to invest in promotion should be geared primarily to the goal of profitability.

The master goal of the modern corporation should be maximum profits in the long run. More explicitly, it should be to maximize the present worth at the corporation's cost of capital of the future stream of benefits to the stockholder.

All other objectives—such as growth or market-share or eternal life—

should be either intermediate or subsidiary to this overriding corporate objective.

D. Business-Getters

How does promotion relate to other ways of getting business?

A company has three ways to augment its sales: by cutting price, by spending more on promotion, and by bettering its product. The three members of the business-getting threesome pull together. But being alternatives, they are at the margin rivalrous substitutes.

The three reinforce each other in a complex symbiotic relationship. For a product that is superior to rivals in wanted ways, promotional outlays will be more effective than for an inferior product. A given amount and quality of promotion will produce more sales of a product priced in correct economic relationship to buyers' alternatives than for an overpriced product.

Each of the three business-getters can have delayed impacts and hence be a business investment. Their delayed and interwining effects on sales, now and in the future, increase the problem of measuring the effects of promotional investment.

E. Determinants of Capital Productivity

What are the determinants of the productivity of capital invested in promotion?

These need to be identified to find out whether capital tied up in advertising will yield enough profits to earn its keep. Its yield must pay for the cost of this capital in the marketplace, or its opportunity costs in benefits passed up by not investing the money somewhere else.

The productivity of an investment in promotion is the relation of its earnings to the amount of capital tied up. This relationship requires explicit recognition of four economic determinants to be measured: (1) the amount and timing of *added investment*; (2) the amount and timing of *added earnings*; (3) the *duration of the earnings*; and (4) the *risks and imponderable benefits* associated with the project.

1. *Added Investment.* The appropriate investment base for calculating rate of return is the added outlay which will be occasioned by the adoption of a promotion project as opposed to its rejection.

The investment should include the entire amount of the original added outlay, regardless of how it is classified on the accounts. Any additional outlay for point-of-purchase displays or for distribution of samples to consumers should be included in the investment amount, as should future research expenses caused by the proposal.

The timing of these added investments has an important effect upon true profitability and should, therefore, be reflected in the rate-of-return computation.

2. *Added Earnings.* Concern with capital productivity implies, of course, that the company's goal is profits.

The productivity of the capital tied up is determined by the increase in earnings or savings, that is, net cash receipts, caused by making the investment as opposed to not making it. These earnings should be measured in terms of their after-tax cash or cash equivalents.

Only costs and revenues that will be different as a result of the adoption of the proposal should be included. The concept of earnings should be broad enough to encompass intangible and often unquantifiable benefits. When these have to be omitted from the formal earnings-estimates, they should be noted for subsequent appraisal of the project.

3. *Durability of Earnings.* The duration of the benefits from a promotional investment has a vital effect on its rate of return.

Economic life of promotion depends (a) on frequency of purchase; (b) on loyalty-life-expectancy, that is, longevity of customers; (3) on gestation period of the purchase decision; and (d) on erosion by the promotional efforts of rivals.

For advertising investments, durability is often the most difficult dimension of project value to quantify. But the problem cannot be avoided. Some estimate is better than none; and estimates can be improved by well-directed research.

4. *Risks and Imponderable Benefits.* Appraising the risks and uncertainties associated with a project requires a high order of judgment. It is only disparities in risk among projects which need to be allowed for, since the company's cost of capital reflects the overall risks. Although measurement of this sort of dispersion is difficult, some headway can sometimes be made by a necessarily arbitrary risk-ranking of candidate projects or categories of projects.

Most projects have some added benefits over and above the measurable ones. If excessive weight is given to those imponderables, then there is danger that rate-of-return rationing will occur. When a low rate-of-return project is preferred to a high one on the grounds of imponderable benefits, the burden of proof clearly should rest on the imponderables.

F. Concepts of Measurement

For calibrating these four determinants of return on investment, what concepts of measurement are needed? Four are particularly useful:

1. *Alternatives.* The proper benchmark for measuring added investment and the corresponding added earnings is the best alternative way to do it.
2. *Futurity.* Future earnings and future outlays of the project are all that matter.
3. *Increments.* Added earnings and added investment of the project alone are material.
4. *Cash flows.* After-tax cash flows (or their equivalents) alone are significant for measuring capital productivity.

1. *Alternatives.* There is always an alternative to the proposed capital expenditure.

The alternative may be so catastrophic that refined measurement is unnecessary to reject it; but in any case, the proper benchmark for the proposal is the next profitable alternative way of doing it.

2. *Futurity.* The value of a proposed capital project depends on its future earnings.

The past is irrelevant, except as a benchmark for forecasting the future. Consequently, earnings estimates need to be based on the best available projections. The outlays and earnings need to be estimated year by year over the economic life of the proposed promotion, and their time shape needs to be taken into account explicitly.

3. *Increments.* A correct estimate of both earnings and investment must be based on the simple principle that the earnings from the promotional proposal are measured by the total *added* earnings by making the investment, as opposed to *not* making it . . . and that the same is true for the investment amount.

Project costs should be unaffected by allocation of existing overheads, but should reflect the changes in total overhead and other costs likely to result from the project. No costs or revenues which will be the same, regardless of whether the proposal is accepted or rejected, should be included and the same goes for investment.

4. *Cash flows.* To be economically realistic, attention should be directed exclusively at the after-tax flows of cash or cash equivalents which will result from making the promotional investment.

Book costs are confusing and immaterial. But taxes do matter, because advertising investments are favored over depreciable investments in after-tax rate of return.

G. Yardstick of Financial Worth

The productivity of capital in a business investment is the relationship between its earnings and the amount of capital tied up. To measure this productivity for promotional investments, we not only must have a correct conceptual framework of measurements, but also must choose the most appropriate yardstick of investment worth.

The concept of advertising as an investment already has some limited acceptance in new-product introduction. The measure of productivity of capital often used is the payout period—a crude yardstick. The cutoff criterion is also set rather arbitrarily to get the original outlay back in two years or three years. Such standards have no objective justification as compared with corporate cost of capital.

What is the best yardstick of economic worth for investments in persuasion? Clearly, the yardstick that is economically appropriate for investments in promotion is true profitability as measured by discounted-cash-flow analysis.

1. *Discounted-Cash-Flow Analysis.* The discounted-cash-flow (DCF) method is a new approach to measuring the productivity of capital and measuring the cost of capital.

The application is new, not the principle. Discounting has long been used in the financial community, where precision and realism are indispensable. The essential contributions of discounted-cash-flow analysis to management thinking about investment in promotion are three:

a. An explicit recognition that time has economic value—and hence, that near money is more valuable than distant money.
b. A recognition that cash flows are what matter—and hence, that book costs are irrelevant for capital-decisions except as they affect taxes.
c. A recognition that income taxes have such an important effect upon cash flows that they must be explicitly figured into project worth.

The discounted-cash-flow method has two computational variants.

The first is a rate-of-return computation, which consists essentially of finding the interest rate that discounts gross future after-tax cash earnings of a project down to a present value equal to the project cost. This interest rate is the rate of return on that particular investment.

The second variant is a present-value computation which discounts gross future after-tax cash earnings of all projects at the same rate of interest. This rate of interest is the company's minimum acceptable rate of return. This should be based on the company's cost of capital. Special risk should be reflected either by deflating project earnings or by adjusting the cutoff rate for projects of different categories of risk. The resulting present-value is then compared with the project cost investment. If the present value exceeds it, the project is acceptable. If it falls below, it is rejected.

In addition, projects can by this variant be ranked by various kinds of profitability indexes which reflect the amount or ratios of excess of present value over project cost.

Both variants of the discounted-cash-flow approach require a timetable of after-tax cash flows of investment and of gross earnings which cover the entire economic life of the project.

In practice, the timetable can be simplified by grouping years in blocks. For projects for which investment is substantially instantaneous and gross earnings are level, simple computational charts and tables can be used to estimate the discounted-cash-flow rate of return directly from estimated economic life and after-tax payback. For projects with rising or declining earnings streams, this conversion is more complex.

2. *Superiorities of DCF.* The discounted-cash-flow method of analysis is particularly needed for measuring the profitability of promotional investments, for two reasons.

First, the outlays are usually spread out. Second, benefits, mainly incremental profits from added sales in the future, are always spread out and usually have a non-level time-shape.

The superiorities of discounted-cash-flow analysis over rival yardsticks for measuring the productivity of capital in promotional investments are imposing:

a. It is economically realistic in confining the analysis to cash-flows and forgetting about book-allocations.
b. It forces guided thinking about the whole life of the project, and concentration on the lifetime earnings.
c. It weights the time-pattern of the investment outlay and the

cash earnings, so as to reflect real and important differences in the value of near and distant cash-flows.

d. It reflects accurately and without ambiguity the timing of tax-savings.
e. It permits simple allowances for risks and uncertainties, and can be adapted readily to increasing the risk allowance over time.
f. It is strictly comparable to cost-of-capital, correctly measured, so that decisions can be made quickly and safely by comparing rate of return and the value of money to the firm.

H. Rate-of-return Rationing

How should rationing of capital work for persuasion-investments?

Rate-of-return "battling" among capital proposals is the essence of capital rationing. The standard of minimum acceptable profitability should (after proper allowance for special risks and for imponderables) be the same for all, namely, the company's market cost-of-capital or its opportunity cost-of-capital, whichever is higher.

Market cost-of-capital is what the company probably will pay for equity and debt funds, on the average, over the future. For a large publicly-held company, this cost can be measured with adequate precision for rationing purposes. There is no better cutoff criterion.

Opportunity cost-of-capital is the sacrificed profit-yield from alternative investments. Only when a company refuses to go to market for funds can its opportunity costs stay long above market cost-of-capital.

PRACTICAL VALUES

Will putting advertising in the capital budget do any good?

Granted that as a matter of economic principle much advertising and other forms of promotional spending are investments . . . and granted also that conceptually correct and pragmatically proved techniques for optimizing investment outlays are available for promotional investment . . . the question is whether this sophisticated and powerful mechanism, applied to promotional investments, will have any practical value.

Most business investments are not made in ignorance of their probable impacts, whereas, many of the outlays for persuasion now are. Characteristically, the amount and timing of the effects of advertising are unknown. The duration of their impact on economic life is unknown, and the probabilities of effectiveness are also unknown. Quite possibly, attempting to estimate these unknowns cannot improve overall results.

The problem of how much to invest in promotion can be solved either by intuitive and perhaps artistic processes, or through a more formal and more systematic study of objective evidence. Quite possibly men of experience and good judgment can determine how much the corporation should invest in promotion by subjective judgment, regardless of whether advertising is formally put in the capital budget. This article is nevertheless confined to a consideration of ways in which sophisticated economic models and systematic quantitative study can help to find the appropriate size of the appropriation for corporate persuasion.

IN SUMMARY

1. Much advertising (and other corporate persuasion) is in economic reality partly an investment. The investment-mix varies over a wide spectrum.

2. Investments in promotion are different from conventional capital expenditures; but these distinctive characteristics do not disqualify promotion for investment treatment.

3. Profitability must be the basic measurement of the productivity of capital invested in promotion. Despite the multiplicity of conflicting corporate goals, the overriding objective for decisions or investment of corporate capital should be to make money.

4. The main determinants of profitability of an advertising investment that need to be estimated are the amount and timing of added investment and of added earnings, the duration of advertising effects and risks.

5. The measurement concepts of capital productivity that must be estimated are future, time-spotted, incremental, after-tax cash flows of investment outlays and of added profits from added sales.

6. Discounted-Cash-Flow (DCF) analysis supplies the financial yardstick most appropriate for promotional investments. By comparison, payback period, although widely used, has no merit.

7. Advertising belongs in the capital budget. Promotional investments should be made to compete for funds on the basis of profitability, that is, DCF rate of return.

8. The criterion for rationing scarce capital among competing investment proposals should be DCF rate of return. The criterion of the

minimum acceptable return should be the corporation's cost of capital —outside market-cost or internal opportunity-cost, whichever is higher.

9. Putting advertising into the capital budget will not perform a miracle. Judgment cannot be displaced by DCF analysis and computers. But judgment can be economized and improved. The most that it can do is to open the way for a research approach which is oriented to the kind of estimates that are relevant and that will permit advertising investment in promotion to fight for funds on the basis of financial merit rather than on the basis of personal persuasiveness of their sponsor.

10. An investment approach to produce practical benefits will require fresh concepts, substantial research-spending, and great patience.

33. DECISION THEORY AND MARKETING MANAGEMENT*

Robert D. Buzzell and Charles C. Slater

The term "decision theory" refers to a body of methods by which complex problems of decision under uncertainty can, in effect, be reduced to a limited number of simpler problems for purposes of analysis. A more specific term for the method recommended here is ***individual decision-making under risk.***[1] By this is meant a formal analysis of decision alternatives and their consequences when the effects of the decision are not known with certainty.

DECISION THEORY APPROACH

The basic elements of decision-making under risk may be summarized briefly.[2] A decision maker (person or firm) must choose among several "acts" or "strategies" which we denote as A_1, A_2, . . . , A_n. Each act is a well-defined series of actions or procedures; thus, "Act 1" may mean, "Build a new retail outlet at X location with 20,000 square feet of floor space." "Act 2" may represent the reverse, "Build no new retail outlet." Insofar as possible, the set of acts employed in the analysis should include *all* reasonable possibilities in a given situation. Experience, judgment, and creativity are required to identify the decision possibilities in a marketing problem.

Choice among the various possible acts is difficult because the consequences of an act depend on certain *conditions* which cannot be

*Reprinted from the *Journal of Marketing,* national quarterly publication of the American Marketing Association (July, 1962), pp. 7–16.

1Compare Duncan Luce and Howard Raiffa, *Games and Decisions* (New York: John Wiley and Sons, Inc., 1957), pp. 12–15.

2See Robert Schlaifer, *Probability and Statistics for Business Decisions* (New York: McGraw-Hill Book Co., Inc., 1959); and Luce and Raiffa, same reference as footnote 1.

predicted with certainty. These conditions may be termed "states of nature" and designated $s_1, s_2, \ldots, s_m$. The "state of nature" concept includes all factors which determine the effects of a marketing decision (for example, the responses of customers, general business conditions, and competitors' reactions). For example, "State 1" may represent "population in the trading area increases 10 per cent in the next five years, and competitors build three new stores." As in the case of decision possibilities, *all* relevant states of nature should be included in the analysis of a decision, so far as possible. In a literal sense, of course, this can never be attained, so that "complete" optimization is not feasible.

The states affecting the outcome of a decision may *be related to* the particular decision chosen. For example, a decision to use a specific advertising strategy might lead to a defensive response by competitors which could not occur if a different strategy were selected. Consequently, the relevant "states of nature" must be identified for *each* possible act A, although, of course, the same states of nature *may* apply to several or all acts.

Assuming that a given act is selected and that a given state of nature prevails, it is possible to determine the "payoff" to the decision maker. By "payoff" is meant the monetary and other consequences of the decision. A difficult problem is presented when nonmonetary "payoffs" must be incorporated. In relatively simple problems, it may be possible to assign "cash equivalents" to these consequences. More generally, modern utility theory provides a mechanism for assigning numerical measures to the results of a decision, including monetary and other effects. These payoffs should be estimated on a *net* basis; that is, the costs of carrying out the decision (if any) should be deducted from its estimated revenue.

Determining the payoff of an act under a given state is not an easy task, since a decision of any real importance has far-reaching indirect consequences, in addition to its immediate impact on profits. For example, a decision to market a new product has effects on the long-term sales patterns of existing products, in addition to its own success or failure. Estimation of payoffs is further complicated by the fact that, if they are to be realistic, payoff measures must reflect the particular values of the decision maker, and these vary among persons. While the treatment of payoffs in this example is straight-forward, it does not imply that the problem is this simple in practice.

Because the outcome of a decision is shrouded in uncertainty, a key element in the analysis of a decision is to assign *probabilities* to the various possible "states of nature." In some cases, especially those involving *repetitive* decisions such as routine buying and inventory control, it is relatively simple to determine the probabilities of occurrence for various "states" through analysis of quantitative evidence. For example, sales data may reveal that demand for an item is between 10 and 19 units per week 20% of the time, between 20 and 29 units 15% of the time, and so on. These *relative frequencies* may then be used directly as probabilities of occurrence for the various states of demand (assuming, of course, that no basic changes take place in the market, seasonal variations have been accounted for, and so forth.)

In most cases involving basic marketing policy problems, however, determination of probabilities for the relevant "states" is not so easy. In most cases, major policy decisions are not repetitive problems, and past experience may provide only a rough and rather ambiguous guide. *Nevertheless, even very crude approximations of probabilities for the various states affecting a decision still are better than none at all.*

The probabilities assigned to the various states represent the decision-maker's "betting odds" as to the probable responses of customers, competitors, and so forth. Admittedly, it is very difficult to assign odds or probabilities to such events. But even in the most informal kind of decision-making, this is precisely what managers *must do.* Any risky decision implies some assessment as to what will ensue from the decision. The real difference between "decision theory" and present management practice is the formalization of this "intuitive" process of choosing among various possibilities. While this may not improve the judgment of the individual decision maker, it improves his communication with others and facilitates the collection and analysis of further information. More important, it forces an executive to examine his problem in concrete terms, and thus serves as a stimulus to more systematic thinking on his part.

Given the various possibilities, the relevant states of nature and estimates of their probabilities of occurrence, and the payoffs for each act given each state, some act must be selected as the "best" of those available. Several different criteria have been proposed for selection of the "best" or "optimal" act, depending in part on whether or not probabilities are assigned to the states. The one adopted in this analysis is that of selecting the act with the *highest expected payoff*. The expected payoff of an act is defined as the average of its (net) payoffs under all possible states of nature, each weighted by its probability of occurrence.

To illustrate the concept of expected payoff, consider the following simple problem.

States of Nature	Decision Possibilities A_1: Build a New Store	A_2: Do Not Build	Probability of State
s_1 : New Subdivision is Built	$1,000,000	0	0.3
s_2 : New Subdivision is Not Built	−500,000	0	0.7

Here the payoffs, as previously explained, represent dollar profits to the decision maker, with future profits discounted to present values. The probabilities are based on management's assessments of such factors as population growth, real estate markets, and zoning. The expected payoff of A_2 is obviously zero, since this decision has no payoff regardless of what happens. The expected payoff of A may be computed as follows:

$$\$1{,}000{,}000\ (0.3) - \$500{,}000\ (0.7) = \$300{,}000 - 350{,}000 = -\ \$50{,}000$$

Under this criterion, then A_2 should be chosen, and the new store should not be built. This is equivalent to saying that the chances of success are not good enough to justify the risk.

The logic of selecting the act with the maximum expected payoff is clear-cut in the case of repetitive decisions. Since the decision is repeated over and over, we expect (by definition) the average return per decision to be the expected payoff as computed above. Hence, we should select the act that produces the highest average payoff per decision and the highest total payoff in the long run.

On the other hand, when a decision is to be made only once, the rationale of the expected payoff criterion is not so obvious. This criterion leads to the optimal decision in the sense of yielding a decision consistent with the decision maker's preferences, as summarized in the payoff table.[3]

DISTRIBUTION PROBLEMS OF THE BAKING INDUSTRY

Wholesale bakers, in common with many other types of firms, face difficult marketing problems as a result of changes in the character of their markets. These problems arise from substantial excess capacity on the one hand, and concentration of buying power among corporate chains, voluntaries, and cooperatives, on the other hand.

[3]Luce and Raiffa, same reference as footnote 1, pp. 20–23; also Schlaifer, same reference as footnote 2, Chap. 2.

DEVELOPMENT OF MARKETING POLICIES

The present-day marketing policies of wholesale bakers can best be understood in the context of the historical factors underlying their development and modification.

The commercial baking industry emerged during the latter half of the 19th century. During this period, as commercial bakers expanded their distribution beyond the immediate neighborhood of their plants, they developed a set of marketing policies geared to the needs of the small independent grocers. Among the more important of these were[4]:

1. Frequent deliveries were made to individual stores.
2. Bakers assumed responsibility for returned stale goods.
3. Retails customarily stocked several brands.
4. Bakers provided display equipment, stocked displays, and deliberately overstocked shelves in order to increase brand exposure.
5. Price competition was abandoned in view of the oligopolistic character of each retail market. In addition, "flat pricing" became customary; that is, each customer was charged the same unit price regardless of quantities purchased or terms of sale.

These marketing policies, developed for the most part in the early 20th century, largely comprise the "rules of the game" in the baking industry today. While each policy can be explained as a rational response to market conditions prevailing at the time, many of them have become less and less appropriate as market conditions changed. The impact of these changes has been made all the more severe because of the inhibiting constraints of labor unions and competitive retaliation in response to change.

RESPONSES TO CHANGING MARKET CONDITIONS

Wholesale bakers in a given market tend to charge identical or nearly identical prices for white bread and other staple bakery products. The explanation lies primarily in the oligopolistic interdependence of the sellers, although illegal price-fixing agreements have been discovered or alleged in some cases.[5] Unit costs are sensitive to

[4]William G. Panschar, "Baking in America," Vol. 1, *Economic Development* (Evanston, Ill.: Northwestern University Press, 1956), pp. 71–84, 93–99.

[5]For example, *Continental Baking Company v. United States*, U.S. Court of Appeals for the Sixth Circuit, No. 13865 (decided July 18, 1960); *Bakers of Washington, Inc., et. al.*, FTC Complaint, Docket 8309 (issued March 7, 1961).

changes in output, since fixed production and distribution costs represent a substantial proportion of the total cost for modern bakery plants. Declines in sales in some markets have had the effect of reducing profits substantially. The response of the larger and more efficient competitors has been, in many cases, to *raise* prices and thus hold an "umbrella" over their weaker competitors. Obviously this policy has tended to aggravate the problem of shrinking demand by increasing the cost gap between chain bakeries and purchased baked goods.

An even more important aspect of pricing is the policy of "flat pricing." Typically, no quantity discounts are offered, nor are lower prices available for customers who are willing to forego the traditional store delivery and display services. But chains and other large buyers feel they are entitled to such discounts, and have exerted considerable pressure for them. The evidence is clear that substantial *potential* cost savings are associated with large purchases.

A systems engineering study showed that drivers' product handling rates (units handled per minute of driver time) are directly related to the number of units delivered per route stop.[6] The handling rate was more than 50% greater for stops at which 200 units are delivered than for stops at which 100 units are delivered. *Realized* cost savings are not this great, since drivers are paid on a commission basis so that improvements in driver efficiency are not reflected in lower unit wage costs. Even under the commission system, however, substantial savings in unit distribution costs are associated with larger drop sizes. (The systems engineering study also revealed that limited-service methods of distribution permit significant reduction in costs.)

Despite evidence that lower costs are associated with quantity sales and limited service distribution methods, most wholesale bakers have resisted demands for differential pricing. This resistance is based in part on the commission system of compensation typically part of the companies' union agreements. Another factor underlying the resistance to change is the fear that doing so would alienate the small outlets which require full service and which (it is believed) would resent any preferential treatment for their larger competitors, even if justified. Also, it is feared that initiation of quantity or service discounts might lead to chaotic price competition unrelated to any economic justification.

Wholesale bakers have also resisted making private brands for chains or voluntaries because of fear of being boycotted by independents.

[6]*Distribution: The Challenge of the Sixties*, a report prepared for the American Bakers' Association (Cambridge, Mass.: Arthur D. Little Inc., March, 1961).

As a compromise measure, many bakers have developed "secondary" brands of bread which are sold at lower prices than the regular brands, although little difference exists in product characteristics. The price differential is not, however, great enough to equal chain-baked brands, and the main result has been a reduction in average profit for the bakers.

In summary, wholesale bakers have responded to the twin challenges of large-scale retailing and declining per capita bread consumption by attempting to maintain the *status quo.* As output has declined, prices have been raised to maintain the profitability of marginal operators. A uniform local system of pricing and customer services has largely been preserved, despite persistent pressures to deviate from it. Territorial expansion has taken place with the result of higher unit distribution costs. Apart from the general inertia of any established marketing system, several specific factors have tended to impede a more flexible response.

The commission system of driver compensation has discouraged quantity and service discounts. Fear of retaliation by small retail customers has prevented bakers from dealing more realistically with chains. Because of the existence of excess capacity, bakers have feared and sought to avoid the chaotic price competition which might ensue if the traditional ground rules were discarded.

The method of analysis which this article recommends is that of statistical decision theory. The application of this method to a specific bakery marketing policy problem is outlined in the following section.

DECISION THEORY ANALYSIS APPLIED

For purposes of this exposition, a "model bakery market" has been developed, consisting of three competing wholesale bakers, several retail food chains and voluntary groups, and a number of independent food retailers. For obvious reasons, the other possible acts, appropriate states of nature, and the payoffs must be identified or estimated for a specific firm. Different firms, even in the same local market, might conceive of different acts and states, and almost certainly would have different payoffs for a given decision and state.

In the context of this model market, the analysis is directed to the resolution of a specific decision problem, that of responding to a customer's request for provision of a private brand. Although this analysis is incomplete in the sense that we have not traced the *full* implications of each possible decision, suggestions for a continuation of the analysis are made in a subsequent section.

THE MODEL BAKERY MARKET

The hypothetical bakery market was designed to reflect typical market and operating conditions in many metropolitan areas in the United States. In this market there are three wholesale bakers, designated as A, B, C; and to chain bakeries, those of the Green Chain and the Red Chain. Wholesale Baker Z, located in a nearby city, is a potential "outside" competitor. The customers served by these bakeries are designated as follows:

Blue, Red, Yellow and Green corporate chains
Retailer cooperatives I and II
Voluntary chain I
Independent supermarkets
Small independent stores
Sales outside the market to various customers

The white-pan bread sales of each bakery to each customer are shown in Table 1. Bakery A has the dominant market position, with sales of approximately 400,000 units per week; competitors B and C sell approximately 250,000 units and 100,000 units, respectively. The two chain bakeries produce 250,000 units per week. Thus, the total bread market amounts to about 1,000,000 units per week.

It is assumed that the total market is fixed in the short run and that demand is sufficiently inelastic so that it will not be quickly affected by bakers' marketing decisions. Selling or transfer prices per unit for each bakery are also given in Table 1. It is assumed that each bakery follows the typical industry policy of "flat pricing," with no systematic price differentials for quantities purchased or services required. An average difference of one cent per loaf in *realized* price exists in favor of large customers, primarily on account of their greater utilization of advertising and other allowances.

The cost structure of Bakeries A, B, and C is shown in Table 2. Operating costs are classified as fixed costs (administration, production, and distribution), and variable costs (production and distribution). The relationship of costs to sales volume is a simple linear one: Total Cost = Fixed Cost + Variable Cost per Unit (Output in Units). This equation for bakery operating costs provides a reasonably good approximation to their actual cost structure.

TABLE 1

WEEKLY SALES BY CLASS OF CUSTOMER, SELLING OR TRANSFER PRICES PER UNIT, AND DOLLAR SALES VOLUME FOR COMPETING BAKERIES IN "EVERYTOWN, U. S. A." MARKET

	White Bread Sales in Thousands of Units by Customer and Price per Unit Sales to												
Bakery	*Yellow Chain*	*Blue Chain*	*Red Chain*	*Green Chain*	*Coop. I*	*Coop. II*	*Vol. I*	*Small Chains*	*Indep. Supers*	*Small Indeps.*	*Outside Market*	*Total*	*Dollar Volume*
A	22@.19	50@.19	10@.19	7@.19	114@.19	76@.19	60@.19	22@.20	11@.20	22@.20	. . .	394	$ 75,410
B	15@.19	36@.19	8@.19	3@.19	72@.19	48@.19	39@.19	15@.20	8@.20	15@.20	. . .	95	17,920
C	3@.19	14@.19			24@.19	16@.19	11@.19	3@.20	1@.20	3@.20	20@.18	95	17,920
Red Chain			162@.155									162	25,110
Green Chain				90@.165								90	14,850
Z												. . .	
Total	40	100	180	100	210	140	110	40	20	40	20	1,000	$183,205

The assumed fixed and variable costs have been used in Table 2 to compute net profits for each of the three competing wholesale bakers under the "initial market conditions" of Table 1. For example, Baker A has sales of 394,000 units per week. This level of sales results in total weekly variable costs of $54,474, plus fixed costs of $12,662 per week, or a total cost of $67,136.

Hence, net profit before taxes amounts to sales of $75,410 minus operating and fixed costs of $67,136 = $8,274. Profits of Bakeries B and C have been computed in similar fashion in Table 2. While Tables 1 and 2 present a simplified picture of revenues and cost, they are accurate enough for the illustration.

ANALYSIS OF A DECISION

In the context of the "model bakery market" described in Tables 1 and 2, the application of decision theory to a policy problem may now be illustrated. In this analysis the viewpoint of Baker B, the second largest wholesale baker in the market, is taken.

Let us assume that the Blue Chain asks Baker B to produce a private brand of bread for sale in the Blue Stores. The problem is, how should Baker B respond to such a request? The decision theory approach may be summarized in six "steps" as follows:

1. *Identification of different possibilities.* Baker B has at least five different basic courses of action open to him, in response to the Blue Chain's request:

A_1 Ignore the request; that is, refuse it outright, or delay any response so long as it amounts to a refusal.

A_2 Make a counter-offer to produce a "secondary brand" bread to be sold at a lower price than the regular "B Brand" Bread.

A_3 Reduce price on the regular brand.

A_4 Accede to the request of the Blue Chain.

A_5 Institute a system of price differentials based on quantity and service rendered by Baker B. Such price differentials would necessarily (under the law) be offered to all buyers in the market; but in view of the Blue Chain's size and personnel capabilities, this would presumably result in somewhat lower prices to Blue than to most others.

Identification of these possibilities implies a considerable knowledge of the nature of the wholesale bread market and the motivations of the customers therein. It is assumed that the Blue Chain wants a private brand so as to improve its competitive position relative to the Red Chain, which has its own bakery plant. If this is true, the real

TABLE 2

WEEKLY COSTS, SALES, AND PROFITS OF COMPETING WHOLESALE BAKERIES IN "EVERYTOWN, U.S.A." MARKET

Sales, Cost, or Profit	*Baker A*	*Baker B*	*Baker C*
Fixed Cost–Baking	$ 4,310	$ 3,732	$ 1,384
Fixed Cost–Routes	1,741	1,429	559
Fixed Cost–Marketing	2,277	1,743	538
Fixed Cost–Administration	4,334	2,261	862
Total Fixed Costs	$12,662	$ 9,165	$ 3,343
Variable Cost–Baking	$.09641/unit	$.10545/unit	$.11053/unit
Variable Cost–Routes	.03072/unit	.02928/unit	.03007/unit
Variable Cost–Marketing	.01113/unit	.01115/unit	.01122/unit
Total Variable Cost	$.13826/unit	$.14588/unit	$.15182/unit
Initial Market Conditions:			
Sales	$75,410	$49,590	$17,920
Total Cost	67,136	46,955	17,767
Net Profit	$ 8,274	$ 2,635	$ 153

question is, What possibilities are available to Baker B that might enable the Blue Chain to attain this goal? Possibilities A_2, A_3, and A_5 have little to do with private brands, but all are designed to help the Blue Chain achieve its presumed objective. Perhaps still other possibilities could be identified.

2. *Enumeration of states of nature.* For each possibility, it is necessary to identify the possible "outcomes" or states of nature governing the effect of the decision. In this problem, the states must take account of the responses of Baker B's customers and competitors to any action he takes.

If Baker B follows possibility A_1 and ignores the Blue Chain's request, there are six possible outcomes:

S_{11} Blue is supplied by outside Baker Z. Having achieved a foothold in the market, Z also supplies private label bread to the Yellow Chain and to Coop I.

S_{12} Blue is supplied by Z, but Z fails to get any other business.

S_{13} Blue is supplied by local Bakery A or Bakery C.

S_{14} Blue acquires its own bakery plant and decreases its purchases from B.

S_{15} Blue decides to wait; but resentful of B's refusal, adopts minor counter-measures, including reduced display space and less careful maintenance of B's display stocks.

S_{16} Blue decides to wait and does *not* adopt any counter-measures.

In similar fashion, the possible outcomes of each of B's decision possibilities have been enumerated. Some of these outcomes are common to some or all of the decision possibilities; but in general the relevant "states" or outcomes depend on the particular decision made by B. The whole range of decisions and outcomes is summarized in Table 3.

As was suggested in the general discussion of decision theory, the number and nature of the outcomes differ for the various decision possibilities, since these outcomes consist in part of *responses* to a particular decision. This also implies that the *probabilities* of the various outcomes differ from one possibility to another, even if the possible outcomes themselves are the same.

3. *Exploration of further possibilities and outcomes.* The analysis of the decision process usually cannot stop realistically with a single "round" of actions and their outcomes. In order to appraise the consequences of each decision possibility, it is necessary to explore the whole chain of effects and reactions that would ensue from a given action by Baker B.

For example, suppose B refuses (A_1) and Z supplies the Blue Chain as well as the Yellow Chain and Coop I (S_{11}). Then B is confronted by a new set of possibilities: he can retaliate by supplying retailers in Z's own market, hoping to drive Z out of the local market; or he can meet Z's competition locally. If he retaliates in Z's market, the outcome will again depend on the "state of nature." The possible outcome, for instance, is that legal action will be taken against B for geographic price discrimination.

This process can be conceived as a "game" in which the decision maker takes "turns" with a fictitious opponent ("Nature") representing the whole complex of personal and impersonal market forces bearing on his decisions. An illustrative series of moves is depicted in a tree diagram in Figure 1. In this example we have traced out two "rounds" of the game: first, B makes a move by choosing A_1; then Nature "chooses" (in a statistical sense) one of the states or outcomes; then B moves again by choosing an action from a new set of possibilities; and, finally, Nature moves again.

The game could, of course, be traced out beyond the second round through a third, a fourth, and so on; but if the analysis is ever to be completed and used, it must be cut off somewhere. Also, it is clear that as the analysis is carried further, the estimates of payoffs and probabilities become more and more speculative, so that the value of analyzing further rounds probably diminishes rapidly.

FIGURE 1

Illustrative Analysis of Decision Possibilities and Outcomes—A_1: B Refuses Blue's Request (Payoffs in thousands of dollars)

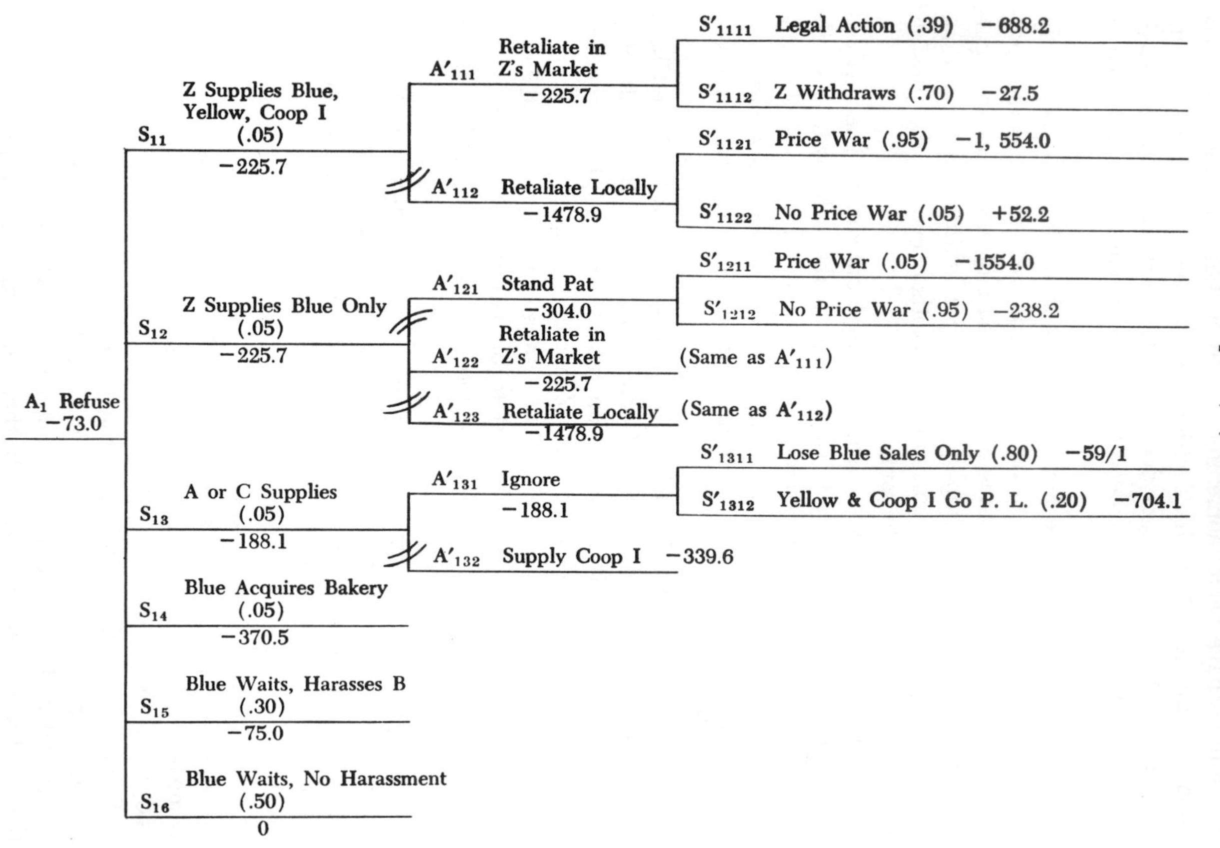

TABLE 3
Decision Alternatives and Possible Outcomes

A_1 *Ignore Request*	A_2 *Offer Secondary Loaf*	A_3 *Reduce Price*	A_4 *Accede to Request*	A_5 *Price Diff. System*
S_{11} Z supplies Blue, Yellow & Coop I.	S_{21} (same as S_{11})	$S_{31} = S_{11}$	. . .	$S_{51} = S_{11}$ (Blue rejects counter-offer)
S_{12} Z supplies Blue only	S_{22} (same as S_{12})	$S_{32} = S_{12}$	. . .	$S_{52} = S_{12}$
S_{13} A or C supplies Blue	S_{23} (same as S_{13})	$S_{33} = S_{13}$	. . .	$S_{53} = S_{13}$
S_{14} Blue acquires own Bakery	S_{24} (same as S_{14})	$S_{34} = S_{14}$	. . .	. . .
S_{15} Blue waits, harrasses B	S_{25} (same as S_{15})	. . .	. . .	. . .
S_{16} Blue waits	S_{26} (same as S_{16})	. . .	. . .	. . .
. . .	S_{27} Blue accepts offer; A & C follow suit	. . .	. . .	. . .
. . .	. . .	S_{38} Blue accepts offer; A & C do *not* follow suit	. . .	. . .
. . .	. . .	S_{39} Blue accepts; A & C follows; B retains slight advantage	. . .	. . .
. . .	. . .	$S_{3,\ 10}$ Blue accepts; A & C follow; market returns to original division		. . .
. . .	. . .	. . .	$S_{4,\ 11}$ Blue accepts; A & C offer secondary loaf	. . .
. . .	. . .	. . .	$S_{4,\ 12}$ Blue accepts; A & C lower prices; B is forced to meet	. . .
. . .	. . .	. . .	$S_{4,\ 13}$ Blue accepts; A & C offer private labels to Yellow & Coop I.	
. . .	. . .	. . .	. . .	$S_{5,\ 14}$ Blue accepts; A & C follow suit
. . .	. . .	. . .	. . .	$S_{5,\ 15}$ Blue accepts; A & C lower prices

4. *Estimation of payoffs.* The payoffs for each decision and each applicable outcome have been estimated by tracing through the effects on Baker B's sales, costs, and profits.

These payoffs are shown for the illustrative moves and countermoves in Figure 1. Consider, for example, the branch of the tree corresponding to the series A_1, S_{11}, A'_{111}, S'_{1111}. This represents a decision by B to refuse Blue's request; an invasion of B's market by Z; retaliation by B in Z's market; and legal action against B as a result of the retaliation. It is assumed that this chain of events results in Z attaining a fairly permanent niche in B's market.

Based on past experience with private brand sales, it is estimated that Blue, Yellow, and Coop I will shift to at least 40% private brand volume, and that B will lose about this same percentage of his former sales to them. This implies a loss of about 52,000 units per week for B; and each unit represents a loss in gross contribution (price minus variable cost) of $.04412. Hence, B's revenue would be reduced by about $2,300 per week. When this weekly loss is converted to its present value, based on a yearly discount of 10% over a five-year period it is equivalent to an outright cash loss of $688,200.

In a similar manner, the payoffs for each possible chain of decisions and outcomes have been estimated and are shown in Figure 1. These estimates are used, together with the estimated probabilities for "Nature's" plays, to derive expected payoffs for each of B's possibilities. Of course, this method of estimating payoffs is oversimplified. In practice, two other factors would have to be considered:

1. In addition to the direct effects on revenue and costs, some of the outcomes might involve nonmonetary consequences, such as the stigma and the inconveniences of litigation.
2. Some of the monetary losses may be so great (for example, the sequence A_1, S_{11}, A'_{112}, S'_{1121}) that they imply bankruptcy for B. In such a case, the loss is really greater in relation to less drastic outcomes than is implied by the payoff measures.

5. *Assessment of probabilities.* Now it is necessary to assign probabilities to each outcome under each possible decision. As suggested previously, this is a very difficult task, but one that must be done at least implicitly in every decision of this kind. The assessments shown in Figure 1 are based on the experience of one of the authors in studying the wholesale bakery market over a number of years, together with conversations with several leading bakery executives.

6. *Computation of expected payoff and choice of optimal decision.* Given the individual payoff and their probabilities, computation of

the expected payoff for each decision possibility is a straight-forward matter. This is illustrated in Figure 1.

In this analysis, it is necessary to start at the *end* of each chain of acts and outcomes (the extreme right in Figure 1) and work "backward" to the initial set of decision possibilities. Consider, first the branch corresponding to A_1, S_{11}, A'_{111}. If B chooses A_1, then A'_{111}, there are two possible outcomes: S'_{1111} and S'_{1112}. The payoff under S'_{1111} is–$688,200 and under S'_{1112} it is–$27,500. The estimated probabilities are 0.30 and 0.70, respectively. Hence, the *expected* payoff at the "fork" representing A'_{111} is .30 (–$688,200) + .70 (–1,554,000) = – $225,700.

Similarly, the expected payoff for A'_{112} is – $1,478,900. Obviously A'_{111} is preferred to A'_{112}. Hence, in Figure 1 the branch corresponding to A'_{112} has been blocked off; it would never be followed if A'_{111} were available.

It follows that the expected payoff for S_{11} is – $225,700, the "better" of the two second-round decision possibilities available to B. In similar fashion, the payoffs for S_{12}, S_{13}, and so on have been estimated and are shown in Figure 1.

Now the expected payoff for the initial decision Alternative A_1 can be computed: it is .05 (– $225,700) + .05 (– $225,700 + . . . + .50 (0) = – $73,000.

The same procedure has also been followed for A_2, A_3, A_4, and A_5; and the results are summarized in Figure 2. In this diagram the second "round" has been omitted and only the initial choices by B and "Nature" are shown. The figures were derived, however, by an analysis of the second-round payoffs and probabilities as illustrated for A_1 in Figure 1.

The analysis shown in Figure 2 suggests clearly that the optimal act for Baker B is A_5, the price and service differential system. This does not, of course, imply that this policy is optimal for all wholesale bakers, since it reflects the specific market conditions, cost structure, and payoff-probability estimates of Baker B which may not be valid in another context.

Examination of Figure 2 also sheds some light on the market behavior of wholesale bakers during the postwar period. The most common response, of course, has been "A_1" a refusal to produce private brands or to offer acceptable alternatives. While this response has been generally unsuccessful, and wholesale bakers have lost market position, it does have the merit that it avoids any of the possibly disastrous consequences of A_3 and A_4. The specter of price war has tended to domi-

Decision	Outcome	Payoff	Subsequent Outcome	Payoff
A_1 Ignore or Refuse −73.0			S_{11} Z Supplies Blue and Others (.05)	− 225.7
			S_{12} Z Supplies Blue Only (.05)	− 225.7
			S_{13} A or C Supplies Blue (.05)	− 188.1
			S_{14} Blue Acquires Bakery (.05)	− 370.5
			S_{15} Blue Waits, Harasses B (.30)	− 75.0
			S_{16} Blue Waits (.50)	0
A_2 Counter Offer −265.2	S_{21} Z Supplies Blue and Others (.02)	−225.7		
	S_{22} Z Supplies Blue Only (.03)	−225.7		
	S_{23} A or C Supplies Blue (.01)	−188.1		
	S_{24} Blue Acquires Bakery (.01)	−370.5		
	S_{25} Blue Waits. Harasses B (.01)	− 75.0		
	S_{26} Blue Waits (.02)	0		
	S_{27} Blue Accepts A and C Follow Suit (.90)	−275.1		
A_3 Reduce Price by .02 −1337.0			S_{31} Z Supplies Blue and Others (.03)	− 225.7
			S_{32} Z Supplies Blue Only (.04)	− 225.7
			S_{33} A or C Supplies Blue (.02)	− 188.1
			S_{34} Blue Acquires Bakery (.01)	− 370.5
			S_{35} Blue Accepts, A and C Do Not Meet (.05)	− 456.6
			S_{36} Blue Accepts, A and C Meet, B Retains Advan. (.10)	−1249.2
			S_{37} Blue Accepts, A and C Meet, Return to Original Share (.75)	−1554
A_4 Accede −260.7	S_{41} Blue Accepts, A and C Offer Secondary (.70)	− 22.2		
	S_{42} Blue Accepts, A and C Reduce Prices (.10)	−1442.7		
	S_{43} Blue Accepts, A and C Supply Coop I and Yellow (.20)	− 504.3		
A_5 Price Differential System + 125.2			S_{51} Z Supplies Blue and Others (.05)	− 225.7
			S_{52} Z Supplies Blue Only (.05)	− 225.7
			S_{53} A or C Supplies Blue (.05)	− 188.1
			S_{54} Blue Accepts, A and C Follow Suit (.60)	0
			S_{55} Blue Accepts, A and C Reduce Prices (.25)	+ 628.5

Figure 2
Summary of First Round of Decision Possibilities, Outcomes, and Payoffs for Wholesale Bakery Private Label Decision (Payoffs in thousands)

nate industry thinking. It is difficult to understand the reluctance to establish price and service differentials for large customers. It may be, of course, that bakery executives have feared price war as a possible outcome of this policy as well as of A_3 and A_4. The restraints imposed by the commission system of driver compensation (which limits the potential savings of limited service) have no doubt also played a part.

VALUES OF DECISION THEORY APPROACH

Among the most important values of this formal approach to decision problems is that it serves to focus attention on the critical issues involved. In the present example, some of the key questions that naturally arise from the analysis are the following:

1. If a wholesale baker supplies chains with private brands, will other customers retaliate by partial or complete "boycotting?" Is this response permanent or transient? Surveys and limited test markets can answer this.
2. Under what circumstances can a chain (or coop or voluntary chain) "afford" to acquire its own bakery plant through backward integration? If these conditions can be identified, we can assign more meaningful probability estimates to the outcome, "Blue gets own bakery plant," as well as better evaluations of its payoff. Cost analysis and careful assessment of the volume needs of Blue Chain may shed light on this.
3. If a bakery forestalls a request for a private brand by offering a secondary brand in its place, does this diminish the future probability of the chain renewing its request? If a secondary brand is offered for sale, what percentage of former regular brand buyers (ultimate consumers) will shift to the lower-priced brand? How does this depend on the amount and type of advertising and sales promotion, if at all?
4. If price differentials based on quantity and service are established, which customers will be able and willing to take advantage of them? What will the impact on average revenue per unit be?
5. How does a given decision affect possible future courses of action? For example, does the introduction of a secondary brand at one time make the decision to supply private brands in the future more or less feasible? Do secondary brands have any effect on the assumed "resentment" of independent retailers toward bakers who supply chains with private brands?

Although these questions cannot be answered now, at least partial answers to some of them could be obtained through properly designed research efforts. A major advantage of structuring a problem in formal terms is to indicate the directions that research efforts should take.

It is natural to ask whether or not formal decision theory is "practical." Is it feasible to carry out such an analyses of marketing problems, and does the use of such an approach offer any advantages over current practice?

In conclusion, there are side benefits. The process need not be time-consuming; however, by preventing a hurried selection of the most obvious conclusion, the way is paved to creative thinking in a manner that fosters dispassionate communication about the problem. There is a strong probability that through such an approach research activities necessary for solution of the problem will be more clearly defined and their application explicitly anticipated.

Finally, the principal advantage of formal decision theory over informal executive judgment is implied by the word "formal." The type of analysis illustrated here requires the decision maker to *formalize* his thinking regarding a problem—to structure his judgment and to "put it down in black and white." That this is likely to improve the quality of executive judgment seems self-evident. Whenever a decision must be made and its outcome is not known with certainty, some informal equivalent of the decision theory must be employed.

34. BAYESIAN STATISTICS AND PRODUCT DECISIONS*

Paul E. Green

In today's fast-moving technology the need for good decision-making in the development of new and improved products is only too apparent. Typically, development of a new product from invention to commercialization is expensive and fraught with uncertainty regarding both technical and marketing success. On the one hand, it is not uncommon to find that development costs exceed discovery costs by fifteen or twenty times. On the other hand, the ratio of products successfully commercialized to total products placed on the market (let alone those that reached at least some stage of development) has been variously quoted as ranging from one in five to one in twenty.

As apparent as the need for improved decision-making in this area is, there has been a dearth of good analytical techniques for dealing with the uncertainties that plague the development manager. While the product developer can (and usually does) enlist the aid of such data gathering services as market, process, and cost research, a formal apparatus for integrating these various sources of information has been conspicuous by its absence.

In recent years, however, a growing body of quantitative procedures for dealing with decision-making under uncertainty has emerged from the disciplines of applied mathematics, statistics, and the behavioral sciences. Under the generic title of "statistical decision theory," these techniques show promise for assisting the decision maker in making rational choices under uncertainty. One of the most relevant and complete sets of tools is known as Bayesian decision theory. The pioneering development of this approach, as applied to business problem solving, is credited to Robert Schlaifer.[1]

*Reprinted from *Business Horizons* (Fall, 1962), pp. 101–109.

[1]Robert Schlaifer, *Probability and Statistics for Business Decisions* (New York: McGraw-Hill Book Co., Inc., 1959). In addition, two excellent expository articles

The purpose of this article is to show the relevance of the Bayesian approach to product development decision-making. More specifically, we shall illustrate how these techniques can be used to help answer two persistent questions related to each stage in the development of a new product:

1. Should we make a decision *now* (with respect to passing a product along to the next development stage vs. terminating the project), or should we *delay* this decision until some future date, pending the receipt of additional information regarding the new product's chances for commercial success?
2. Given a decision on *when* to make the decision, *what* action ("go" vs. "stop") should we take?

The power of the Bayesian approach as applied to these basic questions is described in two parts. First, we shall review the nature of the costs associated with moving too slowly vs. too quickly through the product development process. Second, an illustrative case will show how these groups of costs can be introduced within a Bayesian framework to guide both the "when to" and "what to do" classes of decisions. However, the richness of Bayesian statistics goes well beyond the scope of this illustration. The concluding section of this article discusses some of the more general aspects of Bayesian decision theory.

TIME-RELATED COSTS

The ultracautious decision maker tends to incur sizable costs when he delays each development decision until he has assembled enough information to make the choice patently clear. These costs are partly associated with time and partly associated with the cost of the information gathering activity itself (which also takes time to accomplish).

An illustration should make clear the nature of these time-related costs. Assume that a new chemical product has reached the development stage where the company must either (1) decide now whether to construct a semiworks unit or to terminate the project, or (2) delay, pending the receipt of additional information regarding the anticipated outcomes associated with the alternative to proceed. Apart from sunk costs (that is, historical costs, not relevant from an economic stand-

---

dealing with a description of Schlaifer's work are: Harry V. Roberts, "The New Business Statistics," *Journal of Business*, XXXIII (January, 1960), 21–30, and Jack Hirshleifer, "The Bayesian Approach to Statistical Decision—An Exposition," *Journal of Business, XXXIV* (October, 1961), 471–489.

point), termination at this point would result in a payoff of zero. The decision to proceed, however, is related to a series of future decisions up to and including commercialization before a positive payoff could be forthcoming. From the standpoint of delay, the decision maker should be concerned with how these conditional payoffs would be expected to change between now and some future time for viewing the same set of choices that he presently faces. Moreover, in multistage decisions, a present commitment does not demand that the project be continued in subsequent periods, should later information suggest project termination.

If the decision maker decided to delay his choice, pending the receipt of additional information, it should be clear that at least three groups of costs can be associated with delay.[2] First, as a function of delay time, the present value of all future revenues attendant with commercialization would be reduced as a consequence of delaying the start of the receipt of these revenues until a more distant time. This type of delay cost merely gives recognition to the time value of money.

Second, also as a function of delay time, the present value of all future revenues attendant with commercialization could be lowered as a consequence of the increased risk of competitive imitation or supersedure of the product (at the hands of competitors or conceivably of a future product of the decision maker's own research organization).

Finally, gathering the information obviously costs money and incurs time for its development. If one assumes some linear relationship of money spent for information with the period required to obtain the information, then this cost also can be associated with the time variable.

Certain implications obviously stem from the preceding listing of delay costs. If required target rates of return are low (that is, a low opportunity cost of the company's capital exists), and/or the threat of competitive retaliation is low, and/or the costs of data gathering are low, a relatively small penalty is attached to delay. Conversely, when these costs are high, a larger penalty is attached to the delay option.

On the other side of the coin, an impatient decision maker who eliminates or gives short shrift to vital steps of information gathering runs the risk of incurring sizable costs associated with acting under a

[2]In the case of interdependent activities, a fourth category of cost could include the penalty associated with delaying some other necessary activity not in the project directly affected, that is, equipment design groups might not be able to switch efforts easily over to another job, thus incurring costs of transition.

high degree of uncertainty (and perhaps costs associated with "crashing" the program, that is, telescoping development steps, as well). The behavior of these groups of costs can be viewed as a function of time, which, in turn, is a function of the amount of information collected.

Again, discussion of the preceding illustrative problem should make clear the nature of the costs associated with moving too quickly. Building a semiworks is related to a series of future actions leading to ultimate commercialization. In point of fact, however, these future actions may never be undertaken. The decision maker may delay any single decision while awaiting new data and, in multistage decisions, he will frequently have the opportunity to reevaluate the venture before making subsequent commitments.

Thus, the decision maker must view the change in payoff associated with the go vs. no-go decision now vs. the payoff associated with delay of this decision, pending receipt of additional data. Why collect additional data at all? Additional data would be collected for the purpose of reducing the variance associated with the estimated distribution of payoffs related to acting now. A simple example should clarify this concept.

If the option to build the semiworks now is a "sure thing," that is, no matter what information that could conceivably be developed on, say, potential sales, could change the decision, then it is obvious that additional information (cost-free or not) is irrelevant. On a more realistic basis, however, some potential sales levels (say, zero sales) would obviously favor the option of no-go. The essence of this concept can be expressed in Bayesian terms as the expected[3] cost associated with acting under uncertainty. That is, the difference in payoff between taking the best act now (in the light of current uncertainties) and taking the best act under perfect information about future events represents the expected value of perfect information; and, hence, the upper limit that the decision maker should spend for additional information if it could be collected immediately and would be without error.

Other things equal, it is clear that when the costs of uncertainty are large the decision maker could suffer by moving too rapidly to the next stage of the development process. On the other hand, if the costs of wrong decisions are low, he should move rapidly.

It is thus implied that gathering additional information would at

[3]The adjective "expected" is applied here in the usual statistical sense. That is, expected costs are weighted averages found by multiplying each admissable cost by the probability of incurring it and then adding these products. The weights (probabilities) sum to unity.

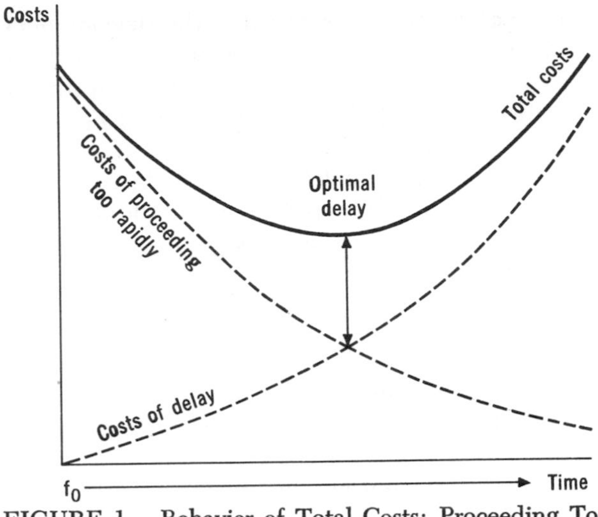

FIGURE 1. Behavior of Total Costs: Proceeding Too Rapidly vs. Too Slowly

least reduce, if not eliminate, the cost of uncertainty; otherwise the information would not be gathered. It is further implied that time and money would be spent on the information gathering activity until the sum of the expected costs associated with information collection and delay and the expected costs of acting under uncertainty was minimal. Otherwise, a shorter or longer delay period would produce lower expected total costs. Figure 1 represents conceptually the behavior of the costs associated with moving too slowly vs. moving too quickly with respect to some stage in the development of a new product.

APPLYING BAYESIAN THEORY

While the preceding remarks have focused on the nature of the costs associated with moving too quickly vs. too slowly at any stage in the development process, we must still illustrate how Bayesian decision theory utilizes these costs to provide a rationale for answering both the "when to" and "what to do" questions. The following example is deliberately simplified to deal with the simplest of cases, a one-stage choice.[4]

[4]In more realistic (but more complex) illustrations, a multistage decision process—for example, pilot plant to semiworks to commercial plant with possible information steps in between—may have to be used. The techniques of dynamic programming are frequently appropriate here. See R. Bellman, *Dynamic Programming* (Princeton, N. J.: Princeton University Press, 1957).

Assume that a point has been reached in the development of a new product regarding whether or not a semiworks should be constructed now vs. delaying this decision (pending receipt of further market information). To be more explicit, three options will be considered:

1. Build a semiworks vs. terminate project now
2. Delay this decision until one period (year) into the future
3. Delay this decision until two periods (years) into the future.

Options 2 and 3 imply, of course, that better marketing information than now exists could be secured over the next year or two and that the more extensive this inquiry, the better the quality of the information. However, the development of the additional marketing data will cost something itself and will delay subsequent steps toward commercialization.

Some present marketing information, which is rather imprecise, indicates that four alternative forecasts of potential sales, given commercialization, bracket the possible levels of future sales. Subjective probabilities[5] have been stated for the occurrence of each forecast and, given each forecast, it has been possible to calculate the payoff, given commercialization. These data are noted in Table 1 where F_1 stands for each sales forecast deemed admissible and $P(F_1)$ stands for the likelihood that the decision maker assigns to the occurrence of each forecast.

Under the go alternative, Table 1 indicates that if forecasts F_1 or F_2 actually occurred, negative payoffs (in present value terms) would result, while under the more optimistic forecasts, F_3 or F_4, payoffs would be positive. According to the Bayesian approach the expected payoff (EP) of the go option is found by summing over the product of each payoff times its probability. The present value of future returns of the no-go alternative (termination) is, of course, zero.[6] In

[5]The term subjective probability refers to the degree of belief the decision maker wishes to assign to the occurrence of each admissible event. This degree of belief is expressed numerically along a scale ranging from zero to one and reflects the experienced judgments of the decision maker. All weights are assigned so as to obey the postulates of probability theory. For a full discussion of the so-called school of personalistic or subjective probability, see the excellent book by L. J. Savage, *The Foundations of Statistics* (New York: John Wiley & Sons, Inc., 1954).

[6]A project payoff of zero, on a present value basis, would imply that the project's cash flow back (over its anticipated life) would just be sufficient to pay back all cash outlays and to earn some net rate of return, say 10 per cent, on the present value of those outlays. Adoption of the no-go alternative thus assumes that other projects exist that could just earn this return; an opportunity cost concept is involved here.

TABLE 1

CONDITIONAL PAYOFFS AND EXPECTED VALUES
(Millions of dollars)

Acts	F_1	$P(F_1)$	F_2	$P(F_2)$	F_3	$P(F_3)$	F_4	$P(F_4)$	EP
Go	−$12	.15	−$1	.30	$5	.45	$10	.10	$1.15
No-go	$ 0	.15	$0	.30	$0	.45	$ 0	.10	$ 0

this oversimplified problem situation, the decision maker–in the absence of the opportunity to collect additional market information–would go with the project, that is, construct the semiworks. The expected payoff associated with this alternative is $1.15 million.

More realistically, however, the decision maker frequently has the option of delaying his decision pending the receipt of additional data regarding the occurrence of the alternative sales forecasts. These additional data will cost something to collect, delay construction time, and rarely, if ever, be perfectly reliable.

ONE-YEAR DELAY OPTION

We shall first consider the one-year delay option.[7] For purposes of illustration we will assume that a delay of one year in construction would have the following results: (1) the cost of delayed revenues amounts to payoffs that are only 91 per cent of the former payoff (interest rate equal to 10 per cent annually); (2) the firm's market share would drop from 100 per cent, under the no-delay case, to 75 per cent because of the resulting greater lead time for competitive imitation; and (3) the cost of collecting additional information concerning fu-

[7]Although not explicitly shown above, it is relevant to note that the expected value of perfect information (EVPI) is $2.10 million. As mentioned earlier, this provides an upper limit on funds that could be spent on the collection of additional data, which could be collected immediately and would forecast perfectly which event would actually occur. To obtain EVPI, subtract the expected payoff of the best act in the light of current uncertainties from the expectation of the payoffs associated with the best acts (given the actual occurrence of each event):
EVPI = [.15 ($0 million) + .30 ($0 million) + .45 ($5 million) + .10 ($10 million)] −$1.15 million
The result is $3.25 million − $1.15 milion, or $2.10 million.

This calculation may be interpreted as follows. If the decision maker could purchase a "perfect" forecasting device that would tell him which event would actually occur, it is clear that before the purchase he must still apply his prior probabilities as to which event the device would indicate; he would then be able to take the best act associated with the event specified.

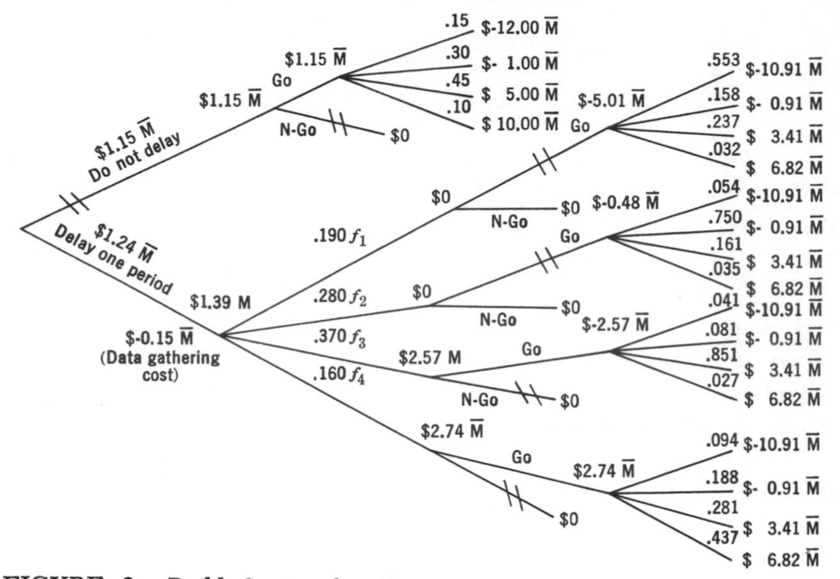

FIGURE 2. Build Semiworks: Terminate Project Now vs. One-Period Delay

ture sales would be $150,000. However, information obtained at this early stage of development is assumed to be only 70 per cent reliable. That is, if the market survey results indicate f_1 (namely, that forecast F_1 will occur), there is a 30 per cent chance that this information could have been assembled if the true underlying sales potential were not F_1 but really F_2, F_3, or F_4.

All of the assumptions of our simple expository case can be summarized in Figure 2, which should be examined by working from right to left. To illustrate, the upper branch (do not delay) summarizes the results of Table 1. The conditional payoffs under each forecast, given go, are – $12 million, – $1 million, $5 million, and $10 million. Multiplying these payoffs by their respective probabilities and summing the results yields, of course, the expected payoff of $1.15 million. Since this is clearly higher than the $0 associated with no-go, this latter alternative is blocked off, and the best alternative, *given no delay*, is go.

However, the second main branch of the tree is still to be evaluated. The conditional payoffs, – $10.91 million, – $0.91 million, $3.41 million, and $6.82 million at the extreme right of the lower branch, reflect the penalties associated with (1) the discount penalty for delay and (2) the effect on the firm's market share due to delay if the product were successful (see author's note).

TABLE 2

MARGINAL AND JOINT PROBABILITIES UNDER THE ONE-PERIOD DELAY OPTION

Survey Results	Joint Probabilities				Marginal Probabilities
	F_1	F_2	F_3	F_4	
f_1 …………	.105	.030	.045	.010	.190
f_2 …………	.015	.210	.045	.010	.280
f_3 …………	.015	.030	.315	.010	.370
f_4 …………	.015	.030	.045	.070	.160
	.150	.300	.450	.100	1.000

AUTHOR'S NOTE: Notice that several sets of new probabilities appear along the sub-branches of the lower main branch of Figure 2. These probabilities are derived by application of Bayes's theorem, a central tenet of this approach. We shall need to compute marginal, joint, and posterior probabilities. Their meaning will be made clear in the computations to follow.

First we consider the calculation of the *marginal* probabilities, .190, .280, .370, and .160 appearing beside the market survey results f_1, f_2, f_3, and f_4, respectively. These calculations are shown in Table 2. The cell entries represent joint probabilities (the probability assigned to the joint occurrence of each survey result f_i and each underlying event F_i). For example, the joint probability of survey result f_1 and event F_1 occurring is found, under the oversimplified assumptions of our problem, by multiplying the conditional probability, $P\ (f_1|F_1)$, by the prior probability, $P\ (F_1)$, which the decision maker assigned to F_1; $.70 \times .15 = .105$. The conditional probability of observing survey result f_1, given the fact that the true underlying forecast is F_2, is assumed equal to .10. (Similarly, for sake of simplicity, the probability of obtaining the survey result f_1 if the true forecast is F_3 or F_4 is also assumed to be .10.) Hence the joint probability of survey result f_1 and event F_2 occurring is, by way of illustration, $P\ (f_1|F_2) \cdot P\ (F) = .10 \times .30 = .030$ as shown in the second column of row f_1. The other cell entries are computed analogously.

The *marginal probabilities* f_1, f_2, f_3, and f_4 are then found by merely summing over the column entries for each row–$P\ (f_1) = P\ (f_1 \text{ and } F_1) + P\ (f_1 \text{ and } F_2) + P\ (f_1 \text{ and } F_3) + P\ (f_1 \text{ and } F_4)$ or $.190 = .105 + .030 + .045 + .010$. Also note that the marginal probabilities, found by summing over rows for each column F_i, are simply the prior probabilities that the decision maker had originally assigned to the occurrence of these four events.

We can next proceed to the calculation of the *posterior proba-*

bilities, $P(F_i|f_i)$, and to a brief description of how Bayes's theorem can be used to derive them. These calculations are shown in Table 3.

Table 3 can be explained as follows: Under the assumptions of our problem it was noted that each survey result was deemed to be only 70 per cent reliable in correctly "calling" the event assumed to be most strongly associated with it. Suppose, however, that we really did observe a particular survey result, say f_1. Under our assumptions it is more likely that event F_1 "caused" this specific result than events F_2, F_3, or F_4. Still, the other events could have caused this result. We would like to reason backward, so to speak, in order to determine how likely it is that F_1 was the underlying event, now knowing that f_1 has occurred.

Given that we have observed f_1, it is clear that only the joint probabilities along row one of Table 2 are now relevant. We would next wish to partition the total (marginal) probability associated with f_1 (.190) among the four events, F_1, F_2, F_3, or F_4, which could have produced this survey result. Hence the first row of Table 3 is derived by merely dividing each entry in Table 2 (.105, .030, .045, and .010) by the marginal probability (.190) associated with f_1. In summary, *before* observing f_1 we would have assigned the prior probabilities. .15, .30, .45, and .10 to events F_1, F_2, F_3, and F_4, respectively. *After* having observed f_1 we would then revise these probabilities to .553, .158, .237, and .052, respectively, so as to reflect the fact that the observance of f_1 was deemed more likely under F_1 than under F_2, F_3, or F_4. Analogous considerations apply to the calculation of posterior probabilities shown in the remaining rows of Table 3.

TABLE 3

POSTERIOR PROBABILITIES UNDER THE ONE-PERIOD DELAY OPTION

Survey Results	*Posterior Probabilities*				
	F_1	F_2	F_3	F_4	*Total*
f_1	.553	.158	.237	.052	1.000
f_2	.054	.750	.161	.035	1.000
f_3	.041	.081	.851	.027	1.000
f_4	.094	.188	.281	.437	1.000

Bayes's theorem formalizes this notion in terms of the following formula:

$$P(F_i|f) = \frac{P(f|F_i) \cdot P(F_i)}{\sum_{j=1}^{n} P(f|F_j) \cdot P(F_j)}$$

In terms of our problem, the posterior probability assigned to, say, event F_1, given that survey result f_1 was observed, is:

$$P(F_1|f_1) = \frac{.105}{.105+.030+.045+.010}$$

$$= \frac{.105}{.190} = .553$$

The appropriate marginal and posterior probabilities (as derived in Tables 2 and 3) appear along the subbranches of the lower main branch in the tree diagram of Figure 2. We can now proceed to discuss which act we would choose, given the occurrence of each admissible survey result:

If the market survey information indicates f_1 (that forecast F_1 is the best estimate), then, as noted earlier, some probability exists that this survey information could have been developed if the true underlying sales forecast were not F_1 but F_2, F_3, F_4. If f_1 is observed however, the best action to be taken after the survey is no-go—terminate the project. Hence, the go alternative branching from f_1 is blocked off. Similar results pertain to survey results f_2. Under survey results f_3 and f_4, however, the resulting best action is to build the semiworks. On an expected payoff basis, collecting the additional information produces a gross payoff of $1.39 million. From this gross figure must be subtracted the $0.15 million cost of collecting the information, yielding an expected payoff of $1.24 million associated with the one-year delay option.

The power of this technique is found in the recursive nature of solution. That is, the two payoffs, $1.24 million and $1.15 million, *summarize completely the whole series of moves along the decision tree.* Moves have been optimally planned from this point forward by, in effect, solving the problem backward. Thus, the decision maker is assured that the best decision now (which happens to be delay one period) has been derived by considering the relationship of this decision to the future decisions that the decision maker visualizes.

TWO-YEAR DELAY OPTION

We now consider the third option: delaying the decision pending a two-year inquiry into the sales potential of the product,[8] in this case we will assume that: (1) cost of deferred revenues amounts to payoffs that are only 83 per cent of the payoffs under the no-delay case; (2) the anticipated market share would drop to only 50 per cent of the market; (3) market survey costs increase to $300,000; but (4) the reliability of the resultant information increases to 90 per cent.

Figure 3 summarizes this second analysis. The upper main branch of the decision tree, covering the no-delay case, is exactly the same as that in Figure 2. All payoffs and probabilities in the lower main branch, however, are adjusted in accordance with the changed assumptions just enumerated by developing tables analogous to Tables 2 and 3. Solution of the problem again proceeds from right to left, always choosing the best alternative for each subbranch of the tree.

The upshot of this analysis is that the two-year delay option produces a lower expected payoff than the no-delay option. In other

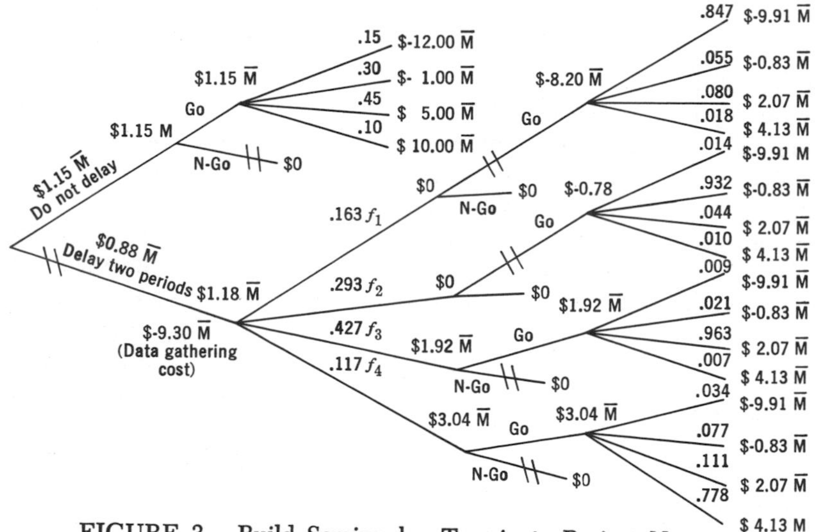

FIGURE 3. Build Semiworks: Terminate Project Now vs. Two-Period Delay

[8]Numerous other combinations could be evaluated ranging from the case where construction of the semiworks and start of the marketing studies are begun simultaneously through various degrees of overlap in timing. No new principles would be involved. Payoffs would, of course, reflect the cost of project "take-down and salvage" if the marketing survey results were to indicate a change in action from go to no-go after construction had already been started.

words, the costs associated with delaying the venture more than outweigh the gains expected through increased reliability of the sales information. For this reason the lower branch of the tree is blocked off in Figure 3.

In summary, it has been shown, via the preceding simplified examples, how costs associated with delay can be balanced against the costs associated with the higher costs of uncertainty related to moving a development along too quickly.

The preceding illustrative case has touched upon some aspects of Bayesian decision theory but has by no means exhausted the many facets of this approach.[9] As could be inferred from our preceding example the Bayesian approach to decision-making under uncertainty provides a framework for explicitly working with the economic costs of alternative courses of action, the prior knowledge or judgments of the decision maker regarding the occurrence of states of nature affecting payoffs, and the conditional probabilities of observing specific events, given each state of nature.

The Bayesian approach to decision-making under uncertainty provides a rich set of techniques for dealing with the complex problems that attend new product development. This is not to say that the relevant probabilities used in this approach can be developed easily or quickly. Rather, granting that decisions must be made in any event Bayesian analysis represents a rational procedure for including all relevant data and for dealing explicitly with the gains vs. costs associated with the option to "purchase" new information bearing on the problem. Coupled with ancillary techniques such as computer simulation and sensitivity analyses, it seems fair to say that this set of tools constitutes the most powerful analytical apparatus of its class currently available to the product development manager.

[9] A full and lucid description of these features can be found in *Probability and Statistics for Business Decisions.*

Index